# Spirit of Enterprise

## The 1987 Rolex Awards

# Spirit of Enterprise

## The 1987 Rolex Awards

Foreword by
### George Van B. Cochran
*President, The Explorers Club, 1981-1985*
*Professor of Clinical Orthopaedic Surgery, Columbia University*
*Director, Orthopaedic Engineering and Research Center, Helen Hayes Hospital*

Preface by
### André J. Heiniger
*Chief Executive Officer and Managing Director, Montres Rolex S.A.*

Edited by
### David W. Reed

**VNR** UK  Van Nostrand Reinhold (UK) Co. Ltd

Photographs and artworks have been submitted by the entrants except where indicated in the captions

This book was produced in Great Britain for Rolex
by Van Nostrand Reinhold (UK) Co. Ltd
Production coordinator: Gavin McDonald

Typeset in Palatino 9 on 11pt by
Columns of Reading, Berkshire
Printed by Jolly & Barber Ltd, Rugby, Warwickshire
Bound by T.J. Press (Padstow) Ltd, Cornwall

First published in 1987 by
Van Nostrand Reinhold (UK) Co. Ltd
Molly Millers Lane,
Wokingham,
Berkshire, England

ISBN 0 7476 0003 1

# Rolex Laureates

# The Rolex Awards for Enterprise 1987 Members of the Selection Committee

André J. HEINIGER, Chairman                                        SWITZERLAND
Chief Executive Officer and Managing Director, Montres Rolex S.A.

George Van B. COCHRAN                                                      USA
Professor of Clinical Orthopaedics at Columbia University, New York, and Past
President of The Explorers Club

Fleur COWLES                                                                UK
Painter and authoress and Member of the World Wildlife Fund International
Council

Xavier FRUCTUS                                                          FRANCE
Specialist in hyperbaric physiology and Scientific Director of COMEX, Marseilles

Yoshimine IKEDA                                                         BRAZIL
Oceanographer specialized in Antarctic research and Professor at the Oceanographic Institute of the University of São Paulo

Kisho KUROKAWA                                                          JAPAN
Architect, President of Kisho Kurokawa Architect and Associates, and Director
of the Institute of Social Engineering, Inc., Tokyo

Hans Joachim PANITZ                    FEDERAL REPUBLIC OF GERMANY
Telecommunications engineer and Payload Operations Manager at the German
Aerospace Establishment − DFVLR, Cologne

Carlo RUBBIA                                                             ITALY
Physicist, 1984 Nobel Laureate, and Project Spokesman at the CERN (European
Laboratory for Particle Physics)

Robert STENUIT                                                        BELGIUM
Underwater archaeologist and author

# Contents

指 indicates a Rolex Laureate

指 indicates an Honourable Mention

## Section 2 – Exploration and Discovery 143

## Section 3 – The Environment 293

xiv

# Foreword

As the human race evolved from its ancestors, many factors affected its survival and the course of evolution. While we lacked strength and speed, we were endowed with intelligence which enabled us to acquire first weapons and shelter, then fire, art, domestic animals, crops, medicines, sciences, machines and, finally, all the blessings and curses of modern society.

Throughout history, our race has been industrious and resourceful, driven by instinct to explore and discover, to invent and to improve and protect our ways of life. Of course, these instincts exist to varying degrees in all people, and are essential to the survival of our civilization – but alone they are not enough. Major progress has always called for individuals to lead the way with inventions, voyages of discovery or other projects that have gone that one step farther. Often these endeavours received little support when they were initiated; typically, they were called difficult or impossible, untried or too risky, eccentric or even worthless. But the bold and energetic people who undertook them overcame adversity, succeeded and, eventually, were recognized for their achievement. Then the words used to describe them changed, and they were admired for their originality, inspiration, courage and tenacity! Why did these individuals succeed? It was because all of them possessed an extra measure of that quality which has been the *catalyst* of virtually all progress in our history – the "spirit of enterprise".

With enterprise we can surmount any obstacle to progress, but if that spirit should die, civilization could drift into a new age of darkness. Rolex has recognized the importance of highlighting the "spirit of enterprise" in a world which tends to encourage conformity and mediocrity, and in which individual efforts are often overshadowed by bureaucracy and the industrial machine. While enterprise is important in every field, The Rolex Awards single out three especially relevant categories: Applied Sciences and Invention; Exploration and Discovery; and The Environment.

As judges, we were privileged to share the efforts of many hundreds of applicants. Choices were difficult, and all the best projects submitted were characterized by exceptional originality, organization, scholarly effort and dedication to a well-defined goal with a significant impact for improving our world. The outstanding projects had, in addition, an abundance of the deciding factor: a clear demonstration of extraordinary enterprise in efforts past, present and planned for the future. Often, as judges, we found ourselves in the classic dilemma, struggling to answer a key question about a highly ambitious or unusual proposal. Was the project truly impracticable or would the applicant's "spirit of enterprise" win through?

This book presents over 240 of the most meritorious projects – endeavours of incredible diversity ranging from massive scientific expeditions to individual efforts to save an endangered species. The purpose of publishing them is to extend the impact of The Rolex Awards for Enterprise far beyond the direct financial support given to the five Laureates. The projects have been selected for inclusion because they deserve wider recognition and support. Finally, it is hoped that this volume will inspire future endeavours by serving as a reminder to us all of our priceless heritage – the "spirit of enterprise".

New York,
November 1986

George Van B. Cochran

*President, The Explorers Club, 1981-1985*
*Professor of Clinical Orthopaedic Surgery,*
*Columbia University*
*Director, Orthopaedic Engineering and*
*Research Center, Helen Hayes Hospital*

# Preface

For the fourth time in succession, it is my pleasure and privilege to offer readers the opportunity of exploring a worldwide panorama of achievement – past, present and future – and of undergoing the rewarding experience of sharing both the satisfaction of those who have advanced in programmes of outstanding endeavour, and the aspirations of those whose projects still await fulfilment.

This has been the experience of the tens of thousands of readers who have read previous books on The Rolex Awards for Enterprise and it was also what awaited the members of the Selection Committee when they launched themselves into an analysis of the many hundreds of projects that were submitted prior to the spring 1984 closing date for the fourth round of the Awards.

Those of you who have followed the course of our activity and have perused the previous books of the 1976-1977, 1981 and 1984 Awards will know what awaits you. Those of you who are joining us for the first time will have the delight of discovering the enthusiasm, courage and perseverance that characterize the candidates whose spirit of enterprise has made and continues to make The Rolex Awards for Enterprise a multidisciplinary and cross-cultural success.

In 1976, Montres Rolex S.A. decided to mark in an appropriate way the 50th Anniversary of a "first" that holds a special place in the history of our company – the invention and patenting of the Rolex Oyster case, acclaimed in 1926 as the world's first waterproof watch. We then looked at how best this event could be celebrated. Finally, we agreed that we would give tangible evidence of our support for something that we, at Montres Rolex S.A., hold close to our hearts and that has been a fundamental factor in many of the innovations that Rolex has brought to the world of fine watchmaking. This "something" is the "spirit of enterprise".

The first Awards were launched in 1976 and the immensity of the response showed overwhelmingly that any doubts we might have harboured that modern society has crushed human initiative and drive were unfounded. By the time we had granted the first Awards to the successful candidates in 1978, we were convinced that The Rolex Awards for Enterprise were a valid initiative and offered a unique forum for enterprising individuals to measure themselves against others and present their projects to the Selection Committee to ponder and evaluate. Clearly, the Rolex Awards could not be a one-off affair – we had offered enterprising individuals an opportunity to display their projects and they had responded massively; we had to continue to feed the flame we had kindled. Hence, the Awards were presented again in 1981 and for a third time in

1984. We also saw that the richness and variety of the ideas submitted to us could not be adequately acknowledged solely by the selection of five Rolex Laureates and a number of Honourable Mention winners. Hence our decision to publish a book so as to share with you, our friends and readers, the diversity and sincerity of the ventures that have been devised.

Yet, a matter of considerable gratification to us is that the three previous editions of *Spirit of Enterprise* have not proved to be a one-way process. The reactions of readers have been generous and effective, and many of the candidates whose projects appeared in the earlier books have written to tell of the opportunities that have been opened to them. In addition, numerous institutes and associations – both national and international – have now undertaken to help bring future rounds of the Awards to the attention of an even larger circle of potential candidates.

The ceremony that takes place on 30 April 1987 in Geneva to present The Rolex Awards for Enterprise 1987 will, for the fourth time, bring to the podium five Rolex Laureates who will each receive a cheque for 50,000 Swiss francs and a specially engraved gold Rolex Oyster Day-Date Chronometer. Moreover, there will be an even larger number – thirty-two – of Honourable Mention winners who will attend special ceremonies organized around the world to acknowledge their success by the presentation, to each of them, of a steel and gold Rolex Oyster. Finally, we are once again publishing a book to give a wider audience to the work – in progress or planned – by the Laureates, the Honourable Mention winners and many, many other outstanding candidates – all of whose projects deserve wider dissemination and appreciation. In this way, we are sure that The Rolex Awards for Enterprise will have an ever greater and broader impact on our society.

The Rolex Awards for Enterprise 1987 and the response to them, epitomized by the contents of this book, have further confirmed that the vision that guided us in the inauguration of these Awards was judicious and discerning, and have encouraged us to persevere like our candidates. Let me, therefore, take this opportunity of announcing that the next Rolex Awards for Enterprise will be launched in 1988, and invite you to join us in them.

Geneva,
November 1986

André J. Heiniger

*Chief Executive Officer and Managing Director,*

*Montres Rolex S.A.*

# Introduction

In opening this book, you have opened a treasure chest of fascinating and stimulating ideas born of the inventiveness of a unique group of individuals.

These people form a group because they all share certain outstanding characteristics – they are enterprising, inventive, courageous, tenacious – and, above all, achievers. Nevertheless, they are individualistic because the vehicles they have chosen for their enterprise are so diverse and multifarious – and cover a vast spectrum of the key areas of progress on the frontiers of human achievement. Finally, they are unique in that they are drawn from the many hundreds of candidates who submitted their projects to the Selection Committee of The Rolex Awards for Enterprise 1987.

The fascinating nature of the 243 projects described in this book will become only too clear as soon as you delve into them. Yet it will also be clear that, in their diversity, these projects do have a common theme or, better, a common objective: to bring an improvement to the world we live in and, in particular, to the people, fauna and flora that populate it. It has been said that "there are no problems – only solutions in search of an application"; if this is so, these men and women of "enterprise" have certainly been able to locate some most demanding situations to which to apply their talents.

On 30 April 1987, five of these enterprising individuals will come to Geneva as the guests of Montres Rolex S.A. to attend an Awards Ceremony where they will each receive their Rolex Laureate prizes – a cheque for 50,000 Swiss francs, a specially inscribed gold Rolex Oyster Day-Date Chronometer and a scroll attesting their selection. Shortly after, in different parts of the world, thirty-two Honourable Mention winners will be celebrated in local ceremonies, and each will be presented with a steel and gold Rolex Oyster and a scroll.

However, once again, Montres Rolex S.A. has decided that many of the other enterprising candidates deserved further encouragement and that many of the other projects merited a wider audience. As before, Rolex has therefore undertaken to publish details about them and their projects in this book.

The actual descriptions of the projects submitted by candidates on the Official Application Forms for The Rolex Awards for Enterprise were of widely varying length; they have, therefore, been condensed into a more succinct form to allow even more projects to be presented than in the three previous Rolex Awards books.

The book itself is divided into three sections, each being devoted to one of the categories of The Awards: Applied Sciences and Invention; Exploration and Discovery; and The Environment. The numbers of projects described in each section represent roughly the proportion of projects submitted under each category rather than a breakdown of the winners.

We believe that the enterprising men and women who figure in this book deserve admiration and encouragement, and we sincerely hope they will receive it from you. However – and perhaps even more important – we hope that an appreciation of their endeavours may stir in you your own "spirit of enterprise" and encourage you to give expression to your project and submit it for The Rolex Awards for Enterprise 1990.

Geneva,                                                                      David W. Reed
November 1986                                                                      *Editor*

# Applied Sciences and Invention

The projects described in this section were submitted under the category "Applied Sciences and Invention" which was defined in the Official Application Form for The Rolex Awards for Enterprise 1987 as follows:

*Projects in this category will be concerned primarily with science or technology and should seek to achieve innovative steps forward in research, experimentation or application.*

# The new workers of the sea

## Marc Simon Bollon

18 impasse Tour Buffel, 34000 Montpellier, France

French, born 29 March 1953. Architect, and Founder and Director of the "Architecture, Illustrations Publicitaires" Studio. Educated in France; diploma (Architecture) from Ecole Nationale Supérieure des Beaux Arts, Unité Pédagogique d'Architecture, Montpellier in 1979; currently preparing a doctorate at the Geography/Development Department of Université Paul Valéry, Montpellier.

This project involves collection of material on the subject of "The new workers of the sea – Exploration and development of the underwater world" for a doctoral thesis. It is planned to use the work that has been done so far in order to undertake the preparation of a richly illustrated encyclopaedic book on the same subject for publication in French, English and, perhaps, other languages.

### Combining technical drawing and underwater sports

My university education gave the opportunity of combining my skills in design and technical drawing with interest in underwater sports and studies in which I have obtained a diploma of diving instructor, 1st degree, from the French Federation of Underwater Studies and Sports. In this way, I took for the subject of my diploma as a state-qualified architect "The organization of space in a diving school" and for my specialized studies diploma, my thesis was devoted to "The port installations of Nouadhibou and Nouakchott, Islamic Republic of Mauritania".

In January 1983, I set up my own studio, under the name Architecture, Illustrations Publicitaires – AIP which, although starting as an architectural agency, gradually began to undertake the production of drawings for clients. It has now become an artist's studio following a major expansion of the publicity illustrations sector; the two main fields of activity are architecture and interior design (for interior decorators, architects, etc.) and marine architecture and archaeology (for shipyards, companies doing underwater works, marine apprenticeship schools, specialized magazines, etc.), although I do a variety of miscellaneous illustrations for advertising agencies, etc.

### Preparation of a thesis

In January 1982, I began my doctoral thesis entitled "The new workers of the sea – Exploration and development of the underwater world", which is divided into three sections giving an overview of the history of underwater technology (both

3

civil and military) since ancient times, and a description of the sea's resources and their exploitation by man. This task is already well advanced, and a substantial part of the text and the illustrations are under way. Moreover, I have systematically collected a vast quantity of documentation by contacting numerous organizations and companies in the field in Canada, Denmark, Finland, France, West Germany, Italy, Japan, Norway, Sweden, the United Kingdom and the USA; I now have 4,000 pages of text and picture material, have classified 8,000 pages of prospectuses and technical descriptions and have compiled a large bibliography.

My thesis still requires a considerable amount of work, and the mass of material I have collected so far is far from fully digested. My current plan is to base the defence of my thesis on a slide show with a recorded commentary backed up by a number of posters taken from my documentation or prepared by myself.

## Developing an encyclopaedia from the thesis

However, I believe that this thesis material has considerable potential beyond the academic realm, and my plan is to produce an encyclopaedic work on the sea, similar in design and content to recent publications that have appeared in English and French on the subject of space technology and exploration. The encyclopaedia would be generously illustrated with both drawings and photographs: the illustrations shown, which were produced for the magazine

Amas (circa 1780)

*The Amas of Japan have been diving for shellfish and edible seaweeds for some 2,000 years. An illustration, showing Amas at work towards the end of the eighteenth century, produced by Marc Bollon and published in* Océans.

4

*Océans*, Marseilles, are typical of the approach that would be used. I believe that the book should be marketed by an English-language publisher; French publishers often buy the translation rights for popular scientific works from publishers in other countries, since they consider – rightly or wrongly – that the French-language market for this type of book is too small to justify the financial risks involved in producing the work from scratch.

A Rolex Award would give me the publicity I need to have a reasonable chance of success in canvassing British or American publishers.

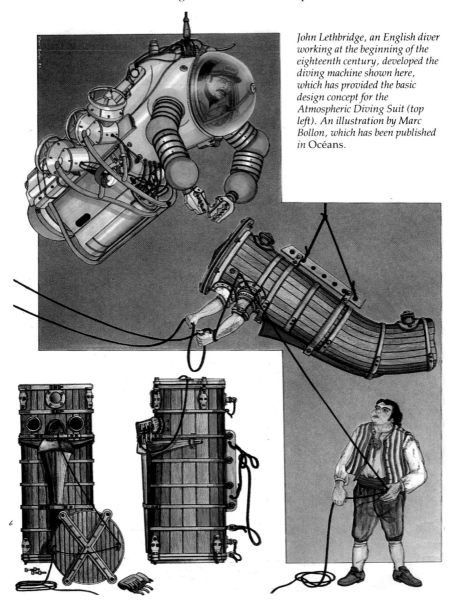

*John Lethbridge, an English diver working at the beginning of the eighteenth century, developed the diving machine shown here, which has provided the basic design concept for the Atmospheric Diving Suit (top left). An illustration by Marc Bollon, which has been published in* Océans.

# Can we turn back the wheel of evolution and produce extinct forms of life?

## Keizō Kamata

Hatoyama-machi, New Town 31–5, Hiki-gun, Saitama-ken 350–03, Japan

Japanese, born 31 March 1938. Practising gynaecologist. Educated in Japan; M.D. (Gynaecology) from Juntendō University, Tokyo in 1964.

Although it is said that the process of evolution is irreversible and that hereditary elements, once lost, cannot be retrieved, my experience in the cross-breeding of endemic Japanese lilies has shown that there is the possibility of reversion to a more primitive form – now extinct – of the common parent species of two extant lilies. My project proposes to reproduce the common parent of all seven endemic Japanese lilies – which certainly once existed.

### Evolution of the endemic lilies of Japan

There currently exist some 100 species of lilies; 16 of these are growing wild in Japan and seven are endemic. It is said that lilies are amongst the oldest angiosperm plants and that the seven species endemic in Japan (*Lilium japonicum, L. rubellum, L. Alexandrae, L. platyphyllum, L. auratum, L. nobilissimum,* and *L. speciosum*) display some of the lily's most ancient features. These seven lilies have a specific factor that distinguishes them from continental lilies; during the Ice Age, the continental species had drastically shortened vegetative periods and therefore dispensed with forming a leaf stalk; the Japanese lilies, on the other hand, were surrounded by warm currents, enjoyed long summers and kept their original leaf stalks. It was just before the Ice Age that Japan separated from the continent.

In the prototype of the Japanese lilies, adaptation was restricted to development of pigments to protect the generative cells from frost damage. However, even such a small change means a (permanent) genetic mutation. In its warm native environment, the flower was white in colour; but the farther north it moved to colder areas, the more the colour became yellow (flavone pigments) or red (anthocyan pigments) since a colour change from yellow to red increases low-temperature resistance. An example of this relationship between cold climate and pigmentations is *L. platyphyllum* from the subtropical island of Aogashima 37 km south of Tokyo; if we try to grow these bulbs in the frost-affected area of Tokyo, the yellow dots on their petals become light brown. Seedlings from plants that have budded, blossomed and fruited in the south

6

will, if sown in Tokyo, die affected by frost. On the other hand, seedlings from plants that budded, blossomed and fruited in Tokyo will nearly all thrive in Tokyo but the dots on their petals will become light or dark brown. Only seldom will they remain yellow as in their home habitat. Seedlings from Izu-Toshima (150 km south of Tokyo) that budded, flowered and fruited in Tokyo, will grow well but will have red-brown spots and resemble *L. auratum*. This proves that, if *L. platyphyllum* suffers frost damage in its budding period (mid-April), its chromosomes will undergo change to allow the generative cells to produce cold-resistant seeds. In other words, as long as it grows on the Izu Islands under the influence of warm currents, it remains *L. platyphyllum*; however, if it is transferred to mainland Japan, it will, as a result of frost, change to *L. auratum*.

As for *L. auratum*, its native zone is the warm south coast of Japan where mandarines are grown. If, in a given year, the mandarine trees are damaged by frost, a special variety of *L. auratum*, with red stripes and containing numerous anthocyan pigments, will also be found growing. Once again, this can be explained only as a chromosomal change intended to enhance cold resistance.

## Genealogy and distribution of lilies

Cross-breeding *L. auratum*, with its red dots on white petals, and *L. speciosum*, with purple dots on pink petals, results in a high percentage of pure white flowers without any dotting. Self-fertilization will never result in dotless flowers and only seldom in white flowers. This astonishing finding became the starting point of my research which, over 15 years of cross-breeding experiments, has allowed me to draw up a genealogical table of the seven endemic lilies of Japan. Moroever, I have discovered in the Izu Peninsula a natural hybrid whose existence I had forecast on the basis of geographical and genealogical factors.

From this I deduced that the ancestral form of *L. Alexandrae* took a northern route, changed to *L. japonicum* and settled in the Izu Peninsula, then took a southern route and became *L. platyphyllum* which eventually also reached the Izu Peninsula. Here it changed to *L. auratum*, but, according to my theory, before doing so it naturally hybridized with *L. japonicum* and produced the Izu-lily.

## My plans for future study

My project is by no means confined to theoretical knowledge on the botanical or geological field. After all, I want to actually reproduce the real prototype of lilies which must have existed millions of years ago. A success in this project would, of course, confirm and endorse the theory. To do this, I must figure out the exact details of the supposed ancestral form, and then, by planned cross-breeding, revive the original lily along the lines of evolution. What is possible with two of the species, must be feasible with all of the seven.

The project I have before me will involve a number of different tasks. In particular, it will be necessary to: carry out a search for the appropriate plant materials (i.e. bulbs and seeds) throughout the whole of southern Japan; construct suitable hot house cross-breeding facilities in which it will be possible for me to artificially reproduce a subtropical climate; and also to develop the correct soil conditions for the plants.

*The outcome of the cross-breeding of* L. auratum *and* L. speciosum *(below) has been this white lily without any dotting. Self-fertilization will seldom produce white flowers and never result in dotless ones.*

*From cross-breeding* L. auratum Lindl. *(left) with its red dots on white petals, and* L. speciosum Thunb. *(right) with its purple dots on pink petals, Keizō Kamata has obtained a high percentage of pure white flowers without any dotting as shown above.*

On the basis of past experience, I estimate it will take about ten years to reach this goal. A success would certainly demonstrate similar possibilities, at least theoretically, for other plants, too. However, whether such extinct forms can be reproduced beyond the limit of a genus, is more than I would dare venture to assert.

# Research and development of robotic components

## Mark E. Rosheim

1565 St. Paul Avenue, St. Paul, Minnesota 55116, USA

American, born 28 June 1960. Technologist with the Sperry Corporation.
Educated in USA; self-educated in the area of mechanical engineering, drafting
and machining, and currently taking extension courses at the University of
Minnesota.

Since childhood, I have had an intense interest in mechanical devices and
gradually progressed from building blocks to working models of telephones and
radios, until during adolescence I began applying my talents to robotics,
intuitively recognizing that the robotic wrist was a fundamental mechanism
needing improvement. I have now worked for several years on designing new
improved robot wrists and have taken inventions in this field to the patent stage.
In doing so, I have installed my own fabricating equipment, including a metal
lathe and a small milling machine, have taught myself machining for producing
my models, and draughting and technical writing for my publications. Through
publications and lectures, I have striven to educate the engineering community
and market my designs.

My goal now is to further develop my wrist actuator technology, thereby
increasing the precision and dexterity of industrial robots, and opening the way
to domestic personal robots and advanced prostheses. It will entail the
establishment of a suitably equipped workshop to build prototypes, and then
involve me in writing, publishing and presenting papers describing these
prototypes.

### Three new designs in wrist technology

I have developed three new state-of-the-art wrist actuator designs which are of
singularity-free, pitch-yaw-roll morphology, and which will enhance the
performance of industrial robots; patents are pending for all three. My project
will further develop these designs.

The compact pitch-yaw-roll wrist features 180° of pitch and yaw motion about
two closely spaced centre points, singularity-free motion, high precision,
mechanical efficiency and back-driveability. These attributes make it ideal for
joints in tele-operator systems, industrial robots, walking robots and prostheses.
Two unique gimbals coupled by spur gears comprise the basic structure. Each

9

gimbal has two perpendicular and coplanar shafts held by bearings in the housing. One of the shafts is formed into a bail and has an internally facing groove. This groove receives a cam follower from the clevis, which pivots with the clevis about the centre point of the gimbal yaw-axis shaft. A bridge attached to each clevis permits connection of the gimbals to the action arms. Spur gear pairs on the front pitch axis bail and yaw shaft mate with the corresponding gears on the back gimbal. Setting the spur gear pairs on each axis slightly out of phase with each other eliminates backlash, while introducing only minimal friction due to the high mechanical efficiency of the spur gears. As one gimbal moves, the gimbal opposite it moves in an identical vector. Limited rotation between the bridges and bails occurs when the wrist is in a compound pitch-yaw mode. This is necessary to decouple the two gimbal axes.

The pitch-yaw-roll wrist construction features the use of simple rings, bearings and gears. Pitch and yaw range is 180° of singularity-free motion, with 360° of continuous bidirectional roll rotation of the tool plate. The design of the wrist consists of two unique gimbal mechanisms, each capable of 90° of pitch and yaw motion. These are held in a cylindrical housing. Each front and back gimbal is concentrically positioned and rotates about spaced centre points placed along a primary axis running longitudinally through the housing. Both gimbals include an inner and outer bearing assembly. The inner bearing and outer bearing of the gimbals are rotatable about individual rotation axes and intersect at the respective front and back gimbal centre points. In each gimbal, the inner bearing assembly is connected to the outer bearing assembly by two pivotal pins so that when the inner bearing is rotated, the outer bearing is rotated. Similarly, when the outer bearing is rotated about its axis, the inner bearing pivots about its axis. Two pairs of spur gear sectors transmit rotary motion from the back gimbal to the front gimbal.

The tendon wrist has 100° pitch motion and 100° of yaw range about a common centre point. Singularity-free, it is back-driveable for walk-through

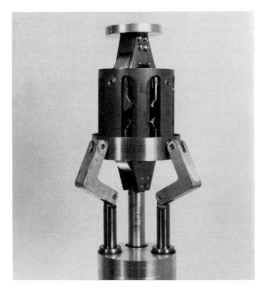

*A prototype of the pitch-yaw-roll wrist, designed and manufactured by Mark E. Rosheim.*

10

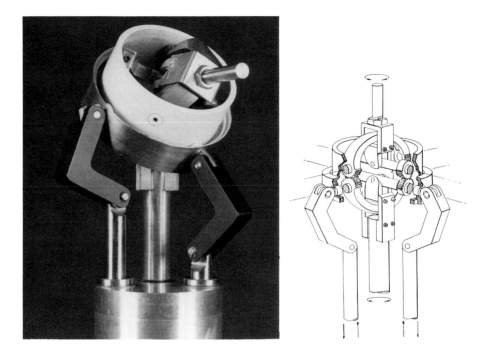

*The compact pitch-yaw-roll wrist designed and manufactured by Mark E. Rosheim with, on the right, an exploded view of the wrist mechanism.*

programming. Consisting basically of a ball and socket joint, with the socket driven by tendons, it is simple and rugged. Low manufacturing costs and easy miniaturization are features. Immediate applications are found in anthropomorphic joint design, including hand knuckles and personal robots.

### Future impact

Future development of more sophisticated, human-like robots depends on advances in wrist-actuator technology. Three of the six axes in industrial robots are in the wrist and these three-degrees-of-freedom joints are essential not only in higher-articulation arms for spray painting and welding but also in legs for walking robots. Master/slave tele-operator systems need improved anthropomorphic joints for high dexterity, and a simpler interface between operator and robot slave. Prostheses too would benefit from improved three-axis actuators since this type of wrist is also critical for the development of neck, shoulder, hip, spine and ankle joints for anthropomorphic robots.

# A waste-recycling biogas generator for farm self-sufficiency

## Felix D. Maramba

Liberty Flour Mills, Inc., Liberty Building, Pasay Road, Makati, Metro Manila, Philippines

Filipino, born 7 January 1897. President, Liberty Flour Mills, Inc. Educated in Philippines and USA; M.Sc. from Iowa State University in 1922.

Biogas is a fuel gas composed of methane, carbon dioxide and small quantities of other gases, produced by the decomposition of organic materials (such as animal manure and crop residues) through the action of methanogenic bacteria in the absence of oxygen. Biogas may be used as a direct substitute for both gaseous and liquid fuels. A biogas plant has two major components – the digester where the slurry of organic materials is charged and retained to ferment under anaerobic conditions; and the gasholder where the biogas that is generated inside the digester is collected and stored pending use.

### Developing a biogas plant at Maya Farms

When Maya Farms, a 36-ha integrated livestock-meat processing enterprise located in the outskirts of Metro Manila, Philippines, was established in 1972, its farm waste was disposed of through a conventional lagoon method. Subsequent expansion programmes posed a pollution problem and it was decided to develop a biogas system attuned to local conditions and the specific needs of a major agro-industrial venture (waste disposal, pollution control and fertilizer production). A prototype incorporating features of different existing models, as well as revolutionary concepts, was eventually constructed.

The installation is fed with a slurry comprising manure and waste water which ferments for 20–30 days. The fermented residue exits from the biogas plant in the form of sludge; the solids are collected for use as organic fertilizer and feed material while the sludge liquid goes through a series of sludge-conditioning lagoons to ensure that it is safe for discharge into public waters.

The rapid rise in energy prices brought about by the 1973 crisis led us to maximize the use of biogas as an alternative source of energy by digesting hog pen washings, and by 1983, with 50,000 head of hogs and more efficient equipment, Maya Farms became totally self-sufficient in energy. The biogas system is now the core of a total waste recycling process which handles not only our total production of manure and waste water but also all the waste products

12

from the slaughterhouses.

The biogas operation at Maya Farms currently produces 6,500 m³ of biogas per day, generating power equivalent to 6,500 kWh of electricity. Biogas fires the burners for the cooking vats, scalding tanks and retorts in the processing plants, and runs the engines which serve as prime movers for various pumps, machines, refrigeration equipment and electricity generating plant.

## Sludge as fertilizer and feed material

The digestion process results in sludge with a high concentration of plant and animal nutrients which, when processed, gives a practically odourless, innocuous, humus-like material. The coarse solids are pelletized and used as fertilizer. The fine solids are dried, ground and recycled as feed material in the feedmill. At present, the biogas system at Maya Farms processes daily over 75 t of manure and 1,000 m³ of waste-water from 50,000 hogs.

The biogas system is the core of the Maya Farms total waste-recycling system which processes a large volume of animal manure, pen washings and industrial waste water. The daily production of manure and waste water are charged into the biogas plants. The biogas that is evolved is used as fuel for the integrated operation. The sludge effluent from the biogas plant is pumped into settling basins to recover the solids for recycling as feed material and organic fertilizer. The remaining fluid flows through the sludge-conditioning lagoons. Ducks are raised to feed on the scum that forms over the surface of the lagoons together with leftover feed from animal pens. The conditioned liquid passes through a fishpond where it stimulates the growth of algae and plankton which serve as food for the fish. Fish life is also an indicator that the liquid is acceptable for use as fertilizer-irrigation water for the crop fields. Crop residues like rice straw and corn stovers are fed to the cattle. The slaughtered pigs, ducks and cattle are processed into ham, bacon, sausages and other meat products. The blood, bones

*A fully integrated system. One of the farm's pigs, which helped supply the manure to generate the biogas, is cooked in a roaster fired by the gas.*

13

*A panoramic view of one of the biogas units at Maya Farms, in which can be seen the biogas digesters, gasholders and a sludge-conditioning system.*

and meat scraps are converted in the rendering plant into feed ingredients for recycling through the feedmill. Blood meal has a high protein content, while meat and bonemeal are good sources of calcium, phosphorus and animal protein.

**Technology transfer**

The benefits offered by our achievements are considered too good to be kept for the sole welfare of Maya Farms and this technology is now being disseminated free of charge to small farmers and social institutions, and on-farm training courses have been organized. It has now been decided to use the biogas system as the basis of an integrated farming system aimed at raising the agricultural income of small farmers with limited land resources. A pilot farm using this system is now run by a volunteer family which owns a 1-ha crop field and a 0.2-ha lot for the farmhouse.

The recent economic crisis in the Philippines has pushed interest rates up, making it difficult for poor farmers to borrow the necessary capital funds. In view of this, I am now exploring ways of gradually building up towards total integration by stages with different possible combinations depending on existing resources on the farm. Work is also being done to reduce the cost of the biogas plant through design simplification and through the use of alternative construction materials. It is further planned to establish demonstration communities in selected rural communities to propagate the concept.

# Precolumbian musical instruments of the south and central-south Andes

## *José Vicente Pérez de Arce*

Museo Chileno de Arte Precolombino, Bandera 361, Casilla 3687, Santiago, Chile

Chilean, born 21 April 1950. Designer and investigator at the Museo Chileno de Arte Precolombino. Educated in Chile; studied music (1969–1973) and the organ (1977–1978) at the Facultad de Ciencias y Artes Musicales y de la Representación, Santiago.

This project forms part of a more ambitious programme for the study of musical instruments throughout precolumbian Andinoamerica. This geographical region has been divided into seven areas and each phase of the programme will cover one of these. The project proposes to survey two areas: the south and central-south Andes which are made up of northern Chile, north-west Argentina, western Bolivia and southern Peru.

These areas contain an extraordinary wealth and diversity of ancient cultures; however, a more comprehensive understanding of these cultures is impeded by our lack of knowledge of their music. Having now carried out 11 years of research in this field, I am convinced that this deficiency is due to the fact that: a significant part of the musicological items from these areas lies undescribed in museums and private collections; difficulties in describing such specialized artifacts as musical instruments have led to incorrect or incomplete descriptions; most of the research is related to regions which reflect current political boundaries and not entities as they were in precolumbian times.

The two areas to be researched were chosen because they contain a wealth of available material which has so far been only poorly documented; thus in view of the amount of work done so far, the project would be relatively easy to implement.

### Planned methodology

The project consists of four consecutive phases: inventory, documentation, evaluation and the presentation of conclusions. The first step will be to establish as comprehensive an inventory as possible of the musical instruments from the area. It will entail designing a filing system to record the essential information about each specimen of instrument to be studied, and making a thorough survey of musical instruments and representations of musical scenes from archaeological sources in museums and private collections. File cards,

15

photographs and tape recordings will be made for each item, and an archive of the material will be compiled.

The second phase will be devoted to a review of all the literature and sound recordings relating to the project; and, in phase three, the specimens will be placed in their historical context, grouped by type, and a study will be made of the nomenclature, variety, use and function of each type. Finally, the fourth phase will attempt to arrive at some general conclusions, with the development of a tuning table for the instruments included. In addition, in order to consolidate the findings and render the different time and space relationships more readily intelligible and accessible to future researchers, it is planned to incorporate the data into a map.

## Project impact

In view of the interdisciplinary character of the project and the novelty of much of the material, a number of spin-offs may be expected. My own knowledge in this relatively rare field of study for our continent will be intensified and expanded. Information which is currently widely dispersed will be centrally compiled – a factor of significance for future studies. The interdisciplinary perspective given to this field of study may open up new avenues of research. Wide publication of the results would disseminate valuable educational material and spread knowledge about ancient musical art, the use of ancient musical instruments and the artifacts involved in instrument manufacture; this would be of influence throughout contemporary culture, whilst the retrieval of a wide range of musical expressions and sounds could influence current musical creativity.

*The ceramic trumpet in the form of a conch shell was used in the geographic area that is now Ecuador in the period between AD 750 and 1250. This drawing represents the use of this trumpet by a native of the period. (Property of Museo Chileno de Arte Precolombino)*

*Ethnographic evidence of the use of the four-holed transverse flute, Mapuche, Chile. (Photo by Ernesto González)*

## Progress to date

To date, considerable progress has been made in various aspects of the programme as a whole. The design of the file card is the outcome of several years of study, and provides for a complete description of musical instruments including dimensions, materials, ornamentation, notation, musical range and signs of use, drawings and photographs. Museums and private collections in numerous towns in Chile and Bolivia have already been surveyed between 1976 and 1985, and a bibliography of over 600 titles has been compiled, together with an archive of over 10,000 file cards describing instruments, bibliographical materials, etc., and a thousand instrument recordings. The study of the first area (the extreme south or Mapuche area) has been completed and will soon be published.

## Tasks for the future

Completion of the project entails photographic and audio recording work and determination of absolute instrument pitch. Finally, visits still need to be made to a number of museums and private collections in Argentina and Peru and various publications need to be purchased to supplement the literature already compiled for the bibliography. Having established a unified catalogue, evaluated its contents and related the findings to present-day traditions, it will be possible also to detect influences and interrelations with other areas which would give a more profound vision of the prehistory of Andoamerica.

# Novocel – An invention to save jute from the fate that befell indigo

## Abu Raihan Mahiuddin Muhammad Manzur-i-Khuda

B/2/1 Humayun Road, Mohammadpur, Dhaka 7, Bangladesh
Bangladeshi, born 1 October 1933. Director, Bangladesh Council of Scientific and
Industrial Research. Educated in Bangladesh, UK, India and West Germany;
Ph.D. (Organic Chemistry) from University of London in 1958.

The delta of the Ganges and the Brahmaputra, known as Bengal, was the birth place of the indigo vegetable-dye industry which paid rich dividends to the cultivators until the advent of synthetic indigo took away the market. It also produced the cotton for the world-famous muslin fabric and, subsequently, the jute fibre that supplied the jute industry for manufacturing hessian and gunny bags. In 1947, the then East Pakistan produced 90% of the world's jute and was the backbone of Pakistan's economic growth. Gradually, competition from other jute manufacturing countries has reduced the share of the world's jute and jute goods market held by the new country of Bangladesh, which today produces scarcely 50% of the world's jute. The competition from synthetics, particularly polypropylene, has lowered market prices to levels which do not cover even half the production costs.

### Finding other uses for jute

This research project was launched in response to threats from jute substitutes to diversify the uses of jute and to upgrade the jute fibre for higher-priced textile uses. In 1967, I developed a process for producing wool substitute from jute, by exploiting the crimping or "woollenization" that occurs in jute when treated with caustic soda. A number of patents and publications have now established a chemical process for converting jute to a fibre termed "Novocel" which can be effectively blended with wool, acrylic fibre, polyester fibre, rayon and cotton under suitable conditions. In addition, when certain conventional jute products such as lightweight twines and hessian cloth are treated by the process used for the production of Novocel, they are transformed into excellent knitting wool substitute and a textile product which could be used for suiting, tapestry, drapery, jean fabric or wall covering. Although these novel products from jute twine and hessian are not of the quality of woollen or acrylic fibre knitting wools and textiles, better jute spinning facilities on more acceptable frames (e.g. flax spinning frames) would result in a superior product.

The key to the invention is the crimping that caustic alkali treatment causes in

18

jute; this crimping can be stabilized or suitably modified by resin bonding or chemical cross-linking, thus creating fibres which can be blended with other natural and synthetic fibres. Bleaching followed by optical brightening can eliminate yellowing and produce a snow-white jute which can be dyed economically using the dyes used for cellulosic fibres. Finishing with the surface-bonded softening agents used with cotton textiles gives the jute a delicate soft feel.

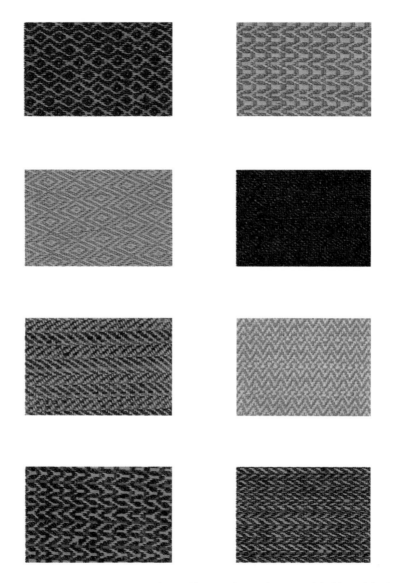

*Examples of Novotex union fabric manufactured from a mixture of cotton and the Novocel developed by Mr. Manzur-i-Khuda.*

## A product with novel features

The novel features of the invention include: the conversion of jute – a bast fibre – to Novocel a textile fibre: stabilization of this woollenization by resin or chemical cross-linking; multiple-stage bleaching and optical brightening to prevent or arrest yellowing and produce white fibre or textile; economic and fast dying of the converted jute using dyes not suitable for normal jute; chemical and softening treatment to eliminate harshness and coarseness of the bast fibre; and the blending of Novocel with matching natural and/or synthetic fibres such as wool and/or acrylics to produce attractively priced materials which can be spun on normal woollen machinery. The resulting Novocel fibre retains its cellulosic character, has dyeing characteristics similar to those of rayon but physico-mechanical properties closer to those of wool with considerable resiliency and elasticity; however, chemical treatment can give it a coarse cotton fibre character.

Resin treatment can be used to upgrade pile carpets made from Novocel or partially treated jute fibres to a quality carpet resistant to fibre shedding on vacuum cleaning – which could allow them to compete with woollen carpets.

Fabric produced from Novocel yarn blended with other textile fibre or Novocel union fabric is called Novotex fabric. It has been shown that Novocel blended with acrylic wool top can be spun on standard wool spinning frames, and that worsted cloth or knitting wool substitute can be produced from such blends. However, commercial production cannot be started until the necessary chemical processing facilities are available. Trial production of Novocel textiles has also been carried out on standard textile machines and it has been shown that frames for cotton blankets are suitable for producing blankets from Novocel yarns.

Novocel yarn quality can be improved by using higher quality jute yarns produced by superior spinning techniques. However, the blending of Novocel with other synthetic and/or natural fibres, already demonstrated in laboratory scale, still awaits production trials. The Bangladesh Jute Research Institute is currently planning further research and laboratory trials but no commercial production of any of the products has started in Bangladesh. It is difficult to overcome apathy or resistance on the part of public sector industry to the introduction of an experimental product.

## The need for production trials

In 1977, all the Novocel patents were made open in the public interest. Financial backing and entrepreneurship are sadly lacking in developing countries and such negative forces may retard progress. The author is currently awaiting suitable opportunities for some private developments to make various production and marketing trials possible. Successful Novocel production can push jute into the cotton and wool fibre blends and such textile products. After allowing for the conversion cost, it can still leave a good margin because of the large price difference with cotton or wool fibres being 10 to 30 times the price of jute.

This project has invented a patented process for chemically modifying jute to an acceptable range of textile fibre. This modified fibre, based on the woollenization of jute, blends well with wool, acrylic fibres, polyester fibres, rayons and cotton. The process holds out new horizons for jute, the economic backbone of Bangladesh. An organized production trial needs to be carried out.

# Maintaining biological tissue viability by preventing prolonged energy-production arrest

## Guy René Raymond Jean Renault

**Honourable Mention**
**The Rolex Awards for Enterprise – 1987**

Appartement 1147, 107 rue de Reuilly, Paris 75012, France

French, born 14 April 1949. Fellow at the French National Institute of Health and Medical Research. Educated in France; M.D. from the Paris XII Faculty of Medicine in 1978 and Ph.D. (Human Biology) in 1986.

To function and multiply, the body's cells need energy which they obtain by breaking down certain molecules in our food, primarily glucose, and absorbing or more accurately "recovering" the energy they contain. A major part of the energy recovery occurs in cellular organelles called mitochondria and takes place within a series of biochemical processes called the "respiratory chain". The main "supplier" of the "respiratory chain" is a coenzyme called nicotinamide adenine dinucleotide (NAD) which transfers hydrogen atoms from the target molecule to the first link in the respiratory chain. At the other end of the chain, the hydrogen atoms form water molecules with the oxygen breathed in by the body, and all the time hydrogen atoms are being successfully transferred along the chain, the cell can, in the meantime, store energy in chemical form, and largely as adenosine triphosphate (ATP) – the major "carrier" of chemical energy in the cells of all living species.

### Disturbance of the cell's respiratory chain

Because they are constantly transporting hydrogen atoms, the numerous NAD coenzymes inside the cells continually pass from a hydrogenated state (NADH) to a dehydrogenated state (NAD+), with the relative amounts of NAD+ and NADH in the cell being dependent on the cell's metabolic activity. However, if it is found that all the NAD in cellular tissue is in the hydrogenated form (i.e. 100% NADH), this means that the cell's respiratory chain is no longer functioning normally and the NADH-suppliers can no longer rid themselves of their hydrogen atoms; the result being that the cells are no longer capable of storing the energy they need. This is the situation that may occur in the cells of an organ when it receives de-oxygenated blood – or no blood at all – or when a poison impairs certain processes in the respiratory chain. In any event, the organ's cells are in more or less imminent danger because they have to draw energy from reserves which are not being replenished.

The aim of this project has been to develop a method by which clinicians can

21

rapidly detect such a state of "100% NADH" and thus have a chance to restore the conditions of cell viability before irreversible damage occurs.

## Principles and practice of NADH laser fluorimetry

The method that has been developed exploits research showing that NAD has certain specific optical properties and that, in particular, NADH, unlike NAD+, absorbs ultraviolet light at a wavelength of about 340 nm, and thereafter becomes fluorescent and re-emits the light at a wavelength of 480 nm (i.e. in the visible spectrum). The amount of light emitted from the cell is directly proportional to the number of excited NADH molecules the cell contains.

The equipment developed comprises: two lasers; an optical fibre for conducting the ultraviolet laser light to the target tissue and picking up the fluorescent light produced by the NADH, and for carrying a second light which allows blood flow to be taken into account; an optical module (with photo-receptors); and a microcomputer for analyzing the signals before they are displayed on a monitor. Thus laser fluorimetry makes it possible to monitor the NADH metabolism of an organ *in situ* and in real time, and, since only one optical fibre is needed, the clinician can reach any part of the body by simple contact, catheterization, puncture or endoscopy.

## Current and future applications

From the first laboratory set-up, three industrial prototypes have now been constructed and placed in medical centres for clinical evaluation. Initially, the method has been applied in heart surgery where, until now, there has been no reliable way of detecting the extent of ischaemia in the heart – a key factor in various kinds of heart surgery. The method has also been used experimentally to

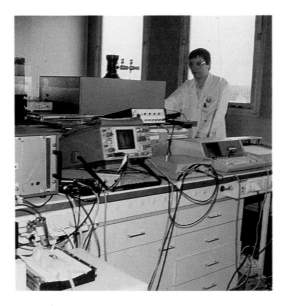

*First laboratory set-up of the in situ laser fluorimeter, operated by Dr. Guy Renault at INSERM UNIT U13, at the Claude Bernard Hospital, Paris.*

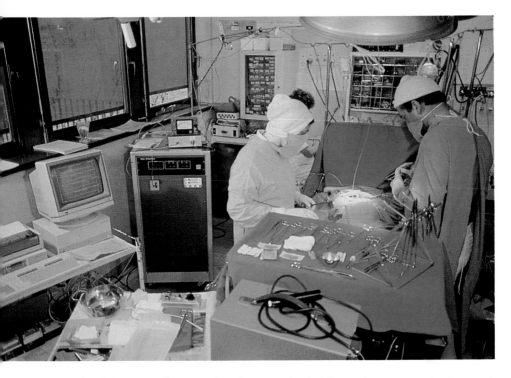

*Industrial prototype of the in situ laser fluorimeter (on the left) used for monitoring the efficiency of myocardial protection by cold cardioplegia during heart surgery. Experiment on a dog at the Marie-Lannelonge Hospital, near Paris.*

measure intra-myocardial NADH during the critical phase of aortic clamping and for monitoring high-risk patients under anaesthesia. In the field of cardiac pharmacology, the long-term implantation of a very thin optical fibre will be a major advance by allowing pharmacological intervention studies to be monitored in real time – an important factor in minimizing the number of research animals that need to be sacrificed. Possible use of the instrument in neurophysiology, brain surgery, ophthalmology and nephrology is also being investigated. Furthermore, its application in monitoring the viability of organs removed immediately after death for the purpose of a graft may reduce the number of graft failures.

The possibilities brought about by *in situ* NADH laser fluorimetry in clinical practice are so great and the underlying concepts offer such potential, that this method is expected to shatter medical habits and introduce the same kind of revolution in the field of health care as those brought about in the previous decade by computerized axial tomography (CAT) scanning or ultrasonics.

23

# New candidates for the prawn culture industry

## I-Chiu Liao

Tungkang Marine Laboratory, Tungkang, Pingtung 92804, Taiwan

Taiwanese, born 3 November 1936. Senior Specialist and Director, Tungkang Marine Laboratory. Educated in Taiwan and Japan; Doctor of Agriculture from University of Tokyo in 1968.

World prawn landings since 1977 have stagnated at around 1.6 to 1.7 million tonne, and this is thought to be close to the upper limit. The establishment of culture techniques, accompanied by decreasing profitability in the existing prawn fishing industry, has stimulated interest in prawn culture. The species used most widely for culture in Taiwan is *Penaeus monodon*, commonly called the grass or black tiger prawn, and its annual production has risen very rapidly from 150 tonne in 1975 to more than 30,000 tonne in 1985. The five principal prawn exporters are Bangladesh, India, Indonesia, Philippines and Taiwan, and the majority of cultured prawn is exported to Japan.

### Our contribution to the prawn culture industry

Perhaps the major contribution that the Tungkang Marine Laboratory (TML), which I head, has made to the explosive growth of the prawn culture industry in Taiwan has been the development of reliable larval-production and grow-out management techniques. The breakthrough came in 1968 when two colleagues and I succeeded in the propagation of *P. monodon*. The techniques were soon made available to local entrepreneurs and the industry was born.

My research into larval rearing and prawn culture has continued and I have published 95 papers in local and international scientific journals, including 35 prawn-related papers. I regularly attend meetings, workshops and conferences, and give speeches on prawn culture methodology and the prospects for growth in this industry. I have also been instrumental in the transfer of Taiwanese prawn culture technology to many parts of the world, particularly South-East Asian countries. Some of these countries are experiencing rapid growth of their prawn culture industries, to the benefit of their people and their national economies.

At present, *P. monodon* remains the most cultured species in many tropical countries and, despite its excellent biological characteristics, *P. monodon* has a dual disadvantage as a culture species, i.e. its growth rate both at high salinity

24

*A panoramic view of the success of the Taiwanise prawn culture industry – a success in which Dr. I-Chiu Liao has been largely instrumental.*

and at low temperature is relatively slow. The potential for further expansion of the prawn culture industry will be ensured only if it proves possible to establish culture techniques for species that will grow rapidly in conditions of high salinity and low temperature. The introduction of new culture species will also meet the market needs for the wide range of commodities.

**In quest of new cultured prawn species**

Preliminary work suggests the two species which show promise, from the above point of view, are *Penaeus semisulcatus*, the bear or flower prawn, and *Penaeus penicillatus*, the red tail prawn. My research efforts will be divided into five areas. In investigations on reproductive physiology, the physiological mechanism of sexual maturation will be studied by monitoring vitellogenin (egg yolk precursor) in blood serum. Based on this information, methods can be established to replace unilateral eyestalk ablation techniques in securing a reliable supply of spawners. In the development of hatchery techniques, we will define optimal environmental parameters such as temperature, salinity and light intensity along with the ontogenetic development of larvae, and then examine the suitability of two existing culture methods, i.e. separate and community culture.

An evaluation will be made of the environmental parameters required for optimal growth and yield, including water temperature, salinity, dissolved oxygen, pond substrate composition and stocking density. The parameters will be evaluated individually and also in combination with each other. From the point of view of nutritional requirements, the development of artificial compound feed is indispensable in prawn culture and information on nutritional requirements will be used to develop formula feed in collaboration with a few qualified Taiwan feed manufacturers. Finally, in the field of aquabreeding, it will be necessary to undertake research into interspecific hybridization for improved

25

growth, low-temperature tolerance, high-salinity tolerance, disease resistance and attractive colour (for market preferences).

It can be appreciated that there remains a tremendous amount of work to be done. Under my guidance, there are teams researching all the areas that have been outlined. TML has come to be recognized as one of the leading aquaculture research institutions, if not the mecca of prawn culture, and it has been training many aquaculture specialist from many parts of the world.

## Prawn culture for the maintenance of rural communities

In conclusion, it may be said that the development of prawn culture technology has many positive impacts, such as increased employment opportunities and efficient exploitation of inhospitable coastal areas. In fact, the drift of rural and village people from the countryside to the cities is a cause of enormous concern in developing countries. Prawn culture provides a means for these people to stay in rural communities, earn a good living and eventually contribute to the advancement of their national economies. The work proposed here would be an important step in increasing and diversifying the prawn culture industry, and a significant contribution to the "Blue Revolution".

Penaeus monodon *(left) has been the mainstay of the prawn culture industry in Taiwan and the South-East Asian countries for two decades. Two new promising species are* P. semisulcatus *(centre) and* P. penicillatus *(right).*

# Capuchin monkeys as aids for high-level quadriplegics

## Mary Joan Willard

19 Robins Road, New Rochelle, New York 10801, USA

American, born 20 March 1950. Behavioural psychologist and Assistant Professor of Rehabilitation Medicine, Albert Einstein College of Medicine. Educated in USA; Ed.D. (Educational Psychology) from Boston University in 1975.

This project began in 1977 when as a postdoctoral student at the Tufts New England Medical Centre in Boston, Massachusetts, studying the application of behavioural psychology to the treatment of medical problems, I made the acquaintance of a young spinal cord injured patient and conceived the idea that intelligent dextrous animals such as monkeys could be trained to perform useful everyday tasks for quadriplegic patients; a partnership in which the patient would be the brain and the monkey the hands and feet.

### A pilot project with Robert

In November 1979, Robert, who had at the age of 18 been paralyzed from the shoulders down in an automobile accident, began to participate in a pilot project to test the feasibility of using Hellion, a 2.2 kg female capuchin, as a helper. Robert communicates his needs to Hellion by aiming a small harmless laser pointer he holds in his mouth at the object he wants her to manipulate and tells her what she is to do with the object. When Hellion has completed a task, Robert rewards her with both verbal praise and the release of a food pellet from the dispenser mounted on his wheelchair. Over the past six years Robert has employed five different home attendants but only one monkey. Although Hellion occasionally makes mistakes, her overall task reliability is 94%. Her life expectancy is 30 years.

Since 1981, seven additional high-level quadriplegics have received simian aides and each placement has functioned as a mini-experiment as new types of living situations, training techniques, and methods of placement are attempted.

Simian aides are taught to return to their cages to urinate or defecate. A human attendant is needed to change the newspapers in the cage pan daily, but this task requires no more than two to three minutes. In addition, to ensure that the monkeys cannot aggress a visitor or other person, they undergo a full-mouth teeth extraction when they reach maturity.

## The psychological impact

Although the primary goal of this project is to increase the ability of a quadriplegic to perform the tasks of everyday life, this unusual intervention has had a strong psychological impact on disabled participants. Most quadriplegics lead very restricted lives, often spending weeks at a time within the confines of their homes. An affectionate, responsive and entertaining capuchin can be a very welcome addition to an unstimulating environment. One owner described the monkey's place in her life as somewhere between that of a pet and a child.

In addition, ownership of a monkey conveys a certain status on the recipient. Monkeys outside of zoos are rare. Monkeys who perform chores like small humans and readily play with visitors are even more unusual. Quadriplegics acquiring a monkey aide have reported that overnight they feel as if they became a mini-celebrity in their neighbourhood. Ownership of a monkey provides an obvious and interesting topic of conversation. It can minimize the discomfort the able-bodied feel when relating to the disabled, and allow for the more natural development of friendships. Considering the circumstances in which many quadriplegics find themselves, the importance of these social factors cannot be overestimated. For psychological reasons as well as financial, it is fortunate that these monkeys have a life expectancy of 30 years.

## Helping Hands – Simian Aides for the Disabled

By 1982, it was clear that, functionally and psychologically, simian aides were effective for at least some quadriplegics and a non-profit organization called Helping Hands – Simian Aides for the Disabled was established to meet the goal of providing simian aides to quadriplegics – much like guide dogs are now offered to the blind. With fundraising now proving more successful, it has been possible to establish a breeding colony of *Cebus apella* monkeys (which we found

*Henrietta, the capuchin monkey and Sue, her mistress, have an affectionate relationship and are good companions for each other.*

to be more suitable than the *Cebus albifrons* species to which Hellion belongs) producing 20–30 babies per year and arrangements have also been made to acquire 15–20 babies per year from Argentina. We have also set up a network of foster homes where volunteers raise the monkeys in their homes and a training programme to socialize monkeys to quadriplegic candidates and establish the monkeys in their homes.

A history of limited and unpredictable funding has forced me to rely as much as possible on donated goods, services, and labour. I have found that financial survival has taken as much creativity and enterprise as the resolution of any technical or programmatic difficulties. However, there are now a considerable number of organizations contributing to the project.

Helping Hands is currently the only service organization in the United States to train and place simian aides. Within the past year, rehabilitation centres in Israel, Argentina and Canada have begun their own programmes with our assistance. This project has the potential not only to help American quadriplegics, but also to serve as a model for similar efforts in other parts of the world.

*The capuchin monkey Henrietta brings a drink to the table, twists off the lid and inserts the straw for her paraplegic mistress, Sue.*

29

# Astronomical observatory in southern France

## Luc Vanhoeck

83 Breendonkdorp, 2659 Puurs (Breendonk), Belgium

Belgian, born 2 August 1959. In charge of the analytical laboratory in a pharmaceutical company. Educated in Belgium; studied at Antwerp University from 1971 to 1981.

Newton 406, an organization which has as one of its aims to bring together amateur and professional astronomers, is establishing a modern astronomical observatory devoted in particular to research areas that professional astronomers at major observatories have neglected owing to their short observing runs. The areas include lunar and planetary observations, photometry of long-periodic variables, peculiar variables or stars suspected to be variable, astrometry, meteor research and the like. The observatory will depend to a large extent on dedicated non-professionals willing to spend their time on long-term projects but, already, it is clear that it is destined to become the forum where non-professionals and professionals will meet each other.

### The establishment of an observatory at Puimichel

The history of the observatory goes back to 1981, when a noted telescope builder and astrophotographer from Belgium, Dany Cardoen, saw the need to remove his high-quality 16-inch reflector from the widely light-polluted Belgian skies, and with Arlette Steenmans, amateur astronomer and artist, was looking for a suitable dark-skies location for a larger instrument he planned to construct. Puimichel, a small village in southern France, where the skies are extremely clear, was chosen, an old farmhouse purchased and, with the aid of amateurs and even some professionals from all over Europe, work was started on the construction of the observatory. This has now become the centre of European amateur astronomy but, in order to expand its horizons and attract professional observers, it plans to add to its facilities several photovisual 16-inch telescopes, completely computerized 16-inch telescopes, large Schmidt cameras, a meteor research programme and, most important of all, a 42-inch research telescope which, it is expected, will be operational in 1987.

Puimichel is an ideal site for an astronomical observatory with very good meteorological conditions, dust-free, dry and extremely clear skies, and the absence of man-made light sources, and observation is possible for up to 200 nights per year. In addition, it is an economically underprivileged region and the population is falling owing to rural migration; consequently, the observatory project is attractive to the local authorities as a basis of cultural and scientific development and a possible source of job opportunities.

Initially, the farmhouse site comprised little more than four walls and was totally lacking in creature comforts. However, visitors now have a range of instruments at their disposal and the main activities at Puimichel include: a meteor observing programme; photography; photographic research; deep-space photography and the construction of the 42-inch telescope.

Newton 406 is self-supporting and has painfully acquired the financial means to complete the 42-inch telescope and its observatory. Dany Cardoen and Arlette Steenmans are permanently involved in running the project. They took the risk of staying in Puimichel and have kept it that way for over four years now. Numerous volunteers from all over Europe are contributing as much as possible. Their combined efforts made possible what has been realized so far. The way is long, however, and much still needs to be done. Some projects are advancing rather slowly due to the lack of funds. There is no doubt that the necessary know-how is present and that all of them can be realized, sooner or later. Present realizations prove that the observatory project is feasible and that it has every chance of success.

## Who will benefit from the observatory?

To start with, for the first time in Europe and possibly the whole world, advanced and experienced non-professional astronomers have access to high-

*The 42-inch glass disk set up on the grinding machine. This glass blank will eventually become the primary mirror of the largest non-professional telescope in the world.*

quality, large-sized telescopes under exceptional skies. As soon as the 42-inch collects light, an undreamed of instrument will be at their disposal. With the instrumentation available, non-professionals will have a chance to prove their skills by doing research. Puimichel observatory would like to be complementary to major observatories in that it will support long-term projects (even those without immediate results), so that the whole astronomical community will benefit from the project.

Second, Newton 406 will make its equipment available to professionals. Of course, it is clear that astronomers, regularly visiting Palomar, La Palma or La Silla, may not be interested in a 42-inch telescope in southern France. But it is a fact, too, that observing requests far exceed observing time, and what is more important, astronomers from small institutions that are not in the forefront of astronomical research, just do not have any chance of sending astronomers to these observatories. A great number of astronomy students get their Ph.D. without ever gaining real-life experience behind a sophisticated instrument. Puimichel observatory will certainly be an interesting alternative for people in this situation. Last but not least, the electronic devices that are to be built may represent a challenge to students of local high schools, thus getting their credit-hours by building useful items.

## Conclusions

Puimichel observatory is not a proposal; it is a reality. Or better – it is becoming a reality. Much has still to be done, and funds need to be found to acquire microcomputers, photometers, modems, a library, measuring and test equipment, etc. The observatory itself, however, is probably unique. Nowhere, as far as we know, has such an enthusiastic community joined forces to build such a large observatory at a fraction of traditional costs and with such a good chance of success.

*An amateur astronomer preparing one of the Puimichel observatory's photographic instruments for the night's observation.*

# Small medical first-aid unit

## Simón Patricio Ponce

**Honourable Mention**
**The Rolex Awards for Enterprise – 1987**

San Juan 549, Torre B–1, Piso 3, Depto. 14, 5500 Mendoza, Argentina

Argentine, born 6 January 1954. Self-employed furniture designer and builder. Educated in Argentina; qualified (Industrial Design) from Universidad Nacional de Cuyo, Mendoza in 1985.

This project evolved from an analysis of the first aid and rescue needs of a person who falls sick or is injured at an inaccessible location. This analysis revealed considerable deficiencies in the equipment currently available even to special emergency teams and instigated work on the design of a Small Medical Unit (SMU) incorporating everything required for first aid and rescue purposes in a compact and easily manhandled system.

### Design criteria and solutions

It was necessary to design a unit which would act both as a container for diagnostic and therapeutic equipment and supplies and as a stretcher for the patient; moreover, it had to be readily transportable, light, easy to handle, aseptic, impact and weather resistant, and foldable but rigid. The unit therefore comprises a container and a stretcher which can be separated and used independently but which, when folded, fit inside each other. The stretcher has two wheels and the container a carrying handle whilst the complete unit is fitted with a hook to hang it on a vertical surface and a harness so that it, or the container alone, can be transported as a backpack. It is made from plastics and aluminium, weighs 27 kg and measures 82 cm x 50 cm x 24 cm.

The container itself was designed around an inventory of essential diagnostic and therapeutic items drawn up in consultation with physicians and the Red Cross. It is divided into sectors that are accessed independently and sequentially starting with those having the least requirements of asepsis (diagnostic and resuscitation equipment) and finishing at those with the greatest (surgical instruments, bandages, syringes, etc.). The contents may vary according to local factors but would normally include a stethoscope, sphygmometer and thermometer for diagnosis; oxygen cylinder and mask for respiratory support; alcohol, hydrogen peroxide, analgesics, antibiotics, etc., for emergency disinfection and medication; syringes and needles for injections; instruments for minor surgery; and surgical dressings, splints, etc. Wherever possible, these items are

*The prototype small medical unit (SMU) on field trials, showing the backpack design and the deployed stretcher.*

of standard design although modifications proved necessary.

The stretcher is rigid with an anatomically shaped surface to prevent the patient from moving when being carried over rough terrain. Integral provision is made for an oxygen cylinder, an intravenous drip pack, pneumatic splints and a metallized emergency blanket. Straps are incorporated to immobilize patients with a suspected fracture of the spine, ribs, shoulder or hip.

### Ergonomic factors

An ergonomic study was made to ensure maximum convenience for operators in the transport of the closed unit and the deployed stretcher. People accustomed to backpacking and mountain treking were interviewed to determine the maximum acceptable weight, and a figure of 27 kg was selected; a lower figure would have impaired efficiency and functionality. The backpack was designed around a hypothetical male operator with a height of 174 cm and a bodyweight of 70 kg in such a way that the carrier can remain as upright as possible, with the harness directing most of the weight to the carrier's hips and ensuring an adequate air space between the pack and the carrier's back, etc. The contents of the container are laid out in a logical sequence and care has been taken to ensure visibility for checking and safety purposes.

### Materials and construction

The container is made from plastics laminates and mouldings, and strength and rigidity are further enhanced by the seams between the mouldings and the use of honeycomb reinforcement for compartment panels. The stretcher comprises a combination of interlinked mouldings, panels and tubes with the three components being combined to enhance strength and rigidity.

The main components are made from injection-moulded rigid polyurethane foam (RPF) and extruded aluminium. The RPF is used for the container and its support and lids and for the surfaces and side panels of the stretcher. Aluminium tubing of a standard circular cross-section is used for the container handle and the stretcher supports, whereas the shafts are of an oval cross-section. Various small components and items in the container are made from polypropylene; the wheel treads are in Neoprene and the housings nylon.

## Further development and testing

The next step will be to build a prototype to test and evaluate the unit's actual performance, determine its physical and financial feasibility and obtain the necessary funding. Testing will take place in both ambulance and mountain rescue environments which present completely different challenges, and modification will probably prove necessary for use in an ambulance.

We will need to review the diagnostic and therapeutic contents in the light of experience and then produce one or two prototypes in manually moulded reinforced polyester resin to replace the model illustrated which was built from wood, plastics, aluminium, etc. The prototype would be used to manufacture dies for the larger reinforced polyester mouldings whilst the smaller components would be injection moulded. Certainly the prototype built will differ to some degree from the model shown in the illustrations.

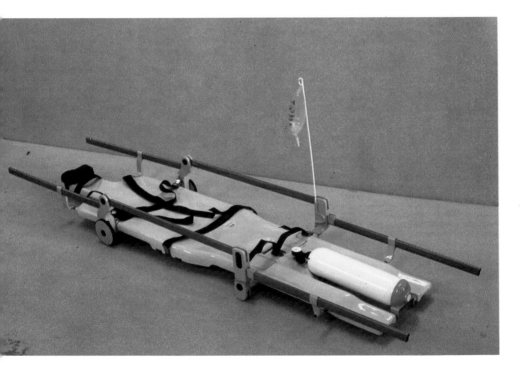

*The deployed stretcher showing the oxygen cylinder, the retaining straps, the intravenous drip support and the contoured, moulded horizontal surfaces.*

# Daedalus – A human-powered flight from Crete to mainland Greece

## John Sholar Langford, III

2509 St. John Place, Alexandria, Virginia 22311, USA

American, born 20 May 1957. Programme Manager, Daedalus Human-powered Flight Team. Educated in USA; Ph.D. candidate (Aeronautics and Public Policy) at Massachusetts Institute of Technology.

History records many more poetic, romantic and mythical references to flight than descriptions of vehicles capable of achieving it. Perhaps none is more famous than the Greek myth about Daedalus, a master craftsman who flew to freedom from imprisonment on the island of Crete using wings he had fashioned himself. Until very recently, such a voyage remained purely in the realm of the imagination: from Crete to a major land mass is a distance of more than 100 km. Only in this century has man found the capability for true heavier-than-air flight, and the greatest achievement to date in human-powered flight is about 35 km.

### Feasibility of a 100-km human-powered flight

Recent advances in aircraft structures, aerodynamics and propulsion may now make it possible, however, for Daedalus' flight to be turned into a reality. A small group of students, faculty and recent alumni from the Massachusetts Institute of Technology (MIT), assisted by the Smithsonian Institution's National Air and Space Museum, have conducted a one-year study to evaluate the feasibility of such a flight and concluded that it is technically, physiologically, meteorologically and politically feasible, and that such a flight would have important benefits in terms of education, research and increased cultural awareness.

This judgement of feasibility is supported not only by detailed analyses and theoretical calculations, but also by an experimental research programme designed to reduce uncertainty in key areas such as: aerodynamics, where members of the study team have developed an airfoil with 30% less drag than that used on previous human-powered aircraft; structures and materials, where we have designed and built an advanced all-composite wing structure, and tested sections in the laboratory; human endurance, where, in co-operation with the Yale University School of Medicine, we have conducted investigations into the factors that limit human athletic endurance and successfully demonstrated a flight-power, full-duration (four hours) test on an ergometer; and meteorology, where we have reviewed detailed historical data in the region and concluded that flight opportunities do indeed exist. Coupled with our experience from two previous human-powered aircraft, the *Chrysalis* and the *Monarch*, we are confident that the chances for completing this historic flight are good.

### Beneficial spin-offs of the venture

There are numerous reasons for undertaking such a venture. Perhaps the most important is education. Through MIT, this project would provide a hands-on interdisciplinary design experience for undergraduate and graduate students. In addition to involving students in aeronautical and mechanical engineering, the project also draws together students and faculty from such diverse fields as classical literature, archaeology and anthropology, meteorology and the medical sciences.

Another benefit will be scientific research in aeronautics, physiology and meteorology. The project will advance aeronautical technology, providing a stimulus for improvements in aircraft structures, aerodynamics and energy-efficient vehicle design. The project will continue to advance our understanding of the limits of human performance, especially in tasks involving both physical and mental workloads. Micro-meteorological data recorded using automatic weather stations deployed at the take-off and landing sites will expand the data base for the Mediterranean region.

*The* Michelob Light Eagle *long-range human-powered aircraft shortly before its formal roll-out on 15 October 1986.* Daedalus, *its companion aircraft, will attempt to make a flight of over 110 km from Crete to mainland Greece in fall 1987 or spring 1988. (Photo, Peggy Scott)*

A third benefit will be cultural awareness. In our experience, this is an extremely rare project with the ability to excite specialists in the humanities, science and engineering. We believe that, properly structured, the project can help increase awareness of the long-standing relationships between art and science, and between the roots of technology and the roots of Western culture. Further, the project will promote international understanding and goodwill. We have received a warm and enthusiastic reception from the Greek Government and from numerous private citizens in Greece.

We believe that, together, the elements of imagination, adventure and youthful enthusiasm will capture the public imagination.

**Project implementation**

The project itself has three phases. The first phase was a feasibility study, with emphasis on aerodynamics, structures, physiology and meteorology, and was completed in April 1986. The second phase verified the design and helped in recruiting and training pilots and in the construction and testing of a prototype aircraft. The third and final phase will revise the aircraft design and operate it from Crete; it could begin in 1987 if financial support is available.

In summary, we believe that the proposed celebration of Daedalus through a human-powered flight from Crete to mainland Greece is feasible in terms of aircraft technology, human factors, weather and international co-operation. The project is uniquely interdisciplinary and promises to capture the imagination of people around the world. It would have important benefits in terms of education, research and increased cultural awareness.

*The* Michelob Light Eagle *long-range human-powered aircraft on test flight. This prototype's successor, to be named* Daedalus, *is planned to symbolically recreate the mythical flight of Daedalus, by flying under human power more than 110 km from Crete to mainland Greece. (Photo Peggy Scott)*

# Vision substitution for congenitally blind children in Mexico

## Paul Bach-y-Rita

Department of Rehabilitation Medicine, E3/346, University of Wisconsin Hospital and Clinics, 600 Highland Avenue, Madison, Wisconsin 53792, USA

American, born 24 April 1934. Professor and Chairman, Department of Rehabilitation Medicine. Educated in USA and Mexico; M.D. from the Escuela Nacional de Medicina, Universidad Nacional Autónoma de México in 1959.

Persons who are blind from birth, or who have become blind at an early age, do not develop visual spatial concepts – which results in both developmental delays and longer-term cognitive and perceptual alterations in their representation of three-dimensional space, the objects that populate it, and their self-representation.

Although it is not possible to replace sensory systems, developments in electronics and perceptual psychology now allow congenitally blind persons to have access to visual information. Thus, although practical substitution systems are not yet available for everyday use by blind persons, it is now possible for a blind person to perceive previously inaccessible information. Our objective is to establish a pilot programme in Mexico to use this newly available technology in training congenitally blind children to understand the visual world.

### Developing a vision substitution system

For a number of years, we have been developing a tactile vision-substitution system (TVSS) in which an optical image captured by a television camera is converted into a tactile display and delivered to the skin of the trunk, with each stimulated point on the skin representing one small area of the image captured by the camera. After sufficient perceptual and motor training, users reported the perception of objects and events in space (not against the skin) and learned to make perceptual judgements using what appeared to be visual means of analysis.

However, it was not until our recent development of a simple modification of a commercially available instrument that the planning of training programmes for congenitally blind children became possible. This modified Optacon is a second-generation device functioning in the same way as the original TVSS.

The Optacon is a commercially available reading device for blind persons that uses the skin of the finger as a receptor surface for optical information. It consists

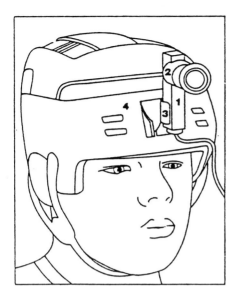

An overall diagram of the standard Optacon device (1), modified by a lens attachment (2) and attached to a light headpiece (4) by means of an adjustable clasp (3).

A detailed view of the standard Optacon device (1) modified by a lens attachment (2) and attached to a light headpiece (4) by means of an adjustable clasp (3). The zoom is located at (5). (opposite)

of a matrix of photocells and a corresponding matrix of skin stimulators. The blind person passes an array of photocells across a line of print on a page and receives the output on a stimulus array of piezo-electric driven vibrating tips on the fingertip. Preliminary work with early blind subjects has demonstrated that much of the information provided by the original TVSS can also be accessed and used via the modified Optacon.

## A training programme in Mexico

Having demonstrated that the congenitally blind can thus learn a great deal about the visual world – and can, in particular, learn to use such spatial concepts as perspective, parallax, looming, zooming and subjective localization in space – we are now developing the curriculum material that would enable this to be taught to blind children in various institutions and countries. My goal is to establish such a programme in Mexico. There are many more blind children in the developing than in the developed countries, and a programme in Mexico would serve as a model for other developing countries. It would, hopefully, enable us to teach congenitally blind persons in many countries to understand and appreciate the world of the sighted.

The main goals of the work are to: develop the methodology and procedures for teaching visual spatial concepts to congenitally blind children in order to overcome some of their perceptual and psychological deficits; and evaluate the benefits and costs of achieving the above-mentioned goals in Third World countries.

The training programme in Mexico will be developed in collaboration with a family development agency in the State of Roelos, called Desarollo Integral de la Familia (DIF). A trainer will be recruited in Mexico, and brought to the University of Wisconsin for training. One of the researchers from the University of Wisconsin will go to Mexico to help to start the project.

40

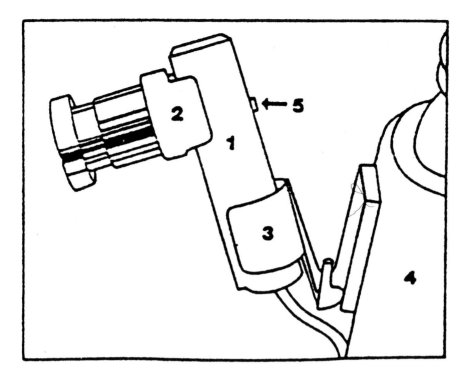

## Programme design and evaluation

The subjects will be congenitally blind children and adults. For the purposes of the project, we will define the congenitally blind as being those who were diagnosed as blind prior to six months of age and who have no visual memory and no more than minimal light perception. We plan to train four groups of children plus a group of adults. Our goal will be to train between four and six subjects in each age group over a period of three years. Each subject will receive between one and two hours of training per week. A comprehensive evaluation programme will be built in.

The training programme in Mexico would serve as a pilot project from which we would develop the knowledge base to extend the training programmes to other Third World countries. In particular, we would collect data on: the costs of setting up a training programme in a Third World country; teacher training requirements; the optimal ratio of trainers to blind children, and the practical geographical extent of each project; travel considerations – such as the relative merits of bringing children to a central location for training, or having the training person travel to various locations on a regular schedule; and, in particular, the usefulness that this training will have for the blind children.

One instrument and trainer (or small training team) can serve a number of blind children. Thus, total costs for training each child should be quite reasonable. Assessing the results of the proposed project should enable us to provide useful input to international agencies and Third World governments on the establishment of further programmes.

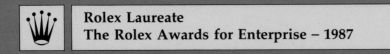
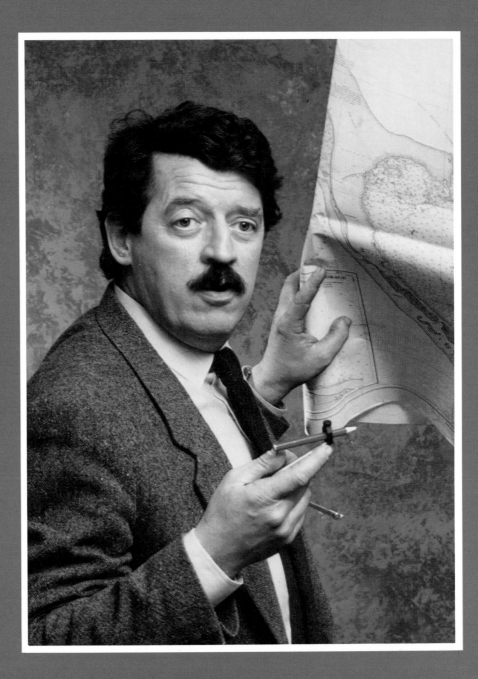

# MFV *Listaos* – Medical and technical aid for the Indian Ocean archipelagos

 *Jacques Luc Autran*

La Grassie, route des Milles, Le Pont de l'Arc, 13090 Aix-en-Provence, France

French, born 16 April 1943. Founder and president of the "Marins Sans Frontières" association, and captain and chief engineer of MFV *Listaos*. Educated in France: studied (Economics) at Faculty of Law, Paris and (Theology and Philosophy) at Institut Catholique, Paris from 1965 to 1968.

---

Several years of navigation in various archipelagos have given Martine Le Fur, a physician, and myself, an engineer, an insight into the problems that are endured by populations isolated by the sea, and induced us to take up the challenge of using our combined knowledge, skills and energy to improve the way of life and the standard of living of these people. Our first step was to set up an association entitled "Marins Sans Frontières" (Seamen without Frontiers) to put our objectives into effect and acquire a motor fishing vessel, the MFV *Listaos*, for sale at scrap-iron price in Cherbourg harbour. Though the boat looked very badly rusted, closer investigation revealed that she had retained the qualities of strength and seaworthiness that are characteristic of traditional motor fishing vessels. With her medium tonnage, large hold, engine power and accommodation for 20 people, she seemed to be what "Marins Sans Frontières" was looking for; and in 1981 we purchased her.

## Making MFV *Listaos* ready for sea

Using salvaged tools, equipment and other materials and obtaining the help of many friends kept the cost of rebuilding the boat to only one-tenth of the 5 million or so French francs that would have been charged by a shipyard. Over 50 different companies have helped by giving or lending tools and salvaged materials, by providing valuable advice or even, at times, doing certain jobs free of charge. The MFV *Listaos* is subject to stringent legal requirements, and to obtain the necessary official certificates and permits, all the work has had to be inspected as for any large ship. However, at the end of 1985, many thousands of hours of work were finally rewarded by the signing of all official papers. Subsequently, MFV *Listaos* sailed 3,200km from Cherbourg to Marseille via

*Jacques Luc Autran, Rolex Laureate – The Rolex Awards for Enterprise 1987, explaining some of the navigation problems to be faced by the MFV* Listaos *in its humanitarian mission.*

43

Gibraltar and proved she was ready to undertake her faraway missions.

Marins Sans Frontières is a registered not-for-profit organization in France, and can receive tax-deductible gifts and apply for grants from official bodies. However, such external resources cover only a third of the association's budget, and applications are being made to various French Ministries for subsidies. Yet even if these fund-raising efforts fail, the team is determined to pursue its aims, if necessary by working to earn the money needed to help the islanders.

## Planning our missions

Recently, it was decided to undertake a 1987–1991 long-term mission to the Maldives archipelago in the Indian Ocean where the majority of island people are calling for better living conditions. The local physicians are all in Male, the capital, and a patient from an outlying island may have to travel five days by boat to obtain medical care. When I visited the Maldives in 1983 and 1984, the Government requested us to undertake – in collaboration with such bodies as the World Health Organization, UNICEF and the United Nations Development Programme – an immunization and health education campaign on the islands. Recently, the Director of Health of the Maldives visited us in Cherbourg to encourage us in our work and confirm his interest in our project.

The MFV *Listaos* is ideally suited for work amongst the atolls in this region. With a fuel capacity of 25,000 l, she has a cruising range of 6,500 nautical miles and this range will be increased by wind propulsion fore and aft, a rigid sail amidships and a series of kites. Three wind-powered generators, a photovoltaic solar battery system, two systems using waves and currents for electricity production and an outboard desalination unit all go to increase the vessel's autonomy. Furthermore, the boat has been fitted with the refrigeration equipment needed to ensure adequate cold storage for vaccines, and has sufficient accommodation space for the 15 Maldivians who will join the medical team. During the campaign, *Listaos* will drop anchor off an island reef and the four or so western physicians and nurses, together with the Maldivian team, will set up a light dispensary on shore. Difficult cases can be treated on board the *Listaos* which has a small operating theatre, a complete pharmacy, a well-equipped laboratory, sterilizers, etc. Local midwives and family health workers will be trained in vaccination, diagnosis and simple treatment procedures, and will be able to continue this work even after the *Listaos* has moved on.

A programme such as this would, of course, be too much for the *Listaos* crew to undertake alone, but several other non-governmental organizations (Médecins Sans Frontières, Volontaires du Progrès, Terre des Hommes, Bioforce, etc.) have already offered their help. We have also been asked to undertake programmes in the Comoro Islands, Madagascar and the Mauritius archipelago, and hope to be able to follow the age-old wake of the dhows of the Indian Ocean on a schedule laid down by the monsoon cycle: from December to June, during the dry winter monsoon, north of the equator and the other six months to the south.

Operating costs for extended cruising are estimated at 2,000 French francs per day and, while on mission, funding will be met by the charterer; however, the priority task is to raise some 200,000 French francs required to cover the bunkerage, port, canal and victualling costs for the outward journey from Marseilles to the Indian Ocean – and this currently is the centre of our efforts.

*Jacques Luc Autran (left) at the wheel of the MFV* Listaos *giving explanations to Dr. Samad Abdullah, Director of Health of the Republic of the Maldives.*

*Jacques Luc Autran, in his blue overalls, leans against an electricity distribution box and takes a break from his work on the refitting of MFV* Listaos *behind him.*

# "Living contact lenses" to correct childhood and adult functional blindness

## Marguerite Bridget McDonald

Louisiana State University Medical Center, Eye Center, 136 South Roman Street, New Orleans, Louisiana 70112, USA

American, born 14 October 1950. Associate Professor of Ophthalmology, Louisiana State University Medical Center. Educated in USA; M.D. from Columbia University College of Physicians and Surgeons in 1976.

Most patients who have had a cataract removed can see only light and dark and vague shapes because the incoming light is not focused properly on the retina. The natural lens that has been removed can be replaced by very heavy spectacles, contact lenses, or intraocular lenses; however, such devices are not suitable for some patients. It is for these people that our project has developed epikeratophakia, a technique that offers a permanent form of correction which becomes a part of the eye – in effect, a "living contact lens".

### Restoring adequate vision after cataract removal

A person with a cataract cannot see because his lens is cloudy, and light cannot get through to the retina from which the visual signals are sent to the brain. The function of the lens is to bend incoming light to focus on the retina. After the cataract has been removed, the patient still cannot see, because the incoming light is not bent enough and the point of focus is somewhere way beyond the back of the eye.

Although the patient who has had a cataract removed can see light and dark and some vague shapes, useful vision requires a replacement lens such as cataract spectacles. However, these have very thick unattractive lenses that cause visual distortion, give good vision only in the central area of the lens, and enlarge what the patient sees by about 20 to 35%, which causes objects to "pop" in and out of focus as though seen through binoculars. Moreover, they are impossible to use when a cataract has been removed from only one eye; the image seen through these glasses is so much larger and so distorted compared with what is seen by the other, normal, eye that the brain usually cannot match up the two images and suppresses one entirely.

Contact lenses are also used but certain patients are unable to manipulate them as a result of arthritis, poor vision in the other eye or some other debilitating disease; some simply cannot tolerate contact lenses at all. Intraocular lenses are another solution but, in particular, there has been some reluctance to implant these lenses in very young patients because of the increasing risk of complications over long periods of time.

### The advantages of epikeratophakia

In epikeratophakia, a piece of donated cornea is frozen and shaped to the patient's specification, much like a contact lens. The top layer of cells on the patient's cornea (the epithelium) is removed and the "contact lens" is sewn on to the front of the cornea. Eventually, the epithelium grows over the added tissue, and cells from the patient's cornea move into the new tissue and make it a living part of the eye. The added tissue bends the incoming light to focus on the retina, replacing the function of the lost natural lens. Many patients have achieved 20/20 vision after epikeratophakia with only slight additional spectacle correction from ordinary "reading-type" glasses.

Epikeratophakia grafts have been used in newborns and very young children with congenital cataracts and cataracts caused by injury to the eye. In a baby or young child, an eye which has no vision during the critical period of development may become permanently blind, even though there is nothing organically wrong. Restoration of useful vision is relatively urgent here; however, though surgical removal of the cataract is fairly simple, improving vision in these tiny patients has been very difficult. Spectacles or contact lenses are difficult to fit and put a heavy burden of attention and constant care on the parents. By the time such a child is six months old, he can usually pop a contact lens out of his eye at will, and this can be costly and hinder visual rehabilitation. In contrast, the epikeratophakia graft is permanently attached and allows the child to see with the affected eye. Then, the unaffected eye is patched for most of the time the child is awake, so that he is forced to use the weaker eye.

Epikeratophakia can also be used for keratoconus, a hereditary disease in

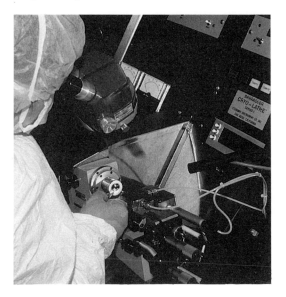

*In the production of "living contact lenses" to correct functional blindness, a donor cornea is frozen and cut to a specified dioptric power and keratometric reading on a complex machine called a cryolathe.*

which the cornea bulges and becomes thin and weak. An epikeratophakia graft of uniform thickness is sutured tightly over the bulging cornea, reinforcing the weakened cornea and reducing the irregularities in shape so that a contact lens can be worn comfortably. Epikeratophakia can, furthermore, be adapted to the correction of myopia (nearsightedness) where, although there is nothing organically wrong with the nearsighted eye, vision is impaired because the light focuses too far in front of the retina. The major difference between this kind of correction and that for cataract patients is the shape of the graft. For cataract patients, the graft is thicker in the middle and thinner on the edges, in order to increase the amount the light is bent. For myopia, the graft is thinner in the middle and thicker at the edges, to "unbend" the light somewhat and move the point of focus farther back in the eye.

## A boon for the functionally blind worldwide

The technique of epikeratophakia has added a new dimension to the treatment of cataract and a number of other ophthalmic disorders and has now been performed by more than 300 surgeons throughout the world. In the course of development, the living contact lens has saved the sight of hundreds of children and adults, and with further refinement, will provide visual rehabilitation to many more.

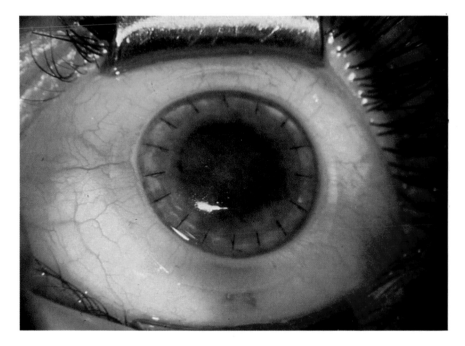

*A Kerato-lens completely sutured in place.*

# Using large amateur telescopes in the visual search for comets

## *Rolf Georg Meier*

4A Arnold Drive, Nepean, Ontario K2H 6V9, Canada

Canadian, born 24 July 1953. Electrical engineer and telecommunications circuit designer. Educated in Canada; B.Eng. (Electrical) from Carleton University in 1977.

As an amateur astronomer, I have aimed my project at discovering comets and, to date, I have myself independently discovered four new comets. Although experts originally considered my technique inappropriate for comet hunting, it has proven vastly superior to previous methods, and has since been adopted by other comet hunters in other parts of the world with similar success. I am currently developing a new observatory which will expand the possibilities for continuing this work. Briefly, the technique involves the use of a large telescope, visually, at relatively high power. Previous visual searches have relied on smaller apertures, which yield lower power but a larger field of view. The scientific benefits to be derived by using the new technique are important.

### A new approach to comet hunting

During the twentieth century, comet hunting by amateur astronomers evolved into visual sweeping using low-power, small-aperture telescopes and, by the 1960s, the typical comet-hunting instrument was a 15 cm reflector, working at a magnification of between 21x and 30x or binoculars measuring 14 x 100 or 18 x 125. Larger telescopes were considered to yield too small a field of view since a new comet may appear anywhere in the sky, and a wide field of view is required to cover as large an area of the sky as possible.

My answer was to use a larger telescope at low power (i.e. aiming at a magnification of less than 1.4x per cm of aperture to ensure that light is not wasted outside the pupil of the eye (which is about 7 mm in diameter when fully dark-adapted). The opening in 1971 of an observatory with a 40 cm reflecting telescope by the Ottawa Centre of the Royal Astronomical Society of Canada offered the opportunity of putting my concept into practice on an instrument which was – especially at that time – large by amateur standards. It soon became apparent that its extra light-gathering power could be put to good scientific use and, in 1974, finding that a number of the telescope's features made it well adapted to my project, I began an earnest programme of comet hunting.

On 26 April 1978, I discovered my first comet, Comet Meier 1978f, after about 50 hours of sweeping. My searching continued and, on 19 September 1979, I made my second discovery, Comet Meier 1979i, after 29 more hours of sweeping. The next discovery came after a further 25 hours of sweeping, on 6 November 1980. This is Comet Meier 1980q. Finally, after 82 more hours of sweeping, the latest discovery took place, on 17 September 1984. This latest find is Comet Meier 1984o. Thus, in a total of 191 hours, I discovered four comets whereas the literature indicates that the comet hunter using smaller telescopes can usually expect to spend at least 200 hours sweeping before finding a single comet.

## The advantages of larger telescope apertures

Essentially the superiority of my new technique over the classical approach is attributable to the fact that, although doubling the telescope aperture reduces the visible area to one-quarter of the size, it does at the same time increase light-gathering capability by a factor of four, since the objective area is proportional to the square of the diameter. So the two factors appear to balance each other out. Double the aperture, and you observe one-quarter the area of sky, and you have one-quarter the chance of seeing a comet. However, double the aperture, and you have four times the light, and comets four times dimmer are visible, and so there are four times as many comets to be seen.

However, there are in fact far more than four times as many comets to be seen if you can see four times fainter. If you can see objects four times fainter, a comet twice as far away can be seen. However, a comet occupies three-dimensional space in the solar system and the volume of space enclosed by a sphere of double the diameter is actually the cube of 2, i.e. 8. If one assumes that comets are evenly distributed in space, then it is clear that a doubling of aperture

*The 40-cm telescope used by Rolf Meier for his comet-hunting programme.*

*Rolf Meier with a model of the observatory he is planning to build to continue and expand his comet-hunting programme.*

actually brings eight times as many comets potentially into view. My own experience has borne out my theory. However, there are other observers who have followed the same philosophy deliberately with success.

### Building an observatory to continue the search

My future plans call for the construction of an observatory for a 45 cm f/4.5 telescope which has already been built but which is currently mounted on a trailer for portability. The observatory will be of unique design with the telescope optics outside the dome and the observer remaining inside, protected from the elements and insects and with a comfortable working environment. A microcomputer will be used to perform the tracking functions and provide position read-out. Using a database, it will be possible to quickly identify objects which are encountered in a visual sweep of the sky, and eliminate non-comet objects much more quickly than before. The observatory will be built on a 32 ha site about 40 km west of the city of Ottawa. The site is sufficiently remote and has a large enough local buffer zone to ensure dark skies.

The benefits to science of using large apertures for comet hunting should be apparent. If a new comet can be discovered early, when it is faint and far out, there is more time for detailed study by the astronomical community. Comets are relatively rare phenomena, so the sample size available for study is small. Actually, most comets never become bright enough to be seen in smaller amateur instruments. Nevertheless, professional astronomers are keenly interested in observing all comets.

# Device for taking photographs from a point high above the ground

## Claude Lambolez

14 rue de la Chapelle, 88160 Le Thillot, France

French, born 2 September 1946. Construction draughtsman.

This project has invented and patented the Lambolair – a device for taking photographs from a point high above the ground without it being necessary for the photographer himself to leave ground level.

### The need for photographs taken from the air

Aerial photographs taken from airplanes or helicopters are nowadays common practice; the photographer is installed in the aircraft with his equipment and takes his photographs as he flies across or circles around the target. However, photographs of this type have to be taken from a relatively high altitude since neither airplanes nor helicopters can fly at very low levels in all the vicinities where photographs are required such as, for example, town and village thoroughfares, public spaces, etc. Nevertheless, it is often desirable to photograph a house, building, monument, or open air gathering, etc., from a point higher than the ground, for example, from a height of some 5 to 15 m, or may be somewhat higher still. However, it is not at all practical to have recourse to an airplane or a helicopter for the purpose in question.

It is also often useful to be able to photograph, from a point at some height above the ground, the details of a building façade, a statue or a roof, etc., and for practical reasons, the use of an airplane or a helicopter would be totally out of the question here; this is all the more true for financial reasons when one takes into account the hourly cost of flying.

### Replacing the aircraft by a beanstalk

The system I have invented is intended to provide a rapid and eminently economical solution to the problem of taking this type of photograph from a height without the photographer having to actually leave *terra firma*, and especially in those cases in which the use of an aircraft is out of the question.

The main structure of the device consists of a metal framework which is attached to the roof of a normal family saloon car or station wagon. The upper section, which slides to the rear, holds in place the mast using a jointed collar to retain it in the vertical position. The base of the mast, itself, is fixed to a standard trailer towing ball fitted to the rear of the car. The adjustable metal framework is designed in such a way that the mast can be located in a perfectly vertical position no matter what the angle of the slope on which the automobile is parked. The mast is manufactured from four telescopic elements and, when fully extended by means of its integral pneumatic system, will reach to a maximum height of 12 m above the ground.

The combined video/photographic camera unit is fitted to the top of the mast and is connected to the ground by a number of control cables. The video and photographic cameras are located on a metal platform and are protected by a metal housing which can be raised and lowered, tilted and slewed through a full 360°. The photographic camera is placed in front of the television camera and aims through the lens of the latter. The unit is linked through a cable to a television monitor situated in the car and all the movements of the platform, the focusing and zooming of the lens, and the release of the shutter are controlled from the vehicle. In this way, the attitude of the camera can be modified at will and, in addition, the vehicle can be moved from one location to another without it being necessary to completely dismantle the installation since its only contact with the ground is through the vehicle's four tyres.

The Lambolair mast has a wide range of applications. For example, the still

*The Lambolair L.12 beanstalk viewing system installed on the back of an automobile.*

53

camera can be replaced by a cine or video camera which, in view of the total mobility of the platform, operates exactly as though it were being handled by a human operator. The shot taken from a height of 12 m and from a horizontal distance of 20 m from the subject is exactly at what I call "a good angle".

### A new project for spring 1986

The new development for spring 1986 is a derivative of the original Lambolair system but is designed for manual use. It will be smaller in size than the original design, with a mast that can be extended to a height of 5–6 m, and it is intended to allow the roving photographer to take aerial photographs from the ground without the need for the dangerous gymnastics involved in climbing ladders, etc. In addition to the mast, the installation will comprise: a support for the photographic and video camera; a belt-mounted video monitor with an 8-cm screen; a belt-mounted battery with converter, junction box and a mains charger; an adjustable mast-head platform and the related control box; and the necessary connecting cables. The mast can be fitted with a safety foot if necessary, and the operator will orientate it manually on site, controlling the correctness of the direction by means of the portable television monitor attached to his belt. The azimuth angle is adjusted by means of a motorized control unit. If the viewing angle is more or less correct, the motor is not required and the angle can be adjusted with a slight movement of the hands.

*The Lambolair team exhibiting their automobile-mounted and portable beanstalk viewing system at the Photokina world fair.*

# Design of windpumps for manufacture in Third World countries

## Michael Harries

Karamaini Estate, POB 40, Thika, Kenya

Kenyan, born 29 September 1938. Managing Director of a family farm, and Chairman and Managing Director, Kijito Windpumping Company. Educated in Kenya and UK; M.A. from St. John's College, Cambridge, in 1962.

In the main catchment areas for the great Tana River, rainfall during the 1970s dropped 15% lower than the level for the previous decade; this unfortunately came at a time when Kenya was experiencing an increased demand for electricity. Another result of this lower rainfall was that power on our family farm was rationed for several days a week, which did not make running things very easy. At the same time, Kenya experienced hugely increased foreign exchange payments for its imported oil, and the combination of these factors prompted me to explore the possibilities of using alternative energy devices that would be appropriate not only to the needs of Kenya, but also for manufacture in Third World countries, thus offering the threefold benefit of increasing local skills, generating employment and reducing imports.

### A search for alternative energy sources

Various alternative sources of energy were considered during 1977, including methane gas, steam, micro-hydro and solar. However it was in 1975, when I first saw an operating windpump, that I became convinced that the development of this technology could be instrumental in bringing clean and cheap water to the peoples of Africa and their livestock. Considerable numbers of windpumps had been installed in Kenya up until about 1950, prior to the development of small internal combustion engines, which often ran on very cheap subsidized fuel.

Windpumps had also, of course, spearheaded the early agricultural development of arid areas in the United States and Australia, where several companies are still supplying them to what is once more a growing market. Even in 1977, it seemed to me that in view of the changing situation worldwide, windpumps would once again play a role, especially in the rural and desert areas of the Third World. Diesel engines had been widely installed in these areas in the past, but their reliability and running costs had left much to be desired. Maintenance requirements of the traditional windpump designs were minimal, and if this concept could be combined with local manufacture then the benefit to countries such as Kenya could be considerable.

55

## The windpump project

The "Kijito" project really started in April 1977 when I saw the first Intermediate Technology Development Group (ITDG) prototype windpump working at Reading University in England. Because of the way oil was increasing in price in the mid-1970s I decided to try to develop something that would help my country reduce its reliance on expensive imports, and chose to work on developing a range of windpumps that could be manufactured in Africa. At that time I met a certain amount of opposition from those who felt I was trying to resurrect a discarded technology and that what Africa needed was the modern technology of photovoltaics. Obviously, I do not doubt that such developments will play a very real and increasing role in the future, but I am convinced that, by themselves, they cannot solve the water supply problems of rural Africa.

In recent years the world has become painfully aware of the disasters occurring in some parts of Africa; undoubtedly the provision of clean drinking water is part of the long-term solution to the problem. But even this became a subject of controversy as some felt the nomadic tribes of Africa should be left to wander in their old traditional ways, which was fine when there were few people and much land, but today's situation being exactly the opposite they can no longer live without being introduced gradually to changes and innovations of recent decades. The desert can bloom with a vastly increased population only if

*A powerful "Kijito" windpump fitted with a rotor some 8 m in diameter, which Michael Harries developed from his original shallow-well design.*

*A glimpse of the future. A small "Wananchi" windpump lifting water for a Kenyan smallholder farmer near Thika.*

the people have access to the most efficient ways of utilizing the scant water existing, which must include rain harvesting, crop breeding, drip irrigation and windpumps.

### The future of windpower

There are still many areas in which the use of windpower can be expanded to help the rural poor of the Third World. The growing deforestation problem in Africa, where the main fuel for cooking is wood, is a case in point. In the future, I would like to attempt production of a simple wind generator that could enable these people to cook with wind.

Meanwhile the biggest problem still to be overcome remains the provision of clean, safe drinking water. After eight years of practical experience, I am now selling four different sizes of windpumps, and would like now to develop a much cheaper, smaller windpump, designed so as to enable the smallholder to install and repair it himself, using such appropriate components as wooden bearings, and a simplified pump mechanism.

We have built a few prototype machines but they are still too expensive for the many smallholders who, in Kenya, are responsible for the greater part of our agricultural input. Therefore to produce a machine that will fill their need is our next development challenge and priority.

# Rebuilding a heart from skeletal muscle

## Larry Warren Stephenson

Department of Surgery, Hospital of the University of Pennsylvania, 3400 Spruce Street, Philadelphia, Pennsylvania 19104, USA

American, born 26 February 1944. Associate Professor of Surgery, Division of Cardiothoracic Surgery at the University of Pennsylvania School of Medicine. Educated in USA; M.D. from Marquette Medical School in 1970.

Each year in the USA, an estimated 10,000 patients are diagnosed as having irreversible congestive heart failure and, despite medical and/or surgical treatment, half of them die within one year of diagnosis. Moreover, since neither medical therapy, cardiac transplantation nor artificial hearts can be expected to benefit these patients in the near future, my laboratory has been investigating a potential fourth therapeutic alternative: the use of a patient's own skeletal muscle to augment cardiac performance. A person's own skeletal muscle is not subject to tissue rejection, would not be hampered by a donor shortage and would alleviate the necessity for a cumbersome and expensive external power source.

### Experimenting the use of skeletal muscle

Over the past seven years, animal research in my laboratory has shown that portions of the right or left ventricles – the pumping chambers of the heart – can be replaced by skeletal muscle. Within a month, these skeletal muscle grafts form common blood vessels with the heart and, even one year later, they continue to contract in synchrony with the heart if they are continually stimulated with the appropriate type of cardiac pacemaker. Recently, cardiac surgical teams in Paris, France, and Pittsburgh, Pennsylvania, have used the concept developed in my laboratory to patch human hearts.

These muscles undergo significant biochemical and mechanical changes and become more fatigue-resistant and similar to heart muscle. We have stimulated some of these muscles continuously for as long as one year at rates similar to or higher than the natural heart rate and they continued to contract vigorously and appropriately at the end of that time period. The electrical current required to cause contraction in nerve-stimulated muscle was only about half that needed to power a cardiac pacemaker. Our studies on the effect of various patterns of chronic electrical stimulation have shown that bursts of electrical stimuli cause much more forceful contractions and that long-term stimulation of skeletal muscle with electrical bursts of the type and frequency necessary to actuate a skeletal muscle ventricle makes the muscle much more fatigue-resistant.

## The right type of muscle

The replacement muscles studied all exist in pairs, left and right, in the human body: diaphragm muscle, which is used in breathing; the latissimus dorsi, the large muscles in the back; the pectoralis, the muscles in the upper chest; and the rectus abdominus, the muscles in the abdomen. These are considered non-critical in that most patients can function fairly well without use of one of the pairs of these muscles. In fact, plastic surgeons use some of these muscles for covering soft-tissue defects in the body and for cosmetic surgery.

We have studied the blood supply to these muscles during rest and exercise, thereby allowing us to understand how best to use the muscles for myocardial augmentation or replacement. It was found that the muscles can be conditioned and made fatigue-resistant before removal or after grafting, and that ventricles can be constructed with this fatigue-resistant muscle. Such skeletal-muscle-powered ventricles, when connected to the arterial circulation, are capable of generating significant pressures and of pumping up to 20% of the blood pumped by the heart for many hours.

More recently, we have constructed skeletal muscle ventricles of multi-layered latissimus dorsi muscle which, several weeks later, continued to generate significant pressures and flows without evidence of fatigue. Skeletal muscle ventricles can also be conditioned electrically whilst they are performing useful work as a pump motor – which is important since a seriously ill patient needing a skeletal muscle ventricle for circulatory support may not be able to wait the several weeks necessary for electrical pre-conditioning.

## Promise for the future

A skeletal muscle assist would avoid the problems of energy source, tissue rejection, donor supply and prohibitive cost. Although progress has been made in this basic biomedical investigation of skeletal muscle, until my present research, relatively little effort had been made in the surgical application of skeletal muscle for cardiac augmentation.

The specific contributions made by my laboratory include the pioneering work in demonstrating that full-thickness portions of the ventricles could be replaced with skeletal muscle. We showed that the muscle grafts would form a common blood supply with the heart muscle and would continue to contract in synchrony with the heart up to one year later when stimulated with an R-wave synchronous pacemaker. We were the first to demonstrate that skeletal muscle could be transformed to a very fatigue-resistant type of muscle when the muscle was stimulated directly or through its nerve at the average heart rate of the dog. My laboratory has demonstrated that stimulation at or above the natural canine heart rate is well tolerated by the muscle even at one year. We have been one of only a few groups to have reported on a successful acute model of a skeletal muscle ventricle. To date, the most important accomplishment of my laboratory is that we have developed a chronic autologous biological pump motor.

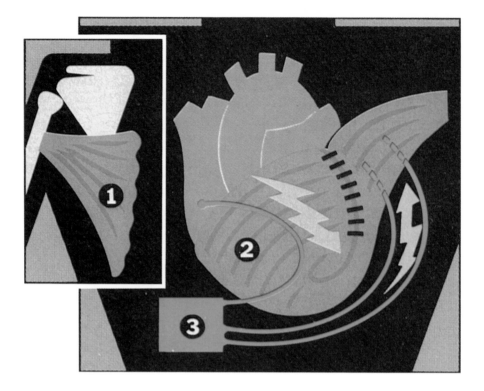

*A skeletal muscle,* latissimus dorsi *(1) taken from the back with the nerve and blood vessels intact. It is wrapped around the damaged heart (2), and a pacemaker (3) is attached to stimulate the muscle so that it will beat with the heart. (Copyright 1986, Time, Inc. All rights reserved. Reprinted by permission from* Time)*

I feel that the use of skeletal muscle to replace portions of the heart, or to function as a non-fatiguing biological pump motor, holds great promise for patients with failing hearts who require chronic circulatory assistance, and may also prove of benefit to children with certain types of complex congenital heart disease. Future prospects may be even greater since there are indications that skeletal muscle might also be used to power an artificial heart or, at a later date, be used to replace the heart as a whole.

# Spinal cord injury disabilities – Prevention, treatment and rehabilitation

## *Suseela Varma*
**Honourable Mention**
**The Rolex Awards for Enterprise – 1987**

Flat No. A.202, O.C.R. Colony, Husainganj, Vidhan Sabha Marg, Lucknow-226001, India

Indian, born 26 September 1928. Director, Rehabilitation and Artificial Limb Centre, Lucknow. Educated in India, UK and USA; M.S. (Orthopaedics) from K.G. Medical College in 1976.

The increase in the pace of life, faster and more dangerous vehicles, natural calamities and lack of knowledge in taking precautions in ordinary day-to-day activities have meant a rise in the number of disabled people with spinal cord lesions resulting in paraplegia or quadriplegia. A paraplegic patient is paralyzed from the waist down and has neither sensation nor movement in the paralyzed part of the body. Such a patient also loses control over his bladder and bowels and, if the necessary care is not provided, will be prone to suffer from many complications such as bed sores, urinary disorders, etc. which, in time, make him or her into a pitiful wreck of humanity lying inert, emaciated, demoralized, beyond help and hope and waiting only for death.

However, over the past 40 years this picture has changed appreciably throughout the world. It has been demonstrated that special units devoted to the treatment, care and rehabilitation of this type of patient not only help in reducing early mortality but also help them to achieve a state of independence physically, socially and economically. Having worked for six years at Stoke Mandeville Hospital, in the UK, under the dynamic leadership of the late Sir Ludwig Guttman, whose pioneering work in the field earned him worldwide fame, I realized that much more can be done for these severely disabled individuals in India too. It was a challenge and a tremendously satisfying project to raise these unfortunate individuals from the human scrap heap to become useful and self-respecting citizens.

### Improving prospects for paraplegics in India

The Traumatic Paraplegia Unit (Spinal Cord Injury Unit) at the Department of Orthopaedic Surgery of the K.G. Medical College in Lucknow, India, was started up in 1967 with six beds. This was one of the earliest units of its kind in India and, even with the limited funds and staff at our disposal, it was possible to demonstrate that with meticulous care, round-the-clock supervision and a

61

*Inauguration of the Spinal Cord Injury Unit at Lucknow, India.*

multidisciplinary therapeutic approach, an 80% mortality rate in paraplegics could be reversed into an 80% survival rate. With the passage of time, even better results were obtained and several of our paraplegics were able to return to useful employment. However, although the knowledge gained in England was of tremendous help, there was no way it could be simply duplicated in the Indian environment, and considerable adjustment and modification had to be made to suit the local conditions and way of life.

Cases were referred to our unit from all over Uttar Pradesh as well as other states in India, and soon we saw the need to develop this field and expand the unit by installing facilities to train personnel from other institutions as well as developing treatment and rehabilitation techniques more suited to local patients. With the help of a handsome grant sanctioned by our late Prime Minister, Mrs. Indira Gandhi, and a research scheme sponsored by the Indian Council of Medical Research, we were able to expand the Spinal Cord Injury Unit to 70 beds, comprising an acute wing with 40 beds in the K.G. Medical College and 30 beds at the Rehabilitation and Artificial Limb Centre in Lucknow. In all, over the 19-year period, the Unit has managed a total of 2,500 cases of spinal cord injury.

### The need for more education

A comparative study I have made of cases managed in India and in Western countries has shown that vascular complications such as thrombosis and death due to pulmonary embolism are far less common in India, the psychological impact of disability on an Indian patient is different – the fatalistic attitude having its own advantages and disadvantages – and other types of equipment and appliances are needed, especially in rural areas, etc. It was also realized that the time and energy spent on the treatment and rehabilitation of the disabled needs to be backed up by greater concentration on augmenting the acceptance of paraplegics by society as a whole.

The Regional Rehabilitation Training Centre set up at our Rehabilitation and Artificial Limb Centre by the Indian Government with American collaboration for the training of rehabilitation personnel, has given us an opportunity to take these services to the rural areas. It would be valuable if our Unit could collect and exchange information and consolidate the work done in a small number of other units that have since been established in India to help in the proper integration of the disabled into able-bodied society. To achieve this it will be necessary to educate both the medical community and the public at large. We do not have any comprehensive Indian text book on spinal cord injuries and the few text books published abroad are not readily available here. Moreover, since the complications that occur in Indian patients and the way they respond to management differ from those in Western countries, a book written specifically with the Indian patient in mind is essential as a guide to the young physicians who are to work in spinal cord injury units. It has been suggested that with 25 years' experience in this field in both England and India, and having visited similar units in the USA, Japan, Germany, France, etc., I would be able to undertake the writing of such a book. It is also essential to supply the lay public (the paraplegics and their relatives) with booklets giving advice on how to live with their disability and avoid complications, and to instruct them on what preventive measures to take.

## The production of educational materials

The work that remains to be done is considerable. It will be necessary to collect information and exchange views with those working in the various spinal cord injury units in India, and other countries if possible, to help the proper integration of the disabled with the able-bodied. Further studies should be made on complications, treatment results and the needs of the paraplegics in the various parts of India, taking into account the differences between their social and cultural background and that of patients in Western countries. All the information should then be compiled in a book for those specializing in this discipline in India, and booklets should be produced on the basic care to be taken by these wheelchair-bound patients to avoid complications.

I myself will need to undertake lecture tours to the various units in India and other developing countries if necessary, and guide the medical and paramedical personnel in the management of spinal cord injuries and, if necessary, help organize units to meet demands in each state. Finally, I plan to visit the spinal cord injured in their homes and places or work, study the difficulties that they meet in their day-to-day activities in their social and cultural background.

This is certainly a major task but one that can bring great relief to the suffering of these unfortunate people.

# A quick, economical and effective solution to prison overcrowding

## Donald Leo Kiselewski

4705 Holly Drive, Palm Beach Gardens, Florida 33418, USA

American, born 3 July 1935. Engineer and certified general contractor. Educated in USA; B.S. (Architectural Engineering) from Washington University, St. Louis in 1958.

Overcrowding in penal detention facilities is a growing social problem in many countries, and the necessary response to one aspect of the problem is the provision of more prison cells at the right place, at suitable cost and in a minimum construction time. However, prisons are often built at a distance from urban areas and, although off-site production of complete cells has frequently been attempted, this has not provided a satisfactory solution to the problem owing to transport, quality control factors, etc. My project has, therefore, been to develop a system for the construction of a low-cost modular prison cell that can be erected in a minimum of time.

### Creating a design

The criteria I set for the product were numerous. In particular, the unit had to be: low in cost and easy to construct; suitable for off-the-shelf delivery; adaptable to different soil conditions; suitable for year-round construction and installation; designed to meet prisoner-containment and comfort requirements and the relevant fire regulations; suitable for assembly-line production from a small number of durable and maintenance-free standard components; adequate for single- or multi-storey erection for new facilities, or the extension of existing prisons; and easy to assemble by construction manpower without a high level of training.

The patented system that I have developed employs assembly line/mass production methods to manufacture lightweight modules of six or more cells that are completely finished and furnished. These modules are transported by truck to the remote site and set on a perimeter foundation; after this, concrete is placed on the top of the module and then flows below the floor, between the walls and on top of the ceiling, completely cocooning each cell. After curing, the concrete gives the cell the stability, strength, fireproofing and durability to meet the requirements of the regulatory agencies for maximum security detention facilities.

64

*Once the walls have been erected on the cell floor, work can start on placing the ceiling/roof panels on the three-dimensional structure.*

In the factory environment, materials can be adequately stored and monitored, and unskilled labour can perform repetitive tasks under strict quality control. The factory enclosure allows for year-round construction on an even flow, and it is not dependent upon the weather. Jigs, fixtures and equipment utilized to assemble and test products can be more sophisticated and accomplish more of the work because the cost of such items can be amortized over a greater number of units. The factory facility can also store units complete, ready for shipment.

### Rationalized construction

The module is made from light-gauge steel with stainless steel inner panels for the interior floor, walls and ceiling. The necessary steel reinforcement for the concrete is incorporated on the assembly line, and all walls, floors and ceilings are fitted with connecting studs so that they are free of fasteners or other attachments that would be accessible from inside the cell. Six or more complete finished interior cells are interlocked wall to wall, and form a unit weighing around 9 t which can be transported on a flat-bed truck.

At the site, the module is unloaded on to the foundation in any number of random patterns to form the first vertical layers of cells. Pre-assembled special panels are shipped with the units in order to span hallways, enclosed space at the end of the hallway, etc. When all such panels and modules are in place, they are then interconnected, and concrete is pumped down the walls, under the

*The CEL-BLOCK prototype during the construction trial. Workers interlock the exterior wall with the interior module.*

floor, and finally over the top of the ceiling panels. The layer of concrete placed on the ceiling may be sloped for drainage, covered by insulation and capped by a roofing structure. Because the systems have already been installed and checked, the cells are ready for use.

### Producing a prototype and extending the unit's use

To prove the proposed design concept and materials, I constructed a prototype two-cell module in order to evaluate basic assembly, stability, etc. The accessory systems were not fitted, however, since proof of their suitability is already available. Once the module had been assembled it was filled with concrete which flowed uniformly beneath the floor, filled out the walls and was easily struck off on the roof. The unknowns of the design behaved as I had hoped and predicted. The system prototype had confirmed my design assumption. On 12 November 1985, I was granted a US Patent under the name CEL-BLOCK (the acronym CEL standing for Concrete-Encased Liner).

Discussions with officials in seven states have shown that the system meets their needs and have allowed me to determine individual requirements and develop specific design features to comply with the various standards. A preliminary design of the assembly process and the necessary jigs, fixtures and equipment has been completed but the various lifting devices for panels, cells and completed modules are still to be developed.

I have now demonstrated that the CEL-BLOCK system is viable, but I can also see that, although originally designed to deal with prison overcrowding, this system clearly has other potential applications and could be used, for example, in free-standing, automated banking facilities or bank vaults, etc.

# Oxfam water-supply scheme packs for emergency and long-term purposes

*James Charles Howard*

Oxfam, 274 Banbury Road, Oxford OX2 7DZ, England

British, born 11 March 1926. Technical adviser and chief engineer for Oxfam. Educated in UK; Fellow of the Institution of Public Health Engineers.

For many years, Oxfam and other agencies involved in relief, medical aid and development work in many parts of the world have been acutely aware of the health hazards created by an inadequate water supply. In spite of improvements in sanitation, health care, food supplies and housing, the overall well-being of the refugee or any other groups of people relies heavily upon the adequacy and quality of the water supply.

### Developing and testing better water-supply facilities

Where urgent and sometimes difficult emergency conditions prevail, there is a need for simpler and quicker solutions. To provide answers, Oxfam and Imperial College, London, collaborated on a two-year study – with funds from a British trust – to research, design and develop a series of water packs comprising equipment and materials in standard kit form for easy transport to the needy area. Results of the studies have been completed, and some equipment is in extensive use overseas.

In 1982, the water packs were used for the first time to provide a safe water supply in the Mocoron refugee camp for Miskito Indians in Honduras where some 10,000 people were drinking polluted water from the local river, causing much sickness and death. In response to an appeal from the United Nations High Commissioner for Refugees (UNHCR), two water distribution packs (weighing approximately 6 tonnes) were despatched by air, accompanied by a young engineer to ensure correct installation.

Within three days of arrival, the first of the pumps was lifting water from the river to a small emergency hospital about 600 m away, and the first of the storage tanks was filling up. Over the next six weeks, the whole camp was fitted with water collection points, storage tanks were fenced off, and the people were able to start enjoying a safe water supply. A further visit by an Oxfam engineer six months later showed the complete water system to be working most satisfactorily, maintained well by the local people, and most important, the health of the Miskito people was much improved.

*A field engineer using the Oxfam water testing kit, in a refugee camp in the Sudan, to ascertain water quality for human consumption.*

Since they were used for the first time in Honduras in 1982, the packs have been used in Nicaragua, Somalia, Rwanda, Yemen, Zimbabwe, the Sudan, Ethiopia and Mexico. Between 1984 and 1986, the Sudan and Ethiopia suffered severe drought and famine, and Oxfam water equipment was flown in to provide water for up to 700,000 people daily in refugee camps and feeding centres. These have been the largest emergency water projects Oxfam has ever undertaken, involving 50 engineers working alongside Sudanese and Ethiopian colleagues, and the supply of over 140 km of piping, 114 pumps and 206 tanks.

Following the September 1985 earthquake in Mexico City, the Mexican Embassy requested Oxfam to advise on how best to meet the water needs of the city. The earthquake had breached the water supply network in many hundreds of places and destroyed the Water Authority headquarters. Two filtration plants from the emergency packs were airfreighted to treat water from two boreholes.

### Technical specifications of the packs

Each pack serves a particular purpose in providing a water supply. One pack comprises large water-storage tanks, and another contains diesel pump sets for pumping water from a river or lake to the tanks. A third pack comprises the pipework and distribution points for drawing water from the tanks and distributing it around the community being served. Further packs have been designed such as: a water treatment pack using a sand filter to obtain safer water from a polluted source; and a water test kit to measure pollution levels. Eventually there will be eight or nine packs in all, covering a wide range of possible requirements including well digging and underground water surveying.

Each pack is completely self-contained with all the necessary items, including spare parts, tools, instructions for assembly, etc. The packs comprise both tried and tested pieces of standard equipment, like pump sets and piping, and some items specially designed for use in the particular pack. The packs can be added to, to meet particular circumstances, or multiplied for larger communities of people. The water packs are proving to be not only of value in emergencies, but many of the ideas and equipment have shown clearly that they are applicable in providing long-term solutions to people's water needs.

## Future developments

It is our intention to continue these water developments, and we feel very much part of the United Nations Water Decade: we are used increasingly as the lead agency in water supplies by the United Nations High Commissioner for Refugees whom we fully support and our water packs are being used by a wide range of international agencies.

We wish to nurture this outreach in international co-operation with the specific intention of developing these techniques, equipments and skills within the country of operation.

*An Oxfam water treatment pack at work in the Sudan Safawa Camp in 1985-1986. Note the brown colour of inflowing water and the colour of the treated water in the tank in the bottom right corner.*

# Miniature self-imaging stamp device

## Michael John Parkes

67 Kildare Avenue, Glendowie, Auckland 5, New Zealand

New Zealander, born 18 February 1946. Company manager. Educated in New Zealand.

Market research has shown that there is potential demand for a portable stamping device that can apply an image to a substrate for the identification of documents and personal or governmental property, and this project has designed and patented a portable system for making repetitive high-quality printed images. The device is intended in particular to serve the demand for multiple self-images (i.e. images in portrait format) since the system employed can produce fine, half-tone, screened flexographic-plate material which in practice, yields high-definition results.

The small high-fidelity images themselves are surrounded by printed text in order to endorse the subject's identity, and it is envisaged that this concept will prove valuable for: account holders to pre-stamp their cheque books; the stamping of travellers cheques; the stamping of paper articles requiring identification or personalization; and the production of personalized stickers for the identification of personal property, etc.

### Design and manufacture

The starting-point is an original photograph – preferably black and white – which will need to be of passport quality. This photograph is then photo-mechanically prepared for platemaking; at this point, considerable attention must be paid to the incidence of dot-gain in the production of printed half-tones if suitable reproduction is to be achieved. To achieve the necessary quality, Cyrel flexographic plate produced by Du Pont de Nemours has been selected since it is designed to release maximum ink upon contact with the printed medium. The plate is made in accordance with recommendations from the manufacturer, with suitable modifications being made to the criteria for depth of etching, e.g. etch depth can be a lot shallower than recommended for flexo-press printing.

This system employs a patented stamping device to reproduce images of a high quality, such as those in the first illustration. The ink used for the images is of a special low-viscosity type and a particular novelty is the device's ability to control a rapid-drying dribbly ink solution, replenish the transfer pad, and contain the ink in a usable condition for a reasonable length of time. Tests have shown that these devices can produce up to 800 images over a six-month period, before the system is exhausted.

On the basis of experience to date, replacement pads are considered preferable to a system of recharging the ink in the reservoir pad elements. On-going research shows that the pre-soaking of the natural compound selected for the reservoir element tends to result in a higher concentration of the carbon black pigment used and this appears to give the transfer action a dryer surface for the photopolymer to stamp on. The outcome is a reduction in the effect of dot-gain, and gives more latitude to the contrast of the half-tone result.

Optical dot-gain is a major factor in ensuring good image and, to a large degree, it is the optical quality of the paper which will determine the level of the results. However, suitable adjustment to the depth of the photopolymer and the selection of well-manufactured ink will ensure the achievement of very pleasing results on most planographic paper stock. Nevertheless, coarse matt paper surfaces are not suitable.

## Marketing

During initial market research, it has been proposed that the system be developed into a self-inking stamping device which would produce results of similar quality. Consequently, half-tone self-inking options were in fact researched and it was found that there is, indeed, an existing system that can produce coarse-screened results. However, it was observed that self-contained ink systems tend to rely on sticky dye solutions which attract lint and dust particles that are difficult to remove when trapped in fine relief areas.

*Prototype model of the image stamping device showing the inkholder, the stamp and typical impressions made on paper.*

*Two production models of the miniature self-imaging device.*

Moreover, in practice, the stamps need to be impressed on all types of irregular surfaces – and the self-inking devices available today do not cushion the depressing action required for imaging. Finally, the self-inking systems employ matrix transfer technology, which will restrict fine screen use, and lower the high level of fidelity, which is probably the most important feature of this concept. It has been for these reasons that the ink transfer method has been pursued and that photomechanical technology has been employed to overcome contrast difficulties inherent with low-viscosity inks.

It is envisaged that this concept will eventually be offered to a large photographic organization, since the marketing success of the device will rely to a large extent on the quality of photographic conversion and the channels of distribution.

# Input-saving mechanization for small paddy farmers

## Amir U. Khan

International Rice Research Institute, POB 933, Manila, Philippines

American, born 15 June 1927. Agricultural engineer. Educated in India and USA; Ph.D. (Power and Machinery) from Michigan State University, East Lansing, in 1967.

Rice is a basic staple food of a major segment of the world's population. Millions of small farmers are engaged in its production in South and South-East Asia. This project will focus on the development of a wide range of commercially viable input-saving equipment for small scale paddy farming in Asia. Such equipment is expected to help farmers in saving up to 50% in fuel, seeds, fertilizers, insecticides, herbicides and hired labour in rice production.

During the past two decades, high yielding varieties have substantially increased paddy yields in Asia, but they require high levels of purchased inputs such as fuel, fertilizers, pesticides, herbicides and hired labour if they are to attain their full potential. Thus farmers have to spend heavily on expensive inputs to obtain increased yields.

In recent years, scientists have made a number of research breakthroughs which offer potential for substantial savings in farming inputs. Such findings have, however, not benefited farmers because appropriate machines to apply these findings at the farm level are not available.

### Potential input savings

Potential savings can be made in the areas of land preparation, seeding and weeding and fertilizer and pesticide application, and this project is currently attempting to develop a range of input-saving alternative mechanical aids for small paddy farmers.

In land preparation, we are working on minimum-tillage puddlers, minimum-tillage power tillers, and zero-tillage dibbling planters. Comb harrows are popularly used with animals and power tillers for secondary tillage (puddling) in wetland paddy; however, they do not have provisions for controlling tillage depth. Consequently, they till the soil to much greater and often variable depths in the field.

A novel rotary puddler concept, which utilizes conical-shaped rotors, is being developed to minimize tillage depth in soft paddy fields. This new concept is

73

based on the principle that when a conical-shaped rotor with longitudinal blades is rolled along a straight path on the soil, different parts of each blade displace the soil differently with a horizontal soil movement. Thus a machine equipped with two oppositely oriented conical rotors can till soil by a horizontal back-and-forth blade action. This will minimize machine sinkage in soft soils and limit tillage to approximately the top 10 to 12 cm soil layer. A prototype animal-drawn conical puddler has been fabricated and has shown promising results.

Excessive sinkage and bogging of power tillers is a common problem during land preparation in soft paddy fields. I am proposing three new concepts for converting standard commercially available power tillers for controlled depth tillage in soft wetland fields. The proposed concepts will permit farmers to convert existing power tillers for controlled depth tillage in soft paddy fields, thereby enabling them to save fuel and power.

Some years ago a rolling injection planter was developed for zero tillage planting of upland crops. This machine was tried in the Philippines for establishing a second crop, immediately after harvesting wet-season paddy. The machine could not perform satisfactorily due to clogging of injector prongs and seed passage with moist soils. I am now trying to develop a zero tillage dibbling planter which will have separate mechanisms for punching holes in wet untilled soil and for precise placement of seeds into the holes. Such a machine will offer good possibilities for establishing a second crop after wet-season paddy without requiring costly land preparation.

For crop establishment we are developing a low-cost row seeder for seeding

*Two-row plunger auger fertilizer injector being used for deep placing prilled urea fertilizer in flooded paddies.*

*Single-gang animal-drawn cono-puddler for efficient paddy wetland preparation. (opposite)*

pre-germinated paddy on puddled soils. With this 8-row machine, one operator can seed paddy uniformly in neat rows in about the same time (8 h/ha) as broadcasting manually. It is also planned to develop a low-cost multipurpose machine for the three operations of row seeding, fertilizer incorporation and weeding. This would enable small farmers to effectively handle the three important operations which currently require substantial amounts of purchased inputs.

For crop care a range of push type rotor weeders using the novel concept of conical-shaped rotors is being developed and a simple attachment will be developed for the conical weeders so that fertilizer and insecticides could be distributed ahead of the rotors for simultaneous incorporation in the soil during weeding.

In addition, the design of a plunger-auger fertilizer injector has recently been finalized and, during trials, has consistently demonstrated increased fertilizer use efficiency.

Finally, manual and animal drawn equipment will be developed for incorporation of azolla in planted and unplanted fields together with special green manuring knives to utilize the slippage of the power tiller wheels to chop trampled green manure crops before incorporating them with the plough. The proposed equipment will be specially developed for local manufacture by small rural-based shops in the Asian rice-producing countries. This will help in generating new employment in the small scale farm machinery manufacturing sector and will, in general, encourage rural and industrial development. Some of the equipment described is already in an advanced stage of development and has shown highly promising results in field trials.

# Bioconversion of lignocellulose into a protein ingredient for animal feed

## Manuel D. Marcelo

35 M. Viola Street, Area 3, University of the Philippines, Campus Diliman, Quezon City, Philippines

Filipino, born 20 January 1937. Director and technical consultant, Feed Technologist, Inc. Educated in Philippines; M.B.A. from University of Philippines in 1962.

One of the biggest problems facing the poultry and hog industries in the Philippines and other Third World countries, is their high degree of dependence on inputs of foreign exchange. Feed accounts for 70% of the cost of producing eggs, chickens and hogs in the Philippines, possibly one of the highest in this region. As a result, local prices of these food items are often beyond the reach of the ordinary wage-earner; moreover, such production costs render the country uncompetitive in the export market. There is therefore a great need to reduce the cost of feeds and correspondingly that of eggs and meat.

With this in mind, about four years ago I started the Bioconversion Research Project to develop a process to convert agricultural by-products and possibly farm wastes into feed ingredients. Laboratory tests have been completed and partial evaluation conducted. What remains to be done before starting commercial production is large-scale test feeding and biological testing.

### The bioconversion project

To produce protein feed ingredients for poultry and livestock, this project envisaged the use of highly cellulosic and lignocellulosic material, such as copra meal, sugar cane bagasse and rice straw, the most abundant renewable agricultural by-products and farm wastes.

Lignocellulosics have inevitably received considerable attention as ways and means are sought to relieve the world's impending shortages of feed materials. New methods for the chemical processing of lignocellulosics are being studied and older methods re-examined as economic considerations change. Studies on cellulose degradation showed that chemical pre-treatment cannot be scaled up to pilot plant level at present owing to the prohibitive cost of chemicals. The most attractive processes, if they can be developed, are enzymatic and microbial.

The development of microbiological processes for the bioconversion of lignocellulosic wastes into more useful products, such as single-cell protein

76

(SCP), has long been hampered by the general inability of the microbes used to attack substrates with a high lignin content. The fungal or bacterial cultures employed are usually active cellulolytic enzymes, but either do not attack lignin or only slightly alter its structure while accomplishing little real decomposition of the lignin. Usually, the existence of the lignin presents accessibility barriers to attack on the cellulosic fractions of waste substrates by cellulolytic microbes.

The lignin apparently surrounds the cellulosic fibres and forms a protective net. If successful bioconversions of lignocellulose are to be developed, this lignin barrier must itself be attacked microbiologically. This problem can be overcome by employing active enzymes that can attack lignin as well as cellulose. These enzymes should, in addition, efficiently attack lignocellulosics which have not been treated chemically or physically by, for example, NaOH digestion or ball-milling, for even though such treatment increases susceptibility, it tends to be much too expensive. Simple grinding or hammer-milling should suffice.

## Using selected enzymes

In this bioconversion process, a specifically selected group of enzymes are used to break down lignin and cellulose into smaller molecules, making nutrients more available for increased microbial digestion. The enzyme activity does not end with this breaking-down process but also creates new matter by exploiting the ability of the bacterial enzymes to synthesize amino-acids and certain vitamins.

Purely indigneous materials and a certain percentage of recycled wastes are used in this bioconversion process. The enzymes are extracted from protease-rich fish processing waste, i.e. fish entrails; poultry entrails are the source of

*Rice straw – one of the most abundant renewable agricultural raw materials for bioconversion – being pulverized in a hammermill prior to fermentation.*

77

pepsin and proteolytic enzymes; micro-organisms are derived from dairy wastes such as whey from cheese manufacture containing *Lactobacillus acidophilus* and *Kluyveromyces fragilis*, and the waste water from yogurt manufacture, which is rich in lysine-excreting micro-organisms. Fly larvae or maggots that grow during the fermentation are an added source of protein.

In analyzing the raw materials subjected to the bioconversion process, the aqueous solution is placed in a tank and salt is added to lower the pH to 5–6; and then stored at room temperature. This solution contains highly active proteolytic enzymes and pepsin that will later be used in the conversion process.

### The conversion process

The raw materials are chopped and then pulverized with a hammermill; and placed in the reactor; water being added at about 50% of the volume of the material which, when the temperature reaches 75°C, is impregnated with the enzyme solution. Once treated, it is placed in a wooden tray for fermentation and the fermented mixture is subsequently put in a reactor for sterilization at a temperature of 75–90°C to kill the larvae, the fermenting micro-organisms and other bacteria produced by the fermentation process; once sterilized, it is dried in the sun or in a rotary drum dryer, after which the dried, fermented material is pulverized with a hammermill and this becomes an ingredient in the processing of the complete feeds.

*Fermented rice straw with a flourishing population of fly larvae and micro-organisms to augment the protein content.*

# Miniature hand-held and eyeglass-mounted infrared travel aids for the blind

## Forrest Marion Mims, III

**Honourable Mention**
**The Rolex Awards for Enterprise – 1987**

433 Twin Oak Road, Seguin, Texas 78155, USA

American, born 4 November 1944. Writer of magazine articles and books on electronics. Educated in USA; B.A. from Texas A&M University.

---

There is a pressing need for an economical electronic travel aid for the blind to supplement traditional travel aids like the long cane and the guide dog, which could be conveniently carried on or about one's person and used in situations where a cane or guide dog might prove impractical. Such an aid could provide valuable information about the blind person's immediate environment when used in conjunction with a cane or guide dog.

Electronic aids employing both passive and active methods have been proposed and, in both methods, information about the presence of obstacles is given in the form of an audible tone or a tactile stimulus. The passive method employs one or more photodetectors and a focusing lens but, although it is inherently simple, it does not function in low light levels. With the active method, the travel aid transmits a beam of energy (ultrasound, visible light or near infrared), and a part of the beam is reflected back by an obstacle in its path toward a receiver installed within the travel aid. Aids using optical radiation as an energy source can be made much smaller than those using ultrasound. Furthermore, a new generation of opto-electronic components (such as powerful light-emitting diodes, low-cost laser diodes, and ultra-miniature integrated amplifier circuits) are ideally suited for near-infrared travel aids for the blind.

### Design considerations for infrared travel aids

To date I have designed, assembled and tested with blind subjects, a series of hand-held and eyeglass-mounted travel aids for the blind. These devices project a relatively narrow (4–6 degrees) beam of near-infrared radiation emitted by a light-emitting diode or laser diode. A small percentage of the beam striking a nearby object is reflected back toward a receiver lens and focused on to the active surface of a photodiode. The resulting photocurrent is then amplified by a high-gain amplifier and, if the amplified signal exceeds the noise level by a predetermined margin, a threshold discrimination circuit generates a pulse that is applied to a small earphone or tactile stimulator. Since the pulses from the transmitter are repetitive, the audio or tactile output provides a pulsating stimulus to the blind user when an obstacle is being detected.

A major objective, however, is to provide several range-detection zones, with the range information being provided by varying the frequency of the output signal. For example, a low-frequency tone or tactile stimulus will indicate an object beyond about 3 m. A high-frequency tone or tactile stimulus will indicate an object within about 2 m. This range detection method will employ single triangulation; the infrared beam from a single source will be projected outward from the travel aid, two or more detectors will be aligned in a row at the focal place of the receiver lens; the distance between the receiver lens and any objects illuminated by the transmitter will determine which of the receiver photodiodes will be illuminated and the photodiodes will be scanned and caused to control the frequency of the output signal.

### Special design techniques

Design of an effective, practical travel aid requires detailed understanding of the optical properties of obstacles (targets) likely to be encountered by a blind user and in particular their physical cross section and reflectance and whether the target is a diffuse or specular reflector (or perhaps a combination of both). I therefore intend to complete an ongoing study of the optical properties of many common obstacles, and publish the findings in a scholarly paper. This accurate characterization would enable further optimization of the optical radar range equations presently used to predict the performance of the various infrared travel aids I have assembled. Such an important refinement will assist significantly in the development of a computer programme I intend to write that will allow the performance of a hypothetical travel aid to be simulated prior to its construction.

To complete these phases of the project, several special design techniques are

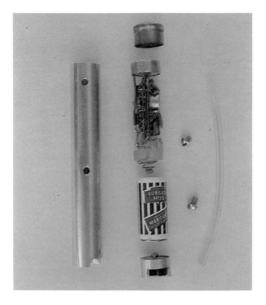

*Disassembled view of the receiver portion of the travel aid for the blind shown opposite.*

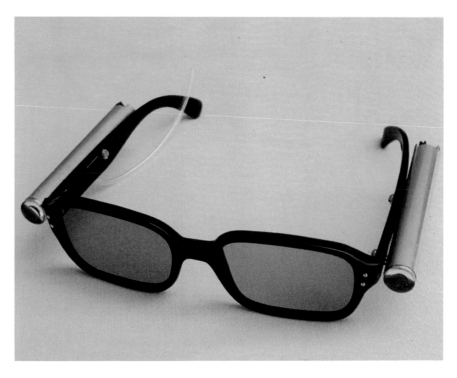

*A prototype infrared eyeglass travel aid for the blind designed by Forrest M. Mims, III.*

required. They include: selection of a set of reliable, calibrated optical reflectance targets having known reflectance properties; use of an optical table to enhance the design process; and connection of the prototype travel aids to a light-emitting diode which will glow when the travel aid is detecting an obstacle, so as to aid in training a blind person.

**Proposed active-infrared travel aids**

Following these preliminaries, several test models of two active-infrared travel aids will be designed, assembled and evaluated using triangulation to provide three range detection zones. One aid will be installed on modified eyeglass frames and provide an audible output signal. The other will be hand-held and will provide a tactile output. Prior to the final design stage, it will be necessary to design the receiver's photodiode array and refine its ability to ignore noise from external light sources, improve the design of the existing tactile stimulator, and make a final decision about whether to use a laser diode or light-emitting diode as a source of near-infrared. Once test versions of the circuits have been fully evaluated, plastic housings for the prototypes will be produced and a test programme will then be launched using selected blind subjects.

# Developing shrimp aquaculture and transferring the technology to developing countries

## Dan Cohen

POB 4330, 91 042 Jerusalem, Israel

Israeli, born 29 December 1942. Director of Research and Development, Aquaculture Production Technology (Israel) Ltd. Educated in Israel and USA; Ph.D. from Brandeis University, Boston, in 1972.

There is an enormous gap between the achievements of modern academic biological research, as conducted in the universities, and the needs of industry in general, and agriculture in particular. This gap is expressed in the self-imposed isolation of many academics and by the attitudes they hold to applied research and involvement in agro-industrial development. However, biological research and biotechnology have considerable potential in the development of new approaches to agriculture and food production, even though the farming community often does not realize it.

### Bridging the gap between research and agriculture

I felt that the value of integrating basic and applied research within the university was underestimated both by the university and by the business community but the mechanisms necessary to rectify the situation were lacking. What was needed was: to identify an agricultural project for Israel; set up a financially independent research unit where basic research can be carried out and post-graduate students can be taken on without depending on limited university resources; bring together the basic and applied research capabilities of the university to enhance the biotechnical process; develop this process to effective economic implementation; and then transfer the technology to developing countries.

### Aquaculture selected to implement the concept

I took upon myself the challenge of demonstrating the feasibility of this approach, and selected the field of aquaculture, the husbandry of aquatic animals, for a full-scale project. Aquaculture seemed to offer a solution to the developing world's shortage of protein-rich foods and, since development here is highly dependent on biological input, I was sure that scientific research and development could facilitate implementation. In particular, I chose the field of

*A prawn and fish farm has now been established in Jamaica using the project's technology. Here, a Jamaican worker sorts harvested prawns in preparation for processing.*

freshwater aquaculture which is already highly developed in Israel and concentrates on the common carp, tilapia hybrids, silver carp, grass carp and mullet – all for the local market. However, the industry was in crisis since the more technologically advanced it became, the smaller it shrank because demand was constant. The solution was to introduce a new product intended solely for the export market but which could be produced using the available infrastructure. In this way, I identified an economic problem which could be resolved by a biological solution.

## A biological solution and a commercial programme

The organism I chose was an unresearched tropical decapod shrimp, the life cycle of which involves a freshwater environment for adult development and a brackish (estuary) biotope for larval development. Then I planned a full programme for implementation of this new enterprise. This entailed: the establishment of a research facility to research the organism; using the know-how acquired to establish a production line, first on a pilot and later at an industrial level; providing technological back-up to facilitate economic production; encouraging first the mixed culture of fish and prawns and then of prawns alone as soon as it became a viable venture; and establishing a science-based biotechnology company, the main asset of which is a long-term agreement with the university and close association with the advanced Israeli freshwater aquaculture system.

It was also necessary to develop a marketing organization specializing in supplying fresh, non-seasonable, high-quality aquafoods mainly to the USA and Europe, where demand is increasing.

I believed that once this had been achieved, it would then be possible to market the technology in developing tropical countries in which conditions (temperatures) are optimal, and land, water and labour are abundant, and in which there is a need for new agriculture crops.

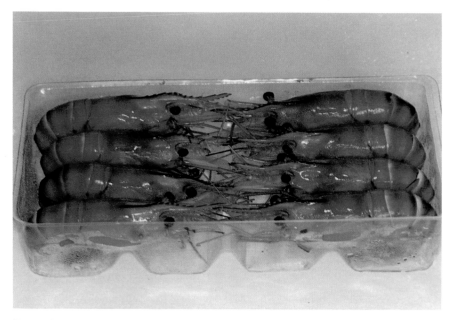

*Processed prawns attractively packaged and ready for shipment.*

### Ten years of accomplishments

During the past ten years, I have accomplished much of my objectives. I have established the Prawn Research Unit within the Life Sciences Institute of the Hebrew University of Jerusalem. This performs basic research, has been responsible for many discoveries and continues to employ several MSc and PhD students researching various aspects of this organism. An intensive production line was set up with a highly automated industrial hatchery, and several commercial hatcheries and nurseries are now supplying juvenile prawns to the farmers. Many of these have now accepted that prawns could be raised in polyculture together with fish and are even starting prawn monoculture. A science-based company, Aquaculture Production Technology (Israel) Ltd., was founded in 1978 with a long-term agreement with the Hebrew University of Jerusalem to invest in technology development and technology transfer. This company has now initiated several prawn aquafarms in Brazil, the Dominican Republic, Ecuador, Jamaica and the Philippines; however, only Israel and Jamaica are currently supplying prawns to the market. Finally, prawn production is also being introduced into the southern part of the USA.

The basic elements needed to achieve my initial goal are now in place. We have a small organization, made up of students and technicians in association with a business partner, which is geared to further develop the technology, implement it effectively and support the various projects with scientific back-up. We are hopeful that we can successfully market fresh, non-seasonal, high-quality aquafoods in Europe and the USA and thus confirm the feasibility of our programme.

# Using locally available plant materials as ophthalmic surgical swabs

## *Erasmus Oluchukwu Chukwudi Oji*

Jos University Medical School, Bauchi Road, Jos PMB 2084, Nigeria

Nigerian, born 2 May 1943. Professor in Ophthalmology, University of Jos, Nigeria. Educated in Nigeria and UK; F.R.C.S. from Moorfields Eye Hospital, London, in 1980.

Compressed hydrocellulose wedges known as German spontex swabs, long used for eye, dental, ear, nose and throat surgeries, are efficient blood absorbers and are easily available in Europe and America at a reasonable price. However, in Nigeria and in many of the developing countries of Africa, these swab wedges are not only difficult to obtain but are also very expensive.

**Selecting potential substitutes**

This, combined with current economic austerity measures, precludes the import of German swabs in adequate quantities even though ophthalmic clinics are full of patients in need of ocular surgery. It has, therefore, been necessary to consider, as sources for ophthalmic surgical swabs materials, such local plant substances as: corn stem, banana leaf frond, millet stem and cane sugar stem, which grow abundantly both in the villages and in the urban areas.

**Test results**

The stems of the selected materials were stripped of their bark and the spongy stem interior was cut into small wedges and studied for autoclaving characteristics, blood absorbing properties and water soaking potential.

It was found that all four types of plant source swabs autoclave very well and none disintegrates on autoclaving by either wet or dry heat. The corn and the millet swabs turn whitish brown after autoclaving, while the cane sugar swab turns creamy white. The banana frond swabs turn dark brown after wet autoclaving and light brown when sterilized in dry-heat. All four types of swabs feel spongy to the touch; the millet and the corn stem swabs being the two most spongy, followed by the sugar cane swabs, while the banana frond swabs were the least spongy after autoclaving.

When used to mop up blood in experimental surgery, the corn millet stem swabs absorb blood very avidly, the cane sugar swab somewhat less; however, the banana frond swab absorbs blood only moderately. It was found that the standardized swab wedge of millet absorbed 16 drops of blood on average before saturation whereas the corresponding figures for corn, sugar cane and banana swabs were 15, 12 and 10 drops respectively. All four types of swabs swell up after blood absorption and retain the blood within their spongy fibres. The absorbed blood can be squeezed out of the swabs, and the swabs re-used for reabsorption without the swabs disintegrating.

The four types of swabs soaked up water easily; the corn, millet and banana swabs did so more quickly than the cane sugar. On average, in 1 min, 1 g of the banana swab absorbed 1 ml of water whereas the corresponding volumes for the corn, millet and cane sugar swabs were 0.8, 0.5 and 0.25 ml respectively. Each swab swelled up on water absorption. After squeezing out the absorbed water from the swabs each type of swab could be re-used to either mop up more water or blood. The banana swabs absorbed blood better when slightly wet than when completely dry.

The German cellulose swabs used as control absorbed blood very avidly in the animal experiment surgery. The standard-size wedge absorbed, on the average, 20 drops of anticoagulated human blood before saturation and also absorbed water very rapidly, at a rate of 2.1 ml/min for a 1 g sample.

None of the autoclaved swabs grew any type of microbial organism either in the blood or Saboraud's media, and none of the rabbits' operated eyes showed any post-operative infections. When the corn and millet stem swabs are handled roughly, for example, with toothed forceps small fragments tend to fall off, especially when the swabs are dry; however, this does not occur when the swabs are wet with blood or water. The banana and the cane sugar swabs hardly show this effect, wet or dry.

*Standard compressed hydro-cellulose German swabs used for ophthalmological surgery. Owing to economic austerity measures, these are no longer readily available in many developing countries.*

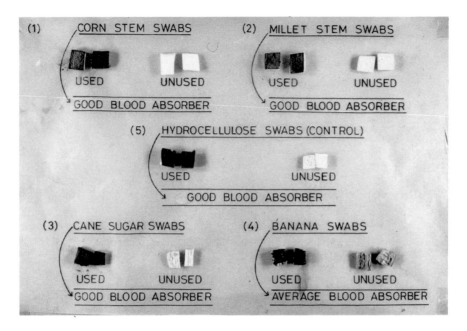

(1) CORN STEM SWABS    (2) MILLET STEM SWABS

USED    UNUSED    USED    UNUSED

GOOD BLOOD ABSORBER    GOOD BLOOD ABSORBER

(5) HYDROCELLULOSE SWABS (CONTROL)

USED    UNUSED

GOOD BLOOD ABSORBER

(3) CANE SUGAR SWABS    (4) BANANA SWABS

USED    UNUSED    USED    UNUSED

GOOD BLOOD ABSORBER    AVERAGE BLOOD ABSORBER

*The blood absorption characteristics of swabs made from a range of natural local substitute materials.*

## A plan for future study and development

The present study, which was motivated by sheer necessity, has demonstrated that three, possibly four, locally available and easily processed plant substances could be used as alternatives to the cellulose spontex swabs which currently are costly and difficult to come by in both Nigeria and many other African countries. Moreover, if these locally available materials are eventually found acceptable for surgical use, swabs made commercially from them would be much less expensive than their imported counterparts.

Research on these materials will be continued to document the effects of subconjunctival and intraocular implantation of the various swabs on New Zealand white rabbits and, hopefully, postulate the effect on humans of accidental implantation into the eye or subcutaneous tissues.

Studies will also be required to determine the optimal methods of processing, sterilizing (for immediate and long-term uses) and packaging of these various swabs. Finally, research should be undertaken to identify similar materials for use in surgery in general.

# Development of artificial-bone tissue

## *Petr Patka*

Department of Surgery, Free University Hospital, 1117 De Boelelaan, 1007 MB Amsterdam, Netherlands

Netherlander, born 1 December 1949. Surgeon (Traumatology). Educated in Netherlands; M.D. and Ph.D. from Free University, Amsterdam, in 1976 and 1984.

Progress in the management and repair of traumatic long-bone defects (including those caused by malignant disease) has created a growing need for suitable material to replace bone tissue. Bone transplantation is now more common than any other tissue transfer, except skin grafting and blood transfusions. Between 1977 and 1979, over 12,000 bone grafting procedures were performed in the Netherlands alone, and the yearly increase is about 10%.

### An artificial substitute for bone

Many artificial materials for bone substitution have been developed, and some are clearly related to bone tissue and biomaterials for bone tissue replacement in places with no or only minimal load-bearing requirements. However, the aim of this project was to develop a material capable of withstanding the compressive, shearing, torsional and bending forces normally applied to the skeleton. Research on biocompatibility has brought to light various ceramic materials made from the calcium phosphate system and, in particular, hydroxyapatite seemed promising in view of implantation experience.

Both dense and porous material made from pentacalciumhydroxide-triphosphate were formed into cylindrical and semicylindrical rods of hydroxyapatite and used to repair relatively large defects in the femurs of dogs; the implants were stabilized by means of an internal fixation (six months for the semicylindrical implants and 18 months for the cylindrical ones). After these periods the internal fixation material was removed. The research was aimed primarily at determining: the suitability of hydroxyapatite, in either porous or compact form, for repairing large segmental-bone defects in animals; the progress of bone-tissue ingrowth into the pores in hydroxyapatite implants under weight-bearing conditions; the interactions between implants and host at the interface between the two, in the case of dense implants under weight-bearing conditions; and the

88

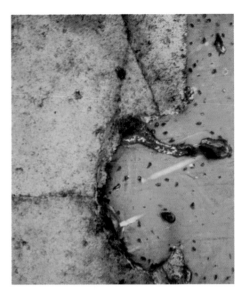

*Photomicrograph of the junction between hydroxyapatite (grey) and bone (red) six months after implantation (magnified 80 x).*

possibility, on the basis of the results from the study, of predicting the clinical applications of hydroxyapatite in bone-defect repair.

## Encouraging study results

Studies on the biocompatibility of these implants showed no changes in the surface structure of dense hydroxyapatite samples. The implant surface was in close contact with the new bone in six-month implants and ingrowth of bone tissue was clearly visible six months after implantation and complete one year after implantation, at which time even the central pores contained bone. Both the porous and non-porous hydroxyapatite implants adhered strongly to the bone but no sign has been seen of an inflammatory reaction, degradation or loosening at the implant surface after two years of follow-up. The pores in parts of the implant which were in contact with surrounding bone tissue were completely filled with bone at six months in contrast to the pores in the central part of the sample.

By using fluorochrome labelling, we were able to show a definite degree of mineralization of bone tissue inside the bores as little as one month after implantation. However, there were no signs of bone growth stimulation. After one year, the pores of the central part of the implant were almost completely filled with bone.

Although there has been no degradation or loosening of the implant surface, failures did occur in dense cylindrical implants; in contrast, porous cylindrical implants had only one implant failure (early after implantation) and one failure after removal of support material. The semicylindrical implants showed no failures at all.

The bend stress test showed an ultimate bending stress of 86% of normal bone tissue in both porous and dense semicylindrical implants. The lack of plastic deformation, and lower values of elastic deformation mean that hydroxyapatite implants have lower ultimate tensile strength than natural bone.

The better values for porous implants, compared with the *in vitro* results, point to a beneficial effect of ingrowing bone tissue. Both types of implants – dense and porous – showed excellent biocompatibility as judged by radiography, bone scintigraphy and histology. However, clinical and mechanical results indicate that the porous form is superior to the dense form and that therefore the porous form should be used for bone replacement.

### Future perspectives

Present studies include the clinical application and the research on bio-degradability of implants made from hydroxyapatite. Furthermore, we are developing a composite material consisting of hydroxyapatite and collagen. The development of such a composite material consisting of the components of natural bone matrix should be advantageous in bone grafting, and will probably result in the creation of artificial bones.

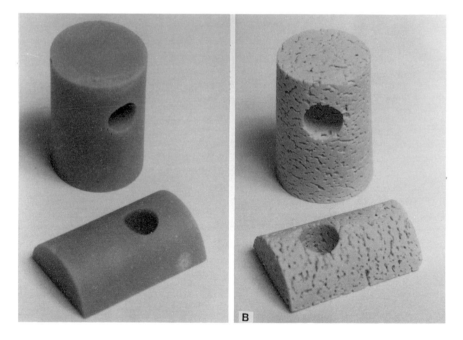

*Cylindrical and semicylindrical implants of dense (A) and porous (B) hydroxyapatite for bone construction.*

# Using appropriate technology for tidal channel and river closures

## *Johannes Van Duivendijk*

21 Adrianaweg, Nijmegen 6523 MV, Netherlands

Netherlander, born 30 October 1934. Consulting engineer. Educated in the Netherlands; M.Sc. (Civil Engineering) from Delft University of Technology in 1958.

On 28 February 1985, the Feni River in Bangladesh was closed off from the sea by the construction of a 1,300 m long bund, made of bags filled with clay. The spectacular closure of a tidal river was achieved by 1,200 labourers who, in seven hours in a single day, placed 650,000 bags of clay to a height of 2 m in the remaining openings over a length of 850 m. The technical design and construction methods used for this closure were developed by a team of specialized engineers under my supervision and were based on the adaptation of century-old Dutch methods to the circumstances in Third World countries. This ultimately led to the success as described above.

### The need to close delta tidal channels and rivers

In deltaic areas, fertile soils are periodically flooded by high tides and storm surges causing damage to the crops and increasing the salinity of the soil and water. This is the reason why the Dutch created "polders" – flat areas surrounded by embankments, inside which the water level is completely under control. The construction of foreshore embankments poses no problem; however, the closure of channels entering the "polder" area is difficult since tidal movement takes place in them. Furthermore, in deltaic areas, the large volumes of water required to irrigate agricultural land are just not available, and to solve this problem, freshwater lakes are formed by closing the mouths of estuaries from the sea. In both cases – for polderization and creation of freshwater lakes – tidal closures are required.

### The technique of closing tidal channels and rivers

This has been developed in the Netherlands over the course of centuries, first, to create polders and second to close breaches in coastal polder embankments which have occurred during high tides or storm surges and which, in many cases, develop into tidal channels. The closure method used up until 1930, the "old Dutch method", was characterized by: very limited project field investigations and hydraulic calculations; use of natural construction materials such as brushwood, reeds, clay, sand, stones; the abundant use of manual labour; limited use of water-borne equipment such as tugs, barges and floating cranes; and an upper limit of 25 million m$^3$ for the tidal volume of channels and basins. From 1930 onwards, the old Dutch method was gradually modernized in the course of a number of major projects such as the enclosure of the former Zuider Zee. In this modernization, emphasis was placed on intensive research and planning, new materials, high technology and the use of capital intensive procedures.

### Development of tidal closure methods in Bangladesh

Having, in 1969, designed and supervised the closure of a small tidal inlet in Ghana using primarily reeds, sandbags and sand together with local labour and a few bulldozers, I was asked in 1976 by the Government of the Netherlands to study the local horizontal closure methods being used in Bangladesh, and found that the work was carried out using solely manual labour and local materials. It was also obvious that the method was applicable only to small channels up to 100 m in width. I subsequently put forward the idea of introducing into Bangladesh the "old Dutch method" suitably adapted to local materials and skills; this proposal was accepted. In the following years, several tidal channels in Bangladesh were closed using a modified version of the old Dutch methods that had gradually been adapted over a seven-year period by experimenting with different construction materials, equipment and working methods.

In 1982, I was asked by the World Bank to advise on the design of the tidal closure of the Feni River in Bangladesh entailing the construction of a 2,500-m estuary dam from loosely packed fine sand and silt in the face of spring tides that are usually 4 m high. Subsequently, Haskoning, the consulting firm for which I

*Closing the Feni River by a 1,300-m long bund with a height of 2 m. This involved the employment of 1,200 labourers in a final seven-hour operation to place 650,000 bags filled with clay. (Photo by Wieger Bruin/Haskoning) (opposite)*

*Final fixing of bamboo and reed fascines to polypropylene fabric mattresses during low tide, for the closure of tidal waterways. (Photo by Wieger Bruin/Haskoning)*

work, was requested to carry out a complete design review and assist in supervising the construction. I was entrusted with final responsibility for design and eventually completely redesigned the closure dam and finally decided on an "instantaneous closure" which involved building a 2-m high closure bund across the full river width (1,300 m) during the ten available hours of a neap tide. Ultimately, this closure bund was constructed in seven hours by 1,200 labourers placing 650,000 bags filled with clay.

## Disseminating the technology

I believe that the old Dutch method can now be applied successfully in other Third World countries and I propose to identify possible areas in which the Dutch method (suitably adapted to local circumstances) could be beneficially implemented for agricultural improvement. This identification work is expensive and is not usually funded by international development agencies; moreover, private consulting firms cannot afford to carry out such identification free of charge.

I consider the method could be valuable in countries such as Burma, India, Viet Nam, Indonesia, Philippines, Ecuador, Brazil, etc., and I propose to visit five to seven countries and make film and slide presentations of Dutch closure technology in general and the "Dutch method" used in Bangladesh in particular. Possible sites would be identified and project proposals drafted. Finally, assistance would be given to Governments in presenting these project proposals to multilateral and bilateral donors for financing of studies.

# Autism in children: Finding the cause and cure

## Bernard Rimland

**Honourable Mention**
**The Rolex Awards for Enterprise – 1987**

4182 Adams Avenue, San Diego, California 92116, USA

American, born 15 November 1928. Director, Institute of Child Behaviour Research. Educated in USA; Ph.D. (Psychology) from Penn State University in 1954.

Autism is a severely incapacitating life-long disability, usually starting at birth, but never later than two-and-a-half years of age. It is characterized by severe learning and communication deficits, little interest in others, withdrawn behaviour, aggressivity and even self-injurious conduct. Despite their profound mental disability, many autistic children display extraordinary talents in areas such as mathematics, music or art.

My involvement with research on autistic children began in March 1956, with the birth of my first son who displayed behavioural characteristics typical of autistic children, although he was then, and is today, a perfect physical specimen. As little was then known about autism, I decided to investigate the condition to see what could be done for him. The high level of public awareness of autism in the 1980s as compared with the 1950s has sometimes been attributed to my own work in this field. After several years, I began to develop a theory of what autism meant, what might be its cause, and where in the brain the disorder might reside. This was done in my leisure hours, as I was then working full time for the Government. In five years I completed a book entitled *Infantile Autism: The Syndrome and its Implications for a Neural Theory of Behaviour* which won the first Century Award in a competition launched by the Appleton Century Crofts publishing company for "A distinguished contribution to psychology". Almost overnight, I became an authority on autistic children, my book having demonstrated that it was in fact a physiological disorder of the nervous system, and not primarily an emotional illness as had been thought. Subsequently I was granted a one-year fellowship at the Center of Advanced Studies of Behavioral Sciences at Stanford University, where I further developed my theories.

### The project

Since autism is a very rare disorder (approximately 4.5 per 10,000 live births), very little information had been collected about it in a systematic, scientific way. To overcome this deficiency, I included, as an appendix to my book, a detailed questionnaire concerning the pregnancy and delivery, and the medical condition of the child at birth and in early life. Parents began sending me completed questionnaires and other information, and researchers and physicians forwarded case histories. I first began collecting data on autistic children in 1964, and today the Institute of Child Behaviour Research has details on almost 9,000 autistic children from over 40 countries.

Some years ago, we published a very preliminary analysis of a small amount of data – *Comparative Effects of Treatment on Child's Behaviour* – which gives parental and professional evaluations of numerous forms of treatment, including certain drugs used on autistic children. As one part of our project involves following up information given by parents who tried vitamin therapy, I undertook a large-scale study (200 children) evaluating four of the vitamins most often mentioned. Published in 1973, it showed that of the four, vitamin B6 was clearly the best, and did produce statistically significant improvement; a subsequent follow-up study was also positive. Our work on high-dose vitamin B6 therapy in autism has been confirmed in a series of studies by Professor Gilbert LeLord of Tours University in France. Our next major research task, will be to explore certain hypotheses concerning the possible causes of autism. Our project also finds carefully diagnosed cases for researchers to enable them to test their own hypotheses.

## Services to researchers and the public

The Institute of Child Behaviour Research provides information to parents, teachers, physicians and researchers who contact us for answers to their questions. Several years ago we were able to help actor Sylvester Stallone and his wife whose infant son was autistic. When they discovered how meagre were the resources available for parents to help their autistic children, they started the

*Autism is a mysterious brain disorder which affects children, usually starting at birth. Autistic children are quite normal in appearance, but appear to live in a world of their own, as though in a glass ball sealed off from normal affection and communication. (Photo by National Society for Children and Adults with Autism)*

Stallone Fund for Autism Research. As Executive Secretary of its Scientific Advisory Board, I have worked with the Fund to allocate money to researchers worldwide.

Because there are few information sources on autism, we have recently begun production of a new quarterly, entitled *Autism Research Review International*. This newsletter will include abstracts and other information from world literature and will be sent free for the first year to the almost 10,000 parents and professionals on our worldwide mailing list. We were able to start this journal with a one-year grant from the Hasbro Toy Company but, long-term, shall have to turn to other revenue to finance it.

Realizing early that parents needed to be able to communicate with each other, I established the National Society for Children and Adults with Autism, with headquarters in Washington D.C., which, among other things, is helping to establish legislation to provide proper schooling and other facilities for autistic children.

The above describes briefly only a small part of our numerous and varied activities on behalf of autistic children and their families and, despite our achievements, much still remains to be done.

*An example of a painting by an autistic child. Such children typically have very poor social and communication skills. They are often said to "live in a glass ball", but frequently show unusual talent in art, music or mathematics.*

# Rectangular container for maturing table wine in wood

## Leslie Ross Macdonald

53 Hackney Road, Hackney, South Australia 5069, Australia

Australian, born 10 September 1936. Company Director. Educated in Australia; studied (Salesmanship, Staff Supervision and Management) at South Australia Institute of Technology from 1954 to 1959.

---

Wine stored in wooden casks reacts with the wood (usually oak) surrounding it, and this reaction may affect the chemistry and taste of the product that finally reaches the table. However, as a conventional cask increases in size, the ratio between the area of wood on the inside surface of the barrel exposed to the wine and the volume of the wine inside the cask itself changes, i.e. there is a reduction in the number of square centimetres of wood surface per litre of wine; consequently, the larger the cask, the less the wood will influence the wine.

### The wood factor in maturing wine

There are three sizes of cask in general use in the world's table wine industry: the barique with a capacity of 225 l, the hogshead which contains 300 l and the puncheon that holds 500 l. In view of its small size, the barique has a higher wood surface area per litre of capacity, and thus the oak transmits its flavour more rapidly to the wine; however, cask manufacturing costs per unit of capacity are higher for the barique than for larger casks, a larger number of bariques are required for a given quantity of wine, and cellaring costs are also increased. Furthermore, casks require regular topping-up to prevent air coming in contact with the wine and causing oxidation, and, when stacked, they are difficult to empty, fill and clean. Even so, many winemakers prefer to use bariques because of the excellent results obtained with them.

### Overcoming the disadvantages of casks

With a view to overcoming the cost and efficiency disadvantages of the barique, whilst preserving all its advantages from the point of view of wine quality, I started work on the development of a replacement for the conventional wine cask. This would have oak staves, exposed on one side to the wine and, on the other, to air; it would, wherever possible, be made from readily available standard-size materials.

The outcome is a rectangular container, 2.5 m high, 1.2 m wide and 20.5 cm in depth with a capacity of 590 l but the same surface/volume proportions as that of a barique (i.e. 80 $cm^2$/litre); standard 110 cm long wood staves, used for the manufacture of puncheons, are employed for the broad surfaces of the vessel and are clamped against the narrow section of the vessel which is made from stainless steel. The staves are compressed together vertically to prevent leakage between them and a gasket is placed at the interface between the wood and the stainless steel. The vessel is supported on a mild steel frame; the base is designed to ease transport by fork lift truck and gives the vessel a 5° slope to facilitate draining.

## A product with added advantages

The design offers a number of attractive features which economize on wood consumption. Since the oak staves used are neither shaped nor bevelled, as in a cask, no timber is wasted; because they are not curved, both sides of the wood can be utilized, simply by turning the staves over to obtain a "new" wood surface. Moreover, since the staves are not under stress, as in a cask, the timber may be shaved to expose new wood, without risk of breakage. Finally, the manipulation of the standardized pieces of wood requires no specialist knowledge of coopering and the staves can be turned, replaced, etc., by normal winery staff.

The vats themselves may be interconnected by fixing stainless steel manifolds to the bottom of each vessel, to make a bank and if the end vessel in the bank is raised slightly higher than the others, and kept "topped up", the other vessels will automatically be kept full as well thus preventing the entry of air which causes oxidation. A heat exchanger can easily be placed within the vessel for low temperature wine maturation, or cold stabilization – a process which is not practical with a cask.

*Final touches being added to the completed wine container prototype. (opposite)*

*A view of the original prototype of the wood maturation container showing the steel frame, the stainless steel side panels, the wooden staves and the filler cap.*

All in all the vat takes less space than a conventional wine cask of the same capacity and its manufacture is less labour intensive than the conventional coopering process for which the costs are likely to increase over time.

### A prototype and improved design

Two prototypes have so far been assembled and tested, with good results and, furthermore, a new design has evolved, using the same basic design tested successfully in the prototypes, but making use of lighter materials which are cheaper and lend themselves to easier and more rapid fabrication.

# Computer-aided design (CAD) and manufacture (CAM) of dental prostheses

## *François Duret*

Draye des Vignes, 38690 Le Grand Lemps, France

French, born 8 December 1947. Dental surgeon, and scientific adviser to Hennson International. Educated in France; Docteur en Chirugie Dentaire et en Sciences Odontologiques from UER des Sciences Odontologiques in 1980.

On 30 November 1985, at an international congress organized by the French Dental Association at the Palais des Congrès in Paris, we, for the first time, carried out the design, manufacture and fitting of a dental crown in a single sitting; the sitting lasted less than an hour and did not involve the use of either paste or moulds. The "patient" for this demonstration was my wife. It convincingly demonstrated the total feasibility of a revolutionary system that has resulted from 15 years of research, and has grown out of a partnership between myself and Hennson International, which started in 1971 when I first developed a complex association between three-dimensional optics, computer-aided design and the manufacture of dental crowns on a numerically controlled machine tool.

The November 1985 demonstration was the outcome of a long process of basic and clinical research and industrial development, and showed in real time that a portable apparatus completely suited for use in the dentist's surgery could be used to define the shape of the patient's mouth and design a fixed prosthesis for manufacture and immediate insertion. This has been achieved by using threshold technologies and has pioneered the application of CAD/CAM to the automation of combined diagnosis and therapy, whilst still allowing the clinician to intervene at any time and modify the course of the process in the light of his specialized knowledge. Moreover, since the technology developed can be used in other areas, it has once again proved that dentistry is at the forefront of progress.

### CAD/CAM and its application to dentistry

Computer-aided design and computer-aided manufacture (CAD/CAM) are techniques which have recently been developed to exploit the power of the modern computer for the far-reaching automation of manufacturing processes. In 1971, whilst still a young dental surgeon in Grenoble, I dreamed of a computer allowing specialists to automatically design and manufacture high-quality dentures so fast that the dentist would be able to design, machine and fit a prosthesis in a single sitting. However, for this, it would be necessary to equip the machine with an "eye" so that it could "see" the relief in the patient's mouth and with a machine tool which would, under the computer's control, manufacture the prosthesis on the spot.

In this new process, an optical probe captures a three-dimensional image of the inside of the patient's mouth, covering the site intended to receive the prosthesis and the neighbouring teeth on both the upper and lower jaws; this image is converted to digital data and transmitted to a CAD computer which can display a reconstruction of the missing teeth on the screen, using a technique for the theoretical memorization of dental shapes; finally, the computer guides the cutter head of a numerically controlled micro-milling machine which carves the prosthesis from a small blank of the selected material (metal-composites or ceramics).

The new process offers numerous advantages: it eliminates the tedious, unpleasant and relatively inaccurate process of impression taking, it significantly reduces the dentist's operating time and, even more so, the time taken to design and manufacture the prosthesis, it guarantees better shape and more accurate fitting and permits the use of newer more suitable, attractive and cheaper materials such as the new composites that I and my team have been working on.

### Industrial and commercial development

In 1984, once a technical feasibility model had been developed, I signed an exclusive rights contract with Hennson International for the industrial development of the process and a team was set up with my support to transform my model into a reliable apparatus for mass production.

It is planned that the first full-scale production units will appear in the second half of 1986 after the apparatus has undergone extensive clinical testing.

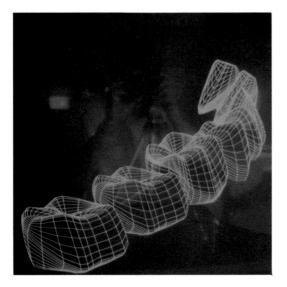

*The power of modern mini- and micro-computers is now available to the individual clinician. Graphics and design programmes allow on-screen visualization and manipulation of complex shapes such as the molars, canine and incisors.*

101

*In the computer-aided design process, the computer displays on the screen a reconstruction of the patient's dentition. The missing-teeth shapes are sent to the micro-milling installation for machining.*

Demand for this revolutionary equipment is already strong and comes from individual dentists and dental mechanics in both France and other countries. However, we are also negotiating distribution and manufacturing rights with companies involved in the dental market.

A variety of equipment configurations are foreseen since a number of dentists in a group practice may each wish to have their own surgery equipped with an independent optical impression-taking unit which is, in turn, connected to a single central machining installation. Prices will range from 150,000 to 500,000 French francs depending on the configuration.

CAD/CAM has fundamentally changed the ground rules for dental prosthetics, offers less discomfort, better fit and more attractive appearance for the patient, and greater efficiency for the dentist. However the principles employed and the know-how acquired hold out enormous potential for progress in a whole range of other fields.

# Illuminated tip for positioning endotracheal tubes

## Richard Moss Heller

Vanderbilt University Medical Center, Nashville, Tennessee 37232, USA

American, born 13 July 1938. Professor of Radiology, Vanderbilt University Medical Center and Associate Professor of Paediatrics. Educated in USA; M.D. from Northwestern University Medical School, Chicago, in 1963.

An endotracheal tube may be used to assist the breathing of certain babies shortly after birth, or in emergency situations; however, the correct positioning of this tube is of critical importance since if it ends above the larynx, ventilation will be impaired and if it ends below the carina, not only will ventilation be impaired but there is increased risk of iatrogenic damage to the lungs (e.g. pulmonary interstitial emphysema, pneumothorax and pneumomediastinum).

### High cost and unnecessary X-ray exposure?

As Professor of Radiology at Vanderbilt University Medical Center and Associate Professor of Paediatrics, one of my main responsibilities is to "read" the radiographs obtained in the Neonatal Intensive Care Unit. Many such radiographs are obtained simply to determine the position of the endotracheal tube. It occurred to me that there had to be a better way to harness technology and science to reduce the number of radiographs obtained for this purpose. Additionally, I read radiographs made in the emergency room on children who have been brought to our hospital from accident scenes where they have been intubated, and the endotracheal tube has been either too far down or not down far enough.

This, I decided, needed to be investigated and studied because, at accident scenes, X-rays are not available to aid in positioning endotracheal tubes. Finally, it occurred to me that, in developing nations, simply the cost of a radiograph and the equipment required to obtain the radiograph might be excessive and that, if I could determine the position of an endotracheal tube without any radiographs it would be of great economic benefit. Furthermore, if the radiologic modality could be disposed of entirely there would be a marked saving in the amount of ionizing radiation the children received, especially in the case of premature babies who receive a considerable number of such X-ray studies.

In essence, then, my present occupation is that of a paediatric radiologist. The challenge that I accepted was to determine if a better way could be found to

103

identify the position of endotracheal tube tips and thereby decrease the cost of medical care and markedly reduce the amount of ionizing radiation our children receive.

## Light as a substitute for X-rays

To tackle this problem, we have incorporated into an endotracheal tube a fiberoptic strand connected to a high-intensity light source terminating at and illuminating the tube tip, thus allowing the position of the endotracheal tube to be identified accurately by the light through the chest wall without radiologic assistance.

Initial fluoroscopic studies were made using a rigid bronchoscope light source placed in the lumen of a conventional endotracheal tube introduced into puppies, kittens and young pigs. Here the light source was readily visible through the neck skin and chest wall.

Subsequently, a number of endotracheal tubes of different internal diameters and fitted with a fiberoptic strand in the wall were manufactured and made available to the paediatric house officers to use as an alternative to the standard endotracheal tubes. The procedure employed was to introduce the tube, connect the fiberoptic strand to a high-intensity light source and dim the nursery lights briefly to facilitate observation of the light through the neck or chest wall. A standard anteroposterior chest radiograph was made to document the position of the tube.

## Trials demonstrate adequacy of procedure

A study made on the use of the illuminated endotracheal tube in 25 infants showed that the tube was safely positioned in all the babies and that, in no instance, did the fiberoptic strand break or the system fail to yield adequate light

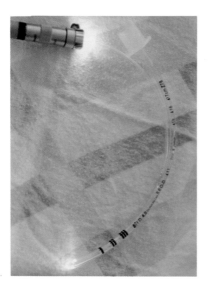

*The illuminated endotracheal tube is constructed so that a fiberoptic strand passes, in the wall of the tube, to the tip. When illuminated by an incandescent light source, the tip of the endotracheal tube glows brightly.*

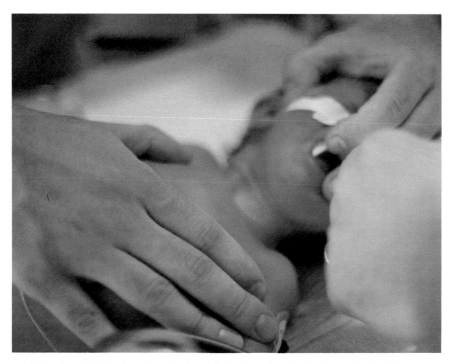

*A baby in whom the illuminated endotracheal tube has been placed. The glow at the tip of the endotracheal tube indicates the termination of the tube, and shows that it is in the safe position.*

for positioning when the lighting in the nursery was dimmed.

This study has shown that it is possible to see the light transmitted from the illuminated end of an endotracheal tube to the surface of the skin of all babies examined, and that the tip of the endotracheal tube can thereby be positioned in the appropriate region of the trachea. The system does not, however, make it possible to differentiate between oesophageal and tracheal intubation since, in both cases, the circle of light seen on the skin is similar.

Further studies are required to determine whether this system reduces the incidence of pulmonary complications such as interstitial air, pneumomediastinum, pneumothorax, and atelectasis. Furthermore, additional studies are needed to provide documentation that this system actually reduces the cost of medical care and the amount of ionizing radiation the baby receives by a reduction in the number of radiographs obtained.

# Navigation and fisheries research project for the sightless

## Andrew Gilbert Henry Hay

35 Star Route, Naalehu, Hawaii 96772, USA

French, born 6 January 1942. Farm worker. Educated in France, Switzerland and USA; M.T.S. degree from Gordon-Conwell Theological Seminary in 1978.

It all began on the shore of New England when I went deep-sea fishing with a group of friends. I did not know on that early morning as we were cruising from Rockport Harbor to the fishing grounds that, on that day, I would catch several fish, one of them measuring over 90 cm and weighing some 7 kg. That first deep-sea fishing trip was the beginning of two exciting summers spent in Massachusetts. At times I spent the night in my sleeping bag on the hard deck of the boat so that I would be there when the boat left early the next morning. I found it was easier to ask my friends for a ride during the day or in the evening than at four or five o'clock in the morning.

### The joys of sailing and fishing

It is a pleasant feeling to be on the ocean, to stand on the deck and sway with the boat as it goes up and down with the motion of the waves! Except when you are seasick! We were 120 km off shore the first time it happened to me. There was a gale blowing and nothing but white caps all over. Then I wished I was on land. During those two summers I learned techniques for bottom fishing as well as how to filet and skin fish. Then, in 1979 I moved to Hawaii. That year, a friend took me on his sport fishing boat and even let me steer the craft for a while; however, every so often, he had to tell me to turn the wheel to the right or left because being blind I was unable to read the instruments. Can something be done, I pondered, to make a blind person independent at the wheel? From then on I began considering the possibility of fitting out a boat with navigational instruments adapted to the needs of the blind – a project which a number of scientists, engineers and fishermen I consulted confirmed as being a feasible endeavour.

Thus, for the past six years, I have been researching and working on this project for it is my desire to further extend the frontiers of the sightless into navigation and the commercial fishing industry. The final outcome is a project comprising four components: the acquisition of a suitable boat; its equipment with navigational instruments adapted to the needs of the sightless and their

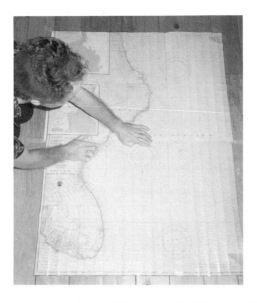

*Navigating with a chart that you cannot read is a major task. This nautical chart of the north-west shore of the Big Island of Hawaii was put into Braille form for Andrew Hay so that he can study it with his fingers.*

testing; analysis of the type of fishing and fisheries most suitable for the blind fisherman and development of special tools to increase his independence.

**The boat and its equipment**

Acquisition of a boat was essential for carrying out the practical phases of the project and a 10.35 m aluminium craft and trailer has been designed and will be built by Delta Marine of Deltaville, Virginia, USA. Throughout the research phase my sighted crewman and myself will use the boat to catch fish and thus provide a source of income to fund our studies, service the boat, purchase new equipment or cover the cost of modifying instruments.

This decade is producing a multitude of new and highly sophisticated electronic and computerized navigational instruments which lend themselves well to the needs of the sightless. A number of these suitable or modified navigational instruments will be installed and tested aboard the boat for safety, accuracy, reliability, quality and clarity of audio systems, quality of hardware and whether or not the audio systems convey all the data displayed on the instrument's screen. The instruments will also be evaluated as to how easily they can be operated by a blind person.

**Fisheries research**

The small boat fisheries in Hawaii and other parts of the world offer a wide range of possibilities to the blind fisherman, either for recreational or commercial fishing. My experience in and research about ocean fishing during the past nine years have led me to believe that a blind person assisted by a sighted crewman is capable of commercial fishing. Therefore, it is my desire to demonstrate that it can be done by getting involved in four hook and line fisheries that are, in my opinion, suitable for blind fishermen. Finally, there is the shark fishery which is

*Fishing equipment with rods, lines and hooks may prove insurmountably complicated for the blind fisherman. The fishing rig above was designed by Andrew Hay, himself blind, to overcome these obstacles.*

also suitable for the blind fisherman, but needs considerable experience and the right equipment. During this phase, I will collect data with a view to establishing which fisheries are most suitable and safe for blind fishermen and to providing information that will be beneficial to them; at the same time, I will also examine trap fishing for lobsters, crabs and shrimps and pot fishing for octopus.

### Information dissemination

To allow other sightless people to benefit from our research, articles will be published in different magazines and data will be compiled on fisheries and navigational instruments. Copies of the reports will be sent to organizations and services for the blind in the USA and other countries; tape recordings will be made by the Honolulu Library for the Blind and made available to the blind and physically handicapped.

### Conclusion

May God use this project to bring motivation into the lives of many sightless and physically disabled persons, to help them turn their eyes from their handicaps and face life's challenges and obstacles with the determination and the will to overcome them. We must use the abilities given to us by God by living a dynamic and active life, enjoying the achievements of successful enterprises, and contributing something worth while to society and for our fellow men.

108

# Deep Flight: A new class of underwater research and exploration vehicles

## Graham Hawkes

**Honourable Mention**
**The Rolex Awards for Enterprise – 1987**

1431 Doolittle Drive, San Leandro, California 94577, USA

British, born 23 December 1947. Chief Engineer, Founder and Chief Executive Officer of Deep Ocean Engineering, Inc. and Deep Ocean Technology, Inc. Educated in UK; HND (Mechanical Engineering) from Borough Polytechnic Institute, London, in 1969.

Over the past century, tremendous advances have been made in aerospace technology, while development of equipment for ocean exploration has lagged far behind. I have already designed and developed a variety of equipment for this purpose, which has proved successful, practical and cost-effective in most cases; however, the majority of these systems have been applied primarily for commercial purposes and have been funded accordingly.

The Deep Flight project aims to develop a new class of lightweight high-performance vehicles and is the only system I have ever designed for the specific purpose of exploration and research. I have been working on the Deep Flight design for the past three years, using my own time and resources for development. It is expected that the first two systems will be completed in early 1987.

### Vehicle design and construction

The two Deep Flight vehicles currently under development are small, autonomous submersibles designed with a range of 50 km at depths of up to 1,000 m for such tasks as photodocumentation and data and specimen gathering. They are designed to be highly portable and deployable from various kinds of ships or from the shore, thus overcoming the problems of dependence and limited intervention capability associated with the existing underwater systems. Design studies and computer modelling eliminated the possibility of using a tether, and demonstrated the advantages of having a human pilot rather than "artificial intelligence"; they also led to the adoption of a highly modular approach including interchangeable instrument packages and manipulators.

The pressure hull is designed to meet or exceed certification standards for manned submersibles with the forward section being in aluminium and an acrylic section that accommodates the pilot, and an aft body in glass-reinforced plastic. The key operating specifications include a weight of 1,225 kg, a

*Graham Hawkes in the diving system, WASP, which he designed.*

maximum payload of 250 kg, an overall length of 4 m, an operating depth of 1,000 m, a working speed of approximately 8 km/h, a basic range of some 67 km and an extended range of some 167 km.

### Pilot, payload and controls

The pilot is in a head-up reclining position and, even though his natural forward view is restricted in this position, this is compensated by camera images displayed on a screen, and the use of a corrective prism mated to the clear hull. In general, the pilot's preferred view for direct, visual inspection will be the clear natural view above, below, and sideways through the acrylic housing. The payload is divided among internal system modules in the pressure hull within reach and view of the pilot, two droppable wing pods, the flooded streamlined nose section and the trim weights in the nose, tail and port and starboard wings. At cruising speeds, the vehicle will be "flown", i.e. controlled by varying hydrodynamic control surfaces rather than by varying buoyancy or differential thrust, and a pair of upswept canard planes on the nose are the main control surfaces. However, for manipulative tasks, use will be made of differential thrust or "manoeuvering" thrusters on the wing and/or nose pods together with variation of buoyancy. Deep Flight vehicles will be fitted with a modified version of manipulators designed by the applicant for other applications and provided with tactile, motion and force feedback.

### Propulsion, life support and safety

Low drag and high propulsive efficiency are achieved by stream-lining and the use of a slow (150 rpm) high-efficiency 12-bladed main forward thruster. For normal use a 1-hp permanent-magnet motor will be used and for higher speeds, this will be replaced by a 7-hp brushless design. Energy will be derived from a

110

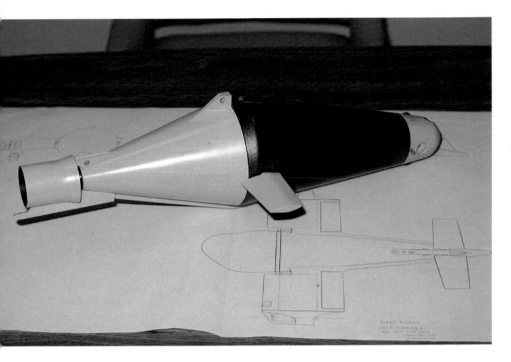

*Model and plans for the Deep Flight lightweight, high-performance vehicle for underwater research and exploration.*

fixed main battery located in the main hull profile. The vehicle will employ atmospheric diving systems for carbon dioxide removal and automatic oxygen make-up that have been tested and proven over thousands of hours of routine use; the life support design specification is for a minimum of 90 hours. Deep Flight vehicles are designed to be deployed readily from a "ship of opportunity", from the shore and, under certain circumstances, may even be deployed and retrieved from a helicopter using suitable tow, lift and sling points. An "operating cradle" will be provided to facilitate entry and exit, and vehicle maintenance and transport.

The safety of one-man atmospheric diving systems has been largely demonstrated and the safety of the Deep Flight vehicles will be further enhanced by the fact that they are being developed as a pair and that, although they are fully capable of operating singly, their combined use ensures immediate "back-up" and enhances working and observational capabilities.

As with all other systems that I have designed, the pressure hull of the Deep Flight vehicles is detachable from the rest of the system and forms a buoyant escape system for the pilot. Once the hull has risen to the surface, the pilot can either remain inside until he is retrieved or release himself from the unit.

# The quest for tropical paraplegia

## Gustavo Campos Román

Texas Tech University Health Sciences Center, School of Medicine, Lubbock, Texas 79430, USA

Colombian, born 7 September 1946. Associate Professor of Neurology, and Acting Chairman, Department of Medical and Surgical Neurology, Texas Tech University Health Sciences Center. Educated in Colombia, France and USA; M.D. from National University of Colombia, Bogotá, in 1971.

Tropical paraplegia (TP) is a disease of unknown cause, manifested by paralysis of the legs, which is highly prevalent in many equatorial countries where, due to a shortage of trained neurologists, it is often not even diagnosed let alone adequately treated. A further point that makes the deeper study of TP a matter of urgency is recent evidence that it could be caused by an infection of the nervous system with the human T-lymphocyte virus type 1 (HTLV-I), a retrovirus closely related to the causative agent of acquired immune deficiency syndrome (AIDS). Moreover, observations on antibodies in the serum and spinal fluid of multiple sclerosis patients open up an exciting new area of research into the possible relationships between tropical myeloneuropathies and multiple sclerosis.

**Progress so far**

To date, I have been largely responsible for the study of two widely separate tropical geographic isolates of TP. In the first, I examined over 200 suspected TP patients, established strict diagnostic criteria, performed spinal taps, obtained blood and spinal fluid samples, and initiated the treatment of these patients. In the second, I led a team of investigators to screen 56 suspected cases using diagnostic criteria defined on the basis of previous experience; and 20 of these were found to be suffering from the disease.

From these studies performed in two areas of the tropics, sufficient information has been gathered to justify the following preliminary conclusions. First, TP appears to be one and the same disease in these two widely separated areas of the tropical world. Second, TP is an extremely common disease in the two areas of the world where it was studied. In the first study, we recorded an estimated prevalence of 98 cases per 100,000 population. If only the population 25 years of age or older is considered at risk, the figure increases to 2.8 cases per

1,000 population. In the second, the estimated prevalence figures range from a minimum rate of 30.8 per 100,000 population to a value of 127.7 cases per 100,000 population (1 case in 783 population). The magnitude of this problem can be accurately perceived when these prevalence ratios are compared with those for non-traumatic paraplegia in developed countries, that range from 2 to 4.3 cases per 100,000 population, or when compared with the prevalence ratios for multiple sclerosis which range from 20 cases per 100,000 in Finland to 129 per 100,000 in the Shetland Islands.

However, despite the magnitude of the problem very little research is being currently done for the study of tropical paraplegia. Many foci of TP have been described throughout the tropical world. The main difficulty in the evaluation of this data originates from the fact that multiple diagnostic criteria have been used for the reporting of these patients and in some instances it is difficult to obtain solid conclusions from the sketchy information provided. Only an experienced clinical neurologist, applying strict criteria, could separate cases of TP from other conditions that mimic this entity.

**Proposal for the worldwide study of tropical paraplegia**

My project is to complete the worldwide study of tropical paraplegia. To this end, I propose to visit the different geographic areas of the world where the disease has been previously described, but not completely studied. The most expensive item of this proposed project is the cost of airline fares. However, I am confident that if the project is approved, the benevolent co-operation of an international airline could be obtained to secure a significant reduction, or even a full donation, of the transportation cost for the principal investigator.

I have corresponded extensively with physicians interested in the study of tropical paraplegia in a large number of countries. Specific contacts have been made with regard to the possibility of study of TP in the different geographical

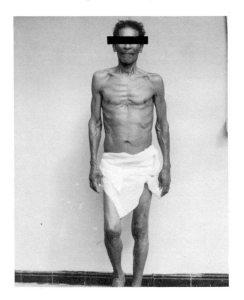

*A patient affected by tropical spastic paraparesis, a disease characterized by progressive difficulty in walking and eventual paralysis of the legs.*

areas. A simplified questionnaire has been tried in earlier field work and can be easily applied by local nursing personnel. The general physical and complete neurological examination will be performed by the principal investigator. The information obtained will be collected on the Mayo Clinic forms for neurologic examination previously used. Blood and spinal fluid samples will be obtained from these patients and, with their informed consent, transported in dry ice and hand-carried by the principal investigator for analysis in the co-operating institutions.

Preliminary contact has already been made with physicians in most of the areas where clusters of TP have been described. Selection of a particular area of study will be made on the basis of availability of a number of patients that could be studied in a central location over a relatively short period of time. The typical length of study in a particular area is between three to four weeks. It will be possible to visit four to five areas of the world in one year. By sampling different regions of South America, the Caribbean, Africa, India and the Far East, the study could be completed in two to three years. The information obtained will be stored in magnetic media, analyzed and presented to the scientific community in the usual manner.

*Tumaco, a port town of the Pacific Lowlands of Colombia, where Dr. Gustavo C. Román carried out a paraplegia study in 1982.*

114

# Using computerized vocal synthesis in measuring instruments for blind people

## *Rinaldo Canalis*

c/o Ser. Mi. G., 61 Piazza Borgo Dora, 10152 Turin, Italy

Italian, born 29 August 1952. Designer and quality-control technician in an electrical appliance factory. Educated in Italy; diploma (Industrial Technology) in 1971.

This project has been undertaken by Restitution of Technology (RE.TE.), a volunteer, not-for-profit group which has as its objective the establishment of communication between people who possess technological knowledge and people who need to benefit from it. It has endeavoured to disseminate various types of equipment, either produced by the group itself or brought in from outside, and which are based on either tried and tested conventional technology or modern sophisticated procedures, with the target users being inhabitants of the developing countries or the handicapped.

### Meeting with blind couple initiates project

The project was started early in the summer of 1985 when we met a blind couple who explained how their life could be made easier by the ownership of a few items of equipment; however, such items were not always readily obtainable and/or their cost was prohibitive. The three appliances that we decided to develop for them were a light sensor, a thermometer in which a synthesized voice reads out the temperature, and a machine that reads printed characters and translates them into Braille.

The first of these has just been completed, and the last one is at a very early design stage. However, it is the second, with some modifications, which is the subject of our project.

### Development of a talking thermometer

Initially, we considered only the thermometer function but soon realized that, with only a few changes, we could develop a complete and integrated instrument for a variety of measuring tasks and even though the actual prototypes incorporate only the thermometer function, we believe that, in the future, the voice synthesizer (the most expensive component in the unit) can be linked with a wide range of devices such as scales, light sensors, blood pressure

115

gauges, medicine droppers, etc. We also believe that we will soon be able to use the unit to read out the frequency to which a radio-set is tuned, and the figures displayed on a calculator, or for connection to a Braille device to meet the needs of both the blind and deaf-and-blind. The unit itself is small (13 x 13 x 5 cm), light (0.3 kg), and powered with a 9V battery, and is readily portable in a suitable shoulder bag. Currently, the synthesizer speech output is in Italian; however, by modifying the programme in the read-only memory (ROM), it is possible to select any other language desired. On subsequent versions, it will be possible to select the language output simply by resetting a few switches placed at the rear of the device.

## Instrument design and circuitry

The circuitry of the unit is in two parts: a board containing the computerized voice synthesizer and the analogue-digital converter, and a series of interchangeable probes for measuring the various parameters such as temperature, weight and pressure. The main board also comprises a number of low-cost and readily available electronic components, including an eight-bit central processing unit (a Z80 chip), a read-only memory (27128 chip), a speech synthesizer (SPO256-AL2 chip), an audio-amplifier, an analogue-digital converter (ADC0804) and a number of logic ports. Since the central processing unit has a large number of internal registers the programme will run without the use of random access memory chips, which means a saving in both money and space. All the components are very cheap and very easy to find. A key feature of the speech synthesizer used is that it is allophone-based and can therefore reproduce any word in any language.

The slave circuit (probe) comprises a sensor connected to an appropriate analogue interface generally consisting of a Wheatstone bridge. Each probe is connected to the master circuit by means of a nine-pin Cannon connector. Since only three of the nine pins are used to encode the sensor, eight different types of probe can be used.

When the electronic voice output device is powered up and the speech synthesizer initialized, the programme interrupts for about one second to allow the oscillator of the analogue-digital converter to stabilize and thereafter, the converter is ready, and its datum is temporarily stored in an internal register of the central processing unit.

The central processing unit encodes the digital output from the appropriate three pins of the probe, checks which one is connected and thus ensures correct conversion of the previously stored datum. The datum is now ready to be converted into allophones that will be spoken by the SPO256-AL2 chip, and the programme loops back almost to the beginning and goes on repeating (every two seconds) the value read from the probe until it is switched off.

## Future prospects

We believe that this device will be of considerable value to the blind in its present configuration and that, linked with a variety of other measuring problems, it offers a wide range of new facilities for the visually handicapped.

116

*An external view of the voice-synthesizer unit fitted with a temperature probe.*

*An internal view of a prototype of the computerized voice-synthesizer unit.*

117

# Project Rainbow – New Rice™: For better use of world food resources

## Jeanne M. Cox

246 East Bartlett Road, Lynden, Washington 98264, USA

American, born 5 November 1939. Mother, inventor and food technology consultant. Educated in USA; self-taught in the field of food technology.

Rice is the second most abundant cereal crop in the world, preceded only by wheat. It accounts for 20% of global grain consumption, provides 25% of the entire caloric intake of the human race and it has been estimated that 2 billion people (approximately half of the world population) depend on rice for 80% of their food. An average of 100 kg of rough rice will yield 50 to 60 kg of whole kernels. The rest will be hulls, bran and brokens. It may therefore be estimated that 30–50% of world rice crops are lost to broken grains which means a staggering loss in cash value and direct loss from the food chain. If some way could be found to put this rice back into the direct food chain, there would be enough to feed all of the hungry of the earth.

### Setting out to upgrade broken rice grains

This project set out with the aim of finding a way in which this vast pool of potential raw materials could be reformed in a way that would meet criteria for hunger relief food laid down by the Food and Agriculture Organization, namely that it should: have a proper balance of amino acids; be free of any toxic factors; be subject to minimal processing damage; be acceptable to parents; and, where possible, come from local crops. In addition, a number of criteria were added for research and development purposes, namely that the product must: be cross-culturally acceptable; be easy to prepare; contain all the essential nutrients (not just amino acids), be cheaper to prepare than other foods, keep well, not require special or expensive packaging, not require expensive or complex capital equipment, have a good taste which is compatible with local preferences, and be available in a variety of flavours made from high volume waste or value-degraded products and, where possible, be suitable for indigenous processing.

The outcome of the research carried out is called New Rice™ which meets all the above criteria. It comprises powdered grain, legume or pulse material, is mixed with a fluid binder containing algin, seaweed derivative, albumin, chitin derivative, gelatin, gluten, pectin, agar-agar, carrageenin, carob gum, guar gum and/or gum tragacanth to form a dough that is moulded or extruded and the

118

*In a laboratory test run, beautiful whole-grain New Rice ™ is manufactured from a final mix of broken grains using a conventional pasta machine fitted with special rice-shaped dies.*

extruded material severed, to form synthesized kernels. These kernels are deposited in an aqueous setting or gelling liquid, preferably containing calcium chloride or calcium lactate, to set the fluid binder, and then cooked and either dried, canned or frozen. If the kernels are cooked for a few minutes after being formed they will be quick cooking. The grain, legume or pulse material may contain additives of protein, amino acid or amino acid analogue, oil or fat, colouring and flavouring material. New Rice is all but indistinguishable from regular rice.

### Other products

Several important aspects of the invention, which developed from the basic work for hunger relief, became so significant in their own right that the various phases of the work have been given their own project titles. Thus, hunger relief foods are referred to collectively as "Project Rainbow", synthetic rice both for hunger relief in underdeveloped countries and consumer food products for exploitation in developed countries is referred to simply as "New Rice", and those products with a substantial medical application have been designated "Rx Rice".

An example of the medical use of Rx Rice has been in patients suffering from azotaemia, a condition in which the patient is unable to clear sufficient quantities of nitrogen which then builds up to toxic levels in the body. These patients may be treated with hydroxy or keto acid analogues of essential amino acids which

119

are, however, so vile-tasting that few, if any, patients can or will willingly take them orally. These analogues have been sequestered, in exactly the right proportions, into New Rice kernels and the dishes made with this product can easily be flavoured to yield a wide variety of tasty meals, which further alleviates the oppressive nature of these disorders.

## Exploitation and market development

It was originally intended to market the invention in the USA first, with Rx Rice being licensed separately from New Rice products and a portion of the licence income being used to develop Project Rainbow. However, it was finally decided to press ahead in India and other developing countries, and not wait for the developed country markets. Nevertheless, not-for-profit implementation posed problems since it was perceived that government interference has, in many cases, unwittingly exacerbated the problem (by supplanting free enterprise), and that the distribution systems offered by church groups did not seem to offer viable alternatives.

It was finally concluded that the development of such an ambitious plan can be served only in a spirit of enterprise. To give Project Rainbow its fair chance, it has been determined that, wherever possible, it will be brought to market by principles of free enterprise under simple licences, but with controls that will provide production incentives and prevent oppressive mark-ups. In countries where the product may be needed, any vestigial- or neo-capitalistic systems that exist will be used to encourage maximum production for maximum profit.

The licence fees or earnings will be used entirely to further the objects of Project Rainbow – to make the world better by improved utilization and upgrading of waste and wasteful practices.

*Jeanne Cox at work in her food laboratory on the development of New Rice ™. High-protein soya flour is being added to give life-sustaining properties to the finished product.*

# Belihuloya hydropower project

## *Gamini Samarasinghe*

**Honourable Mention**
**The Rolex Awards for Enterprise – 1987**

390 Araliya Gardens, Nawala Road, Rajagiriya, Sri Lanka

Sri Lankan, born 4 January 1940. Farmer and vegetable seed production researcher. Educated in Sri Lanka and Sweden; studied for Ph.D., Institute of Zoology, University of Lund in 1971–1974.

In December 1976, with my Swedish wife and my son, I came to Sri Lanka, and set up a 2.5 ha research/production farm at an altitude of some 2,000 m in one of the most inaccessible mountain areas of Sri Lanka where for the first year and a half, we did agricultural research on cauliflower and broccoli which were exotic vegetables in Sri Lanka. My wife started a free health service for the poor and isolated workers on a nearby tea plantation, and we were able to provide a useful social service.

A huge ravine 1,000–1,600 m deep, lay in front of the farm, offering us a spectacular view of about one-sixth of Sri Lanka, with the south and south-east coast being visible on clear days. Behind us was montane tropical forest with leopards and monkeys and deer and beautiful trees on which exotic orchids bloomed. The closest main road and village were nearly 20 km away, and our beautiful secluded site was accessible only via a terrible road.

### The hydropower project is born

During my wanderings, I came across the beautiful Belihuloya River flowing through the jungle about 1 km behind our house. One day, sitting contemplating the world, I was suddenly struck by the idea of diverting the river into the ravine and using the fall for electricity generation. Consultation of maps confirmed that the river fell only slowly along its course. I observed the water flow rate at different times of the year, did some simple hydrological calculations and approximate measurements of weekly water flow. Thereafter, equipped with an altimeter, I descended the precipitous slope, measuring altitude differences at intervals. I found a direct drop of some 1,000 m, a drop of 1,400 m down to a stream called Kiriketioya flowing in the ravine bottom, and a drop of a further 200 m another 2 km on; a stupendous 1,600 m in about 5 km. My calculations showed that even a run-of-the-river project could produce a large amount of electricity for a country in which only 20% of the population is served with electricity.

*Gamini Samarasinghe surveying towards the bottom of the Kiriketioya ravine, with the mountain range rising to an altitude of 1,400 m in the background.*

I decided to approach the Government and wrote a report on my observations and calculations to the Secretary for Plan Implementation. This was followed by a visit by the engineers from the Ceylon Electricity Board (CEB) who checked my observations – a surprise to many since the hydroelectric potential of Sri Lanka had supposedly been researched exhaustively! They confirmed my findings but made a very conservative estimate of the energy available.

I nevertheless obtained Government permission to build a measurement weir at the approximate site of the dam, appealing for aid to a Swedish company building a large dam elsewhere in Sri Lanka. This company not only built the measurement weir, but also made a private survey of the entire project – which they found fascinating. From then on, I was able to regularly monitor the river water flow rate, and now have daily flow figures from April 1982 to August 1985 showing an annual average of some 2,000 l/s. The survey done by the Swedish firm established that a 30-m high dam would produce a reservoir of some 6.5 million m$^3$ of water, with a dam crest of only 135 m in length. A penstock of 3-3.5 km would give an immediate head of some 1,194 m and a further 2-3 km would give a head of some 1,600 m. A feasibility study would evaluate the cost of different heads but a drop of approximately 1,600 m was available within a distance of 6-7 km; this is exceptional, and is exceeded only by the Reisseck dam in Austria and the Grande Dixence in Switzerland with 1,758 and 1,738 m respectively. The Ceylon Electricity Board then got the services of the Chief and Principal engineers of the Norwegian Electricity Board to do a short preliminary pre-feasibility study of the project; however, the report produced considers only the direct drop available without extending the penstock.

### The challenge of going it alone

In view of enthusiastic expert opinion about the economic viability of the project, I considered taking up the challenge and going forward privately, as a

122

*The 30-m wide three-notch weir built by Gamini Samarasinghe on the Belihuloya, with the help of the Swedish construction company Skanska.*

joint state-private enterprise project, or with a limited time of ownership so that I could be personally involved in the building work. With this in mind, I published a series of articles in the Sri Lankan daily press about private involvement in the construction and ownership of a hydro-electric project. Since all the utilities in Sri Lanka are owned and operated by the State, my action was considered highly provocative; however, with the State giving more prominence to private enterprise, I thought it could very well be interesting and even wrote a letter to the President which was acknowledged, although no definite decision has been made.

The project is, in fact, now included in the electricity generation plan; it should be completed around 1990 at the latest and may be done even earlier. However, I am keen to have the possibility of going ahead with this as an innovative private project in Sri Lanka, with international collaboration. Many reputable firms in different countries have already shown interest in this project. However, at the time of writing I am still awaiting Presidential approval and the Ceylon Electricity Board will, I believe, start the official feasibility study soon.

# Diver's position-fixing and telemetry system

## Bryan Woodward

5 Burton Street, Loughborough, Leicestershire LE11 2DT, UK

British, born 11 February 1941. Lecturer in Electronic and Electrical Engineering, Loughborough University of Technology. Educated in UK; Ph.D. (Physics) from University of London in 1968.

Existing diver navigation systems are designed for offshore commercial situations where all the equipment is sited above the water and operated by a surface supervisor. Positions are computed with respect to fixed receivers which detect, at different relative times, pulses from an acoustic source carried by the diver. Communications are maintained by a directly wired telephone link which is an integral part of the umbilical line carrying the diver's breathing gas.

By contrast, there are many scientific applications for which this is not a practical possibility, mainly on account of the cost and bulk. The alternative is a unit which allows a free-swimming diver to do his own position-fixing. He takes the entire system with him and can monitor his position continuously in three-dimensional space with respect to an array of fixed receivers. The method, which I and others have used, is to make measurements with a hand-held sonar rangefinder measuring the ranges to three (or more) fixed transponders. Done manually, this is time-consuming and, consequently, a great improvement would be to compute any position automatically by this principle.

### Developing a design

In my design, the system carried by the diver is battery-powered and self-contained in a small pressure housing attached to a conventional aqualung. The prototype comprises digital circuits to measure the acoustic pulse transit times between the diver's transmitter and three transponders, and a microprocessor programmed to do the triangulation calculations. The diver simply views a liquid crystal display on a wandering cable; this shows the $x$, $y$ and $z$ co-ordinates of his position, updated every second, as conventional seven-segment decimal numbers. Alternatively, for a future version, this information can be presented on a small liquid-crystal display screen showing any position as a spot with respect to a plan of the transponder array. With this method, the diver can see at a glance his relative position. By incorporating a velocimeter to measure the sound velocity in the region where the measurements are made, the system becomes self-calibrating as well as automatic.

The co-ordinates can also be monitored at the surface, if required, by transmitting them as digital data which is detected by a hydrophone and processed for display. The surface equipment proposed is essentially ancillary, is all battery-powered and may be used in a small boat. With the addition of a telephone line, radio link, or even a satellite link to a remote terminal, the diver can be put in touch with a non-diving specialist, for example an archaeologist, geologist, biologist or oceanographer. So far as is known there is no other system enabling a diver to do automatic position-fixing completely unaided by any surface direction. If three (or more) receivers are placed at widely spaced locations on the sea bed, i.e. a "long-base line array", the position of a sound source carried by the diver can be determined by the principle of triangulation, as applied widely in civil engineering and radio navigation applications. After deriving several sets of position-fixing algorithms, I adopted the one requiring the fewest input values and the simplest equations for programming.

**Progress so far**

My past and present work relating to this project has resulted in the design of many types of diver-portable systems, in particular a self-calibrating sonar (patent applied for), a velocimeter, acoustic beacons and transponders, an underwater telephone, a dive-profile recorder, a differential depth meter, a diver homing system, and a system for monitoring a diver's physiology by digital data transmission. Future effort requires the synthesis of all past experience in this work to realize the proposed project objectives.

At present the microprocessor circuit, which is the central feature of the design, is complete and working in the laboratory. In its present form, the time inputs, which are proportional to the distances required for triangulation, are simulated to generate realistic values on the displays. Tests carried out have verified that the algorithms programmed in the microprocessor's memory give co-ordinates to a very high precision.

The next stage in the development will be to replace the simulated time inputs with the real flight times of a sound pulse from an air transducer source travelling to three air transducer receivers connected directly to the timing

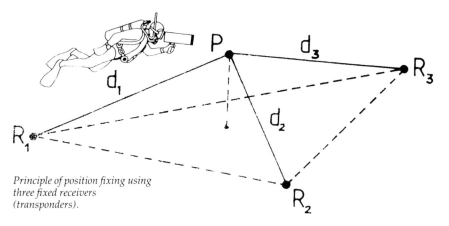

*Principle of position fixing using three fixed receivers (transponders).*

125

*Prototype position fixing system, showing circuits and pressure housing ready for laboratory testing. The housing will be carried by a diver who will monitor his position underwater by reading a display on a wandering cable.*

circuits. A natural development of the project is then to replace the air transducers with hydrophones so that the system can then be taken underwater. When this stage has been reached, the hydrophones will be replaced with transponders so that the diver is free of all leads. The hydrophones then become the receiving and transmitting elements of the transponders; these are the most expensive components of the design. The next phase will be to extend the system by adding an acoustic link, including voice communications, to allow remote monitoring at the surface.

With the inclusion of an acoustic link to the surface, further circuits can be added to allow monitoring of other parameters. For example, by providing the diver with suitable sensors, his breathing rate, heart rate and skin temperature can be remote-monitored in real time: all the information needed, including his position, is transmitted to the surface for permanent recording, yet it is all derived from a small unit carried on the diver's back.

### Potential for the future

The final system envisaged could be used by any type of diver in any depth of water. The possibility of monitoring a diver's position, and talking with him, from some remote location by digital data transmission techniques has great potential for applications in which non-diving specialists can participate from their own laboratory or office. With the present sophistication in large-scale integrated circuit design, the diver's unit could ultimately be reduced in size to enable it to be worn like a wrist watch. In this configuration, it would have no leads and be truly self-contained. Like the decompression computers presently coming on to the market, it could be a standard piece of equipment for underwater scientific work.

# Roadways that "talk"

## Hugh Bradner

1876 Caminito Marzella, La Jolla, California 92037, USA

American, born 5 November 1915. Professor of Engineering Physics and
Geophysics, University of California, San Diego. Educated in USA; Ph.D.
(Physics) from California Institute of Technology in 1941.

This project proposes the production of passive roadway surface texture
markings which will "speak" to drivers to warn of dangerous curves,
intersections, etc. Operation will be completely automatic and no modifications
will be required to the automobiles. The invention could also be used to give
map directions, for advertising and many other applications.

Drivers motoring along a highway have certainly noticed the different sounds
produced by various types of road surface. Sometimes these sounds seem to be
just a noise, soft or loud. Sometimes they seem to be a tone, especially when the
road has been given transverse grooves to improve the slippery surface – and
the tone changes with changing car speed.

### New use for speaking-toy mechanisms

Such observations, coupled with my memories of the "speaking toy" which
reproduced a simple "verbal" message when a thumbnail was pulled along a
plastic ribbon, led to the idea of making a road surface that speaks to automobile
drivers. The ribbons on the toys were about 1 cm wide and 15 cm long, and had
transverse grooves on the surface like coarse mechanical analogues of the
varying magnetization lines on familiar magnetic tapes. One end of the ribbon
was attached to a box, doll, greeting card or "secret society" badge. When a
thumbnail was pulled along the ribbon the toy vibrated to produce the sounds.

The tone produced by regularly spaced transverse ridges or grooves in a road
is caused by the vibration induced in the tyres which then transmit this vibration
to the car; the tone is merely the result of vibration at sonic frequency. If we take
the example of an automobile travelling at a velocity of 80 km/h across a set of
ridges spaced 5 cm apart, the resulting tone will be 444 Hz, i.e. close to "A" on
the musical scale. With an automobile travelling at 120 km/h the frequency of the
tone will be 50% higher (a fifth on the musical scale) and should be louder
because of the more violent impact of the tyres against the ridges.

At 53 km/h the frequency of the tone will be 50% lower and probably not as

*These road signs piled on top of one another seem to have been arranged more with the object of confusing the motorist rather than aiding him. Hugh Bradner's "talking road" is designed to overcome this kind of visual confusion. (Photo IVB-Report)*

loud. Loudness can also be changed by changing the dimensions of the ridges or grooves and the pitch will be in direct proportion to the number of ridges or grooves per metre along the road. Therefore, by marking the road with grooves or ridges that have varying spacing and dimensions, a modulated tone can be produced. However, the modulations should be made slow enough to ensure that the front and rear wheels are vibrated at approximately equal frequency; for example, in the case of a car with a wheelbase of 3 m, the modulation at 80 km/h can be made as fast as 0.13 seconds.

## Instructions that demand attention

An intriguing aspect of the speaking highway is the way that the roadway "voice" will change with changing automobile speed. Let us assume that the message "Go slow" – "Dangerous curve" has to be delivered at normal pitch and speaking rate when a car travels over the grooved section of the road at a speed of 80 km/h. If the car is travelling faster, the message will be higher pitched and quicker until, at very high speeds, it becomes an urgent, high-pitched, loud warning, "Go slo – Dangerous Curv".

However, for a car travelling at lower speed, the message becomes a low-pitched cautioning drawl, "Gooo slooww. Danggeerrouss currvve". Similar changes from mild caution to strident warning would occur for messages such as "Stop ahead" or "Stay awake"; or the voice could be made to deliver a sharp message such as "Don't enter" or "Wrong way, turn back", even at speeds below 80 km/h.

## Need for a trial model

It would be possible to construct a scale model to demonstrate the Talking Highway since, if velocity and all dimensions are reduced by the same factors, the sound frequency would be unchanged. The model speaking strip could be made using commercially available equipment by digitally recording the message, time stretching it, then producing the desired surface by a digitally controlled milling machine. Alternatively, a ribbon could be formed by extruding plastic through a slit of controlled aperture width.

Obviously, in addition to enhancing highway safety, the technique could also be used to give map directions or for communicating other information.

# Developing live electronic holography

## Ronald L. Kirk

2809 North Main Street, Findlay, Ohio 45840, USA

American, born 17 May 1952. Chairman of the Board, The Holotronics Corporation. Educated in USA; attended Ohio State University and Bowling Green State University.

This project has as its overall objective to develop an electronic system capable of capturing, transmitting and reconstructing live holographic data and/or three-dimensional images, and also proposes a first step toward the full exploitation of a new technology.

### Holography – A revolutionary technology

Although many methods of creating holograms have been developed since Dennis Gabor first proposed his theory in 1947, certain fundamental factors still hamper full exploitation of the tremendous potential of holography. A hologram created utilizing the coherent light from a laser beam is then split by a partially silvered mirror into two beams each of which is dispersed by a lens or other means. The first or "object" beam illuminates the subject of the hologram. The second, or reference beam, is directed to the film plate directly, setting up a reference of undistorted phase periodicity or a carrier frequency. The object beam also maintains its coherence until it strikes the three-dimensional object. Since each ray of the object beam strikes a different portion of the object, its point of reflection determines its phase relationship with each of the other rays reflecting from the object. Therefore, the wavefront reflecting from the object, through phase distortion, carries the three-dimensional information to the film plate. Since the film plate itself is incapable of recording phase relationship directly, it is the reference beam, heterodyning with the reflected object beam, that records the phase wavefront as a pattern of fringe lines which are recorded on the film plate.

### Current shortcomings in holography

The pattern of these fringe lines can, in one sense, be considered the product of the object multiplied by the reference beam. To reconstruct the original three-dimensional image (the solution), one merely needs to illuminate (divide) the

130

hologram (product) by the reference beam (multiplier). Heretofore, the difficulty in doing this by electronic methods lay with the size and number of these fringe lines. State-of-the-art photodetectors, and more importantly, electronic displays cannot achieve resolutions that are one-tenth of the minimum requirement for high resolution optical holography.

## Enter the optical tunnel array (OTA)

Until the development of my invention, the optical tunnel array (trademarked as the OTA), available electronic systems did not support the recording of light patterns in the holographic range of 200 to 2,000 lines of data per millimeter. The OTA now has a major role to play in the development of the world's first truly electronic holographic system. The applications for such a system are vast and include holographic television, robotics, artificial intelligence, optical computing/processing, medical imaging, CAD/CAM, biological research, three-dimensional tele-conferencing, adaptive optics, non-destructive testing and ultra-accurate automated quality control.

The OTA was developed using a new and innovative approach to the problem and will be capable of decoding, transmitting and reconstructing holographic wavefronts in real time. This is made possible not by the use of very small detectors but, rather, by an array comprised of crossed electrodes and a proprietary fluid. It is based on the principle that a longitudinally applied electric field can open a transparent tunnel in a normally opaque fluid. By using discrete, ultra-small electrode pairs, it has been possible to achieve switching of 2-micron diameter pixels located at 4-micron centres. This is equivalent to a programmable transparency.

## Status and potential of the OTA

After four years of research and development, the OTA has reached the point where the first commercial devices can be put into production. A proprietary new fabrication technique has been developed that enables the mass production of high quality, highly reliable devices of sufficient resolution to be used in the recording and reconstruction of optically recorded or computer-generated holographic images. These first devices represent the minimum requirements of 200 lines per millimeter; recent prototypes have achieved a resolution of 250 lines per millimeter and research indicates that 1,000 lines per millimeter will eventually be achieved.

## Taking holography from the laboratory to the real world

While the OTA in itself may represent a major breakthrough, the commercial applicability of such a device lies in the development of systems that employ its outstanding capabilities. We feel that the shortest route to commercialization and use of the device lies in the area of artificial intelligence as a robotic vision system which can take advantage of the OTA's present state of development. The device will simply replace the film plate in existing optical-pattern recognition systems and will not be subject to the problems involved in recording and reconstructing holographic data with film plates. The robot vision system would combine vision and artificial intelligence in pattern recognition, and the OTA would act, here, as an incoherent-to-coherent converter.

We feel that, by using our OTA devices to produce an electronic, holographic, artificially intelligent vision system for use in a robot assembly system, we can move the power of holography from the laboratory to the real world where it belongs.

## Towards a broader understanding of the athlete in motor racing

*Kurt Lewis Borman*

Motion Technology Inc., 703 Giddings Ave., Suite M6, Annapolis, Maryland 21401, USA
*American, born 7 August 1949. President and founder of Motion Technology Incorporated. Educated in USA; studied (Electrical Engineering) at University of Maryland from 1967 to 1972.*

Professional, and in particular Formula 1, motor racing is a major international sport; however, little is known about the actual performance of the athletes involved. This project plans to use electronic instrumentation to scientifically analyze the human performance characteristics of these athletes using, in particular, the Formula 1 racing driver Keke Rosberg as the research subject.


## A substitute for petroleum and wheat for tropical countries

*Karsten Werner Jochims*

Apartado postal 2389, Carretera vieja a León, km 13½; Reparto Maromo, Managua, Nicaragua
*West German, born 10 March 1934. General Manager and President of Jicaro S.A. Educated in West Germany; Doctor of Economics in 1964.*

The fruit of the calabash tree, *Crescentia alata*, yields ethanol (as a gasoline substitute), vegetable oil (as a diesel fuel substitute) and charcoal (as a fuel oil substitute), in addition to oil-cake, dry fruit pulp and tannic acid. This project has developed technology to exploit the calabash fruit; a plant to process 5,000 tonne/year of fresh fruit and its byproducts will come on-stream in 1987.


## Immunoassays for developing countries

*Alister Voller*

21 Castle Hill, Berkhamsted, Herts HP4 1HE, UK
*British, born 1 June 1937. Reader in Immunology of Parasitic Diseases, London School of Hygiene and Tropical Medicine. Educated in UK; FRCPath (London) from Royal College of Pathologists in 1984.*

Modern diagnostic techniques, e.g. radioimmunoassay and fluoroimmunoassay, have revolutionized early detection of pathogenic conditions; but they are expensive. This project plans to develop simple diagnostic systems specifically for use in the impoverished countries of the world, and aims to provide general methods, based on immunological reactions, to detect biological materials of diagnostic importance in man, animals and plants.


## Popular biodigestor family for developing countries

*Bela John Edward Zettl*

98 Praia do Flamengo, Apto. 403, 22210-Rio de Janeiro-RJ, Brazil
*Brazilian, born 15 November 1920. Senior researcher and consultant to Head of Research Department, Brazilian Naval Research Institute. Educated in Hungary; entered Military Institute of Technology, Budapest in 1938.*

By their design and construction, conventional biodigestors are often unsuitable for certain terrains or remote regions. This project has developed a family of three kinds of inexpensive biodigestors for use in remote regions. They can be employed for domestic, farm or community purposes and can be submerged or semi-submerged in water or placed on solid soil. All generate usable biogas.

# Determining the bio-effects of ultrasound on embryonic cells

*Nicole Bournias-Vardiabasis*
City of Hope Medical Center, 1500 East Duarte Road, Duarte, California 91010, USA
*American, born 24 July 1954. Research scientist, Division of Cytogenetics, City of Hope Medical Center. Educated in USA and UK; Ph.D. (Developmental Genetics) from University of Essex in 1978.*

Concern has been expressed that ultrasound techniques used in diagnostic examinations on pregnant women may have foetal teratogenic, mutagenic or carcinogenic potential. This project proposes to examine the morphological, biochemical and molecular effects of diagnostic ultrasound on Drosophilia embryonic cells with a view to proper assessment of the relative risks of such diagnostic exposure of the foetus.


# Using an artificial gill for underwater life support

*Joseph Bonaventura*
Pivers Island, Beaufort, North Carolina 28516, USA
*American, born 15 February 1941. Associate Professor, Department of Physiology, Duke University Medical Center; and Co-Director, Marine Biomedical Center, Duke University Marine Laboratory. Educated in USA; Ph.D. from University of Texas, Austin in 1968.*

This project is developing an artificial gill which will extract dissolved oxygen from aqueous fluids and make it available in gaseous form for use in biological life-support systems or as an oxidant for internal combustion engines. This device will enable man to breathe underwater and establish underwater habitats free from restrictions of battery power or tethered linkages to the atmosphere.


# Cardiomyoplasty – A new approach to cardiac assistance

*Juan Carlos Chachques*
29 rue des Rossays, 91600 Savigny-sur-Orge, France
*Argentine, born 8 January 1944. Physician. Educated in Argentina; M.D. from University of Rosario.*

This project has researched the use of skeletal muscle for biological cardiac assistance by "dynamic cardiomyoplasty" and sequential, progressive electrostimulation, and the possibility of left or right ventricular myocardium reconstruction. Cardiomyoplasty is expected to offer an alternative to heart transplantation or artificial heart replacement in severe cardiac insufficiency and extensive myocardial infarction.


# Communication of technical information with simple visual aids

*Ove Kurt Nordstrand*
11 B Herlevgårdsvej, 2730 Herlev, Denmark
*Danish, born 19 February 1929. Principal Conservator of the Royal Library, Copenhagen. Educated in Denmark; largely self-taught in the conservation of ancient manuscripts.*

This project proposes that simple visual aids (cartoons) could be used by Western technical experts working in developing countries to communicate technical information in spite of language barriers. The organization of a pilot project for bamboo papermaking at the village level is put forward as a means of illustrating the feasibility of this proposal.

## Nuralam Institute for Applied Research on Plants

*Christine Rohani Longuet*
3576 Kampong Duyong Besar, Kuala Trengganu, Trengganu 20100, Malaysia
*French, born 23 December 1943. Independent ethnobotanical consultant. Educated in France;*
*Maîtrise d'histoire from Sorbonne in 1969.*

In Malaysia, medicinal knowledge is a mixture of Arabic, Indian and Chinese healing traditions combined with the indigenous herbalism of South-East Asia. Malaysia also has a wealth of unexploited plant resources (some 8,000 plant species have been recorded). This project proposes the establishment of a regional phytopharmaceutical industry to utilize these botanical and related cultural resources.

## Apparatus for patients with pulmonary oedema and myocardial infarction pain

*Dimitris Joannis Stankourakis*
23 Hatzidaki, 74100 Rethymnon, Crete, Greece
*Greek, born 8 May 1942. Cardiologist in private practice. Educated in Greece; M.D. from Athens*
*University in 1970.*

This project has invented a transportable support device for patients presenting with acute heart failure (pulmonary oedema), anginoid pain or emphractic pain. The device retains the patient in a posture that reduces by at least one-half the flow of blood to the heart from the lungs, improves respiration, decreases cardiac effort and provides the physician with more time for effective intervention.

## Standardization of Malawian medicinal plants for local drug production

*Aubrey Harry Mvula*
Department of Personnel Management and Training, Box 30227, Lilongwe 3, Malawi
*Malawian, born 24 September 1957. Civil servant. Educated in Malawi; B.A. (Public*
*Administration) from University of Malawi in 1984.*

This project proposes to select a number of Malawian medicinal plants that have been thoroughly studied for the therapy of certain selected diseases, and to standardize them for local production of drugs that can be dispensed to the rural community as part of the Malawi National Primary Health Care Programme. The project also foresees the production of a range of excipients.

## "Peace" and other economical "I.Q." board games

*Roberto Ortaleza Kee*
17 Ofarrel Street, Pasay City, 3129 Metro Manila, Philippines
*Filipino, born 31 January 1949. Mechanical engineer in private practice. Educated in Philippines;*
*B.Sc. (Mechanical Engineering) from University of the East, Manila in 1970.*

This project has developed "Peace", believed to be the world's first board game that advocates human existence without violence. As a complement to this, other board games are being invented which emphasize intellectual growth in an environment without violence. All of these games have been designed with emphasis on economy so that many of the Third World peoples can afford to buy them.

## Identification of natural pesticides in vegetable epicuticular waxes

### Patrick Moyna

11634 Missisipí, Apto. 104, Montevideo, Uruguay
*Uruguayan, born 1 November 1938. Professor of Pharmacognosy and Natural Products Chemistry. Educated in Uruguay, UK and Canada; Ph.D. from University of Birmingham in 1968.*

Certain components of the epicuticular waxes forming the external protective layers of plants have fungistatic and insecticidal properties. It is proposed to study these auxiliary compounds in waxes and, by suitable breeding programmes, bioengineer crop cultivars to incorporate genetic material related to wax auxiliary compounds and thus obtain crops which have greater pest resistance.


## Controlling the parasitic weed, *Orobanche ramosa*, in the Sudan

### Faiz Faris Bebawi

Faculty of Agriculture, University of Khartoum, Shambat, Sudan
*Sudanese, born 9 April 1944. Associate Professor, Faculty of Agriculture, University of Khartoum. Educated in Sudan and UK; Ph.D. from University of Aberdeen in 1977.*

The parasitic weed, broomrape, *Orobanche ramosa*, is a major agricultural problem in the Sudan since it severely reduces broadbean crop yields; it can lie dormant in soil for up to 12 years and then germinate only when stimulated by a chemical exuded from the roots of the host crop. This project will study the potential of ethylene as an artificial germination stimulant for broomrape.


## Refractory bricks using indigenous raw materials and alternative technology

### Muhammad Ikramul-Haq

172 Ataturk Block, New Garden Town, 16 Lahore, Pakistan
*Pakistani, born 7 July 1945. Metallurgical engineer. Educated in Pakistan and U.K.; Ph.D. (Metallurgy) from Teesside Polytechnic, Middlesbrough in 1976.*

The high cost of refractory bricks imported into Pakistan led this project to develop labour-intensive processes for producing refractory bricks from local raw materials. To improve brick quality the project has also developed an alternative technology for manufacturing chemically bonded bricks which are cured *in situ* during the steelmaking process. Trials are awaited for bricks made using the alternative process.


## Vortex method of submerging, entraining, melting and circulating metal charge

### Raymond Joffre Claxton

Materials Analysis, Inc., 10338 Miller Road, Dallas, Texas 75238, USA
*American, born 15 July 1943. Founder and President of Materials Analysis, Inc. Educated in USA; Ph.D. (Metallurgical Engineering) from Case Eastern Reserve University in 1971.*

The Vortex System was designed to significantly reduce the melt loss of scrap material (e.g. aluminium beverage containers) during the metal recycling process. It also significantly increases the rate at which the scrap can be melted without increasing melt loss by producing a vortex that submerges shredded scrap (that would normally float) immediately upon contact with the molten aluminium.

# Digital image processing and computer graphics in archaeological research

*José Jacobo Storch de Gracia y Asensio*

Cátedra de Arqueología, Facultad de Filosofía y Letras, Edificio A, Ciudad Universitaria, 28040 Madrid, Spain

*Spanish, born 31 March 1959. Assistant Professor of Archaeology, Complutense University. Educated in Spain; graduated (Geography and History) from Complutense University, Madrid in 1981.*

This project has applied digital-image processing and computer graphics techniques to archaeological research, in particular for enhancing the image of incorrectly exposed photographs of archaeological interest, the interpretation of objects which have been subject to severe surface degradation, the plotting of level curves for excavations, etc. The analysis and elucidation of a medieval bas-relief has been taken as an example.


# A thermodynamic approach to immunology

*Stanislas Safaïssou*

POB 6829, Yaoundé, Cameroon

*Cameroonian, born 18 November 1952. Physician. Educated in Cameroon; M.D. from University Centre for Health Sciences, Yaoundé in 1977.*

This project states that classical immunology is in deep contradiction with genetics and that, by a thermodynamic approach, it has been possible to achieve a general synthesis of immunology and thermodynamics by involving the action of the hypothalamus into immune reactions. It is claimed that this new concept will have important consequences in developing new models for the treatment of cancer and female infertility.


# Adaptation to water stress in *Kalanchoe daigremontana*

*Juma Athumani Kapuya*

POB 35060, University of Dar es Salaam, Dar es Salaam, Tanzania

*Tanzanian, born 22 June 1943, Associate Professor of Botany. Educated in Tanzania, UK and Netherlands; Ph.D. from University of Wales, Aberystwyth in 1975.*

This project has studied *Kalanchoe daigremontana*, a plant which responds to drought and waterlogging by accumulating ethylene, to determine how it survives under these stress conditions. The plant was found to accumulate an unidentified compound, possibly an amino acid, and it is proposed to concentrate, purify and identify this compound which could help crop plants cope with water stress.


# Rotary sails – Old wine in a new bottle

*Kenneth Arthur Austin*

3 Longlands Spinney, Worthing, Sussex BN14 9NU, UK

*British, born 17 October 1920. Retired chartered mechanical engineer. Educated in UK; Corporate Member, Institution of Mechanical Engineers, London, in 1952.*

This project has developed and patented a rotary sail for ships, consisting of a tall, shapely cylinder rotating on an upper deck and utilizing the Magnus effect to generate thrust. The sail preferably rotates on a single roller bearing within which is nested a direct-drive electric motor. It can be installed for either main or auxiliary propulsion and takes advantage of wind power to reduce fuel burn.

# The real sequence of the exploits of Hercules

## Dimitris Anagnostopoulos

6 Kerkyras, Kastri, Near Erythrae, 14671 Athens, Greece
*Greek, born 1 May 1931. Physician and surgeon. Educated in Greece; graduated from Athens University Medical School in 1964.*

Ancient Greek writers differ on the sequence of Hercules' exploits. This project reviews the literature and shows that the number and sequence of the exploits constitute an ancient calendar. It proposes to produce a book documenting the true sequence of the exploits of Hercules from ancient Greek writings and archaeological remains.


# Development of a silk industry in Malaysia

## Yusoff Mohd Nik

Permint Suterasemai Sdn. Bhd., Kawasan Perindustrian Chendering, Kuala Terengganu 21080, Malaysia
*Malaysian, born 25 May 1947. Managing Director of Mermint Suterasemai Sdn. Bhd. Educated in Malaysia, New Zealand and USA; Bachelor of Horticultural Science from Lincoln College, University of Canterbury.*

Attempts to introduce silkworm rearing into Malaysia between 1973 and 1984 and to establish a silk industry proved unsuccessful. This project launched a new approach to the establishment of commercial silk production and has instigated a whole new agrobase industry in Malaysia potentially providing Malaysian farmers with better income from silkworm rearing, and putting Malaysia amongst the world's silk producers.


# Late-flying European drones – A solution to the African bee problem?

## Orley Robert Taylor, Jr.

Department of Systematics and Ecology, University of Kansas, Lawrence, Kansas 66045, USA
*American, born 28 August 1937. Professor, Departments of Entomology, Systematics and Ecology, University of Kansas. Educated in USA; Ph.D. from University of Connecticut in 1970.*

In studying the mating dynamics of European and African bees, this project has found that most virgin queens of both races mate with African drones, and that African drone dominance tends to eliminate European stocks. It proposes to develop a stock of European bees in which the drones fly late enough to mate with African queens, dominate matings and "Europeanize" any low-density invasion of African bees.


# Food dehydration by osmosis

## Angel María Jadán Peralta

307 Luis Martínez, Ambato, Ecuador
*Ecuadorian, born 28 May 1936. Professor of Biology and Biochemistry in Nutrition, University of Ambato. Educated in Ecuador, France and Argentina; graduated from School of Chemical and Natural Sciences, Central University of Quito.*

Current food preservation techniques are inefficient since they break down proteins, vitamins and lipids. Moreover, the use of ionizing radiation may be carcinogenic. This project has invented an osmotic food-dehydration process which uses natural reagents such as saccharose, leaves no toxic residues and permits the rehydrated foods to regain their natural juiciness.

# Active principles of medicinal plants and cancer treatment

## Diana Teresa Erujimovich de Wainberg

Virrey Loreto 2433, piso 6°, Departamento "A", 1426 Buenos Aires, Argentina
*Argentine, born 12 March 1947. Clinical physician in private practice. Educated in Argentina; M.D. from National University of Buenos Aires in 1971.*

The object of this project is to carry out further investigations on the cytostatic action of a drug developed from a number of medicinal plants. It is stated that the drug can be administered parenterally, intramuscularly, by endovenous drip or even orally, and that it stimulates the immune system, increases patient weight, returns blood count to normal and has no side-effects.

# Tympanic thermosensor for monitoring body temperature

## Peter Lomax

Department of Pharmacology, UCLA School of Medicine, Center for the Health Sciences, Los Angeles, California 90024, USA
*American, born 12 May 1928. Professor of Pharmacology. Educated in UK; M.D. and D.Sc. from University of Manchester in 1964 and 1971.*

The clinical techniques commonly employed for measuring body temperature are useless in severe hypothermia or heat stroke since the thermoregulatory system protects deep core temperature. This project proposes to design a device comprising a thermosensor fitted in a hearing-aid prosthesis to accurately measure and monitor tympanic temperature in hypothermia and heat-stroke victims pending transfer to treatment facilities.

# Production and publication of computer light curves of southern variable stars

## Frank Maine Bateson

POB 3093, 18 Pooles Road, Greerton, Tauranga, New Zealand
*New Zealander, born 31 October 1909. Astronomer, Director of the Variable Star Section, Royal Astronomical Society of New Zealand. Educated in New Zealand and Australia; Honorary Doctorate from the University of Waikato in 1978.*

More than 2.5 million observations have been made of southern intrinsic variable stars over 60 years, and this project is seeking access to a large computer to reduce these observations to light curves. The resultant print-outs would be in camera-ready form for direct publication together with other details of the several hundreds of stars in the programme, to make the results available to the astronomical community worldwide.

# Removable dental appliance for brain-damage and seizures patients

## Luis Katz

POB 8336, Panama 7, Panama
*Panamanian, born 1 March 1959. Doctor in Dental Surgery, and post-graduate student at the Boston University Henry Goldman School of Graduate Dentistry. Educated in Panama and USA; D.D.S. from the University of Panama School of Dentistry.*

Comatose, mentally retarded and other patients with uncontrolled seizure disorders may inflict severe injury on themselves by biting their lower lip. This project has designed the "Katz appliance" consisting of a customized mouth guard fitted to the lower teeth and a pre-formed lip bumper to stop and prevent mutilation and trauma of the lower lip while permitting healing of existing trauma.

# Basic requirements for a master chess computer

## Ioan Muraroiu

55 Avenue Petre Cretu, Bucharest 71328, Romania
*Romanian, born 13 July 1912. Retired electromechanical engineer. Educated in Romania; Diploma from the Polytechnic Institute, Bucharest in 1934.*

Current chess-playing computers are not suitable for master chess. This project proposes a computer hardware modification to manually vary the value of individual pieces at each move during the game so that the piece values are not constant. This will be of advantage for correspondence chess, unofficial chess and for analyzing the situation at the 40th move in official chess when the game is interrupted.


# The development and sharing of advanced surgical techniques for scoliosis

## Benjamin L. Allen, Jr.

C3-66 Child Health Center, 9th and Market, Galveston, Texas 77550–2776, USA
*American, born 11 May 1940. Professor of Surgery and Paediatrics. Educated in USA; M.D. from Duke University Medical School in 1964.*

Recent decades have seen great progress in the surgical treatment of scoliosis (lateral curvature of the spine). Galveston Child Health Center has been to the fore in developing advanced techniques – especially those of pelvic fixation. This project reviews progress made and proposes the endowment of a lectureship to bring scoliosis surgeons from around the world to Galveston to learn these techniques first hand.


# Italian New Renaissance Project – A design philosophy for space habitability

## Daniele Bedini

3 Via della Spada, 50123 Florence, Italy
*Italian, born 4 October 1952. Architect and industrial designer. Educated in Italy; degree (Space Architecture) from University of Florence in 1983.*

Space research and activity have so far considered human factors only as limitations on man's ability to do something well in a minimum amount of time. This project proposes the introduction – by means of space architecture – of strictly human factors into space research to safeguard the mental and spiritual health of man in space. This research should also be useful in improving our way of life on earth.


# High-efficiency drip-irrigation system for the poorest Third World farmers

## Mudumbi Parthasarathy

45 First Avenue, Sastrinagar, Madras-600020, India
*Indian, born 4 July 1924. Engineering consultant to the plastics industry and on water management and drip irrigation. Educated in India; B.E. (Mechanical) from University College of Engineering, Bangalore in 1949.*

This project is attempting to provide small, low-income or subsistence farmers with the benefits of a combination of high-efficiency drip-irrigation, fertigation (use of fertilizer in drip/trickle irrigation) and black polyethylene mulching, previously largely restricted to highly mechanized and automated farmers. The system integrates the relevant technologies into a low-cost standard kit for two 22 m x 22 m plots of land.

# Concrete reinforcement with synthetic cord strap

*Thomas J. Karass*

4645 Circle Road, Montreal, Quebec H3W 1Z2, Canada
*Canadian, born 17 October 1921. Chairman of the Board of Caristrap International Inc. Educated in Hungary; Ph.D. obtained in 1942.*

This project has researched and developed the use of synthetic textile-fibre cord straps as substitutes for steel rods in the construction of reinforced concrete for highway and airport runway pavements, house or factory floor slabs, etc. The results achieved to date indicate that, in this application, synthetic cord strap is stronger than steel and offers better reinforcement for significantly lower cost.

# Movable-frame beehives made from rural materials for developing countries

*Mohamed Aly El-Banby*

Chairman, Plant Protection Department, Faculty of Agriculture, Ain-Shams University, Shobra-Kheima, Cairo, Egypt
*Egyptian, born 21 April 1929. Professor of Entomology and Chairman of Plant Protection Department. Educated in Egypt; Ph.D. (Entomology) from Ain-Shams University.*

In developing countries, the development of beekeeping using modern techniques offers significant economic potential; however, the movable-frame hives required are too expensive. This project has designed a movable-frame and movable-comb hive that can be constructed from cheap rural materials (baskets, crates, etc.), and proposes visits to a number of developing countries to disseminate the construction technique.

# A balloon-borne amateur radio satellite project

*Arthur Cecil Gee*

21 Romany Road, Oulton Broad, Lowestoft NR32 3PJ, UK
*British, born 15 December 1912. Retired medical practitioner, radio amateur and free-lance journalist. Educated in UK; graduated (Medicine) from King's College, London.*

This project aims to use balloons to launch simple recoverable amateur-radio transponders, beacons and telemetry data transmitters into the upper atmosphere so that radio amateurs can acquire experience in the construction of simple hardware for use in space, learn to track this type of equipment and receive and analyze the data transmitted by it. The package would be taken aloft by hot-air or meteorological balloons.

# Biotechnological improvement of alkaline soils for higher food and energy production

*Jorge Samuel Molina Buck*

178 Olaguer Feliú, 1640 Martínez, Buenos Aires, Argentina
*Argentine, born 29 June 1919. Agronomic engineer and Director, Research Center on Biotechnology and Microbial Ecology. Educated in Argentina; degree (Agronomic Engineering) in 1942.*

This project has developed a biotechnological method for the large-scale reclamation of alkaline soils in semi-arid regions, without irrigation or drainage. Since it is based on the influence of carbon dioxide on the pH of alkaline soils, the method operates at low cost and will enable the improvement of huge areas now affected by this problem in the Argentina Republic and other parts of the world.

## Programme of research in natural dye technology

### Tomás Alejandro David del Solar y del Solar

1488 Sierra Leona, Colonia Independencia, Guadalajara, Jal. 44860, Mexico
*Mexican, born 3 March 1945. Craftsman, teacher and administrator. Educated in Peru, Mexico and USA; B.A. from California College of Arts, and specialization studies in arts and crafts.*

This project aims to recover natural dye techniques employing simple, renewable substances not requiring sophisticated training or equipment. It will carry out historical, chemical, dye-practice and ecological studies with a view to providing an adequate technological background for revitalized creative and economic activities in a number of currently marginal regions.


## Improving the beam quality of pulsed gas lasers

### Karl-Heinz Krahn

147 Hustadtring, 4630 Bochum 1, West Germany
*West German, born 8 September 1948. Scientific staff member, Electro-optic Department, Ruhr University of Bochum. Educated in West Germany; Doctorate (Electrical Engineering) from Ruhr University of Bochum in 1981.*

Existing pulsed gas lasers have relatively poor beam quality and, in many applications, the beam acts only as a blunt tool. This project has developed and patented a novel concept of helical electrode geometry which will produce nearly ideal beam characteristics, prepare a new generation of pulsed gas lasers and open up new applications for them. A working model of a helical gas laser will be developed.


## Non-destructive photon backscattering determination of semiconductor wafer subsurface quality

### Robert Michael Silva

4032 Linden Avenue, Dayton, Ohio 45432–3015, USA
*American, born 2 November 1930. President, VTI, Inc. Educated in USA; degree (Geophysics) from University of California, Berkeley in 1955 and degree (Electrical Engineering) from Texas Tech University in 1962.*

This project plans to adapt previously developed optical techniques to equipment for the high-speed, non-destructive quality control of all semiconductor wafers. These quality judgements will help in improving wafer-processing methods, and allow wafers to be selected for higher precision, greater areal density circuits, thus leading to higher-speed computers, better astronomical sensors and more capable circuits.


## Rapid total serum, fibrin and red blood cell separation without coagulation

### Ken Heimreid

446 Brånanveien, 3940 Heistad, Norway
*Norwegian, born 13 August 1930. Retired laboratory technician. Educated in Norway.*

Traditional separation of blood for laboratory analysis entails the blood standing for 30–40 minutes, which causes delay, allows coagulation to occur and gives serum which is not fibrin-free. This project has devised the Fibrinactiv rapid anticoagulation method for total serum, fibrin and blood cell separation by centrifugation of freshly drawn blood.

# Exploration and Discovery

The projects described in this section were submitted under the category "Exploration and Discovery" which was defined in the Official Application Form for The Rolex Awards for Enterprise 1987 as follows:

*Projects in this category will be concerned primarily with venturesome undertakings or expeditions and should seek to inspire our imagination or expand our knowledge of the world in which we live.*

# Exploring the Arctic with small, purpose-built motor sailing boats

## Janusz Kurbiel

**Honourable Mention**
**The Rolex Awards for Enterprise – 1987**

11 rue de Berry, 78140 Vélizy-Villacoublay, France

French, born 2 January 1946. President of Kurbiel Exploraglobe Inc. Educated in Poland; graduated (Master Mining Engineer – specialized in electricity) from Silesia Polytechnic in 1973.

Each winter, I plan a new expedition, with a new objective to a different part of the Arctic region, and the following summer I set sail in my boat *Vagabond 2* to execute my plans. The 1986 mission will be a special one since it will mark my tenth polar expedition over the space of 11 years.

Initially, these expeditions were a childhood dream of independence that I persisted in turning into reality. As a result, I have eschewed sponsorship, be it private or governmental; certainly, it has not made my project an easy one but it has guaranteed my ethical and practical independence. Thus, for example, my first exploration, mapping and hydrographic work was done on the eastern coast of Greenland, on my own account and to prove the design of my polar boat, *Vagabond 2*, which was built with the proceeds from the sale of my first boat *Vagabond* and with the help of the shipyard and some manufacturers. My expeditions are financed by my writing, film making, lecturing and exhibitions which have also made me more widely known both in the specialist and general press. Initially, I took on paying crew members, but now I employ a professional crew and have, over the years, been able to carry out research activities for various organizations.

## The research boat, *Vagabond 2*

Nowadays, polar exploration programmes are of two types: heavy programmes operated from a fixed base, a scientific station, a large ice-breaker or oceanographic vessel, etc.; or light programmes in which a small team is, for example, brought in by helicopter to operate over a small area using a limited range of equipment. However, technological development and the miniaturization of scientific and electronic equipment has made it possible to use a relatively small ship for polar exploration and research projects in areas inaccessible to a larger vessel. This was the concept that lay behind the new design concepts for *Vagabond 2* which was constructed specifically for work in northern seas.

*Vagabond 2* is 15 m overall and has a beam of 4.3 m and a minimum draught of

*Janusz Kurbiel's* Vagabond 2 *moving delicately through the iceflows of Greenland.*

only 1.1 m. The hull is built from high-strength steel, and an aluminium honeycomb structure is used for the inside. It carries a 42 m² mainsail, and a 35 m² jib or a 70 m² genoa and has two 36 hp diesel engines. There is accommodation for six people, and its full tanks give it a cruising range of 5,600 km. Moreover, it was designed for easy handling with a small crew or single-handed, comfort and safety and for silent and clean cruising under sail. *Vagabond 2* is both a polar and deep sea boat, and this means that she is perfectly adapted to sail all seas, including the polar ones.

### The 1986–1987 Northwest Passage expedition

Having left France in October 1984, *Vagabond 2* sailed to the French Antilles, through the Panama Canal, up the west coast of the USA reaching Vancouver in May 1985. From there, we sailed the North Pacific to the Aleutian Islands, the Chuchki Sea, the Bering Sea, along the northern coast of Alaska and Canada and wintered over in Tuktuyaktuk in the Canadian Northwest Territories – which made her the first sailboat to have wintered three times in the Arctic.

The 1986–1987 expedition will start out from Tuktuyaktuk in an attempt to make the Northwest Passage, from west to east, and sail to Baffin Island or even further. The passage is a very difficult one in this direction in view of the head winds and currents and the occurrence of large amounts of ice; moreover, conditions may limit sailing to only a few miles a day, and on some days the boat may make no headway as all. You have to travel as fast as you can since the Arctic sailing season lasts only a few weeks. The Northwest Passage is a vital route but its use is limited by the ice conditions which may vary significantly from year to year and from area to area during a single year. Its economic future depends on a better knowledge of the ice, natural phenomena such as magnetism, and improved or modified vessel design.

Summer 1986 was set aside to conclude two studies started in 1982, namely measurement of the variation, in the vicinity of the magnetic North Pole, of the low-frequency electromagnetic waves (10, 11, 13 kHz) used to determine a geographic position using the hyperbolic Omega navigation system. It is known that the system is less reliable near the ice masses of the Arctic and the Antarctic where it indicates more and more irregular positions. It is also known that this is due to the physical presence of ice and the influence of the magnetic Pole but nobody knows exactly how this takes place. Since the Omega is the only navigation system giving instant positions in the Arctic region, elucidation of this matter is vital for the future of the Passage as a commercial route.

## Prospects for the future

Having acquired a wealth of unique experience and having proved the concept of exploration and research in small vessels, I would like now to build a new boat, *Vagabond 3*, even better suited to our needs and fitted with bigger cranes, winches, etc. to handle more hydrographic and biological equipment. The new boat would also have space for the two or three scientists that would have to accompany the vessel in the new research activities that are being requested of our team.

*Picking a route through the ice is far from easy. Janusz Kurbiel came up with the idea of using a ULM, which can be dismantled and stored on the aft of* Vagabond 2, *to carry out reconnaissance flights.*

# Small cetaceans of the South American sector of the Antarctic and Subantarctic

## Rae Natalie Prosser Goodall

44 Sarmiento, 9410 Ushuaia, Tierra del Fuego, Argentina

American, born 13 April 1935. No fixed employment but actively employed. Educated in USA; M.A. (Biology) from Kent State University in 1959.

The depth of our knowledge of certain parts of the world, of certain of its creatures, in any branch of science, depends basically on one fact – whether a competent researcher has worked there or not. Our knowledge of cetaceans (whales, dolphins and porpoises) is no exception: some species are never sighted at all and are therefore known only from their bones.

Cetaceans are completely aquatic and very little of the animal shows above the surface of the water. They are most difficult to follow around, especially in the colder waters of the world. Nearly all countries have laws against their capture, and this makes it next to impossible to study them at close hand; and of the various methods of studying small cetaceans available to us the examination of stranded animals yields more basic biological information than any other.

During the past ten years, we have studied the stranded cetaceans of southern South America – mainly eastern Tierra del Fuego – but instead of just waiting for material to turn up, we actively go out and look for it, making regular surveys of suitable beaches, at first on foot or horseback, but more recently on Honda all-terrain-cycles. However, although a good start has been made in South America, an enormous amount remains to be learned and our project is not only to continue our activities but also to extend them south, through one or more expeditions to survey the beaches of the South Shetland Islands and northern Antarctic Peninsula.

## Research objectives

Our studies of stranded, beach-cast or incidentally captured animals will cover such basic biological parameters as: distribution, pigmentation, external and internal morphology and anatomy, food habits, reproduction, etc., and museum specimens will be obtained when possible. We will also determine areas in the South Shetlands where there is greater likelihood of strandings and which could be surveyed on a more regular basis in the future. Our efforts will concentrate essentially on species for which there is a growing data base, such as Commerson's dolphin, *Cephalorhynchus commersonii*, Peale's dolphin, *Lageno-*

148

*rhynchus australis*, the hourglass dolphin, *L. cruciger*, and the spectacled porpoise, *Phocoena dioptrica*, as well as the beaked whales of the region. The information we gather will be computerized and prepared for publication.

Periodic and systematic beach surveys will be made either on foot or on an all-terrain-cycle to locate specimens which will be studied or removed to a laboratory. During dissection of the animal, organs will be weighed and examined for parasites and diseases, and samples taken for contamination and histological study. The stomach contents, complete skeleton and other materials will be collected cleaned, labelled and stored. Specimen data forms, complete with tracings of appendages, photographic record, and analysis (stomach contents, parasites) by experts, will be filed by species and archived in the computer. A bibliographic reference file has been built up on each species and will be added to periodically.

## Results to date

Although the waters of Tierra del Fuego are very cold and only nine species of cetaceans had previously been recorded, we have found that, in addition to the seven species of great whales which migrate through the area, at least 20 species of smaller cetaceans strand on these beaches – well over a third of the world's species! Just by being in the right place, where the cool climate keeps stranded animals in "cold storage", we have doubled or tripled the number of museum specimens of several rare species. We have found that between 90 and 110 specimens either strand or are captured accidentally each year, and this has allowed us to gather a great deal of information which is being recorded in our personal computer for preparation for publishing in journals and at conferences. Moreover, we have built up an osteological collection which contains more than 1,300 specimens, many of them nearly complete skeletons.

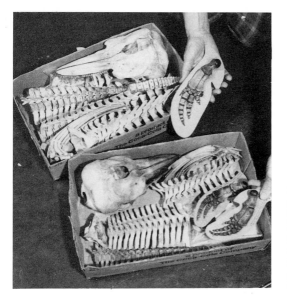

*Osteological specimens of cetaceans are cleaned, numbered, wired in sections and stored in boxes for future study. Each specimen has a folder with measurements, photographs, tracings, stomach content analysis and other data (Photograph T.D. Goodall).*

## Plans for the future

In addition to continuing our detailed studies on selected species in Tierra del Fuego, we also plan several expeditions to the Province of Santa Cruz, to the north, and to the South Shetlands and northern Antarctic Peninsula, to the south. However, although Tierra del Fuego and Santa Cruz can be explored with our existing vehicles and materials, surveys of the South Shetlands must be made by boat and we are planning to make summer (January) trips to the South American sector of the Antarctic aboard small yachts equipped with Zodiacs so that beaches can be surveyed at some leisure. Two yachts have offered their services for 1987–1988.

Only five species of smaller cetaceans have been recognized for the Antarctic south of 60° south latitude but we feel that beach surveys for strandings will reveal other species which reach Antarctic waters.

Although many institutions and scientists may frown on this type of "opportunistic" studies, they have reaped large benefits in our case – and we are sure that the project before us will prove no exception.

*Strandings often occur without anyone observing them. Here, a collection is being made of skulls, many partially buried in sand, of a long-ago mass stranding of 22 pilot whales (*Globicephala melaena*).*

150

# Promoting sports diving for disabled people

## David Royston

39 Rowlands Road, Horsham RH12 4LH, UK

British, born 30 July 1940. Production engineering manager. Educated in UK.

In November 1982, the National Diving Officer of the British Sub Aqua Club (BSAC) asked me, as a disabled diver myself, to help, advise and instruct other disabled people, interested in or already practising diving as a sport. The terms of reference for my project, drawn up by the National Diving Officer, were that I should voluntarily undertake to collate existing knowledge, develop ·new techniques, and make available and distribute information useful in training and diving for disabled people.

### Overcoming my own disability

Having undergone a below-knee amputation in 1957, following a road accident, I joined the BSAC in 1975. completed training as a sports diver and then trained as an instructor; I considered myself qualified for this task since, over the years, I had confronted, assessed and lived for myself the problems faced by the disabled diver. Moreover, I had set myself the objectives of showing disabled divers themselves that they could train and become, in many cases, competent divers and of demonstrating to the diving world that disabled people could become not just people who could dive but also experienced and useful members of the Club.

Originally, I had practised my diving with the minimum of modification to my diving gear, namely a leg had been cut from my wet suit and the end sealed. However, following some six years' activity as an advanced diver and poolside instructor, when hopping was my only means of mobility around the dive site or pool, I took up the suggestion of wearing a fibreglass limb over my wet suit. This proved to be a break-through in mobility but brought certain difficulties since the sealed hollow limb was obviously positively buoyant in the water and had to be weighted with 1.5 kg of lead which made it suitable for use in the water but too heavy on land. This limb was never intended for use whilst diving, only to enhance mobility around the dive sites and for launching and recovering small boats; nevertheless, it was comfortable to use for up to 15–20 minutes at a time and allowed me to follow the course and pass the examinations for BSAC Advanced Instructor in September 1982.

151

## Project realization

When I joined the BSAC National Diving Committee, I was aware that various studies and trials had been carried out in different parts of the world on the physiological and psychological aspects of training disabled individuals to dive but the results were usually contained in scientific papers or magazine articles and the application of this information was in no way organized. Moreover, although the BSAC knew that certain disabled people were practising diving no figures were available of the numbers involved.

Within the Committee, my task was to take the lead in drafting information documents on instructions to help teach disabled people to dive – taking into account their various disabilities – and to keep these up to date by means of feedback from branch clubs. With this in mind, I set out to compile information about equipment currently available for disabled people wishing to dive and those responsible for their instruction, and present it in a suitable form for the two groups.

My initial approach to the project was to consider the publication of a series of guidelines for instructors, but I soon came to the conclusion that the individual disabilities, training requirements and solutions to various problems were overlapping and interdependent. Better, therefore, for individual papers to be grouped together; this resulted in the preparation of a booklet written in an instructive but light vein, with an element of humour introduced. However, it soon became clear that work was first needed on adequately adapting diving gear to ensure that the majority of those who wished to dive could do so with completely manageable equipment.

I first approached my artificial limb manufacturers with a design for a glass fibre limb with a tidal-flow buoyant system, which would be both light on land and neutrally buoyant in the water. This limb was constructed with funds from the Department of Health and Social Security and, having successfully undergone testing, it is now available to others through the National Health Service. This lighter limb was made to fit over a wet suit and proved to be more manageable and significantly more comfortable. However, it could not be worn underwater since the socket would become loose as the wet suit compressed at depth, and I therefore obtained from a supplier a suit with boots attached, and seals only at the wrists and neck; with this I carried out underwater trials wearing a comfortable, everyday artificial limb under the suit which eased the problems of entry and exit from the water over pebbles, soft sand, rocks and heaving ladders on large boats. The effect was magnificent; the limb was balanced underwater, comfortable on land and gave me much more mobility when entering and leaving the water; so much so that I was able to qualify as a First Class Diver and, since the dry suit kept me mobile and dry for long periods, I was able to extend my instructing to small-boat handling.

With the conclusion of this equipment development and testing stage it was possible to complete the booklet and submit it to the National Diving Committee even though I had become convinced that such a weighty text would benefit from some lighter-hearted illustrations. The Committee approved the document but was unable to provide the funds needed for an illustrator and for publication. I therefore wrote to the President of the BSAC, HRH The Prince of Wales, to ask him to write a foreword to the booklet. This he graciously did,

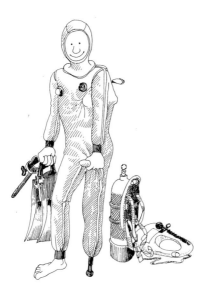

*One of the illustrations by Trevor Andrews from* Diving for Disabled People, *by David Royston (The British Sub Aqua Club, London, 1985).*

which greatly helped with the fund raising and when I had obtained half the amount required, the BSAC Jubilee Trust agreed to loan the balance necessary. My search for an illustrator was less successful until I managed to get a fellow diver, Trevor Andrews, to produce a series of quite brilliant illustrations which gave the booklet the necessary lighter touch. A setback occurred when the BSAC updated and radically changed its diver training syllabus, meaning that our booklet had to be re-written and re-approved. Nevertheless, by March 1985 the booklet was in print and distributed to each of the 1,000 branch clubs, regional coaches, many other individuals and organizations for disabled people in addition to the main national sport diving organizations throughout the world.

The booklet has since been taken up by the Irish Underwater Council and a copy issued to all member Irish diving clubs. A more recent request has also been received to allow a translation to be used by Swedish clubs.

### A more positive outlook

I hoped for, fully expected and am beginning to get, some critical and constructive feedback from those using the booklet so that it can be expanded to provide a better way with which to unlock the physical barriers, often created by lack of awareness and understanding by the able-bodied of what can be done for and achieved by disabled people.

After three years, the project has now reached the end of the first communication stage. It is, by no means, at an end. Much practical work remains to be done by individuals, organizations and equipment manufacturers to improve the adventure sporting activities for the physically disabled individual and to fully explore the degree of assistance that can be provided by the use of diving equipment and skills in swimming training for all disabled people.

# People of the World as they are – where they are – painted by Texana

## Texana

3 chemin Laurence, 1180 Rolle, Switzerland

American, born 8 March 1918. Artist/painter. Educated in USA and Mexico;
attended art schools in Los Angeles and worked with various artists.

In this project, ongoing since 1963, Texana has travelled to this planet's remotest
areas to paint the People of the World, and has worked with individuals from
hundreds of tribes and ethnic groups who are being uprooted into mass
anonymity and whose cultures are vanishing. Her arduous journeys have been
explorations pioneered with the paintbrush, where every painting is a discovery
of people and culture and every sitting a record of the world's population during
the greatest transitional period of history. Her works of art are proof that art is
the universal communication which needs no interpreters, and transcends
prejudice, nationality, race and religion. In the total and absolute face-to-face
communication between the people and the artist, love and understanding are
in the ascendancy, face-to-face with the People of the World. The painting
session provides an affirmation of dignity and unique individuality of each
person, whose pride rises visibly in this regained sense of identity and respect.

Often, it seems that the people find the artist, rather than the artist finding the
people. It is as though they are waiting for the occasion in villages and markets,
along roadsides and on lonely paths. There is a mystery and a magic that
prevails and pervades – unexplainable and unfathomable; it is here, too, that the
greatest discoveries – the unexplained revelations – are made. In this joint effort,
the donor and recipient are one – each giving himself to meet the other's need
and to fulfil a vaster purpose.

### People of the World on display

When these paintings are put on exhibition far from their point of origin, the
distances involved – both mathematically and culturally – are immeasurable.
Faced with barriers to comprehension, each one has the task of establishing
spiritual communion in a brotherhood of humankind. During the exhibitions,
the paintings are displayed with explanatory photographs and texts, showing
the subjects within their own ethnic environments, where possible along with
local artifacts and handicrafts. Educational institutions and libraries find these
exhibitions valuable in stimulating interest in and study of geography and

154

peoples among students from primary through university level.

For one teacher, her pupils learned more in four hours at the People of the World exhibition than they had learned the entire term in school, and parents have reported that this was the first time their children had taken them to an exhibition and then requested to stay on when the parents had to return home.

The paintings emphasize that we are all People of the World, and that we can and must share our global home with understanding and in peace. People are weary of destructions and negations, and yearn for release from the bondage of limitations and for freedom from ignorance. All the armaments in the world have never brought peace. But art can bring peace that unifies people and brings the "healing of the nations". Peace is a community enterprise. Art is the natural environment of people, leading the way to understanding global neighbours. Art is the oldest form of communication, and is still the best. It is the universal communication of humankind and the capacity to think and to dream. Face-to-face, art speaks and the people answer. Time and again, this has been proven by Texana – in the jungles – on mountain tops – islands – seas and oceans – beyond the Arctic circle – wherever the easel is opened, and the Thousand League Canvas is unfurled to paint the People of the World.

## A home for People of the World

The most difficult and longest journey for the artist has been the search for a home base for the paintings and artifacts. But finally she found it and, in spring 1983, brought the collection half way around the world from California to Geneva, Switzerland, where she has since held exhibitions at the European headquarters of the United Nations Organization and many of its specialized agencies. These exhibitions require a home base, a cultural repository and spiritual home for mankind, an advanced idea for a living museum. The

*Afridi Pathan tribal chief painted by Texana inside the Khyber Pass, Pakistan Northwest Tribal Territory. The Afridi Pathans of the Kuki Khel clan are considered the most valiant and ferocious warriors of the Khyber Pass.*

*Texana in the process of painting in the field in her "studio" on the rooftop of Spitok Gompa. Sitting for her is a member of the Yellow Hat sect of Tibetan Mahayana Buddhism, considered to be the Abbot of Spitok from a previous incarnation.*

functions of the museum include painting, sculpture, music, drama, literature, folklore, handicrafts and artifacts, and there are also research facilities for the study of mankind. The artist further envisions the establishment of People of the World Community Art Centres in every part of the world working in co-operation with the parent museum. These Centres will aid people in search for food, housing and work, and in renewing hope for a better life that respects individual dignity.

### Paintings for global unity

The paintings meet people face-to-face, and the viewer finds that there are no alien strangers, but individuals who can learn to love each other, not in spite of – but because of – diversities. Life enriches and expands in culture exchange, and observers at exhibitions respond enthusiastically and eagerly to creativeness, positiveness, and constructiveness, and are motivated to participate in this work of art, consecrated to the heritage of humanity for the attainment of global unity.

# Vegetation survey of Western Australia

## John Stanley Beard
**Honourable Mention**
**The Rolex Awards for Enterprise – 1987**

6 Fraser Road, Applecross, Western Australia 6153, Australia

Australian, born 15 February 1916. Environmental consultant. Educated in UK;
D.Phil. from University of Oxford in 1945.

---

When I moved to Western Australia in 1961 with the task of creating a new
botanic garden for the cultivation of Western Australian native plants, botanical
science in Western Australia was in a primitive state and we were hampered by
lack of vital information. I therefore resolved to achieve two objectives: a census
of plant species and a census of plant communities. The descriptive catalogue of
species was compiled and published relatively easily but the census of plant
communities proved more difficult, and took 20 years to complete: to identify
and localize the plant communities it was necessary to map them, and this has
led to the establishment of a mapping project entitled the "Vegetation Survey of
Western Australia".

### Mapping the plants of Western Australia

The State of Western Australia comprises the western third of the Australian
continent with an area of 2,525,500 km², 40% of which is uninhabited and a
further 40% sparsely inhabited. There were, therefore, peculiar difficulties of
access to remote areas, and of sheer magnitude of the project, so that methods of
rapid survey had to be devised. The project required field surveys, photo
interpretation and mapping, cartography and map production.

As part of the field surveys, I made about two major expeditions a year. I was
the first professional botanist to enter the Great Sandy Desert and, in 1966, made
the first botanical crossing of the Great Victoria Desert. I explored the Gibson
Desert in 1967 and the Nullarbor Plain in 1968. In all, I probably travelled 200,000
km by four-wheel drive vehicle, and collected 7,000 botanical specimens, not
counting those brought in by accompanying botanists. My observations are
recorded in eight books of manuscript notes.

Photo interpretation was carried out at base, at other times of the year, and in
between other duties – making particular use of the aerial photography done by
the Australian State and Federal Governments and especially the mosaics at a
scale of 1:63,360. Basic vegetation mapping was done by me on the mosaics and
reduced and drawn on manuscript sheets of 1:250,000 which were filed in the

map library of the Department of Geography at the University of Western Australia.

## Plans for publication

The intention was to publish a certain number of sheets of the more populated areas of the State at a scale of 1:250,000 and to cover the whole with a series reduced further to 1:1,000,000. At this stage, however, the project was held up for lack of funds, and I left Western Australia to become Director of the Royal Botanic Gardens, Sydney. However, I returned to Western Australia in 1973 to became a self-employed consultant and continue the Vegetation Survey.

I had commenced publication of the 1:250,000 series of maps on my own initiative, doing my own cartography, establishing my own publication firm and producing the maps and accompanying booklets at my own expense; I was also planning to self-finance production of the more expensive colour 1:1,000,000 series. At that moment, a breakthrough occurred when the recently established "Australian Biological Resources Study" provided grants for producing and printing the 1:1,000,000 series. However, I continued with the 1:250,000 series on my own initiative as before, and completed it in 1980; maps at scales of 1:3,000,000 and 1:10,000,000 were also produced by reduction.

The 1:250,000 series comprised 24 black and white sheets, and the 1:1,000,000 series seven sheets in colour. Each was accompanied by a book of explanatory notes, those for the 1:1,000,000 series ranging from 50 to 222 pages. A total of 821 pages of text was printed, including exhaustive data on climate, geology, land forms and soils of the area and as much detail as possible of the floristic composition and physiognomy of the mapped communities.

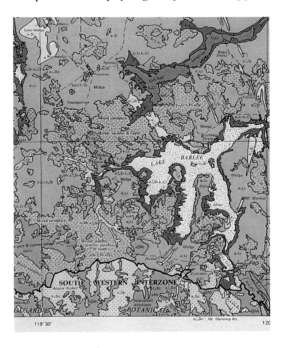

The Central Kimberley Region of the Northern Province that forms part of the area covered by Dr. John Stanley Beard's Vegetation Survey of Western Australia. The escarpment of the King Leopold Range forms the southern boundary of the Kimberley Plateau. (opposite)

A section of one of the sheets in the 1:1,000,000 series of maps from the Vegetation Survey of Western Australia carried out by Dr. John Stanley Beard.

### Achievements and future objectives

I have now mapped the plant cover of a far larger segment of the earth's surface than has ever been done by one person at a comparable scale. Such a coverage does not exist in the other States of Australia (except tiny Tasmania). The work was undertaken on my own initiative, i.e. I was not employed by anyone expressly to do it. Government grants paid only for some of the field work, and for production and printing of the 1:1,000,000 series. After retiring in 1973, I received no salary and supported myself and the other expenses of the survey from my own resources.

I currently need to finance the final and culminating production of the Vegetation Survey, a book to be entitled *The Plant Life of Western Australia*, intended as a lavishly illustrated authoritative work for the intelligent layman, condensing into a single volume the seven regional monographs of the survey and presenting the information in a form understandable by the general public. The book will be extremely costly to produce, it is doubtful whether there will be sufficient market in the small population of Australia for it to be a commercial success, and it will therefore have to be subsidized.

# Himalaya Soaring Expedition to study meteorology in Nepal

## Alvaro de Orleans-Borbon

25 bis boulevard Albert Premier, 98000 Monaco, Monaco

Spanish, born 1 March 1947. Investor with active management participation in various companies. Educated in Italy and Switzerland; Doctor of Engineering from Acoustic Research Laboratory, Italian National Research Council.

The Himalaya Soaring Expedition is an ongoing project designed to: measure atmospheric data at various altitudes in the Kali Gandaki, a Himalayan valley flanked by two 8,000 m mountains (Annapurna and Dhaulagiri), using a highly instrumented powered glider; process and compare this data with computer predicitions obtained by a numerical weather forecasting model; and explore the soaring potential of the world's highest mountains.

### Drawbacks of weather forecasting models

One of the major difficulties affecting weather forecasting models is the scarcity of actual data on the interaction of mountain ranges with synoptic (large-scale) airflows; this leads to early divergence between computer predictions and actual weather development. The acquisition of data on winds and other atmospheric parameters in mountainous regions allows increasingly better understanding of their synoptic effects, and has already begun to improve forecasting results. One of the most extreme examples of mountain-induced local winds had been observed on the bottom of the Kali Gandaki, the world's deepest valley. With a depth of 6,000 m and a width of 35 km, this valley breaks through the Himalayan range, and allows the dry Tibetan airmass to mix with the warm, humid air of the Indian subcontinent. Wind patterns at the valley bottom are well established, with daily peak intensities in the order of 80 km/h.

To evaluate the airmass exchanges induced through the valley, wind and other atmospheric data have to be measured at the valley bottom and above at various times, altitudes and locations. These data, adequately processed in the form of a data set with its own time and space references, allow a comparison with the analogous data set derived from a computer forecast; procedures to minimize the divergence between reality and the numerical model may then be investigated. In our case, the best way to economically sample airmass data from a valley was to use an aircraft. We decided to use a newly developed powered glider and to equip it with sensors to measure temperature, humidity, altitude, wind, position and time.

160

*A view of the cockpit of the powered glider used for the Himalaya soaring expedition, showing the layout of the navigation computer, directional gyro, computer, transducers, etc.*

## Project planning and execution

Project planning, the field execution phase and most of the data processing have already been carried out. A preliminary data evaluation is available, but the final project evaluation and the divergence analysis from the numerical weather prediction model remain to be made.

In three months, we selected the Valentin Taifun 17E powered glider with its instrument package, which two of us flew from Europe to Nepal and back. These two flights took about two weeks each, and represented a major technical and bureaucratic achievement, as did the obtaining of the permit-to-fly in Nepal; this was the first permit of its kind ever to be issued, and required an additional preliminary trip to that country to explain our project to the Nepalese Government.

The temperature, humidity and altitude (pressure) sensors were loaned to us by the Swiss Weather Service. However, the wind sensor comprising a Litton Omega/VLF navigation system, combined with a fast computer, turned out to be a delicate part of the project. A complex arrangement was set up so that a local forecast made by the Global Forecast Center in Washington, D.C., reached us within two hours via Bangkok, New Delhi, Kathmandu, radio to Pokhara, and a 1.5 km bicycle ride to our airstrip. Logistic planning was critical owing to the remoteness of the area; for instance, no aviation gasoline is available in Nepal, and selected spare parts had to be brought along, since it took at least two weeks to have them sent from Europe or the USA.

In February 1985, we arrived at our destination, the Pokhara airstrip, 150 km west of Kathmandu. During two weeks we flew whenever the weather was favourable, and also a few other times, recording about 40 h of data on tape; the equipment, exposed to continuous temperature variations between 900 and 6,000 m, proved to need only minor field adjustments. The data tapes were subsequently read, through a series of signal processing steps, at the Laboratory

*The expedition's powered glider flying at an altitude of around 6,000 m and heading east towards Annapurna, over the southern entrance of the Kali Gandaki Valley, covered by clouds.*

of Atmospheric Physics of the Federal Institute of Technology in Zurich. Current project activity is concentrating on extracting specific data from flight portions in order to analyze single phenomena, and proceed towards the final evaluation.

The soaring potential of the Himalayan range appeared to be more spectacular than conducive to record flights; as a sport, soaring in that region appears to be safe only in a powered glider; the absence of a road and a telephone network would make any outlanding a lengthy and potentially risky undertaking.

### Future project activities

The equipment developed for this project lends itself to other applications; for instance, flights along a microwave beam, to record airmass data, considerably increase the accuracy of the propagation correction; one flying day with our powered glider on 6 June 1985 allowed the Institute for Geodesy and Photogrammetry in Zurich to reduce the measurement error along a 70 km geodetic base from 50 to 5 cm. The current advanced state of this project would never have been achieved without the unfailing support and enthusiasm of the expedition members and the assistance of the Nepalese Weather Service and the Royal Aeronautical Society in London.

162

# Retracing Amundsen's route to the South Pole

## Neil Forbes McIntyre

Mullard Space Science Laboratory, University College – London, Holmbury
Saint Mary, Dorking RH5 6NT, UK

British, born 26 May 1958. Polar Products Leader, Mullard Space Science
Laboratory. Educated in UK; Ph.D. (Antarctic Glaciology and Remote Sensing)
from St. John's College, University of Cambridge in 1983.

The aims of the four-person 90° South glaciological expedition are both
adventurous and scientific. We will ski and sledge to the South Pole with teams
of Greenland huskies; this will be the first time anyone has repeated
Amundsen's route, and the first time a woman has led an Antarctic expedition.
In addition, we will carry out four glaciological studies and one veterinary
investigation.

### The expedition

The expedition will transport itself from Europe to the Antarctic by *Polaris V*, a
53-m research vessel and by helicopter, and the team should be in position at the
Bay of Whales starting-point, ready to set out for the Pole by 15 November 1986.

In the Antarctic, the expedition will travel and camp in two units, each of two
people, one sledge and 11 dogs. Daily targets of 20 km could be exceeded by 10
to 30 km in the first and last parts of the route. Navigation will be by dead
reckoning and celestial techniques and daily radio schedules will be kept with
manned bases whenever possible. In the event of difficulties due to slow
progress or accident, the team will have to turn back before reaching the Pole or
call in the helicopter. The route to be followed in 1986/1987 will be substantially
that pioneered by Amundsen in 1911/1912 and not repeated since. Minor
modifications will be made in the light of more recent knowledge for safety
reasons; and to comply with scientific requirements.

### The scientific programme

The scientific programme is distinctive in that it is designed to take full
advantage of the lightweight, fast-moving field group. It is dependent on an
extended sequence of measurements taken at regular intervals over considerable
distances and so cannot be effectively carried out by anything other than an

overland party. Current near-global satellite coverage and, in particular, Landsat high-resolution imagery and radar altimetry have proven of considerable benefit in the surveying of the Antarctic ice sheet, which has such a major effect on our environment. The expedition will carry out two investigations to enhance the ability of these satellites to study the ice sheets, first by measuring the surface power reflection coefficient of snow and ice at intervals throughout the 2,600 km traverse which will help characterize conditions experienced by present and future satellite altimeters.

Second, a basic requirement for the Landsat programme is to achieve absolute and automatic identification of snow and ice types and this can often be achieved only by field investigations. In order to provide the necessary baseline measurements, 90° South will use a specially built photometer to measure the surface albedo over a wide range of conditions at wavelengths appropriate to Landsat sensors. Although it is accepted that the main mechanism for the loss of mass from Antarctic ice shelves is the calving of icebergs and that oceanographic vibrational forcing is the most likely cause of iceberg formation, we have insufficient data to say whether swell or tides are more important or to indicate how far inland these factors operate. The study that 90° South will make of the flexure of the Ross Ice Shelf will involve investigations of its bending at periods typical of both swell and tidal oscillations. The team will also collect samples of surface snow to gather data which will enable better evaluations to be made of cores taken deep in the ice mass in a search for historical indicators of past prevailing climatic conditions left by snow falls over the millenia. Finally, the team will carry out studies on sledge-dog metabolism. A specially designed diet has been produced for the expedition's dogs and the dogs' body weight will be monitored throughout the 2,600 km journey to assess their nutritional status under documented conditions to verify the suitability of the diet.

*Aerial photograph of the Axel Herdberg Glacier taken from an altitude of some 3,000 m. The heavily crevassed middle step will be the most difficult section in the ascent of the Glacier. (opposite)*

*One of the expedition members driving a team of Greenland huskies in summer conditions.*

## Outcomes

The clearest adventurous outcome will be the very considerable personal tests (both mental and physical) for the four individuals and in particular for the team's female leader. The venture will have demanded great endurance and enterprise, both by way of preparation and on the trip itself. It will be the first expedition to retrace Amundsen's pioneering route and will do so on the 75th anniversary of his conquest of the South Pole, a not-insignificant historical coincidence for both Scandinavian and British participants alike. The art of dog sledging has sadly lapsed from regular use in the Antarctic because of the time required to achieve the skills which make use of dogs so efficient and safe. The expedition is likely to encourage some considerable enthusiasm for and interest in this most-thrilling means of travel. Scientifically, the expedition will be followed through from its field work to a full conclusion, with the results being worked up over the following year and published in the normal academic fashion.

The venture will also have a lasting impact since it will be filmed throughout and recounted in two books. More importantly, however, any residual funds or subsequent income will be directed to the Antarctic Foundation, a charity specifically set up by the expedition members to encourage interest and activities in this remotest of continents.

# Ornithological exploration of New Guinea's mountains

## Jared Mason Diamond

Physiology Department, UCLA Medical School, Los Angeles, California 90024, USA

American, born 10 September 1937. Biologist and Professor of Physiology, UCLA Medical School. Educated in USA and UK; Ph.D. (Physiology) from University of Cambridge in 1961.

Between 1964 and 1986, I have made 11 expeditions to the New Guinea region, each lasting between three and five months, to explore the country's mountains and their birds. I now propose to carry out the final stage of this research by two more expeditions over the course of two years.

### The significance of New Guinea's mountains and birds

Why is the exploration of New Guinea's mountains and their birds important? While New Guinea is conventionally described as the world's largest tropical island, its significance to the ornithologist is instead that of the world's smallest continent. For New Guinea birds, speciation – the process by which an ancestral species splits into two or more daughter species – involves the same mechanism as on the world's major continents, namely the separation of ancestral populations by geographic barriers. However, New Guinea has several advantages over the major continents for the understanding of the process: it is smaller and less complicated; it has enough bird species to be interesting, but not so many as to be overwhelming; and it is a natural unit surrounded by water, whereas each of the major continents except Australia is connected to another continent. In addition, New Guinea's rugged terrain promotes speciation by isolating bird populations in adjacent valleys or on adjacent mountains only a few kilometres apart. Thus, our understanding of speciation in general owes much to the insights that were derived from studies of New Guinea's mountain birds nearly 50 years ago.

New Guinea has several further advantages for the biologist. Because it lies on the equator but has mountains rising to 5,000 metres, it offers a complete range of habitats from lowland tropical rain forest to permanent snow and glaciers as one ascends its mountains. On this isolated island-continent, evolution has proceeded until a higher fraction of New Guinea's birds is unique to New Guinea than is true of the birds of any other comparable-sized area in the world.

## Knowledge of New Guinea montane birds as of 1964

By 1964 ornithologists had explored much of the Central Dividing Range, five of the ten larger outlying mountain ranges, and the mountains of several offshore islands. Available information about the songs, behaviour and ecology of New Guinea montane birds was limited, however.

In 1964, when I mounted the first of my 11 bird-surveying expeditions to the New Guinea region, much still remained unexplored or little explored by ornithologists. Specific goals of these 11 completed expeditions, as well as of the two proposed remaining expeditions, have included: geographical exploration; an inventory of bird species present on each mountain; the habits of each bird species; altitudinal distribution; knowledge that local New Guineans possess of birds; species of particular interest; and conservation (including part of expeditions spent working with the staff of the government wildlife service).

My methods for identifying birds depend heavily on their songs, since one hears far more birds than one sees in tropical rain forest. It is not uncommon to spend an hour in the forest, and during the course of that hour to identify 50 species by voice without having seen a single bird. When I began work in New

*Courtship bower that a male bowerbird erects and decorates with red leaves and other coloured objects, in the forest on New Guinea's Mt. Wandamen. This large, hut-shaped structure is built by birds no larger than a jay.*

Guinea in 1964, little published information was available about New Guinea bird songs, and I have had to devote much effort over the years to identifying the calls of each species. This task is made harder by the fact that some species have different calls on different mountains. I carry a tape recorder and parabolic mirror in the forest for recording bird songs, and the resulting tapes are deposited in the Library for Bird Sounds at Cornell University, Ithaca, New York.

## Tasks to be completed

The major remaining task in this long-term project aimed at understanding New Guinea montane birds is to survey the Jayawijaya Mountains, which constitute the largest remaining block of ornithologically unexplored mountains in New Guinea; they have been proposed as New Guinea's largest nature reserve, yet much of the information needed to establish the reserve is unavailable; and they are likely to harbour many of the least known, most distinctive bird species of New Guinea.

An ornithological survey of the Jayawijaya Mountains appears to present no insuperable problems qualitatively different from those I have encountered on previous expeditions to New Guinea. However, there is no doubt that it is a large task involving surveying birds over an altitude transect extending from lowland forest to the summits of the highest peaks. I thus anticipate that the survey will require two expeditions each lasting several months, and scheduled for 1987–1989. The strategy for gathering field information about birds will be similar to that of previous expeditions but particular effort will be devoted to observing important but little-known species such as the snow quail, green-backed babbler, McGregor's bird of paradise, etc. The scientific results of my studies will be published in ornithological and ecological journals, and a detailed report will be made to the Indonesian Government and the World Wildlife Fund to assist them in planning the nature reserve gazetted for the Jayawijaya Mountains.

# Revitalizing Lake Nipissing's transportation history

*Bessel J. VandenHazel*

**Honourable Mention**
**The Rolex Awards for Enterprise – 1987**

Nipissing University College, Gormanville Road, Box 5002, North Bay, Ontario
P1B 8L7, Canada

Canadian, born 3 May 1927. Professor of Science and Environmental Education,
Nipissing University College. Educated in Netherlands, UK, Canada and USA;
M.Sc. (Outdoor and Environmental Education) from Northern Illinois
University in 1969 and qualified underwater diving instructor.

My interest in the transport history of Lake Nipissing was fired by my discovery
of a shipwreck while scuba diving in the lake near my home in North Bay,
Ontario in 1976. Enquiries in libraries showed, to my amazement, that very little
heritage information was available on the fascinating events that must have
occurred on this lake during the past 1,000 years. I therefore decided that the
history of the native people, the French explorers, the fur traders and the steam
era was not only worth researching but should be brought to life for the people
of north-eastern Ontario. I began interviewing residents of the area who still had
residual knowledge of the logging era, and launched into research in the Public
Archives of Canada, which led to a series of articles in the regional daily
newspaper.

### Creative development

Consultations with the North Bay Area Museum in 1971, led to a decision to
create a thematic exhibition on the history of Lake Nipissing transport
technology. With the financial assistance of the Federal Department of
Manpower six college students with outstanding skills in technology, painting,
drawing, writing and administration were engaged to create the Nipissing Room
in the North Bay Area Museum, which now holds a dugout canoe, a birchbark
canoe and parts of steamers. For tourist purposes, a 50-page booklet was
produced with captions in English, French, German, Italian and Ojibway.

When, in 1981, the city of North Bay celebrated a "Century of Progress in
Transportation" a summer project was developed in co-operation with the
North Bay Historical Society. Funds from the Federal Department of Manpower
were once again used to engage five college students to produce posters and a
monograph entitled *One hundred years of progress in transportation and communication.*

*Adaptation and exploration. A diver archaeologist uses a helmet-mounted light when measuring the wreck of the* John Fraser *in the murky depths of Lake Nipissing. The mounted light frees the hands to manipulate measuring boards, tape and pencil.*

*The Nipissing Room of the North Bay Area Museum. The* John Fraser *exhibit created by student artists in 1979. Preservation work on the iron and wooden artifacts is still continuing. (opposite)*

The next step in developing a multimedia package of information on Lake Nipissing was a number of paintings dramatizing the technology of the turn of the century, and, in 1982, four promising young artists were engaged to produce 28 paintings of steamboats, locomotives and logging scenes which were subsequently presented to municipalities, museums and libraries around Lake Nipissing. The same year saw publication of my book *From Dugout to Diesel* which more or less completed the general history phase of the Nipissing Project and allowed me to move into the more technical aspects of underwater work.

## Underwater archaeology

Over the years 1980–1985, the project evolved from the general history phase into the more demanding task of underwater archaeology, and commenced with the training of a group of certified divers, including my son Mark, in underwater surveying, measuring and mapping at visibilities as low as 50–150 cm.

In the summer of 1983, using a further grant from the Department of Manpower, five students, including two certified scuba divers with experience in low-visibility diving, were hired to survey submerged docks and shallow wrecks. *Underwater Archaeology Report No. 1* was the product of the 1983 diving season. Two native Indian students were engaged to create two dugout canoes which were donated to museums. In 1985, using a government research vessel and a sidescan sonar, the wreck of the paddlewheel steamer *John Fraser* was relocated in the centre of Lake Nipissing. Grants were obtained, novel instruments and methods of underwater surveying were developed and the assistants were also introduced to the techniques used in the preservation of wood and corroded artifacts – all of which was recorded in a second *Archaeology Report* and various published articles.

### Research for the future

A number of Canadian municipalities are now considering raising wooden ships for exhibition purposes, and I have therefore initiated small-scale laboratory experiments on waterlogged-wood and corroded-iron preservation at the Nipissing College, and have been granted sabbatical leave of absence for the 1986–1987 academic year to study shipwreck preservation and museum exhibit technology. My main objectives here will be to collect information on preserving marine heritage resources from sunken ships, and on presenting this heritage in a museum context.

I am planning to spend two weeks visiting some 14 learned locations and draw up a comprehensive report for Canadian museums, archives and heritage conservation agencies. With this experience behind me, I will be well placed to contribute to current discussions in Canada on the feasibility and desirability of raising wooden ships. Therefore, 1987–1990 will be devoted to securing funding for further research on the transportation history of Lake Nipissing especially prior to AD1800 and for a regional conservation laboratory for waterlogged wood and corroded iron artifacts. The unravelling of the Lake Nipissing transportation history has provided me with a series of demanding physical and intellectual challenges involving underwater exploration, archive publications and the preparation of talks and exhibits that appeal to the general public; and I look forward to continuing and expanding this stimulating activity.

# Unlocking the mystery of the underwater columns of the Lost City of Nueva Cadiz

## Richard Sammon

One Fox Road, Croton-on-Hudson, New York 10520, USA

American, born 9 May 1950. President of CEDAM International, a non-profit organization dedicated to conservation, education, diving, archaeology and museums, and Vice-President of Bozell & Jacobs Public Relations. Educated in USA; studied (Music) at Berklee College of Music, Boston.

On his third voyage in 1498, Christopher Columbus explored the northern coast of Venezuela where he met numerous Indians wearing beautiful necklaces of natural pearls from the waters off Cubagua Island. Having briefly explored the area, Columbus continued his voyage to Santa Domingo where the news of the pearls created such widespread excitement that, when it eventually reached Spain, it produced a "pearl rush" to the rich pearl beds of Cubagua.

The city of Nueva Cadiz was founded on Cubagua in 1503, and this exact dating means the site offers historians an almost laboratory situation for studying the culture of the Spanish Conquest. Furthermore, the fact that Nueva Cadiz was the first Spanish settlement in South America, makes the city important from an archaeological standpoint. When the city was at its peak in 1535, some 340 kg of pearls were being taken out of the waters off Cubagua each month but, within the next decade, the pearl beds had been "fished out" and, in 1543, a hurricane destroyed the city and the Spanish abandoned the site.

### Searches to date

The 1940s and 1950s saw major excavations of the site but these were of a less than scientific standard. Moreover, areas of Cubagua have since been excavated by treasure hunters searching for gold, silver and pearls. Today, there is absolutely no supervision of the site, and anybody with a boat can visit and dig on the island. In 1984 and 1985, with the co-operation of the Government of Nueva Esparta, which includes Cubagua and the Margarita Islands, CEDAM International – a non-profit organization dedicated to conservation, education, diving, archaeology and museums – organized two expeditions to the Nueva Cadiz site. The one-week 1984 expedition produced only a preliminary map and survey of the site but the 1985 expedition recovered over 750 artifacts of sixteenth-century Spanish and Indian origin; these artifacts were handed over to the Governor, who directed the opening of the first Nueva Cadiz Museum, on Margarita Island.

## The "mystery" underwater columns

A particularly interesting feature of the Nueva Cadiz site is the columns standing submerged some 1,000 m off the coast of Cubagua, and these were studied in the 1984 CEDAM International expedition. None of the literature researched by CEDAM International makes any mention of these underwater columns which, until 1984, were thought to be either: petrified trees, pillars from a cathedral, pilings from a dock or breakwater, or a natural formation. The 1984 CEDAM International expedition mapped six of the columns and took a core sample of one of them. An analysis showed the sample to be sandy limestone which is not found in the area but only on the mainland, and this is felt to disprove the tree theory; the map revealed that the columns were basically laid out in a straight line and this is felt to disprove the natural formation theory. The 1985 expedition made a more detailed map of all 23 columns and found ten of the columns to be some 180–270 cm high and 13 to be some 60–120 cm high, and basically arranged in a straight line.

## Future expeditions

Although earlier expeditions led to the founding of a Nueva Cadiz Museum in Nueva Esparta and have also disproved three of the popular theories of the underwater columns, preservation of Nueva Cadiz remains a task of major importance. We propose that a team of archaeologists, surveyors, engineers and dedicated volunteers should be assembled to carry out the following land work: make an accurate map of the ruins of Nueva Cadiz; continue excavations under the guidance of qualified archaeologists; train Venezuelans to recover and

*The tallest of the mystery columns of Cubagua was over 2 m tall.*

173

*Underwater metal detectors were used to see if any metal artifacts were in the area of the Cubagua columns.*

restore the artifacts; explore Nueva Cadiz for additional Spanish and Indian sites; work with the Venezuelan Government in preserving the Nueva Cadiz site and developing the Museum.

Archaeological work would be conducted using standard archaeological techniques and equipment; moreover, a future terrestrial archaeological expedition would also include a complete photographic and videotape record of the project and a computerized day-by-day log of activities.

The proposed underwater work would be carried out in two phases. In the first, more exact measurements would be made of the columns to establish an accurate map, and core samples would be taken from each column to help determine whether the columns are pilings from a dock, a breakwater or offshore platform for the pearl boats. The second phase would be devoted to the painted tunicates – tiny marine organisms which have colonized the columns and which have been found to produce a substance effective in treating cancer in laboratory animals. These tunicates would be collected, packaged and shipped to the New York Aquarium/Osborne Laboratories for further study. It is also intended to carry out a complete photographic study of the marine life on the columns which have attracted a wide range of organisms.

It is believed that the project's objectives can be achieved in approximately two months, and the periods of September and October have been selected in view of the weather conditions. Support vessels will be provided by the La Salle Foundation and the SUBES Diving Organization, and the Venezuelan National Guard has offered helicopters and patrol boats if required. The co-operation of Venezuelan contacts combined with the team of uniquely qualified experts from the United States makes accomplishment of the project's goal a very real possibility.

# A centre to study haemorrhagic syndrome due to skin contact with caterpillars

*Carmen Luisa Arocha-Piñango*

Instituto Venezolano de Investigaciones Científicas, Caracas 1010A, Venezuela

Venezuelan, born 5 December 1932. Head, Coagulation Laboratory, Venezuelan Institute for Scientific Research. Educated in Venezuela; M.D. from Universidad Central de Venezuela in 1954.

In 1967, we described a severe haemorrhagic syndrome of extended duration resulting from contact with caterpillars unidentified at that time. All the patients came from Bolivar State, south of the Orinoco River. Since then, cases have been reported to the north and south-east of the river. The caterpillar was identified in 1971 as the larval form of a moth of the Saturnidae family, *Lonomia achelous (Cramer)*, which is widely distributed throughout South America. However, in December 1985 we had been able to study in detail and treat only 200 of the many patients who suffer from contact with the caterpillars.

### A history of the treatment strategies

Until 1981, victims were treated locally, and by the time specialist personnel arrived from Caracas, the majority of the cases had already received some therapy. As from 1982, patients were transferred by air to Vargas Hospital in Caracas, where clinical and laboratory work was carried out under much more controlled conditions.

During the past three years, however, only four patients have been treated under these controlled conditions. Thus, we have so far been unable to obtain a general overview of the pathophysiology of the syndrome, or establish therapeutic guidelines.

Clinical studies have been accompanied by biochemical tests on the haemolymph and hair secretions of the caterpillar in order to isolate and characterize the causal agent, in addition to studies on the habitat and life cycle of the moth with the idea of breeding it in the laboratory; however, since the moth is found in isolated zones far from Caracas, these studies have been very difficult to carry out. Consequently, we have made only little progress with studies on the animal's life cycle, and tests of breeding the moth in the laboratory are at a preliminary stage.

*The instar caterpillar,* Lonomia achelous, *found to be the cause of haemorrhagic syndrome in Venezuela and Brazil.*

*The project team from the Instituto Venezolana de Investigaciones Científicas working in the camp laboratory. (opposite)*

## Situation in Brazil

Surprisingly, in view of the wide distribution of *Lonomia achelous* in South America, the only other country to report cases is Brazil, where the caterpillar appears to be an occupational hazard among the rubber workers of the Amazon Delta.

In September 1985, we were invited to Macapá, capital of the Amapá Federal Territory, where we were able to visit many of the affected areas and came to an agreement with the Secretary of Health that this city would be an ideal place to set up a Centre to study the syndrome, bringing experienced and trained personnel from Venezuela as a contribution to this joint project.

Financing would be necessary for the travel expenses of myself and probably one trained technician from Caracas to Macapá and for basic equipment to set up a laboratory there. During a stay of approximately one year, we would be able to train the local personnel, carry out therapeutic trials with the patients and collect sufficient caterpillar specimens for the biochemical studies. Once the Centre was in full operation, the local personnel would take over, maintaining close ties with our laboratory in Venezuela.

## Objectives and plan of action

The primary tasks would be to: obtain an understanding of the pathophysiological mechanism of action of the venom and, with this knowledge, establish appropriate therapeutic guidelines; map the endemic foci with the aim of educating the local population with regard to the caterpillar and also setting up links to the Centre; investigate the possibility of developing an antitoxin for use in high-risk areas; and, given the potency and long duration of action of the venom (brief contact with a single caterpillar may cause haemorrhage for up to 15 days), isolate and purify the principal active agent which causes the

176

syndrome for possible use as an anticoagulant in cases of thrombosis.

To achieve these objectives it would be necessary to transfer myself and one member of my laboratory to the city of Macapá, Amapá Federal Territory, Brazil; set up a laboratory in the Macapá Blood Bank, with techniques necessary for the study of the clot and fibrinolysis mechanisms; and train local medical and laboratory personnel in the necessary laboratory and management techniques.

Subsequently, the Centre could admit patients and carry out regular biochemical studies, and this biochemical and clinical monitoring would provide invaluable feedback to guide therapy. When results have been obtained on a sufficient number of patients, the correlation between the treatment and the evolution of the syndrome could be analyzed and general therapeutic guidelines drawn up.

An attempt would also be made, using experimental animals, to produce antibodies against the venom, for use as a therapeutic antitoxin. Finally, as a complement to the above studies, it would be necessary to seek the caterpillar or colony of caterpillars which caused the syndrome in each patient, identify the variety and the instar, and also collect the venom for further biochemical studies.

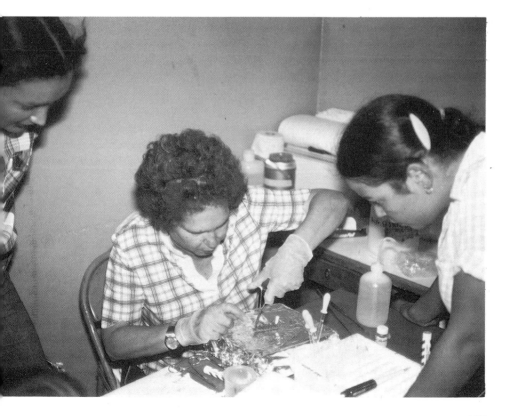

# Roman occupation of West Gloucestershire

## *Maurice Fitchett*

Mariners Cottage, High Street, Newnham-on-Severn, Gloucestershire GL14 1BB, UK

British, born 3 October 1929. Educated in UK; B.Sc. (Economics) from Manchester University in 1953.

Since retiring in 1983, I have been furthering my studies on the Roman occupation of Britain. I soon realized that, as the area between the rivers Severn and Wye had for some time constituted a frontier region at the start of the Roman occupancy and had been rich in natural resources, it must have received considerable attention. Yet, although it was accepted that the Romans had used the natural resources, as evidenced by the remains of their ore mining, there had been little detailed research or excavation, it having been reasoned that little would have been left of anything occurring before the intensive coal-mining and iron-working which took place in the eighteenth and nineteenth centuries. Moreover, as it was fairly easy to discover and excavate Roman remains on the Cotswold scarp which lay to the east of the Severn, as did the Roman town of Glevum, it had also been assumed that the west would not have much to offer.

### The search for Roman sites to the west of the Severn

The only excavated sites to the west of the Severn appeared to be the Temple of Nodens at Lydney and Chester Villa, Woolaston, though there had been scattered finds of Roman pottery, coins, etc., over the years, which indicated a far wider distribution of sites. I therefore looked into all records of such finds and plotted them on a map, marking the two excavated sites. A pattern emerged which pointed strongly to the iron-ore extraction sites and, from the dating of the finds, indicated that, particularly where hoards were concerned, these would not have resulted from chance losses, but the deliberate hiding of large amounts at a time of danger, which could only have related to a period of sea-borne Saxon raids. This was substantiated by the report on the Woolaston Villa site, but did not constitute proof, and there was nothing in the excavation report on the Temple of Nodens site nearby to show that such a phase had occurred there. Believing that other sites might have existed, I undertook a private aerial survey which confirmed, from a variety of crop markings, that this was indeed the case. Publications of local societies and the Gloucester Records Office files provided information on Woolaston and also on villa sites at Huntsham by the river Wye and Park Farm Lydney, adjacent to the Nodens Temple site, as well as brief details of a Roman iron-working site at Popes' Hill. The number of sites on my map had now increased by three, but the work had provided no details from other areas on which the aerial survey had shown markings, so it was then necessary to make an on-the-spot ground examination.

## The excavation phase

Excavation at Littledean Hall, where I had reason to believe a major site existed, yielded an important finding: the foundations of an apsidal temple building, second in size only to that at Colchester. In 1985, I was able to involve my old University, Manchester, and an excavation team confirmed the site as being a Roman-British temple with Celtic origins. Further works awaits funding.

There being a dearth of persons capable of carrying out photography and site drawing to an acceptable standard for publication and recording, I undertook this work myself, assisted by a number of local volunteers, including some members of the Forest of Dean Local History Society. I was invited to join the Society and to become a committee member, responsible for the formation of an archaeological field group. This having had considerable success, and as a consequence of running a lecture course on archaeology through the extra-mural department of Bristol University, I was able to set members a series of field projects which, to date, have resulted in the discovery of a number of possible Roman sites, and the positive identification of two. One, a second-century industrial settlement, is under continuous excavation by a volunteer team; the other, a large villa-type unit in the main iron-working area of Clearwell, has been backfilled to await future excavation as funds and labour become available.

Ground work resulted in the discovering of a villa site at Hadnock Court near Monmouth; and I was also able to confirm one at Boughspring, near Chepstow,

*Ritual burial site at Dean Hall, covered by a layer of fourth-century ox horns.*

*Boughspring Roman Villa. Excavated area of flagged floor of north wing.*

which had been excavated privately. In connection with the preservation of a
Saxon chapel at Lancaut, adjacent to the river Wye, I found that a certain
amount of the church's masonry is re-used Roman stone which, in view of the
situation of the church, is evidence that the Roman site must be on the same
peninsula, just above the 10 m contour. I then checked the spot heights of the
four villas, and all are just above the 10 m mark, indicating that most transport
must have taken place by river.

### Tasks for the future

The project's main future task, among many others, is to ascertain the placing of
other sites in and around this area, and to establish their nature and inter-
relationship, if any.

   In the course of the research I developed a special photographic technique to
enable precise photographs to be taken when and where time and/or conditions
make drawing impracticable; hopefully, a prototype of this equipment can be
produced for subsequent manufacture and general use.

# Ethnoecology of the Bischarin – Documenting a disappearing culture

## Steven Michael Goodman
**Honourable Mention**
**The Rolex Awards for Enterprise – 1987**

Museum of Zoology, University of Michigan, Ann Arbor, Michigan 48109, USA

American, born 3 August 1957. Graduate student and research assistant. Educated in USA; carrying out graduate studies in the Department of Ecology and Evolutionary Biology, University of Michigan.

---

The mountain of Gebel Elba (1,435 m), in the region slightly inland from the Red Sea and skirting the Egyptian/Sudanese border, offers a biological diversity unparalleled by any other area farther north in this portion of Africa. It is also the revered mountain of the Bischarin, a group of pastoral nomads of Hamitic origin, who are believed to have lived in the area since the predynastic period of ancient Egypt. For these people, Gebel Elba is a resource refuge in that it provides water and herbage, and thus plays an important role in their history, folklore and migrations.

### The Bischarin of the past and present

The origins of the Bischarin are not altogether known, but they are clearly an ancient group of Hamitic descent. Their native tongue is a form of *Tu Bedawie*, which is unwritten and shows some affinity to several East African languages. Physical anthropologists and historians have evidence that the Bischarin have been living in this region for over 4,000 years and are derived from or akin to the predynastic ancient Egyptians. Those that remain pastoral nomads have herds of goat, sheep and camel, and spend a good portion of their time tracking water and herbage. The Bischarin are part of a much larger nomadic or semi-nomadic group known variously as the Beja, Blemmyes, and Bedu el Atbai. Their ancestor Bishar, who remains an obscure figure in history, had a grandson or great-grandson by the name of Koka, a holy man who lived in the vicinity of Gebel Elba, and it is believed that he is a portion of the mountain and that the local water and greenery are direct gifts from him.

In the past decade or so, government programmes have encouraged the Bischarin to give up their traditional nomadic life style, settle in coastal villages and learn Arabic. With this change, a considerable amount of cultural tradition has broken down, including the strong ecological/cultural ethic. A small group of Bischarin still live by the "old ways", in that they continue to use *Tu Bedawie*, refuse to assimilate themselves in Arab culture, and live by a strong relationship

*View from a high mountain peak near Gebel Elba; in the foreground there are the characteristic ombet trees,* Dracaena ombet, *of the area. (Photo by Peter L. Meininger)*

*The base camp set up by Steven Goodman at the foot of Gebel Elba during his expedition in April 1985. (Photo by Peter L. Meininger) (opposite)*

to the land. It is these people who see themselves as the cultural and ecological "caretakers" of Gebel Elba and have the utmost respect for its resources.

Since 1981, I have travelled to the Gebel Elba area five times, often for stays of several months and have developed a good rapport with a family that continues the nomadic tradition and especially one son of this family, Hassan Awad, who has accompanied me on numerous excursions in the region. Hassan has now invited me to join his household on my return and share their nomadic life for two years to develop a lexicon of *Tu Bedawie*, document the rock decoration and pharaonic inscriptions, and catalogue the medicinal plants of the Bischarin.

### Documenting the language and rock drawing

To date, little is known about this unwritten language and, since it is being replaced by Arabic, its importance as a spoken tradition is being lost. Using the standard procedure of lexicography I wish to catalogue the local language with particular emphasis placed on the etymology and variety of words dealing with the natural environment, such as names of plants, animals, stars and natural spirits. If indeed the Bischarin are descendants of or akin to the predynastic Egyptians, then a study of *Tu Bedawie* might yield important information on aspects of ancient Egyptian language.

Gebel Elba and other nearby mountains are locally covered with quantities of rock drawings and inscriptions including upper palaeolithic to neolithic drawings and paintings (30,000–5,000 BC); dynastic inscriptions (2,700–945 BC), and Islamic drawings (AD 600–1,200) which I would document in a standardized and comprehensive manner. Several of the dynastic inscriptions have cartouches of the contemporary ruling Pharaoh, and thus can be dated. The majority of these inscriptions document expeditions sent out to the far reaches of the kingdom to look for precious stones or metals.

The palaeolithic-neolithic material is essentially a time capsule. It depicts scenes of wild animals that no longer occur in the area, methods used to capture them and herds of domestic animals – thus forming an important record to assess the continuity of pastoral nomads' culture through time. Whilst I conduct the documentary portions of this project, I will solicit explanations of the depictions from my Bischarin companions.

## Medicinal plants

I will also attempt to document the traditional medicinal plants of the Bischarin. A detailed inventory will be made of the Bischarin pharmacopoeia, including a description of the plants, their Bischarin names, folial and floral portions used, season to be gathered, and therapeutic use. Secondly, a detailed survey will be made of the local flora – which is one of the most diverse in this portion of Africa – and Bischarin names will be equated with scientific binomials.

Further subjects for study include: the general domestic use of wild animal and plant products by the Bischarin; a classification and inventory of the Bischarin natural spirits; the stars as a story telling tradition in the classification and explanation of the cosmos; the distribution and floral ecology of the Ombet tree, *Dracaena ombet*; and the ecology of granivorous birds, feeding ecology of nubian ibex, *Capra ibex*, altitudinal distribution of reptiles on Gebel Elba, and song dialects in local populations of trumpeter finch, *Rhodopechys githaginea*.

The general theme of most of the proposed projects is to learn how the Bischarin assimilate and organize the natural world they live in. This group has coexisted with a relatively harsh environment for thousands of years and have clearly adapted in numerous ways. An understanding of these adaptations reveals how man and environment develop and change in an interactive way. Given that the Bischarin are indeed the descendants of the predynastic Egyptians, then a study of these pastoral nomads and their basic ethnoecological tenets should provide insight into historical land and resource use. With the vicissitudes taking place in the habits and ideologies of the remaining nomadic Bischarin, this information must be gathered in the near future before the vacuum of change makes it impossible.

# Orbiting Unification Ring Satellite

## *Arthur Ray Woods*

21 Im Grund, 8424 Embrach, Switzerland

American, born 26 March 1948. Multi-media artist. Educated in USA; B.A. (Psychology) from Mercer University, Macon in 1970.

Much of our planet's energies and resources are being devoted to the development of increasingly lethal weapon systems and the maintenance of the military establishment. The militarization of space has recently become prominent in the discussions between the superpowers of our planet. I propose to construct and have launched into orbit around the Earth a satellite in the form of a circle visible to the naked eye as a gesture of hope for that future which most of us on this planet desire. This Orbiting Unification Ring Satellite (OURS) will certainly be an idealistic notion but, at this moment in history, some idealism may be our planet's only viable alternative.

As a circle in the night sky, it will be a symbol of the interconnectedness and interdependence of all things. It will remind us that we have a responsibility to preserve the environment and that some form of planetary unity and cooperation must be maintained in order to ensure the survival of our planet and ourselves as a species. As such, it will celebrate our passage into the next millennium.

### OURS – An art work

As an art work, OURS will be very significant in that it may be the largest, most ambitious, the most technologically sophisticated, the most expensive to produce and perhaps the most important art work done by an artist of this century. Appearing as a fine circle, an ellipse or a line above the horizon, it will be seen by more people than any other single art work and it will belong to everyone.

OURS is a pioneering use of space as a cultural medium. It is not the first space art work to be proposed and realized. But as far as I know, OURS will be the first project of this scale that has a realistic chance to be realized. Its form, the circle, is a powerful and universal symbol common to all cultures. It is a symbol of the Self expressing the totality of the psyche in all its aspects, including the relationship of humanity and the whole of nature. The ring sculpture satellite will be formed out of Mylar – a space age product often used in the space environment. This material is strong, highly reflective and extremely light-weight, qualities which are essential for the realization of this project. Approximately 20% of its outer surface area will be painted in a painterly and expressionistic way which is indicative of our century of modernism. Both the inner and outer surfaces will remain highly reflective.

I would be naive to think that an individual, even with sufficient financial resources, would be given the permission to affect the environment in such a way. My plan is to build an international network of sponsors, which I estimate to eventually number more than 100,000 individuals and with the goal of having at least one sponsor from each country of our planet. This will create a "people's satellite" serving the interests of all the nations. It will be necessary to gain the endorsement of governments, organizations, the media and respected individuals.

The impact of OURS on the physical environment, that is, by placing a visible object in the night sky, is not a responsibility to be taken lightly. It is my intention that the satellite will remain in orbit for a limited time. Every attempt will be made to prevent its disintegration in orbit and to ensure its eventual removal after a designated date. My plans call for a mid-1990s deployment and an orbital lifespan that would include the year 2000.

## OURS – Technical specifications and costs

The exact dimensions of the ring are dependent on a number of technical criteria but it is expected to be 158 cm wide, some 3,300 m in circumference, 1,000 m in diameter and approximately 100 kg in weight.

OURS will most probably be delivered and deployed in orbit by the American space shuttle – Space Transportation System – as it is the only currently operational transporter of this type offering manned assistance. A mid-1990s launch date may make the planned European Hermes or even the Russian shuttle system viable alternatives. At this early stage it is difficult to ascertain the exact costs of the project but on the basis of information supplied by NASA, I have arrived at a total cost of $4,100,000.

This money will be raised by selling pieces of the painted satellite material to individual sponsors from all parts of our planet. Each sponsor will receive a piece of the painted ring material equivalent to a paid amount based on a calculated price per square meter. The beginning price is $50 which makes OURS available to a large public. The creation, organization, administration and publicity costs may be equal to the cost of the actual satellite. Therefore, I estimate that the final costs may be approximately $10,000,000.

## Status

The current status of the project, which began in the summer of 1985, is quite satisfactory and I am in contact with experts concerning the OURS specifications and the question of orbital debris. At the time of writing, the OURS brochure has been printed in English, German, French and Italian. The Spanish and Swedish translations have been completed and will be printed in the near future. I plan to have the Japanese, Chinese and Arabic translations complete by June of this year.

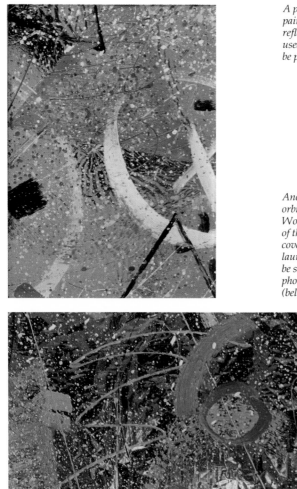

*A piece of the continuous painting done on the same reflective material that will be used on the actual ring that is to be put into space orbit.*

*Another section of the space orbiting ring painting. Arthur Woods is selling individual pieces of this work to raise funds to cover the production and launching costs. Each piece will be signed, numbered and photographically documented. (below)*

I can only offer to those who come in contact with the project the opportunity to consider the global priorities involved and the opportunity to participate if they so desire. Making OURS a reality is precisely this process of considering all of the available alternatives, then choosing and participating in the future of our choice. Hopefully, OURS will one day symbolize and celebrate that choice.

# Maritime archaeology and the search for shipwrecks in the Cape Verde Islands

## Erick Henri-Emmanuel Surcouf

15 rue des Fontaines, 92310 Sèvres, France

French, born 8 May 1948. Director of Agence Erick Surcouf, and Head of Operations, International Maritime Archaeology Group. Educated in France; studied (Management and Economics) at Paris-Dauphiné University.

When, in 1492, Columbus discovered the "New World", he opened the doors to one of the greatest maritime traffics of all times. For more than three centuries, Spanish ships sailed from Spain across the Atlantic to bring back gold, silver, precious stones and many other goods such as tobacco, leather and spices. On 7 June 1494 the Treaty of Tordesillas was signed between Spain and Portugal to settle conflicts arising from Columbus' first voyage. This Treaty set up a line of demarcation from pole to pole, 370 leagues west of the Cape Verde Islands. Spain was given exclusive rights in the region to the west of the line; Portuguese expeditions were kept to the east.

### The Cape Verde Islands and their wrecks

Discovered during two Portuguese expeditions between 1460 and 1462, the Cape Verde Islands, by their geographic situation between Africa, Europe and America, served as a strategic springboard for Portuguese colonial expansion and played an important role in the development of maritime navigation and trade. Between the sixteenth and nineteenth centuries, they were a major port of call for Europe's heaviest maritime traffic. It therefore goes without saying that the waters around the Cape Verde Islands hold an impressive number of wrecks of outstanding interest and significance.

The International Maritime Archaeology Group (Groupe International d'Archéologie Sous-marine) has, since 1980, been preparing a project to search out, raise and study by means of the latest techniques a number of ships that were sunk off the Cape Verde Islands between the sixteenth and nineteenth centuries. I have visited the site several times and it is hoped that final permission for work to start will soon be granted by the political and cultural authories of the Republic of Cape Verde.

The wrecks that we have identified and propose to search are not themselves Cape Verdian but are, nevertheless, the property of the Cape Verde Government, and it is our intention to maintain close collaboration between our specialists and the Islands' officials throughout the programme.

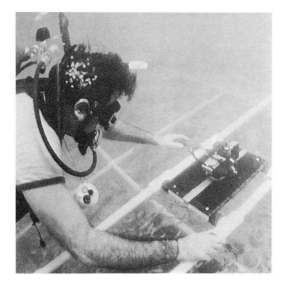

*Stereophotogrammetric coverage of a shipwreck site.*

*Erick Surcouf holding a model of a sixteenth-century Spanish galleon. (opposite)*

## The salvage technique

A shipwreck is a "time capsule" and under no circumstances should the capsule be opened up until we are sure that we can extract from it all the information it contains. Consequently, the recovery must be preceded by adequate archival research to allow comparisons to be made between archival documents (such as ship's manifesto) and on-site findings. Furthermore, before the excavation is commenced, a preliminary survey of the wreck must be made. The expedition itself will be carried out by squaring the search zone using a system of guide marks, precise navigation, etc., with exact positions and locations being marked on the map. The methods that will be used will include aerial photography, scuba diving, closed-circuit underwater television, and a research submarine. Where visibility is poor, a side-scanning sonar may be employed.

Once the artifacts have been brought to the surface they will be photographed, drawn or even X-rayed where necessary. Moreover, we will install an on-site laboratory since many of the artifacts recovered will need immediate preservation and treatment. Conservation and restoration specialists will play an important part in the project and we will even have an expert in naval architecture of the appropriate period available to carry out on-site research.

## Expected outcomes

It is expected that our research and findings will have an impact at various levels. From the historical and archaeological points of view, the discovery and comparative examination of several shipwrecks of different nationalities which were travelling similar missions and sank under similar conditions in a well-defined zone is of considerable interest and significance, and the results of the studies should shed light on an important part of European colonial expansion.

From the point of view of general culture, the study of the remains of hulls,

rigging, armament, navigation instruments and cargoes will give us an insight into the maritime traffic that centred on the Cape Verde Islands, raise general awareness about the country's maritime archaeological wealth, protect the national patrimony and provide the wherewithal for the creation of a Museum and an Underwater Exhibition Centre.

From the point of view of tourism and the media, we plan to develop cinema, radio and television documentaries, and write a book and press articles to widely disseminate the findings. Our team contains specialists in the field of exhibitions and museums and in the cleaning and marketing of marine artifacts, and their expertise will be placed at the disposal of the Government for the development of the museum and the underwater exhibition centre. We also envisage the possibility of a travelling museum which would tour the main towns of Europe.

Finally, from the social point of view, our project will be involved in training men and women from the Cape Verde Islands in the various areas of research technology, such as archival research, archaeological techniques, conservation and preservation procedures, scuba diving and museum organization and operation.

# The Transcanada Expedition

*Stewart Holmes*

The Studio, 41 Moorhouse Road, London W2 5DH, UK

British, born 24 February 1955. Founder and Director of the Scientific Earth Association (SEA). Educated in UK; studied at Thurroch Technical College of Further Education; Fellow of the Royal Geographic Society.

The Transcanada Expedition is a 30-month crossing of Northern Canada, travelling via Hudson Bay and the Northwest Territories by the Scientific Earth Association (SEA). The aim of this Association is to develop a central database collating biosphere information from field projects around the world and to disseminate this information to education centres, research establishments and industry and, over the long term, offer advice and financial support in the planning and development of similar biosphere research programmes and act as an advisory centre for overseas relief agencies. During the crossing, a scientific team will carry out field research in a wide range of environmental areas and provide support for the expedition team. The film team will produce a number of documentaries.

Transcanada will be the first field link with the SEA database and will utilize advanced telecommunications procedures and networks to analyze data on the spot, feed information to universities and research centres for further analysis and reply and allow the SEA headquarters in London to put together education packages to be distributed to schools nationally and internationally.

## The first phase – To the Mistassini Reserve

The first phase of the expedition will involve overland and river travel to the Mistassini Reserve, where contact will be made with a family of Cree hunters and a photographic and film record obtained of the lifestyle and hunting practices of a Cree tracking community. During the summer of 1987, the science team will analyze soils and vegetation around Cree camps to determine the effects of changing Cree lifestyle; a study will also be made of the surroundings to provide a good introduction to most aspects of boreal ecology. In October 1987, the science team will run supplies from Toronto to Thompson, Manitoba, from where they will be airlifted to several points along the west coast of James and Hudson Bays in preparation for the boat trip there in spring 1988, and a secondary base camp at Baker Lake. During the winter period 1987–1988, the science team's research activities will include measurements of snow acidity and conductivity in the area between Toronto and Thompson.

## The second phase – James and Hudson Bays

The main forestry research programme will commence in spring 1988 with ecological and phytosociological studies of the boreal environment in an attempt to demonstrate the importance of climate on both a macro- and micro-scale.

At the same time, a team will travel by inflatable boat some 1,900 km along the west coast of James and Hudson Bay between Moosonee and Baker Lake carrying out a four-part research programme, which includes: a search for *Ascophyllum*, a seaweed normally found in Arctic Norway; entomological studies on mosquitoes and black flies and tick-borne encephalitis; collection of river water and silt samples for qualitative and quantitative pollution determinations; and collection of samples of algae from under the breaking ice.

## The third phase – Baker Lake base camp

The summer of 1988 will be spent at the Baker Lake base camp continuing studies on tick-borne encephalitis in mammals, particularly in caribou; and undertaking a plant search programme to record all the different plant species in large areas around Baker Lake, in an attempt to demonstrate the sensitivity of the tundra ecosystem to human activity. At the end of 1988, a small research and film team will live with a community of Caribou Inuit Indians to record on film the changes that Western influence has had on the hunting techniques and gain an insight into their art. Before the team arrives at Baker Lake, the Expedition will run a competition in which schools in Canada and the United Kingdom will be asked to design their own projects on tundra ecology. A small group of pupils from one school in each country will travel to Baker Lake during the summer of 1988 to carry out the proposed research programme.

*The painting used to illustrate the history section of the Transcanada Expedition brochure. Canoes such as these were used to open the trade routes between Montreal and York Town (now called Thunder Bay).*

191

## Phase four – Across the Barrens

In the winter of 1988–1989, a two-man team will drive Skandic Snowmobiles a distance of 1,600 km across the Barrens from Baker Lake to Yellowknife to commemorate the attempted 1926 expedition led by Englishman John Hornby in which both Hornby and his nephew Edgar Christian died whilst attempting their second west-east crossing. During the east-west crossing – a journey never yet completed in winter – the team will record the climate, take soil and snow samples and film the unique flora and fauna of the Barrens region.

The two-man team will link up with the researchers at Yellowknife, and the Expedition will then continue by road to Prince Rupert on the west coast of Canada and launch a supported boat journey in spring 1989 to follow the coast from Prince Rupert to Vancouver. On route, marine studies will be carried out on remote coastal islands looking in particular at similarities between species of seaweed on the west coast of Canada and those in Japan and the east coast of China. The final film project will involve a small community of Haida Indians on Vancouver Island and a mainland tribe called the Kwakiutl and look at the importance of fishing as their major source of income.

The Expedition will finish in Vancouver in the autumn of 1989 where the various film and research projects will be completed.

*Members of the team preparing the Transcanada Expedition at work stocktaking the expedition equipment prior to moving to the new headquarters.*

# Sarawak 87 – Studying the world's largest known underground karstic room

## Eric Gilli

**Honourable Mention**
**The Rolex Awards for Enterprise – 1987**

13 rue Massena, 06000 Nice, France

French, born 29 May 1957. Geologist and specialist in karstic phenomena.
Educated in France; Doctorate (Geology) from Marseille University in 1984.

---

The Sarawak chamber is located in the rain forest of the Island of Borneo, in Eastern Malaysia. It is the world's largest karstic room and measures 600 m long, 450 m wide and is probably 100 m high; there are no pillars supporting the roof. It was discovered and mapped in 1980 by an English team of cavers who were exploring the caves of the Mulu Mountains. Although another expedition in 1984 collected more information about this room, access problems and difficulties in studying large underground volumes have meant that little else has been discovered.

### A major exploration challenge

Exploration of this chamber offers an unprecedented challenge, and this project plans an expedition under the leadership of Eric Gilli, who has been studying large underground volumes for three years in France and in Turkey and who, during his thesis work, has highlighted the value of a naturalist approach to digging artificial chambers. There is a wide gap between nature and man's experience in this field. The largest artificial limestone cave is only 30 m wide; the Sarawak chamber, at 450 m, is 15 times wider.

A reconnaissance trip was carried out in March 1985 with the financial support of the *National Geographic* and *Figaro* magazines, and allowed us to establish a wide range of information required to pursue the project. However, although we obtained official permits for an expedition in summer 1985, we had to postpone our plans for lack of funding.

The Lubang Nasib Bagus caves in which the Sarawak chamber is located are a relatively inaccessible area of Borneo Island and are reached by flying to Miri, a coastal town, and then travelling by boat to Marudi village, the last civilized place before the jungle. From that point, almost two days' travel are required to reach Long Pala Camp, the entrance to Gunong Mulu National Park and four further hours' march through the forest to the Lubang Nasib Bagus caves.

The caves start with a 500-m lake which can be traversed in inflatable dinghies; next, a 500-m section follows a difficult gallery containing a stream which leads

*Loading the caving equipment aboard a piragua at Mulu during an earlier expedition by Eric Gilli.*

*Lake entering the Labang Nasib Bagus cave at Mulu, Borneo. (opposite)*

to a dry zone strewn with large boulders. Thereafter, the passage widens until the Sarawak chamber is reached at a distance of 1.5 km from the entrance. The journey through the caves takes almost three hours.

### Technology and logistics

Lighting will be a key factor in the exploration of the Sarawak chamber and has been the subject of detailed study. Experience has shown that a lighting level of 1,000 W is sufficient to study La Verna, the largest chamber in France (300 m wide); therefore, we plan to use a source of 6,000 W from three 2,000 W electric generators. Portable batteries will allow 1,000 W floodlights to be taken all around the chamber to study details on the walls. All this will simplify visual and photographic study.

The selected photographic equipment and techniques have already been tested in France to ensure good results and comprise: electric generators and floodlights; flash bulbs and a special high-power powder mixture of barium nitrate and magnesium for which we have developed an opto-electronic detonation system.

Topographical equipment has been loaned to us by Wild and it comprises two theodolites, a beam laser and a distance meter; these items have been used successfully during a training session in the Poudrey cave in the French Jura. The laser beam places a red spot on the wall or the roof of the cave, whilst the theodolites measure the angles, and trigonometric calculations are used to give the position of the red spot in space. This process can be employed to measure any point although, where possible, distances will be measured directly using an infrared distance meter.

### Expedition timing

The timing of the expedition is determined mainly by the equatorial climate of Borneo and its heavy winter rains which we wish to avoid. A reconnaissance trip has already been carried out in March 1985 when two of our colleagues spent 30 days meeting with the local authorities and visiting the Lubang Nasib Bagus caves; this will be followed by an administrative trip by two persons, for 15 days, to Kuching in December 1986.

The expedition itself will take place in summer 1987 and will involve a team of six persons for 60 days. This will comprise an outward journey of one week; a stay on site for 45 days (setting up an advanced camp in the jungle, portering the equipment to the cave); setting up the underground camp; surveying and photography and perhaps further explorations; and a return journey lasting one week.

We believe the expedition will constitute not only a major adventure but will provide much valuable information on a remarkable natural phenomenon.

# Astronomical detection of missing Egyptian 5th dynasty sun temples

## Ronald Allen Wells

1080 Peralta Avenue, Albany, California 94706, USA

American, born 12 September 1942. Part-time publisher's assistant, Freeman-Cooper Publishing Co., and Lecturer in Physics, Computers and Astronomy, Crowden School, Berkeley. Educated in USA and UK; Ph.D. (Astronomy) from University of London in 1967.

The importance of solar religion in ancient Egypt reached its height with the nine Old Kingdom sun kings of the 5th dynasty, six of whom built extensive temple complexes for sun worship, usually comprising a main building, an auxiliary temple and surrounding houses for the priests. The main temple was open to the sun, orientated in an east-west direction and had an altar in front of a large obelisk with facilities for the slaughter of sacrificial animals. This temple was connected by a' causeway to a smaller, north-easterly-facing temple at a lower level about 100 m away, known as the "valley temple", adjacent to which were the priests' quarters. Although ancient records confirm and even name the six temple complexes, archaeologists have found and excavated only two of them, those of Userkaf and Neuserre. My project is to locate the four remaining sites.

### Astronomical detection of the four missing sun temples

The locations of the missing temples are not known, but the possibility exists of limiting the search areas by astronomical investigation; preliminary research into possible astronomical use of Egyptian sun temples has revealed that, of the seven principal sites of interest, one concerns the 5th dynasty temples.

In trying to understand the possible astronomical role played by the sun temples at Abu Ghurab, it was noted that the valley temples faced in a north-easterly direction and were situated at the end of the causeways also having north-easterly azimuths, whereas those associated with the major pyramids face east. Since the causeway ramps of the sun temples could just as easily have been orientated to the east, I have concluded that the valley temples may have been constructed to face a rising astronomical phenomenon other than the sun. At Userkaf's temple, daily sacrifices were offered and were presumably placed on the altar before sunrise; thus the priests had to know when this would occur. I have therefore hypothesized that the valley temples could have faced a series of

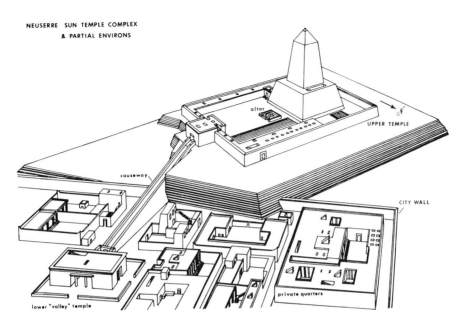

NEUSERRE SUN TEMPLE COMPLEX
& PARTIAL ENVIRONS

altar

UPPER TEMPLE

causeway

CITY WALL

private quarters

lower "valley" temple

*A reconstruction of the appearance of the Neuserre sun temple and part of the priests' city. Adapted from Ludwing Borchardt, Der Bau, in: (F. W. von Bissing, ed.)* Das Re-Heiligtum des Königs Ne-Woser-Re *(1905).*

rising stars so positioned that each took its place as a warning star when the interval time between the latter's rise and sunrise became too long. When not serving as a sunrise warning star, the other stars in the series would be spaced across the sky, marking the other hours of the night.

Therefore, the positions of 719 of the brightest stars were moved back in time by computer to 2,400 BC, i.e. around the middle of the 5th dynasty. The frequency peaks of the number of stars rising within 3° north of a given azimuth were then plotted against the azimuth, the vertical scale being chosen so that the elevation of the stars as they crossed a given temple axis would be in the range of 0–5° above the horizon. The stars on the eastern horizon appear to rise in periodic sequences, and two of the six peaks correspond to the known sun temple valley temple axes; thus, the four others may possibly be related to the four missing temples. The azimuths of the Neuserre and Userkaf sun temple valley temples coincide with the first two significant frequency peaks ("significant" being defined as 12 stars).

The valley temple star clocks would have marked the hours shortly after the star rose as it crossed the temple axis, which would account for the orientation of the valley temples in a specific direction. It is clear from our data that the Neuserre and Userkaf star clocks had a sufficient number of stars distributed in an adequate manner for marking the hours of the night. Researchers have pointed out that the earliest form of telling time by the stars would have used a method depending on rising rather than transiting stars, and thus in the sun temples of Abu Ghurab we may well have the precursors of the Ramesside star clocks.

197

## Star clocks and religion

That each sun temple had its own star clock may have been because the use of different star groupings developed gradually, or have occurred on religious grounds. The coincidence of six Egyptian sun temples of the 5th dynasty with six special groups of rising stars suggests a cause-effect relationship which merits further investigation since, if the star groups were sacred, this could explain why the last kings of the dynasty did not build their own sun temples: there were no more adequate star sequences available! If the stars of each star clock did have a religious significance, it may have been concentrated mainly on the brightest star in each group, leading to the determination of the other stars, which would be considered as "followers". The verification of this possibility must await examination in greater detail of all the stars in each of the other frequency peaks.

## Future research

It is important to determine the rising times throughout the year of all the stars in each of these special peaks in 2,400 BC. If indeed the other four peaks are related to the missing temples, it may be possible to compute their locations, because the declination of each frequency peak can be related to the latitude and longitude of the site from which the stars in the peaks can be observed.

An iterative study with equations of the star data may yield possible site locations which may be further used with satellite infrared and possibly radar imagery of the Nile Valley to choose likely sites for field inspections.

*Ruins of obelisk podium seen from south-east corner. Giza pyramids appear on horizon (right of high-tension pylons).*

198

# Korean butterflies – Exploration and classification

## Kyong Chol Chou

Department of Astronomy and Meteorology, Yonsei University, Sinchon-dong, 120 Seoul, Korea

Korean, born 4 April 1929. Professor, Department of Astronomy and Meteorology, Yonsei University. Educated in Korea and USA; Ph.D. (Astronomy) from University of Pennsylvania in 1962.

The Korean peninsula belongs to the palaearctic zoogeographical realm, and the animal and other biological life in its highland district is closely related to that of the boreal zone of Manchuria, mainland China, Sakhalin and Hokkaido, whereas the lowland area has a milder climate. The peninsula's wildlife and birds have been well observed, studied and classified with the exception of the butterflies, and this is a gap that I and Mr. Seung Mo Lee, my co-worker, have tried to fill.

Over a period of 45 years, we have collected more than 100,000 butterflies throughout North and South Korea, and we have now donated this collection to the Korean National Science Museum where it is housed in a newly built annexe. We now propose to complete the collection of butterfly samples and their taxonomic study, organize a major public exhibition and publish an illustrated book entitled *Butterflies of Korea*.

### Our achievements to date

To accomplish our objectives, we have visited and collected butterflies in almost all districts and provinces of Korea with the exception of North Korea, and a total of 1,170 trips have been made in South Korea alone since 1947. However, of the 100,000 specimens collected so far, only 905 are from North Korea.

We have carried out wide-ranging observations and have carefully classified the material we have collected. By referring to various foreign publications and through private contacts with foreign organizations, we have grouped our collection into the following categories: Papilionidae, Pieridae, Lycaenidae, Danaidae, Nymphalidae, Libytheidae, Satyridae and Hesperiidae.

Although we have made many new discoveries, identified new species and have had several surprising encounters, we still feel that our results are far from complete. We are sure that there is much more information and material to be found, and more specimens to be collected from various places throughout the country.

*Just some of the tens of thousands of butterflies that Professor Kyong and his colleague Mr. Lee have collected but which still need to be processed.*

Much to our regret, however, our work on the classification of our specimens is far behind our intended schedule; this is due primarily to a lack of funds that we need to hire laboratory assistants and to buy the proper instruments we require. Nearly 50,000 specimens, about one-half of the entire collection, are still awaiting processing.

A national television network produced a one-hour television programme describing our work and entitled "Butterflies of Korea", and this was broadcast in August 1985. It took them almost a month to cover the exploration we have carried out in the fields and mountains of several districts of Korea and the work that is being undertaken in the laboratory. The programme won national acclaim but, unfortunately, it did not bring in any financial support.

### Plans for the future

With considerable hope and determination, we have set ourselves the objective of accomplishing a number of further tasks. There still remain about 30 areas of the country to be explored in order to complete our collection, and we still have the 50,000 unprocessed specimens! We hope to finish the sampling work with either voluntary help from students or possibly by hiring a number of assistants. Using the materials we have already processed and the new specimens we are expecting to collect, our intention is to complete and terminate our efforts to classify the totality of the collection.

In April 1987, we are planning to hold an exhibition of our butterfly collection in Seoul, and if this event proves to be a success, we will attempt to organize similar displays in other cities with a view to creating greater public awareness and knowledge about butterflies.

We are also attempting to publish a book describing the 45 years of work we have carried out; however, although the text has progressed slowly but surely, the illustrations have not advanced to the same extent because of the high cost of

*A partial view of the storage area used by Professor Kyong Chol Chou and his colleague Mr. Seung Mo Lee. The empty boxes are awaiting samples to be made up from many tens of thousands of specimens still to be processed.*

photographic materials. If funding can be obtained to publish the book, copies will be distributed free of charge to various libraries and research and educational institutions all over the world.

Over the past 45 years, we have had to overcome numerous difficulties in achieving this much; however, since collecting butterflies is such a lonely and, seemingly, unrewarding task we now find, unfortunately, that we do not have any one to carry on our work. We have gained the impression that we are the only ones to have an interest in this aspect of our national heritage. Nevertheless, in spite of our age, we hope we will be able to finalize our project and leave a complete collection for the coming generations. Establishing the distribution pattern of Korean butterflies will not only offer a valuable range of information, but also, possibly, provide clues to the missing link between longitudinal or latitudinal trends of passage and the eastern or western origin of butterflies.

# Exploring sacred mountains and ancient ceremonial centres in the Andes

 *Johan Gjefsen Reinhard*

c/o Constance G. Ayala, United States Embassy, Casilla 1995, Lima 100, Peru

American, born 13 December 1943. Free-lance anthropologist, writer and lecturer. Educated in USA, West Germany, UK and Austria; Ph.D. (Cultural Anthropology) from University of Vienna in 1974.

My project involves searching for and investigating mountain ritual sites in the Andes at altitudes of up to almost 7,000 m and collecting information on mountain worship in selected Andean areas from Chile to Colombia. Use of such data to reinterpret selected ceremonial centres in terms of sacred geography has already led to reasonable explanations for some of South America's most enigmatic archaeological sites.

Mountain worship was a major feature of prehispanic religion and continues to exist in many areas today. It has been called the "keystone of Andean culture", providing a cultural unity for otherwise divided Andean peoples, and my research indicates that an understanding of the basic concepts of mountain worship is essential for interpretations of ceremonial centres of great antiquity.

I selected three types of sites (Chavin, Nazca and Tiahuanaco) and examined them on the basis of data collected relating to mountain/fertility cults in the vicinity and found that this information allowed a more unified explanation of the sites' functions and locations, and of the meanings of many of the figures found there. This project should further substantiate my theoretical and methodological approach, provide deeper insight into some of the most enigmatic sites in South American archaeology, lead to re-examination of previous theories about prehispanic ceremonial centres and help change our perspectives about ancient religious beliefs and practices in the Andes.

## High-altitude archaelogy and ethnography

Nearly 100 prehispanic archaeological sites have been found at altitudes between 5,200 and 6,700 m in the southern Andes. These are by far the world's highest ruins and, taken together, constitute one of the most awesome accomplishments known to us from ancient times; they are also among the few

*Johan Gjefsen Reinhard, Rolex Laureate – The Rolex Awards for Enterprise 1987, pauses in the fierce mountain sunlight on an expedition to a sacred site in the high Andes. (Photo by Antonio Beorchia)*

203

Inca religious sites to escape destruction by the Spanish. Archaeological finds such as frozen Inca bodies (human sacrifices) and rare metal statues have been among the most important in South America. Yet the origin, distribution and purpose of these constructions were subject to conjecture until I began this study in 1980.

My findings were that mountain deities were perceived as controllers of meteorological phenomena (rain, hail, lightning, etc.) and, consequently, of crop and animal fertility. I have hypothesized that the Incas built the sites in the southern Andes to help increase production and to support the Inca state and religion. To test this hypothesis, I now intend to gather further information in Ecuador, northern Peru and Colombia, since I believe that the reason why high mountain sites have not been found north of 10 degrees south latitude is purely that there has been a lack of research in the northern Andes. For example, I will investigate sites referred to by the chronicler Albornoz (1583), and follow up reports from additional historical and ethnographic sources.

The nature of the work at high altitude has necessitated use of specialized techniques and the acquisition of knowledge not commonly held by an anthropologist; in fact, I have helped develop a special subfield in anthropology called "high-altitude archaeology". As unusual as it may seem, diving has also played an important part in this project since the mountain lakes were often perceived as "doors" to the interiors of mountains where the gods reside, or as the wives of these deities.

### Research programme and funding

For over two years, this project was entirely self-supported, although local institutions often provided valuable assistance. Subsequently, I received grants from the Explorers Club, the National Geographic Society, the American Philosophical Society, Dumbarton Oaks and the Social Science Research Council. However, lack of funds for a vehicle and an experienced assistant have meant the loss of considerable time and made some aspects of the research dependent on resources and personnel that happen to be available.

Ethnographic and historical research will be carried out: on Mts. Pariacaca, in central coastal Peru, and Coropuna, one of Peru's highest mountains; on the lakes of Piura, Moina and Urcos near Cuzco; the mountains near Huamachuco to locate the worship place of Catequil, one of the most important deities in northern Peru; Mollotoro, a mountain near Cuenca, Ecuador; at Cuzco and near Machu Picchu to collect ethnographic data to interpret the centres in terms of sacred geography; and the ceremonial centre of San Agustín, Colombia.

For the ethnographic research, reports will be obtained from local investigators and field studies will be conducted with local scholars, mainly to interview ritual specialists on such matters as reasons for worship, legends, meanings of ritual objects, etc. Current-day ceremonies will be observed where possible. Historical sources dating back to the time of the Spanish Conquest will be studied for information on mountain/fertility cults. The lesser-known "visitas" of the Spanish priests will be examined and historians will be asked to assist in the location of materials.

The archaeological research will be concerned with locating and surveying ruins on or near mountain summits in the areas selected and in utilizing excavation reports where available. Detailed site plans and photographic records of finds constitute the principal means of documentation. Excavations are planned only for selected sites under the direction of investigators with the necessary permits. Research on ceremonial centres at Machu Picchu, Cuzco and San Agustín will be primarily concerned with gathering ethnographic and historical information. The figures at the sites will be examined relative to beliefs found as to the roles they play in mountain/fertility cults (e.g. birds of prey as representing the mountain gods).

In conclusion, it is felt that this research will contribute significantly to understanding the traditional Andean religio-economic beliefs and ancient religious sites.

*From high aloft in the Andes, the lands of the ancient Empire of the Incas stretch away as far as the eye can see, while Johan Reinhard examines the archaeological remains of a sacred mountain site.*

*Surprisingly, diving is one of the skills that Johan Reinhard has had to acquire as a high-altitude archaeologist. Mountain lakes are a potential source of thrilling discoveries since precolumbian populations considered them "doors" to the sacred mountains. (below)*

# Archaeological and ethnographical research in western Tassili-n-Ajjer, Algeria

## Juergen Friederich Kunz

32 Grampersdorf, 8432 Beilngries, West Germany

West German, born 14 December 1935. Supreme Councillor to the West German Government. Educated in West Germany; Diploma (Architecture) from Technical University, Munich in 1961.

Prehistoric rock art is a fascinating phenomenon of cultural and intellectual history and offers a rewarding research subject which reveals many important aspects of man's culture not deducible from his material artifacts. In Africa, rock art – in the form of paintings on walls of rock shelters and engravings on rocks – is to be found over a very extensive area, both geographically and historically; however, no satisfactory systematic approach has yet been made to this subject. Tassili-n-Ajjer – a mountain region in the south-east of the Algerian Sahara – has proved, over the past decades, to be particularly rich in prehistoric rock art but research has been limited to the central and eastern Ajjer area. The western region has been ignored as its morphology is not particularly promising and the area is somewhat inaccessible; before I started my research project, only three rock art sites had been identified in this region.

After two visits to the existing rock art finds in 1967 and 1969, I started investigating the western region in 1971, following a trip there which indicated to me how easy, in this age of space exploration, the discovery of our own planet can be. In the course of nine field surveys, I have been able to uncover a large number of previously unknown rock art complexes, extraordinary both in quantity and quality. My project is now to establish a comprehensive and accurate documentation of the rock art of this area which would then serve as a broad basis for analysis.

The rock drawings are also of great importance in explaining ancient technologies and, consequently, the paint chemistry and painting technique will also be examined with a view to identifying the pigments, binders, etc., highlighting chronological and regional differences and, possibly, determining the causes of any physical and chemical damage.

### Documentation strategy and procedures

The difficult terrain is one of the main reasons why the western part of the Tassili-n-Ajjer has so long been able to keep its treasure trove of rock art to itself.

Even with offroad vehicles, only a few areas of this arid mountain region are accessible, and most parts can be reached only with the aid of Tuareg guides and camels. The Tuareg have indicated some rock art finds to me, but for the most part, maps and satellite pictures will be used to locate promising areas.

The paintings and engravings will be photographed, a method which is now accepted as the most objective, using medium- and small-size cameras with special lenses and orthochromatic film which highlights the contrasts in the red coloration. Attempts to record very faded paintings will be made using infrared and ultraviolet film. The rock engravings will also be documented with colour film so that the degree of patination – which is an important factor in establishing the relative chronology – can be determined. Latex casts will be made of the most significant engravings which should later enable the engraving technique to be assessed in detail.

Where possible, without damaging the rock paintings, micro-samples (exfoliated fragments of 0.1–1mm in size) will be taken for micro-chemical and spectrometric analyses, etc., by participating institutes. Microsections will also be made in order to look at the layer structure of the paintings. Macro-photos of the rock paintings and engravings will be taken to explain the technique of production.

### First results

So far an area of 30,000 km$^2$ has been surveyed and four petroglyph sites and 70 painting sites have been found. Two of the shelters contain paintings of the Round Head period and 37 contain paintings of the Neolithic Cattle period, many of them artistic masterpieces. The Horse period of the Bronze Age or Early Iron Age is represented in 13 illustrations of horses with chariots. Among them, one scene found during my 1971 expedition at Ekatnoucher is of special relevance: it shows a quadriga which corresponds in many amazing aspects with

*Rock painting at Tassili-n-Ajjer.*
*A two-horse chariot galloping*
*across the rock wall.*

207

Greek representations of the fifth and fourth centuries BC. The engraved illustrations of big mammals, anthropomorphic figures with animal heads and spiral or phallomorphic signs at two of the sites can be attributed to the oldest, immediately post-palaeolithic period (Bubalus period).

## Ethnological research on the Tuaregs

Today, exogenous change and foreign infiltration have put the existence of the Tuareg nomads in Tassili-n-Ajjer at risk. For this reason, it seems natural to conduct ethnological research along with the archaeological investigations in order to document at least some aspects of this nomadic culture.

Of the results of ethnographic research work, mention might be made of the recordings of Tuareg traditional music and toponymy and camel brands of the different tribes. An oral tradition was found which shows that the triliths, stone structures discovered for the first time in the Tassili-n-Ajjer by me, are connected with hunting sacrifice rituals.

*An example of one of the animal petroglyphs of Tassili-n-Ajjer.*

208

# In the wake of Sir Francis Drake – A photographic record of his life and voyages

## Michael David Turner

7 Rosewood Avenue, Burnham-on-Sea, Somerset, TA8 1HD, UK

British, born 21 July 1955. Physical education teacher, part-time author and photographer. Educated in UK; B.Ed. (Hons.) (Physical Education) from University of Sussex in 1982.

Sir Francis Drake is one of the most illustrious figures in England's maritime heritage but my studies of his numerous biographies have shown that primary and secondary accounts about him are frequently contradictory and that the only illustrations they contain are portraits, maps and artifacts. My readings left me frustrated because too much was left to the imagination and, therefore, open to misinterpretation. I longed for pictures of places which would show where and how events occurred and, at the same time, reduce the number of contradictions and vague descriptions often characteristic of academic accounts.

Following extensive reading to record minute details of each location, I began in 1981 photographing every place throughout the world visited by Drake using angles and distances which bring life to the primary and secondary accounts; this has yielded several substantial discoveries.

By archival studies and coastal surveys, I have located Drake's careenage in Costa Rica, the village of Guatulco (in what is now Mexico) which he raided during this famous voyage of circumnavigation (1577–1580) and Borburata cove in Venezuela, which will allow historical atlases to be suitably corrected. During the attack on Nombre de Dios in Panama, Drake was wounded and convalesced on an islet which he recounts as being three miles from the town, however, observations showed the nearest islet to be six miles away and I was able to make an exact identification by eliminating islets without a safe landing place.

### Exploiting the resources

My plan is to mould this collection of photographs together with the new facts into a book lavishly illustrated in colour which would be published on the 400th anniversary of the Spanish Armada in 1988. The text will confront practical findings with primary and secondary accounts which can be questioned, corrected, amplified or supported by this pictorial evidence. Readers will view the world as Drake saw it, since most of the photographs have been taken from angles that avoid twentieth century intrusions in a way that will bring life,

209

depth, greater accuracy and realism to this segment of early-modern history and, with the help of this bridge between the past and present, they have a more vivid perspective of the past.

## Using the photographs as teaching aids

As a school teacher, I have devised a series of lessons, incorporating worksheets and slides, for teenage pupils, designed to help them select and interpret evidence in learning and appreciating the significance of Drake's contribution to British history. A publisher has shown interest in publishing this material as an educational text book and wall-chart. In addition, the National Trust, a preservation society, is interested in installing an educational audio-visual unit with worksheets at a residential centre for schools near to Drake's country house – Buckland Abbey – and the owner of Coombe Sydenham Hall, where Drake's wife lived, is planning a similar venture. The Curator of Plymouth City Museum, who is responsible for the displays at Buckland Abbey, is keen to include comprehensive photographic documentation to supplement the museum's exhibits.

Finally, I would like to help develop a series of television documentaries which would narrate Drake's domestic life and the events of the Spanish Armada, unravel the mystery of the exact place where Drake careened in Costa Rica and retrace Drake's 16-day march across Panama which culminated in robbing treasure-laden mule trains on the trans-isthmus jungle trail.

## An exhilarating but hazardous exploit

I believe that this project and its achievements can be of interest worldwide, since Drake anchored in over 30 countries; it may, moreover, inspire others to photographically document further areas of history and thus embellish the world's past.

*The plaque indicating the site of Drake's town house in Plymouth, England. Research at the official records office proved that Drake's house was, in fact, at the other end of the street.*

210

Following in the wake of Sir Francis Drake has not always been an easy task – sometimes, it has involved chartering boats but more often it has been a case of hitchhiking through jungles, mountain ranges and deserts with climate ranging from freezing to sticky heat. Many of the regions are remote and primitive, where travel is slow and food and accommodation exceedingly basic. Some areas are downright dangerous. In three trips to northern Colombia I was physically attacked, was robbed at knife point of my camera equipment and my Rolex watch and I suffered cuts to my ear, wrist and knees. I also spent, unjustifiably, three days in a Guatemalan jail. Another demanding requirement was the five years I have spent learning Spanish, an essential for research here.

The mechanism and directions of this project are now well established and a third of the countries have been visited using my own funds. If I can secure financial support, three journeys could be completed annually, which would accelerate current progress and ensure completion by 1990; furthermore, publicity would give the mature project credence and help entice publishers to invest in its commercial potential. In the meantime, my unshakeable faith, persistence, drive and determination will endeavour to surmount any obstacles in order to achieve realization.

*The fortified anchorage of San Juan de Ulua in Veracruz, Mexico, where, in 1568, the Spaniards massacred most of Drake's men whilst the English fleet was moored by hawsers passed through the iron rings on the walls.*

211

# Surveying the rock art of West Darling, New South Wales

## Robert George Gunn

RMB 2008, Pomonal Road, Stawell, Victoria 3380, Australia

Australian, born 6 December 1949. Consultant archaeologist. Educated in Australia; Bachelor of Education (Art and Craft) from Melbourne College of Advanced Education in 1985.

The West Darling region has some of the most extensive Aboriginal rock art galleries in Australia. These sites are of both national and international importance, and one of them contains over 13,000 individual motifs. At least three techniques have been used in the galleries: engravings, stencils and paintings. The earliest of these (engravings) is over 5,000 and possibly as much as 27,000 years old whilst the most recent (stencils) depict European artifacts and are, therefore, only 100 to 200 years old.

I am currently carrying out a major study of the rock art of south-eastern Australia, and the West Darling region is the only rock art region for which no overall assessment is available. The region covers an area of some 100,000 km$^2$ and lies within the semi-arid belt. It consists of flat plains, interspersed with low rocky ranges and the main land uses are sheep stations and national parks.

My aims in this project will be to: locate and record a representative sample of prehistoric rock art sites in the region; identify and describe the different art styles present; compare and contrast the contents, contexts and distribution of these styles; and disseminate the results in both academic and general publications.

### Survey strategy and time schedule

The first month will be spent studying existing site records and publications and liaising with State authorities and aboriginal communities in the study area. This information will be used in conjunction with topographic and geological maps to determine the areas to be explored. Relevant station owners/managers will then be contacted and their permission and assistance sought. An article will be placed in the local newspaper explaining the project and asking for assistance in locating sites. The local radio will also be approached for assistance.

It is estimated that the field work will take four months, with Broken Hill being used as the base for supplies and a four-wheel drive vehicle with caravan trailer for transport and accommodation. Camp will be struck at each major site

*Pounded engravings of human figures, emus and other designs at Euriowie, Australia.*

complex, and day trips – on foot and by car – will be undertaken until the complex has been explored and recorded. It is not expected that every site will be recorded in detail as the time required for such a survey could not be justified by the present aims; rather, a record will be made of a representative sample of site complexes from throughout the region.

## Survey procedure

All new sites will be recorded using a site record card developed from my previous experience in this field. The art will be sketched to show my interpretation of each motif and the relative positions of the items to one another. Each motif will be individually numbered, measured and described on the record card, and the site will be mapped by tape and compass measurements to show the location of the art and, for rock shelters, the amount of protection afforded to the art and any occupants. Each site and its setting will be photographed as an additional aid for site identification and relocation, and the art of each site will be photographed as a record of its condition and specific form.

On average, it takes about two hours to record a site but a full day is not uncommon for particularly complex locations. Allowing for travel and exploration, this project can hope to record some 400 sites. As the site recordings around Mootwingee are known to be reliable, attention will initially focus on the more poorly documented complexes and on areas likely to contain unrecorded sites. Following the field work, a summary paper will be submitted to an archaeological journal, and a general statement will be given to the press. The results will also be communicated to the aboriginal community. After analysis, the site records will be bound and lodged with the State authorities and the library of the Australian Institute of Aboriginal Studies, Canberra, for use by other researchers.

213

### Analysis of the results

The analysis will use both quantitative (archaeological) and qualitative (art appreciation) approaches. The different art styles will be identified and described by the core and range of their attributes and their artistic quality, and their variation across the region will also be investigated. The styles will then be compared and contrasted to illuminate changes in the art over time; geographic, ethnographic and other archaeological studies will then be used in an attempt to explain these changes and develop a picture of art in Aboriginal society. Finally, the region will be briefly compared with the Cobar region (to the east of the Darling River) and other areas of south-eastern Australia.

Following completion of the programme, a detailed report will be submitted to *Rock Art Research* (journal of the Australian Rock Art Research Association), and a more general article will be submitted to a more popular journal such as *Australian Geographic*.

*Pounded engravings of stylized human figures at Mootwingee, Australia.*

# Early human Pacific settlements – Sea level changes and underwater artifacts

## *John Richard Hutchinson Gibbons*

**Honourable Mention**
**The Rolex Awards for Enterprise – 1987**

c/o Department of Biology, School of Pure and Applied Science, University of the South Pacific, POB 1168, Suva, Fiji

British, born 3 June 1946. Died in a boating accident in November 1986.

This project is based on a recently developed hypothesis that the course of Pacific prehistory, including the development of boat technology and subsequent migrations to far-flung islands of Micronesia, Melanesia and Polynesia, has largely been determined by the massive sea level rise since the last Ice Age. The suggested mechanism is that, at the height of the last Ice Age i.e. about 18,000 years ago, mean sea level in the Indo-Pacific was about 150 m lower than at present with landmasses extending to the very edge of continental shelves. All tropical oceanic island lagoons were totally dried out and surrounded by steep cliffs 100 m or more high – the remains of exposed barrier reefs – dropping away steeply into very deep water. Under such conditions, few marine or coastal resources would have been accessible, and boat technology must have been minimal. Many present-day Pacific islands were then very much larger, and distances between adjacent islands and archipelagos much smaller than today.

### Effects of a massive rise in sea level

The overall 150-m rise in sea level between about 18,000 BP and 4,000 BP had profound consequences for the peoples of South-East Asia, gradually submerging more than 75% of the original land area, forcing people to switch from an agricultural or hunter-gatherer economy to a primarily marine one, and eventually forcing migrations to uninhabited islands just visible from parts of South-East Asia. This fits in well with linguistic data suggesting Papuan movements into New Guinea starting 15,000 BP and continuing for a further 10,000 years. A major consequence of this model is that people may have arrived on the tropical oceanic islands much earlier than is currently estimated (i.e. no more than 3,000–4,000 years ago). However, since studies of underwater archaeology on Pacific islands have been almost totally neglected, these estimates are hardly surprising.

It is therefore essential to explore for human artifacts in underwater caves which people may have used for shelter and which are relatively free of coral growth and extensive sedimentation. The report of apparently human artifacts

215

in a cave on Tuvalu submerged more than 8,000 years ago and now 50 m below present sea level is especially exciting and needs urgent investigation. Even more exciting is the possibility of finding submerged buildings or other structures following claims made recently by the adventurer-explorer, David Childress, that a submerged city exists at a depth of 60 m, at the old site of Nan Modal, in Pohnpei (Ponape). Exploration of underwater sites close to Nan Modal is an essential part of this project.

A second and equally stimulating consequence of our model is the new light that may be thrown on the racial origins of the various Pacific island peoples. Our model suggests that Polynesians are of mixed ancestry, being primarily derived from a mixture of Indo-Malay and Papuan peoples in Melanesia. This is not to dismiss South American contacts, especially in eastern and marginal Polynesia (e.g. Marquesas and Easter Island). This project plans to work closely with research teams using the ultimate genetic marker, HLA blood groupings, and in particular the Australian National University, Canberra, so that these testing techniques can be employed in determining ethnic correlations.

**Project plan and timetable**

The proposed project is therefore designed to investigate whether the model proposed for human settlement of Pacific islands is supported by facts. As a first step, I wish to take unpaid leave from my present Institution and be based in the Department of Pacific Prehistory, Australian National University (ANU) where much of the top-level research on Pacific prehistory is currently undertaken. Underwater archaeological field trips, in the company of a highly experienced scuba diver, would be made to Pacific islands, especially to Tuvalu, Pohnpei (Nan Modal) and New Caledonia, in a search for artifacts and to take radiocarbon-14 samples. In addition, a knowledge would be gained of HLA

*A Pacific island and reef typical of the area in which John Gibbons planned to explore early human settlements.*

216

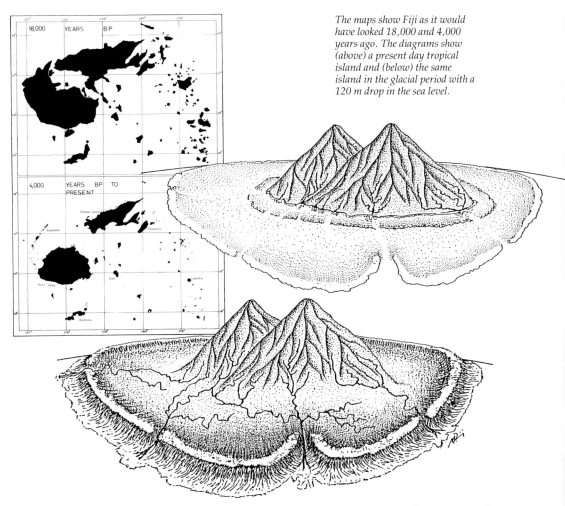

*The maps show Fiji as it would have looked 18,000 and 4,000 years ago. The diagrams show (above) a present day tropical island and (below) the same island in the glacial period with a 120 m drop in the sea level.*

blood testing, with the prospect of obtaining samples during my fieldwork; and my association with the University of the South Pacific (USP) should prove invaluable here, since this would make authorization for research in 13 island countries in the USP region more readily obtainable.

During the project, some time will also be spent at the California Academy of Sciences which carries out research on Pacific prehistory and which has appointed me an Honorary Research Associate. One of the desk tasks will be to construct maps of the entire tropical Pacific at 50 and 120 m below present sea level, giving a realistic approximation of the geography of the region at 10,000 and 15,000 years ago respectively.

However, perhaps the most important – though entirely unscientific – factor in the logistics of this project is that I am gifted in finding things, often apparently stumbling across undescribed species or old artifacts quite by chance. This assertion might well sound arrogant, but intuition bolstered by such a talent is often of paramount importance in a project of this nature.

# Exploration of the caverns of the Maya Mountains of Belize and Guatemala

## Thomas Edward Miller

26 North Washington Court, Cheney, Washington 99004, USA

American, born 7 February 1952. Adjunct Professor of Geology, Eastern Washington University. Educated in USA and Canada; Ph.D. (Physical Geography) from McMaster University, Ontario in 1982.

The Maya civilization of Meso-America made extensive use of caves and left behind a wealth of undisturbed artifacts, burial sites and wall decorations. The caves used by the Mayas in Guatemala and Belize form part of one of the world's great karsts which cover the majority of Meso-America. They have become great historical repositories, preserving in their sediments, artifacts, and cave-adapted life forms a record of the landscapes, climates and evolutionary development of mankind and other species. This project aims to inventory the hydrological, biological and archaeological resources of the Maya Mountains, and to catalogue and salvage from looting as much of the archaeological material as possible.

### Using caves to see back into the past

Past archaeological studies have largely concentrated on the most visible remnants of the Maya: their temple complexes. However, these were works of, and for, the religious elite. Caves were apparently used in folk religious practices: the number and preservation of skeletal burial material (including hundreds of bare footprints) make them important sites for physiological study of the "common" Maya's health, stature, longevity, etc. The types and association of ceramics, lithics, paintings, etc., provide important information about site occupation dates, trade routes and even a look into the minds of the Maya, with an interpretation of how their religious symbols and representations changed with time.

The peoples living in the Maya mountain area have been profoundly affected by the hydrological characteristics of the karst which has created a waterless surface in an area of abundant rainfall, and allows easy transmission of bacteria, toxins and pollutants over large distances. Knowledge of the interior of these karsts is vital in estimating and controlling water resources and minimizing pollution. The karsts of the tropics are among the most spectacular and fascinating phenomena of limestone solution, but their remoteness and ruggedness hamper research. Debate exists over the presence of fundamental differences between tropical and temperate karsts. Study and exploration of the springs and deposits in the caves would directly address these questions. An adequate understanding of solution processes and rates could be easily obtained through water analysis. These researches are of more than academic interest, since they have relevance to the occurrence of bauxite ore (much of it found in karsts) and the distribution of petroleum accumulations in buried fossil karsts.

With respect to the biological research, caves are well known as ecological refugia during periods of high ecological stress (e.g. the glacial Pleistocene), and cave life offers important clues to past changes in climate and rates of phytogenetic evolution. Although Belize possesses the most extensive cave systems known in Central America, its biota is so little known that collection efforts repeatedly expose extremely high ratios of new species, genera and families.

## An exploration plan and schedule

The schedule of exploration would follow three phases: identification of underground networks, visitation and surveying, and analysis.

For the task of identifying suitable areas for study, both Belize and Guatemala have excellent and complete map coverage; however, although aerial photographic coverage is thorough in Belize, it is less so in Guatemala. Using the available resources, a master map of important sites of sinking and resurging streams and rivers will be established and exploration concentrated on caverns produced by the invasion of the limestones and karst by fully integrated rivers flowing from the non-carbonate highlands. Past efforts of this type in Belize have demonstrated that these caves are the largest and the ones most likely to contain salvageable Mayan materials. Hydrologically, they are the master

*A large* hoya *or pot used for Mayan ceremonial purposes, discovered in a Belizean cave. The fracture is probably due to a deliberate ritual "killing".*

*An entire, completely calcite-coated burial from a Belizean cave. Deposition of mineral calcite, in a pool, has coated the remains of a Mayan dating from circa 1,000 BP.*

controls of drainage within the karst, and offer relatively easy access to significant collections of water and sediments.

Physical exploration will be complicated by the remoteness of many of the major caves of Belize and eastern Guatemala, and access will be by mules or backpacking. The major caves will be fully explored and mapped. Maya remains will be sited on the maps and salvaged where necessary, and water, sediment and cave biota will also be collected. Finally, at the analysis stage, maps of the explored caves will be produced, indicating the occurrence of sample locations. It is expected to publish a number of reports to bring results of the project to the attention of the scientific community.

The karst of eastern Guatemala and Belize has not been widely studied or explored: the caverns beneath this ancient, unglaciated surface are among the world's largest. They are important water resources for the peoples of the area, treasure houses of vanished Maya civilization, and refugia of life forms from the Pleistocene. Each of these aspects is individually of world significance, each is presently threatened by expanding farming, hunting, logging, looting and indiscriminate development. To find such a combination of the rare and exotic of three disciplines is probably unique in the world: to explore these caves is to save or salvage an important human heritage. To ignore them will permanently sacrifice knowledge of incalculable value.

220

# A history of Venetian sculpture of the early Renaissance

## Anne Markham Schulz

192 Bowen Street, Providence, Rhode Island 02906, USA

American, born 3 March 1938. Research associate, Art Department, Brown University. Educated in USA; Ph.D. from Institute of Fine Arts, New York University in 1968.

My project – begun in 1971 and likely to last until 1991 – is to recover Venetian early Renaissance sculpture for historical study and general appreciation and enjoyment. This is not to say that Venetian sculpture is lost and requires discovery in the literal sense. It has always been there: affixed to towering monuments inside dimly-lit churches or dotting the rooflines of lofty buildings. Its very inaccessibility, however, has resulted in sovereign neglect.

Ignored by most scholars of the Renaissance, touched on distractedly by a few, unknown to the educated public at large, Venetian early Renaissance sculpture might just as well lie buried in the ground. And yet, it is among the very finest in terms of sheer artistic quality, and that in a period which worked to an extraordinarily high standard. My own fixed purpose, therefore, has been to bring these works back to the light of scholarly and general esteem, by systematically publishing them, first in detail studies that break the material down into manageable increments and make it accessible to specialists, then in the form of a synthetic history of Venetian early Renaissance sculpture that brings the whole rich field to the attention of all who care.

### Why has Venetian sculpture been neglected?

Neglect of Venetian sculpture has several explanations. Very few pieces are signed, and extant archival documentation is extremely fragmentary. The scholar, therefore, confronts a chaos of anonymous and undated works of art from which it is not easy to extract a coherent pattern. Not suprisingly, art historians have preferred to pursue subjects less fraught with difficulties and have published little on the subject. The absence of a substantial secondary literature, in turn, has acted as a deterrent to further study and has confirmed the prevailing but mistaken view of Venetian sculpture's artistic insignificance. But more responsible still for the neglect of Venetian sculpture is the fact that most of the major monuments have remained *in situ*: few pieces are preserved in the museums of Europe or North America, and even within Venice itself there are no public collections where prime examples are assembled and on view.

*Antonio Lombardo, ceiling of the cirborium, Zen Chapel, St. Mark's Cathedral, Venice. This photograph had to be taken with the photographer and camera upside down.*

*Prophet on roofline of north façade, St Mark's Cathedral, Venice. This shows the extent to which Italian stone statues, located out-of-doors, have suffered from weathering. Marble statuary has suffered even more. (opposite)*

Most Venetian sculpture, made for tombs or as ecclesiastical decoration, is situated high on the walls or façades of churches where close inspection is impossible, and where, even with the aid of binoculars, the sculpture can hardly be seen.

### Analyzing the sculptures at first-hand

My first objective was to see and analyze at first-hand the sculptures themselves. Though this must seem so obvious to scientists as not even to require mention, the fact is that, among students of sculpture, I believe I am unique in my insistence upon seeing from anear and from every angle, newly cleaned, and in light that makes close observation possible, the objects which I mean to classify. On more than one occasion, I suspect, I have been the first person to have seen a statue since it left the sculptor's workshop 500 years ago.

In the case of most Venetian sculpture, and, indeed, pre-modern sculpture in general, first-hand observation is possible only from scaffolds, sometimes 20 or 30 metres in height and stretching across an entire monument or façade, and erected at a cost which is not only beyond the means of an individual scholar, but beyond the means of the Italian superintendency of monuments. The erection of scaffolds has enabled me to gather the following data for hundreds of individual statues: measurements, descriptions of figures and facial type, pose, attributes, and costume, identification of materials, and record of inscriptions. In addition, a close study of hundreds of statues has enabled me to distinguish among the styles of different epochs and different sculptors, to assign to their rightful authors a great number of works that were previously anonymous or misattributed, and thus to begin to chart a history of the development of Venetian Renaissance sculpture. A second advantage of scaffolding was that it has permitted a complete photographic record of every work under consideration.

222

However, first-hand study and photography of Venetian sculpture was only the beginning of my work. With the raw data in hand, I had then to discover the historical circumstances surrounding the creation of each work and this has involved wide reading in eight languages and archive combing in numerous cities.

## Collecting the findings together in a book

The fruit of these researches has been two books, two monographs, and 14 articles. In addition, I have more than half finished a book on the early sixteenth-century sculptors Giambattista and Lorenzo Bregno. This done, I intend to write separate studies on Antonio Minello and Giammaria Mosca. My ultimate goal, however, is to combine and synthesize my findings in one comprehensive volume. Central to the purpose of my book will be the tracing of the evolution of the style of Venetian sculpture, as a record of both the internal development of individual artists and the play of external influences.

Even at the beginning, I never doubted the validity of a study of Venetian sculpture. But it was only upon a nearer acquaintance with particular works that I came to appreciate their extraordinary quality. Therefore, for its own sake as well as for the sake of its historical implications, Venetian sculpture deserves to be studied. But if so, it is urgent that it be studied now, for it is especially vulnerable to the ravages of weather and pollution. If these sculptures are not photographed and studied now, it may soon be too late to do so.

223

# Rediscovering the "Paper Age" of antiquity and Man's early flight

## Isadore William Deiches

14 Railway Square, Brentwood, Essex CM14 4LN, UK

British, born 9 September 1933. Free-lance researcher and author. Educated in UK; studied (Archaeology) part time at Morely College, London.

We tend to see technology as something that began with the Industrial Revolution, barely 200 years ago, but there is spectacular evidence that many ancient civilizations attained a level of technological sophistication which may well have surpassed even our own. This project argues that the ancients built and flew aircraft, applying principles and processes which we are only now rediscovering.

### Aviation in antiquity

To most people today, the era of flight dates back to AD 1709, when Father Bartolomeu de Gusmão demonstrated a small hot-air balloon, or to 1783 when the Montgolfier brothers used a much larger hot-air balloon, or finally, to 1903, when the Wright brothers launched the first man-carrying powered aircraft. My rediscovery of the "Paper Age" and of ancient aircraft came quite by accident in 1982, during an attempt to determine whether a picture of a pectoral (breastplate) belonging to King Tutenkhamon (ca. 1,350 BC) could actually be a scale plan of a flying apparatus. The picture was enlarged with the aid of a photocopier, and various component paper parts were dismantled and re-arranged into a flying bird using every part of the plan, without any additions or subtractions except adhesive. To our amazement the bird we had created from the pectoral flew across my study, flapping its wings. This led me to a more detailed analysis of the Paper Age, although I have encountered one major obstacle: even modern books on the ancient world (especially Egypt) are based on the works and the findings of Victorian archaeologists and historians who knew nothing of flight and therefore interpreted ancient artifacts and relics of the past in the context of myths, magic, religion, rites, etc.

Using material from Ancient Egypt, Persia, India, China, Japan, Mexico, Colombia and elsewhere, I have now built over 300 flying scale-models of ancient aircraft, including hot-air balloons and airships together with similar models of boats, portable bridges and flying toys. Paper was pentiful in these countries and proved an obvious construction material for our ancestors. When

*An unusual ancient Egyptian aircraft or glider seaplane evolved by the Egyptians from their study of the waterfowl. This model was reassembled from an Egyptian vignette.*

glued in multilayer structures, using a simple gelatine glue, it is strong but still light and flexible and, on impact, springs back to its original shape. It can also be made fireproof, and is easy to repair.

## The Paper Age

Having made over 300 aircraft and finding them all airworthy, I would have to concede either that I am the world's greatest paper plane designer – or that I have rediscovered an important era of ancient history: the Paper Age. My task has been simplified though by my discovery that there seems to be a code of symbols – understood throughout the ancient world – to help decipher plans in ancient artifacts. The aircraft I have built are extremely strong, and tests with weights indicate that a full-size aircraft could carry a pilot who would control the flight by the movement of his body which was used as a ballast weight.

In ancient times, aircraft were used for the same purpose as they are today, for travel and for war: land travel was difficult and dangerous and the ability to drop bundles of arrows and spears from the air, as was done in the First World War, provided clear strategic advantages. This theory is partially substantiated by the discovery in the Middle East of a mass grave of soldiers whose bodies have been pierced from head to foot by arrows that can only have been dropped from the air.

Nearly all the countries that have used these paper aircraft had a mountainous terrain, and the aircraft were carried and kept aloft by thermal currents; the use of ridge waves may have enabled an early flyer to cover hundreds of kilometres in the same way as today's glider pilots. The aircraft were launched from hot-air balloons and airships or down specially prepared paper runways laid on to the steep inclines of pyramids as in Egypt and Central and South America. I have also discovered three airfields: at Queen Hatshepsut's funerary temple in Egypt, at Baalbek in the Lebanon, and at Kos in Greece.

*Ancient Egyptian flying scale-model aircraft which has been flight-tested and proven. It was taken from a pectoral found in the tomb of Tutenkhamon.*

## Plans for a full-scale flying model

Over the past three-and-a-half years, my studies have attracted considerable attention; I have appeared on international television, been interviewed on the radio, have figured in both the local and national press, and have held two exhibitions of my work. My name also appears in the glider section of the *Guinness Book of Records*. However, my greatest ambition is to build a full-scale flying model capable of taking a pilot aloft and, if I find a suitable workshop, I may be able to demonstrate to the world what it (and I) previously thought impossible. Above all, I believe that the Paper Age is as important as the Stone Age, Iron Age and the Bronze Age. Ancient writings have substantiated many of my theories and, for example, the University of Sanskrit Research at Mysore, India, has recently translated a manuscript recounting details that date back to unknown antiquity and contain 230 stanzas describing every possible aspect of flying – and even how pilots in different aircraft could communicate with each other.

This project tends to turn upside-down traditional interpretations of familiar relics. One can perceive an ancient world linked as a global village with networks of communication and transportation, and I believe that modern aviation may learn from the gliding techniques and aircraft configurations employed by the ancient civilizations. What has been discovered should be approached with an open mind – surely we owe the ancients at least that much.

# Geoglyphs in the Iquique Province of northern Chile

## Sixto Guillermo Fernandez

**Honourable Mention**
**The Rolex Awards for Enterprise – 1987**

Armada de Chile 2211, Iquique, Chile

Chilean, born 23 September 1941. Supervisor, Mining Properties Department, Sociedad Minera "La Cascada". Educated in Chile; graduated (Technical Draughtsmanship) from University of Chile in 1966.

Reports in archaeological publications of geoglyphs (figures carved in planes and slopes of canyons) in northern Chile produced using techniques similar to those employed for the Nazca lines and figures in Peru stimulated us to make a number of major trips through the Atacama desert and familiarize ourselves with the figures described in the literature. However, as our interest grew, we became involved in more serious studies and have now located further sites containing almost 8,000 figures, a large portion being discoveries – although some are rediscoveries.

Our studies have now generated such a large amount of information that we have been forced to design a "methodology" for the orderly and coherent dissemination of data on this invaluable prehispanic heritage to researchers as a whole. The correct processing of this information will permit the compilation of a descriptive file for use as a data base for specialists; the delineation of new target areas for exploration; and chronological and cultural correlation in the field of art, linguistics, astronomy, anthropology, religion, etc.

### A programme for a geoglyph inventory

Our aim is to supplement and classify the information we have collected, so as to finalize the "methodology" we have developed pragmatically over the years. An immediate outcome should be the identification of a number of new target zones for exploration to expand the geoglyph inventory of northern Chile. The various steps involved include: implementing the methodology we have developed for the classification and categorization of geoglyph information; additional desk and field work on data for each figure we have located; expansion of our knowledge of the significance, functions, use and dating of geoglyphs, by correlations and computerized statistical processing of the data; progress in the development of a geoglyph inventory and the dissemination of our findings.

It will first be necessary to prepare a card containing the data for each figure, arranged in geographic order to describe the different styles and allow

227

*The geoglyph at Ariquilda.*

correlations to be made with other forms of rupestrian art in the area. These findings will give us an insight into the way in which prehispanic populations lived and, possibly, show associations between the geoglyphs and contemporary desert water resources. We believe there may be relationships between this form of Chilean rupestrian art and similar examples at other sites on the American continent, such as for example, Paracas, Nazca, Palpa. Nevertheless, the real meaning of these figures may long remain an enigma.

**Building on an already large base**

To date, we have built up a collection of 5,500 slides and 500 cartographic, climatic, topographic, archaeological and geomorphological items. Field trips will be organized to document geographic locations, and record visual findings, take measurements, determine geomagnetic orientations and collect data on soil texture and quality, furrow depth, erosion, and relation with other groups, water sources, archaeological sites, etc. In addition, topographic surveys will be made to determine any intentional deformation of perspective; it is hoped that we will continue to receive the assistance of the Chilean Air Force in aircraft reconnaissance and surveying.

The existing and newly acquired data will be processed to form the complete descriptive and technical inventory. However, in view of the immense quantity of documentation involved, it will be necessary to use a computer to search for correlations. The magnitude of the task can be seen from the fact that the data for each figure comprises 553 characters; for 8,000 figures, we will be handling some 4.5 million characters.

The geoglyphs of northern Chile are unique and the only comparable findings are those of Nazca, Palpa and Paracas in Peru and of the Sonora Desert in Mexico and California. They are under growing threat from erosion and they need to be documented before it is too late. Little research has been done on

*A highly complex geoglyph on the side of Monos Hill.*

them, and no studies have looked at the individual figures in an attempt to establish correlations with archaeological findings, water resources, prehispanic travel routes and other forms of prehispanic art (basketry, ceramics, textiles, silverware, etc.). Nor has anyone studied their orientation in relation to roads, hills, stars, settlements, etc.

## The impact of our research

A study such as ours would expand archaeological knowledge of the area, establish a Chilean inventory which would provide a significant contribution to the work of the International Council on Monuments and Sites, and might stimulate a systematic study of rupestrian art in northern Chile. Finally, the processed data should prove of value not only to archaeologists and students of rupestrian art but also to water resource planners, artists, farmers and craftsmen, tourism authorities and agencies, and various cultural organizations.

# Archaeological and historical remains in southern Iran

## Reinhard Pohanka

35/9 Weinberggasse, 1190 Vienna, Austria

Austrian, born 15 May 1954. Archaeologist. Educated in Austria; Ph.D.
(Archaeology and Ancient History) from University of Vienna in 1981.

The aim of this project is to explore historical sites and archaeological remains in the province of Laristan, between the towns of Shiraz and Bander Abbas in southern Iran. Measuring some 130,000 km$^2$ in area, it is far from the main traffic routes and has never been properly surveyed because of security risks and the difficulties of the semi-arid topography.

### Compiling the history of Laristan

The work involved comprises the collection and/or compilation of all historical sources from earliest times to the present, including: the writings of European travellers of the sixteenth, seventeenth and eighteenth centuries, and histories of the leading Muslim families of Laristan; pictures, maps, drawings and photographs of Laristan, including satellite photographs – since aerial surveys are not currently available in Iran; and small artifacts such as coins, ceramics, books and manuscripts. Archaeological surveys will also be carried out with a view to the production of maps, photographs and tape recordings.

I started the project with the help of the Iranian Commission of the Austrian Academy of Sciences in 1982; thereafter, until 1985, I worked in the region of Laristan several months each year. The first task was to consult all known and available information about Laristan in the libraries of Europe and Iran and this entailed several months in the libraries of Teheran, Paris, London and Vienna.

For the second phase, I moved to Laristan and began an exploration of the ancient traffic routes which were of some considerable significance, because since the time of the Achaemenidae, Laristan has held an important place in the movement of trade between the Iranian Highlands and the Persian Gulf region. The third phase took me to an exploration of the network of the trading towns and resting places (caravanserais) and the old fortresses which were built to protect the commercial traffic. Fourthly, I collected from the local inhabitants as much information as I could about Laristan in the form of myths, legends and oral history, together with facts about little known buildings, inscriptions and places of historical interest.

In the fifth phase, I collected information about the religions of Laristan and of the different sanctuaries like gonbads (mausoleums), imamzadehs (sanctuaries) and mosques, and about the religious customs of the Iranians and Kashgais. In the final phase, I worked together with an architect to compile data on local forms of building in clay, wood and stone, since there is considerable danger that the practice of these art and craft forms will be lost in the near future.

Normally, I like to work alone and independently and try to establish a good relationship with the nomadic people of the Kashgais. The fieldwork itself is done using a Land Rover, but from time to time the topography of the country is such that I have to take to horseback or even make use of my experience as a mountain climber since some of the fortresses are located on high mountain cliffs. The information that is gathered is stored in a small computer using a specially developed programme. I hope that the use of the computer will allow me to establish new correlations between the archaeology of Laristan and that of the adjoining regions.

## First results

The difficulties that Iran is currently going through have obviously not accelerated the completion of my work; nevertheless, it is progressing and I estimate that the research will be completed and the findings published in 1990. So far, I have been able to survey only certain parts of Laristan. However, in the city of Lar, the principal town of Laristan, I have, for example, found more than 20 places of archaeological interest, including two major fortresses and one of the largest existing ensembles from Safavid times in Iran (comprising three important caravanserais, a bazaar and a garden palace). To the south of Fasa, I hit upon the remains of an Achaemenid palace and, in the town of Benaru, an unknown stone relief from Sassanid times. The discovery of over 50 newly found caravanserais, several hundred imamzadehs, old graveyards, mosques,

*Overview of the older parts of the City of Lar, with the Mausoleum of Mir Ali ebn Hosein, dating from the twelfth century.*

231

*Caravanserai near Bander Abbas on the shores of the Persian Gulf, dating from the sixteenth century.*

castles and prehistoric sites have come together to offer a completely new image of the region of Laristan.

It is widely believed that from the earliest times to the present day, Laristan was a desert region, sparsely populated and inhabited only by nomads. The evidence provided by my new finds in Laristan has, however, proven that this was not the case, and it is now clear that, in ancient times, Laristan must have been a very rich country, perhaps equal in status to the famous region of Fars, with its towns of Persepolis and Istakhr. During the period of the Islamic conquest, most of the towns, castles and roads were, nevertheless, destroyed and it was not until trade with India commenced in the sixteenth and seventeenth centuries that Laristan regained, for a while at least, some of its ancient glory. Finally, for the past two centuries, Laristan has been a forgotten country.

## Continuing the efforts

To date, I have now been able to inventory over 1,500 major items of data for publication about the region, and the main document will be published in the next year. Next year, too, I hope to be able to return to Laristan to continue my research.

# Protecting the fossil deposits of the Araripe Plateau

## Alexander Wilhelm Armin Kellner

36 rua Aires Saldanha, Apt. C-01, 22060 Copacabana, Rio de Janeiro-RJ, Brazil

Austrian, born 26 September 1961. Researcher, National Department of Mineral Production. Educated in Brazil; currently doing postgraduate studies (Geology) at Federal University of Rio de Janeiro.

The fossil deposits at the Araripe Plateau (Chapada do Araripe) in Brazil are one of the world's largest. This project aims to warn the scientific community of possible depredation of these deposits due to clandestine fossil trading, and proposes to: organize a library about the region; verify existing information; obtain new data; and publish a book containing an analysis of the trade in fossils in Brazil and photographs of the main fossils of the region.

### One of the world's major fossil sites

The Araripe Plateau is situated on the borders of the states of Ceará, Pernambuco and Piauí, in the north-east of Brazil. The first record of fossil deposits in that region dates from reports by two German researchers in the early nineteenth century but stratigraphic explorations were not carried out in the region until 1913; these revealed, on the lower part of the sequence, a basal conglomerate followed by sandstone and then a calcareous substance which the explorers at the time called the Santana Formation, with sandstone on top. Considerable research has been made of these units, which correspond to the following formations and ages: Cariri (Devonian), Brejo Santo (Neojurassic), Missão Velha (Eocretaceous), Santana (Aptian-Albian) and Exu (Albian).

Nevertheless, exploratory work still remains to be done in the Araripe Plateau region especially on the geological evolution and the fossiliferous content of this basin, of which the Santana Formation is the largest. This stratigraphical unit is divided into three sections (Crato, Ipubi and Romualdo) containing many different species of plants, pollens, molluscs, arachnids (scorpion), fishes, turtles, crocodilians, dinosaurs and pterosaurs (flying reptiles), etc., some of them of great interest to palaeontologists everywhere.

### A clandestine trade in fossils

The fossil deposits in the Araripe Plateau region are significantly endangered by the clandestine trade in fossils. The only Brazilian legislation relating to fossils is

233

a law which prohibits fossils from being dug up without the permission of the National Department of Mineral Production; however, the law is not enforced and, consequently, in recent years the illegal trade in fossils has expanded enormously. In fact, souvenir shops in all the main towns in Brazil freely display and sell fossils from the Santana Formation. Moreover, the smuggling trade is also growing. The situation has become so critical that, during the IXth Brazilian Congress of Palaeontology held in September 1985, an appeal was made to all palaeontologists throughout the world to concentrate their research on the Araripe Plateau deposits before all material is lost.

## A three-part project

The first part of the project consists in establishing a comprehensive library of all the research published on the region. The collection of material has already begun and of the 92 recorded titles, we have acquired 45 so far. We estimate that there are some 150 titles and once these have been collected, they will be deposited with the National Department of Mineral Production in Rio de Janeiro, for use by any research workers interested in the area.

The second part will be devoted to on-the-spot verification of existing information and to collection of new data. As far as the stratigraphic studies are concerned, more field work will be needed to resolve the question surrounding the "Fish horizon", where the majority of fossils are found. Our studies would concentrate on evidence of marine influence in the region during the Cretaceous age, since this is fundamental to a proper understanding of the evolution and history of the Araripe basin. A further requirement would be to map the region and catalogue the main fossil locations, compiling, wherever possible, a complete list of the animal species found there. An important step will be an investigation of the clandestine trade in fossils; we will look at how the major sales outlets operate, calculate the number of fossils extracted annually, etc.

*The major portion of the fossils found in the Araripe Plateau are those of fishes. Shown here is a fossil of* Iemanja palma.

234

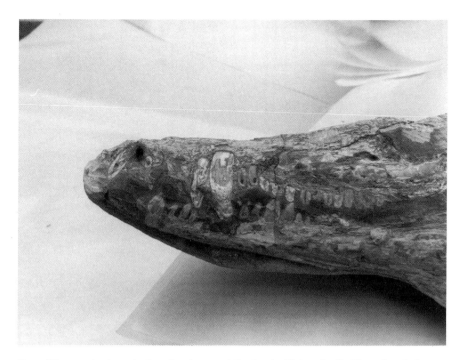

*Crocodilian remains have also been found amongst the Araripe Plateau fossils. Shown here is the second crocodilian fossil to have been discovered* officially. *It was in the hands of an illegal fossil dealer who was asking US$ 50,000 for it.*

Lastly, we will write a book on the Araripe Plateau region explaining the scientific importance of fossils, listing the various types of fossil found on the Araripe Plateau and giving a summary of the main characteristics and photographs of the most important fossils. This will be followed by a history of this fossil basin, its evolution and its inhabitants and their connection with the fossils. A chapter will be devoted to the clandestine trade in fossils, the existing legislation concerning this problem in Brazil and elsewhere, and proposals will be formulated on how an end could be put to the current situation (creation of a fossil park).

## A way of alerting the authorities

We are aware that this project cannot provide the fossil deposits of the Araripe Plateau protection from complete destruction; for only Federal or State action, together with revision of the current legislation and the institution of regulations prohibiting the smuggling of this type of scientific specimens, can do that. However, our project, together with the publication of our book, will serve to alert the responsible authorities and public opinion as to the urgent need for a solution to this question. These fossils are part of the Brazilian national heritage and are crucial to an understanding of past life on this planet; their protection, therefore, is not just a necessity but a duty.

# The Andros Project – The 1987 international Blue Holes project

*Robert John Palmer*

**Honourable Mention**
**The Rolex Awards for Enterprise – 1987**

Department of Geography, University of Bristol, University Road, Bristol BS8 1SS, UK

British, born 18 October 1951. Postgraduate student. Educated in UK; preparing M.Phil. thesis (Human Impact on Blue Holes) at University of Bristol.

Following six years of research and exploration by members of the British Cave Diving Group and the Cave Diving Section of the US National Speleological Society, a major scientific research project will be mounted in mid-1987 to study the underwater cave systems ("Blue Holes") of Andros Island, in the Bahamas group. The scientific programme will be divided into four integrated aspects: exploration and survey; geology; hydrology; and biology. In addition, it will make a contribution to ongoing conservation and management activities.

## Exploration and survey

Of the known Blue Hole sites on South Andros (from the South Bight to the southern extreme of the island), fewer than a dozen have been explored to any significant degree and, consequently, experienced divers from the United Kingdom and the USA will access every known site and survey any passages discovered within. New techniques and equipment will enable expedition divers to work more safely at depth and at increased distances within the caves, allowing the full range of Pleistocene development and deposition to be accessed. Long-distance explorations (in excess of 1,000 m) within the South Bight Caves will enable the more remote environments of marine Blue Holes to be more closely studied.

## Geological programme

The Blue Holes offer an unusual opportunity to physically access the interior of one of the world's largest carbonate platforms. Geological studies will concentrate both on the relationship of Blue Hole development to climatic and sea-level change in response to glacial fluctuations during the Pleistocene, and their relationship to the structural geology and diagenetic processes (by which deposited carbonate material becomes sedimentary rock) at work within the saturated island bedrock. Special attention will be paid to the diagenesis of the mixing zone between fresh and saline waters, thought to be one of the areas in which dolomitization of calcium carbonate may take place. Such studies have considerable significance to the petrochemical industry; the mixing zone environment is one in which oil deposits are thought to initially form, and direct access to such zones has hitherto been impossible. Analysis of wall rock, speleothems (stalactites and stalagmites formed during periods of low sea levels) and sediments from the full, accessible range of cave and rock deposits will be undertaken to provide a comprehensive record of geological and climatic change during the late Pleistocene.

## Hydrological programme

A comprehensive examination will be made of the water chemistry throughout the vertical water column from the top of the freshwater lens (the reservoir of accumulated rainwater that lies below the island surface, floating in suspension on the denser saltwater beneath) to the deep saline phreatic waters which underly the mixing zone (the region of diffusion between the fresh and the saline water at the base of the lens). Studies will be made of the sub-island tidal flow associated with the mixing zone in an attempt to define the causal factors behind this significant hydrodynamic movement. Data compiled will cover salinity, pH values, dissolved oxygen, turbidity and temperatures, and will include chemical analysis to determine other significant factors which may have an effect on the caves, their structure or their fauna. Attention will be paid to the previously unreported bacterial activity immediately above the mixing zone throughout these caves, and the effect its reducing action has on both cave formation, cave deposits and cave life.

## Biological programme

The biological aspects of the Project include an examination of the ecology of the inland and marine Blue Holes, and of the crevicular and surface environments associated with the freshwater lens. In the Marine Holes, the effects of tidally related currents on the biotic structure of the entrance and cave environments will be closely monitored, and the occurrence and distribution of species with increasing penetration into the caves will be examined, as well as studying the relationship of Blue Holes to surrounding marine environments.

Inland Blue Holes have been found to contain an unusual and little studied cave adapted fauna that appears to have very close links with Mesozoic marine fauna. Preliminary studies of South Andros caves have found them to contain a prolific population of these animals, including previously unrecorded species. Their accessibility makes them ideally suited as research sites for such faunal studies, and additional work will be directed at the apparent relationship of this fauna to bacterial activity at the mixing zone. The Andros Project will seek to establish the parameters of the inland "deep cave" environment, in an attempt to gain a more complete insight into the ecology of this peculiar and isolated "Lost World" and the living fossils within it.

Studies of the freshwater fauna inhabiting the crevicular environment within the freshwater lens above will form a link between the deep cave fauna and that of the surface above, and may have a relationship to water quality within the

237

*Blue Holes are underwater cave networks. The stalactites and stalagmites within their passages are relics of the ice ages when sea levels fell by over 100 m and the caves were, for a time, filled by air.*

lens itself. Studies of the freshwater fauna of isolated inland lakes and creek remnants from higher sea levels have, on other islands, revealed unusual relict fauna, trapped in such sites by retreating sea levels. These studies will be extended on Andros, and, together with the biological and geological programmes, should reveal a great deal about climatic and biotic changes in the region in response to glacial fluctuations during the Pleistocene Ice Ages.

## Conservation and management

The Bahamas National Trust is undertaking a long-term conservation and management programme within the Bahamas. The terrestial side is well in the planning stage but, so far, there has been a lack of co-ordination in establishing such a strategy for Blue Hole environments. The Bahamas contain the most important and largest concentration of such sites on our planet, and several have already come under severe pressure from a variety of forms of human impact: uncontrolled tourist diving (both dangerous and destructive), industrial and domestic pollution, bleaching, overfishing and land use change. Arising from the work of the Andros Project – the first co-ordinated scientific examination of the Blue Holes and their related environments – it is hoped that such a conservation and management policy can be established to ensure the protection and survival of one of the most unusual, the most beautiful and the most fascinating environments yet to be discovered beneath our planet.

# A squid's eye view of the mesopelagic ocean

## Ronald Keith O'Dor

1181 South Park Street, Halifax, Nova Scotia B3H 2W9, Canada

American, born 20 September 1944. Professor of Biology, Dalhousie University, Halifax, Nova Scotia, Canada. Educated in USA and Canada; Ph.D. (Physiology) from University of British Columbia in 1971.

Although the oceans are often considered one of the earth's last frontiers, we have acquired some familiarity with the top 50 m – the zone of greatest biological production – and are exploring the bottom 50 m for mineral wealth, etc. The vast volume in between is now the only true *aqua incognita* remaining. What little we know of this mesopelagic zone comes largely from observations of its few commercially important inhabitants such as whales and tuna. The schools of squid, which are food for whales and tuna, graze small zooplankters and have a direct link to the productivity of the sea. Because of their limited reserves and short life cycles, they measure and reflect the condition of the sea with their lives.

### Studying the squid in captivity

The origin of this project was a 1976 study in which we introduced oceanic squid of the ommastrephes genus (*Illex illecebrosus*) into a 15-m diameter sea water aquarium in the Aquatron Laboratory at Dalhousie University for short-term studies on the hormonal control of their reproduction. To our surprise, these delicate animals, which had never survived for more than a few weeks in captivity, did very well in the large pool and, in subsequent long-term studies, we eventually held schools of squid until they ended their life cycle by spawning in captivity.

The species' mating process and spawn had never been seen in nature, and there was only the scantiest information on their reproductive biology. Experiments showing that eggs would not hatch at the temperatures found where the adults are fished, combined with collection of juveniles from the northern edge of the Gulf Stream, led to a hypothesis that adult squid, from as far north as Newfoundland, migrate to breeding grounds off Florida, where they spawn in the Stream to produce larvae which are carried back to the rich feeding areas in the North. Since 1983, I have been testing this hypothesis and developing a survey routine which will allow abundance predictions so that

239

fishing can be adjusted to stock size. The initial hypothesis of a life cycle essentially driven by this great current system has been confirmed, and the tool we developed for studying the population dynamics has proved sufficiently promising that we have been asked to organize a proposal for an International Recruitment Programme on cephalopods for UNESCO. Our proposal was endorsed last year by the Cephalopod International Advisory Council and is currently under consideration as a model for a global programme to study ways of predicting the number of juveniles recruited annually into cephalopod fisheries. The key to this approach is recognition that, while adults of this species are often widely distributed, suitable nursery areas are more restricted. Thus small-scale surveys of nursery areas can produce predictions applicable to commercial fisheries over large areas.

## Verifying a hypothesis on the squid's life cycle

I am neither enterprising nor egotistic enough to claim this ten-year, multi-national project as my proposal, although I do think my personal involvement in various collaborations as an independent university researcher has been and will continue to be a significant factor in its development. The project I wish to claim as my own is the "acid test" of the hypothesis: to actually see and film the spawning process in the mysterious mid-ocean where it occurs. This goal alone, however, does not justify the project. The real justification comes from the fact that, to ensure the survival of the species, these squid apparently must travel thousands of kilometres to a precise point in three-dimensional space to release their eggs into a powerful river flowing through a vast ocean, which, to my senses, has no landmarks. To accomplish this, these animals must perceive, in this world of sameness, a complex and fascinating landscape. I want to follow them and try to understand how one "sees" the mountains and valleys of this new world.

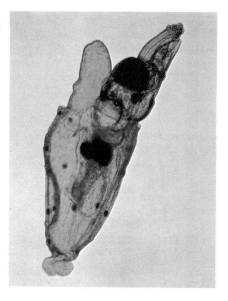

*The world's largest squid fisheries are based on tiny oigopsids like this* Illex illecebrosus, *hatched in captivity. Just over a millimetre long, these minute "jet-setters" have already travelled hundreds of kilometres in current-borne egg masses.*

*Enormous schools of* Illex illecebrosus *and other oigopsid squid navigate the mid-ocean depths largely unseen by man. If we understood their movements, we could tap this underutilized food resource.*

Filming the event may turn out to be relatively straightforward, but it will not be cheap. The identification of numerous newly hatched larvae in the area of the Florida Straits indicate that spawning takes place there, and there is one unpublished report of dead, post-spawning adults of the genus Illex near Fort Pierce, Florida. We have begun discussions with researchers at the Harbour Branch Foundation in Fort Pierce about using the Johnson Sealink submersible, a stabilized plastic bubble with photographic and sampling equipment capable of all the required depths. If funding is found, prospects are good.

### Tagging as a method of tracking squid

If our current beliefs about the site and timing of spawning prove incorrect, and we fail in the initial attempt, we are developing an approach which should eventually guarantee success. We have produced and tested ultrasonically transmitting tags which fit inside the mantles of squid. Squid carrying these tags rejoin their schools, feed and have survived for several days in tests in captivity. This technique should permit the use of tags large and powerful enough to be tracked at sea, and we are working with colleagues in Fisheries and Oceans Canada to fit out a vessel for such work. Since squid heading south seem to have no purpose but to mate, spawn and die, any squid caught and tagged on the southward migration could hopefully lead us to the spawning grounds.

# Preservation of the Chaouia Berbers in the Aurès Mountains of Algeria

## Christian Sorand

8 rue Thomas Edison, 13200 Arles, France

French, born 17 May 1950. English teacher. Educated in France; M.A. (Applied Linguistics) from Provence University, Aix-Marseilles in 1974.

Although a number of studies have already been made and a number of books written on Berbers, much still remains to be done. In particular, the Kabyles and Tuareg – to mention only two of the most noted Algerian Berber groups – have attracted considerable attention, but not so the Chaouia. My intention, then, is to fill a gap on a subject which will undoubtedly prove to be rich both in learning and teaching, and at the same time try to preserve a civilization which is doomed to disappear unless adequate measures are taken.

In achieving this objective my project will aim to complete ongoing studies of the Chaouia Berbers by a further period of field research in the Aurès Mountains with a view to collecting valuable artifacts and reconstructing historical sites. By making a full survey and publishing a book on the results, the project would help preserve the heritage of a dying community, the life and traditions of which may well be of prime importance in the knowledge of the Mediterranean world.

### The Chaouia and their environment

The Aurès Mountains – a sort of inland island – contain what are probably the last vestiges of the Berber antiquity, and are a living testimony to an age-old Berber way of life of utmost importance in Mediterranean and African studies. Moreover, amongst the Berbers of Northern Africa, the Chaouia play a unique role, and it is my intention to situate them more accurately in the long chain of peoples who, from the shores of the Atlantic, to the sands of Egypt and as far away as the Niger, have given birth to a series of modern nations. These people thirst for recognition but political factors have deprived them of that right.

The objectives of my project are to resume field studies and complete the research that I have already commenced, to catalogue utilitarian or decorative works of craftsmanship, to stimulate the Chaouia's interest in their own heritage, to establish a Museum of the Aurès Mountains displaying and preserving artifacts or documents of historical value, and possibly to help restore a small number of historical or architectural sites.

242

## Support from the Berber community

Having spent four years in the area, I can count on the support and assistance of numerous Berber friends who are acquainted with this project and this strengthens my belief that the project can be successfully completed.

My plan would be to live in one of the Aurassian villages and share the life of its inhabitants in order to acquaint them with and interest them in my aims. Some two years would be required for the initial survey, and its start-up would attract the attention of the Algerian Government whose assistance, sympathy and approval need to be sought.

I personally would need to obtain an official leave from the French Ministry of Education and the sponsorship of the French State Department would also be required.

## Answering key questions of Berber history

My study on the Chaouia Berbers would also help answer a number of key questions of Berber history which still remain unanswered, such as why the Aurès Mountains have remained an untouched stronghold for as far as historical records are available, the nature of the impact of the Jewish communities of Northern Africa on the Berbers, whether the mysterious – and as yet still undeciphered – inscriptions at the Cretan ruins of Phaestos are of Lybic origin and, consequently, were the Garamantes the harbingers of Greek civilization for other parts of Africa.

A number of other items of interest would also be dealt with including: the use of fibulae for ornamentation among all Berbers; the carved symbols on the wooden gate of the Sidi Okba Mosque; the relationship between two Berber communities – the Jerba inhabitants (the Tunisian island of Jerba has also a prevalent Jewish community preserving an antique synagogue) and those of the

243

*Young girls dressed in Kabyle costume singing at the Berber Festival of Yenni (Kabylie).*

M'Zab; and the Lybic inscriptions at Dougga (Tunisia).

Clearly enough our proposed project could act as a launching pad for future and more general studies on the Berber populations of Africa.

# Discovering, rehabilitating and protecting reptiles in Burma, India and China

## Nicole Andrée Viloteau

**Honourable Mention**
**The Rolex Awards for Enterprise – 1987**

2 rue Blaise Desgoffes, 75006 Paris, France

French, born 20 April 1946. Journalist and photographer. Educated in France; National Fine Arts Diploma in 1970.

---

Nicole Viloteau has felt an intense attraction for nature and its magic spell ever since she was a child, and time has created in her an unshakeable and determined personality which has further strengthened her taste for the solitary discovery of wild nature. During her adolescence, she also developed a passion for the world of reptiles and amphibians and has, since then, devoted the better part of her apparently inexhaustible energy and enthusiasm to the study and conservation of these animals worldwide.

### Working with reptiles from an early age

Scarcely had she finished her studies than she organized a travelling vivarium with which she criss-crossed France for five years, stirring up public interest wherever she went. Having become an expert on snakes and an active member of the Herpetological Society of France, she finally took a major step towards achieving her dream – and began to travel and explore reptiles in their natural surroundings. Since then, she has visited a number of countries in Africa, Australia and Latin America, crossing deserts and jungles in a search for nature's rare reptiles, braving dangers and discomfort for the satisfaction of finding an unknown species.

Her work consists in capturing the reptiles – most of them venomous – which she then studies, photographs and classifies. Thereafter, she releases them again, although a sick reptile may be kept for treatment where necessary; carefully using her tape recorder, she also takes note of the circumstances and ecological context of the capture so that a description can be written up at a later date.

Nicole Viloteau has put together an outstanding collection of documents – mainly photographs – describing her travels and the reptiles she has encountered and this, combined with her journalistic talents, has enabled her to publish a wide range of articles in various magazines and specialized journals. Her achievements in this sector culminated, in autumn 1985, with the publication of *La Femme aux Serpents* (Snake Woman) a striking work recounting her

245

*Nicole Viloteau, during a recent expedition to Australia, handling a king brown, probably the most dangerous snake in that country.*

adventures. Subsequently, at the invitation of the cultural authorities of Gabon, she visited that country to give a series of lectures which received an enthusiastic audience.

## Danger sometimes strikes

The task of tracking and studying poisonous reptiles does, of course, have its dangers and Nicole Viloteau has not always succeeded in bypassing them. On 23 May 1971, she was bitten on the lip by a lethal American rattlesnake which had been placed in an incorrectly labelled sack. Rushed to hospital in a critical state, she was finally saved after two months' treatment by the administration of a new product, calcium heparinate, which had never before been tried on a human patient. This medication is now in general use and Nicole Viloteau is proud to have helped medical progress in this way.

## Plans for future expeditions

Her plans are now to finalize a comprehensive list of the reptile species in Burma, China, India and Thailand and, at the same time, to compile information on the beliefs and legends that surround them. Many of the turtles, tortoises, lizards, snakes and reptiles in these countries are rare and may be on the verge of extinction; it is her hope that the magazine articles she is writing and the second book that she is planning on the basis of this research will make a significant contribution to reptile conservation. She expects to spend about a year on this project, leaving for India in January 1987, and plans have already been finalized for a stay in the Manas and the Kaziranga National Parks; she will subsequently make an expedition to Bhutan where she proposes to live with the local tribesmen in order to learn their survival techniques. This will be followed

*The* Boiga blandingij, *one of the many poisonous snakes studied and photographed by Nicole Viloteau during an expedition to the Ivory Coast.*

by trips to the Kanha National Park in the Bastar region and the Desert National Park in India.

During these trips she will photograph the reptiles and their environment and the animals in their biotopes, and hopes to discover rare species of reptiles and study areas rich in flora and fauna.

Through her books, articles, lectures and radio and television appearances, Nicole Viloteau has opened up the world of reptiles to an ever wider audience. She hopes that this next expedition, compounded with her personal commitment, will enable the cause of nature conservation to progress even further.

# Exploring the underwater island of Cordell Bank, California

## Robert William Schmieder

4295 Walnut Boulevard, Walnut Creek, California 94596, USA

American, born 10 July 1941. Physicist and marine scientist. Educated in USA; Ph.D. (Atomic Physics) from Columbia University, New York in 1968.

We want to carry out a comprehensive exploration of Cordell Bank, an underwater island some 80 km north-west of San Fransico, California; this island has an exceptional biological community that will soon be designated a US National Marine Sanctuary, and is destined for high visibility as a research site. In spite of considerable exploration since 1978, most of the Bank remains unseen and undescribed and we envisage a series of expeditions over a three-year period to reach and describe the major unexplored areas.

### Previous work and general goals

I organized the first exploratory diving expedition to Cordell Bank in 1977–1978 and subsequently formed a non-profit research association called Cordell Bank Expeditions (CBE) which has carried out expeditions under my leadership every year since. The work done is documented in about 20 published reports and papers, eight films and slide shows, about 35 newspaper articles and more than 50 presentations. To date, CBE is the only group that has carried out research on this site and has found that the Bank supports a biological community that is extraordinarily lush and healthy, and visually spectacular. Recognizing the unique value of the Bank as a resource for conservation and research, the National Oceanic and Atmospheric Administration (NOAA) is granting it the status of a US National Marine Sanctuary, the eighth site to be so designated; this will serve to protect the resources of the Bank and stimulate research on the site.

The Bank is described as an "underwater island" because plants and animals living there are, for the most part, stranded. Deep water all around creates a formidable barrier to migration. The community lives in relative isolation, like an island, albeit underwater. There is evidence that some species have been stranded there for thousands of years, and that the entire community has evolved in a semi-insular state. This condition makes Cordell Bank an exceptionally interesting site for marine research.

The project aims to generate a body of data which describes the topography,

248

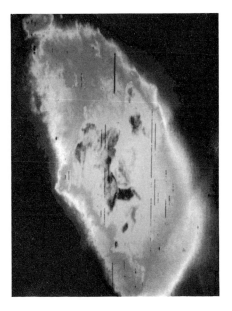

*Image of Cordell Bank generated from the 1985 survey data.*

biota, geology and oceanographic environment of the Bank with a view to understanding the processes controlling the area; perceiving variations in time; and rationally managing the valuable resources on the continental shelf represented by Cordell Bank and other similar areas.

Over the next three years it plans to locate, explore and describe the major unseen areas on the Bank using the newly acquired 12.8 m diving research vessel *Cordell Explorer*. Assuming that this project is completed successfully, we plan to acquire a small manned submersible around 1990 and initiate a new phase of exploration, extending our documentation to deeper waters.

## Methods to be used

The principal method to be used for the field work is scuba diving for the collection of representative specimens and the taking of photographs. Other activities will include direct underwater sketching and verbal description, surface observations, and dredging in areas too deep for diving. Every aspect of the work is thoroughly documented. Diving at Cordell Bank requires considerable preparation and some special techniques. Over the past nine years, we have developed procedures and gear to ensure safety and maximize effectiveness, and the result is a well-organized team focused on the scientific goals of the expeditions.

There is at present no other research group with the ability to carry out this project. Most of the field work has been done with a group of 16–18 divers each making only one dive per day. Most expeditions are completed in two days and, if the weather is good, all divers are able to make dives on both days. The results of a good expedition typically include 300 underwater photographs, 10 kg of specimens, and detailed drawings of the topography.

*A diver from the Cordell Bank Expedition's team checks the time and date after installing a fish trap at a depth of some 45 m on Cordell Bank. With the diver are his specimen collection bag and the descent line anchor.*

During the 1987–1989 period the specific goals will be to: locate as many new sites as possible and examine them by diving; make quantitative measurements of the biota of selected sites; identify candidate sites for long-term study; install preliminary experiments, such as growth platforms, temperature and current meters, etc.; and publish the results.

## Relevance and importance of the project

Offshore and subtidal northern California is practically unexplored and undescribed, and the literature is very incomplete – especially for an area which is an important source of fish and shellfish for human consumption. Cordell Bank itself is in imminent danger of having its fish stocks destroyed by illegal overfishing, of having its invertebrate community damaged by commercial oil development, and of having its fragile and slow-growing hydrocoral forests destroyed by uncontrolled bottom drags and anchors. A large body of data, and development of baseline data for measuring normal conditions, will be necessary before these resources can be comprehended, regulated and conserved.

250

# New evidence on Colonel Fawcett and the lost cities of Brazil

## *René Jean-Antoine Chabbert*

800 Kimberton Road, Apartment H-3, Phoenixville, Pennsylvania 19460, USA

American, born 24 June 1936. Laboratory technician. Educated in France and USA; M.A. (Human Relations) from University of Oklahoma in 1976 and M.A. (Counselling Psychology) from Pepperdine University in 1981.

In 1925, Colonel P.H. Fawcett and his eldest son, Jack, entered the Mato Grosso, north-east of Cuiaba, in search of ancient cities and tribes of light-skinned Indians who, Fawcett believed, were descendants of the survivors of Atlantis. The expedition vanished somewhere near the Rio Tanguro, miles away from where they should have been heading. The goals of the expedition were to locate a city that the Colonel had named "Z" (of which there are no records in the history of Brazil), and to explore the City of 1753 (on which the archives of the National Library in Rio de Janeiro contain a single document). However, I became convinced that if the Colonel was willing to risk his life, and the lives of those dear to him, something must be there waiting to be discovered.

### About the City of 1753

In 1743, a group of Portuguese adventurers left Minas Gerais to find the fabled lost mines of Muribeca, and wandered in the jungles for about ten years. On their way back towards the settlements along the east coast of Brazil, they came upon a large, deserted city nested on a plateau, at the foot of a mountain chain in which the architecture was similar to that of ancient Greece. Some of the buildings had inscriptions on them, which they recorded. The unique feature of the city was a river, which started in front of the main square. Following it, after three days' march, they arrived at some waterfalls. Near them, tunnels had been dug into the side of a mountain. The entrance to one of these tunnels was sealed by a huge stone slab, with strange carvings upon it, similar to the ones seen in the city. The year was 1753, and later, that city became known as the City of 1753. A year later, nearing civilization, the Portuguese sent an Indian messenger with a brief to the Viceroy of Bahia, informing him of the find; but the adventurers never completed the voyage. A century later, that letter became document No. 512.

My research on the lost City of 1753 showed that the few explorers who had searched for it had concentrated in totally different areas, hundreds of

251

kilometres apart. In the 1840s, Canon Benigno investigated the region south/south-west of Bahia. Fawcett felt that the city was roughly south of Xique-Xique, and in 1948, Hugh McCarthy, an admirer of the Colonel, followed the Juruena River, some 480 km west of Cuiaba. The distance between the Juruena and Bahia is almost 2,400 km. Fawcett had stated in his travel notes that the primary target "Z", the Great Objective, was due west of Xique-Xique, and 1753 due south. Why was he starting 1,600 km to the west? The reason given was that he wanted to check out an ancient tower, illuminated at night, and causing great terror amongst the Indians.

To me, this was not a justification, but rather an excuse to conceal the real locations of the cities. From Xique-Xique, both "Z" and 1753 would have been easy to reach. The cities should have come first, and then, the tower, at a later date. If Colonel Fawcett had started from Cuiaba, it was not because of the ancient tower; it must have been because at least "Z", and perhaps 1753 as well, were somewhere between Cuiaba and Xique-Xique. I would work with that assumption in mind.

## Understanding Document 512

Document 512 was Fawcett's only concrete evidence of the existence of a lost city in the Brazilian wilderness. The Portuguese adventurers had realized the great wealth potentials which they had uncovered and, to be assured of their fair share, their report was written to ensure their movements could not be traced. Colonel Fawcett had realized that the document had been written in a deceptive manner; however, he never informed his family. Yet, I was sure that the sequences of geographical features mentioned in the document must be correct, since everything else had been so carefully disguised. The Portuguese had climbed a chain of mountains, from the top they could see a plateau where 1753 stood, a river started within the city, and, following it, you would reach some falls. All I had to do was to find these features, and I would find 1753.

## The search

Since Hugh McCarthy had taken the Juruena River, I decided to focus my efforts on an area extending from the east bank of the Madeira River to the west, and the west bank of the San Francisco on the east. From north to south, the boundaries would be the Equator and the Tropic of Capricorn. Regular maps were not detailed enough, and I chose to use aeronautical charts. Since I did not know the direction the Portuguese were heading when they found the city, I had four choices, the north, the south, the east and the west. The next 16 years were spent going over the charts, and I found that only the north-to-south bearing gave me what I was looking for. In 1981, I had fixed on several areas where the City of 1753 might very well be found.

## The enhancements

To verify my theory, I obtained infrared satellite tapes covering the most promising locations, and had them computer enhanced. The first two tapes showed nothing but mountains and rivers but the third one contained an odd shape which when enhanced to approximately 0.4 ha per pixel, revealed that the shape was almost oval and, about 1.5 km long by 1.5 km wide, and contained what appeared to be large buildings and several squares. Most important, a river started near the largest of these squares, just as the Portuguese had said. The gates, or arches, were visible. It was a fortified city, surrounded by a wall. I had the print of the city analyzed by a reputed geologist and authority on satellite photo interpretation who confirmed that the infrared return seen was man made, and not an odd geological formation. I had finally rediscovered the City of 1753.

## The inscriptions

The last page of Document 512 contains 13 inscriptions – the nine signatures of the adventurers and copies of four inscriptions made by the Portuguese in the city and near the waterfalls. The first, second and fourth were in some form of Greek but I could make some sense of only the first one, Kuphis, which in Greek means Egyptian incense compound. I sought the help of a well-known epigrapher, who concluded that the first, second and fourth inscriptions are in corrupt Ptolemaic Greek, and that the third is in the alphabet of Scorpio, which also belongs to the Ptolemaic Greek family. These scripts were used in Egypt from 100 BC till the middle of the seventh century AD. It is the opinion of the epigrapher that, in view of the very limited knowledge existing at that time about Gnostic scripts (third inscription), the Portuguese could not have made them up; they must, therefore, be genuine.

## The ancient miners of Brazil

My deduction is that the City of 1753 was not built by white Indians, descendants of the survivors of Atlantis, as Colonel Fawcett believed. Rather, it was a harvesting and mining centre, operated by Egyptians of the late Ptolemaic period. I am quite sure that 1753 is not the only such settlement to be found in Brazil and it formed part of an extensive mining project, stretching throughout the country.

## In conclusion

My work is almost completed. I know the location of 1753, its purpose, and the origins of the settlers who built it. The only thing left for me to do is to investigate the target area. I have been notified that the exploration permit which I requested will be most likely granted this year. I will take Brazilian scientists and government representatives to the site. I had planned for a Brazilian/American venture, but the several universities and institutions which I contacted in the United States refuse to agree with my findings. To them, no transatlantic crossings occurred prior to 1492.

It will be a memorable experience to retrace the steps taken by Colonel Fawcett and his party. They are almost forgotten now, but it is my intention to ensure that their deaths were not in vain, and that they will receive the credits they so justly deserve. They started it all, 61 years ago, and I will complete their task, the day that I dedicate the City of 1753 to the lost explorers.

# Women to the Pole – A study of the polar ice

## Madeleine Griselin

1 rue Saint-Epvre, 54000 Nancy, France

French, born 2 November 1951. Research officer at the Physical Geography Laboratory, Nancy II University. Educated in France and Canada; Ph.D. (Geography-Polar Hydrology) from Nancy University in 1982.

The polar region has been my life-long passion. For example, it led me to study geography (specializing in polar hydrology) and to organize, for my doctorate, two expeditions to Spitsbergen to study the rivers on the polar fringe as the subject of my thesis. During my post-doctoral research in a marine dynamics laboratory in Canada, I joined an expedition to the Canadian Arctic ice field and, at that time, it became clear to me that much of the research needed about "sea" ice could be done without extensive funding.

### The idea of a small expedition to the North Pole is born

I began to toy with the idea of a small expedition to the North Pole to expand our knowledge of the polar ice and environment, and I came to the conclusion that no sponsor would be interested solely by scientific research and that only a sporting event would attract the necessary funding. I wanted to study the current of the transpolar ice field, and this would entail a journey across the ice from Spitsbergen to the North Pole, a world premiere in itself. Furthermore, no woman has reached the North Pole by crossing the ice. The idea was born – I would organize an all-women's Franco-Canadian expedition across the ice to the North Pole.

As a research worker, finance and business had always been worlds I had avoided; yet I responded to the challenge and naively launched myself into the task of fundraising. Surprising to say, I found the warmest reception came from businesses in the scientific sector, and numerous laboratories have given us funds or equipment. Submission of the project to the French National Science Centre gained me a research post in geography and a prize from the Académie des Sciences, which spurred me on to greater efforts to raise the remaining 4.5 million French francs. Hundreds of calls and visits to private firms ensued – and this brought me in equipment more easily than finance – but success was in sight and, finally, a letter to the Prime Minister of France opened up access to several of his ministers who helped provide a portion of the missing funds.

Finally, in February 1986 when we left for the ice field, even though we had still not secured all the funds we needed, we decided to continue, confident in the hope that the success of our expedition would bring in the money from the subsequent sale of photographs and invitations to conferences and lectures.

**The scientific programme on the transpolar ice field**

The Arctic Ocean's permanent ice cover is subject to complex drift motions. There are two main patterns: the Beaufort Gyral which moves in a circular fashion past the Pole and through the Beaufort Sea and exits between the Canadian Arctic Islands and Greenland, or joins the other principal drift as it passes near the Pole; and the transpolar drift which moves linearly, originating off Siberia and exiting into the open sea between Greenland and Spitsbergen.

Although we have general information about the motion of the polar ice, specific data are few and far between and, to fill this gap, the expedition will use the Argos polar-orbiting satellite to track – over a period of a year – a set of beacons deployed on the ice. The beacons will be planted on the ice every 100 km along the expedition route and each beacon's position will be accurately calculated and recorded up to six times per day by the Argos central computer system to determine the specific drift velocities of the ice over a major part of the year. A further beacon will mark the expedition sledges so that the satellite can track the expedition, and calculate the drift to which it is subject. In addition, certain of the beacons will transmit meteorological data or ice parameter information.

*Madeleine Griselin plots her position before the team sets off again on its polar expedition.*

The benefits of the scientific programme will be wide-ranging for government agencies, private companies and universities. For example, a technique being developed to measure local ice thickness and consolidation will certainly be of interest to those responsible for offshore structures in ice-covered areas, to harbour managers, etc. Models for pack ice drift currently undergoing trial will be able to forecast pack conditions and thus be useful to offshore operators and to shippers planning arctic routes and schedules, etc.

Finally, the expedition also expects to collect a wealth of medical and physiological information about the expedition members. Studies will be made on human response to cold, physical effort, isolation and physical and mental stress – and provide a unique insight into reactions of a group of women to such inhospitable and arduous conditions.

**Where we stand today**

The first Woman to the Pole expedition did not succeed in reaching its polar objective. However, undaunted we have decided to try again and are recommencing our preparations.

*A sighting with a sextant is not the easiest of tasks when clothed for Arctic conditions.*

# Exploiting cave water for the nomads in Somalia

## Urs Ehrsam

**Honourable Mention**
**The Rolex Awards for Enterprise – 1987**

Viadukt-Strasse 12, 4133 Pratteln, Switzerland

Swiss, born 16 February 1949. Commercial employee. Educated in Switzerland; 20 years part-time activity as a speleologist.

---

Over the years, I have found in the Balkans and in Western regions of Asia Minor that fair-sized caves or cave systems tend to collect and store considerable quantities of water from the winter and spring precipitations, and that this water could, in many places, augment or even guarantee the water supply in small villages during the dry season. In individual cases, the water is already being used in this way.

## The search begins

Having studied the literature about the Jurassic formations in northern Somalia, I became convinced that many caves must exist in these chalk hills, so in the winter of 1981–1982, I organized an eight-month expedition to the area. Initially, we found only one very small cave in the chalk area; however, a stream emerged from it, and supplied water to a small oasis and village. Karstic development here is very far advanced, but only on the surface, and there is little cave formation so, on the advice of a Somali archaeologist, we moved to the region of Burao, Erigavo, Las Anod and the adjacent Nogal-Valley, where the hills and plains are virtually devoid of vegetation and the gypsum (alabaster) layers descend several hundred metres and contain thousands of enormous caves and cave systems. At Huddum, we found a large, very warm cave in which the air had a relative humidity of 100% and water condensate collects in puddles.

Nomads we encountered led us to further holes north of Huddum where the plain of marble-like gypsum (alabaster) is devoid of all vegetation except for a few small trees kilometres apart. At regular intervals there are dolines or sinkholes, and in about half of these we found water at a depth of some 15 m where we encountered a dense network of underground channels hollowed out by the slowly flowing ground or karst water. The lowest levels of communicating shafts were all half-filled with slowly flowing water. It became clear that there were hundreds of enormous cave systems beneath the Erigavo high plateau, and half of the 30 caves investigated contained lakes; these were seldom near the entrance but usually less than 20 m below the surface. Jackals, porcupines,

*One of the expedition team
standing in a water-collecting
alabaster cave in the area near Las
Anod.*

*A typical panorama of the
alabaster mountain scenery in the
vicinity of Las Anod, under
which there are networks of caves
containing pools of condensed
water. (opposite)*

hyenas and big cats may sometimes live in the entrance area.

Shortly before the end of our first expedition we found a further big cave near Eil-Afwein in which there was a gradient of 80 m over a distance of some 1,500 m. This complex acts like a huge water distillation plant and even when the outside air is at its driest, it "supplies" about 2 $m^3$ of top-quality fresh water per day. Unfortunately our final and most promising discovery occurred right at the end of our first expedition, too late for any further work to be done.

### ... And continues

Our second expedition, in the winter of 1984–1985, was aimed at finding caves similar to the one at Eil-Afwein and installing as many watering places as possible. Once on site, we explored every cave with a gradient, and found that every one contained water. Caves such as these may yield up to 4 $m^3$ of water a day, and must exist in large numbers. A valuable indicator in locating water-containing caves was the existence of a large isolated fig tree which, in this climate, would have died long ago were it not for its roots reaching down to storage water or drip patches. We soon named these "cave trees", and found that every second tree is by an open entrance, and every third entrance leads to a cave negotiable up to where the water lies. Some of these caves contained enormous quantities of water and, in one, the lake extended over more than 600 m.

Unfortunately political factors cost us considerable time during our second expedition, and closed frontiers and civil war held us up in the Sudan for more than three months; at one point, we were even imprisoned as Russian spies.

### Plans for the future and problems to be solved

Although the Somali nomads already exploit some of these caves where water

258

comes to the surface, there are various problems impeding more widespread use of these resources. First, apart from their justifiable fear of wild animals (and especially big cats), the nomads do not have torches or other equipment needed to explore the caves. Second, after a time, the cave water absorbs such large quantities of lime that it is unsuitable for human consumption. Last but not least, the underground water is contaminated by excreta from grazing animals; in some cases, the water was made unusable by deposits of excrement, metres thick and kilometres long. Nevertheless, I am convinced that the condensate in these caves can ensure the survival of many nomads and their animals, provided they continue their nomadic way of life. Moreover, exploitation of the water requires no machinery or expensive equipment. However, the watering places themselves must be easily accessible, and grazing animals require a second, deeper water basin or similar installation, fenced in to avoid pollution.

We are now preparing our third journey in which we can use our findings to work more systematically: for example, only caves with a gradient need to be explored for their development potential. Yet, the main task on our third expedition will be the installation of watering places. Publicity for the new wells will be unnecessary – we found that news of our work sometimes spread much faster than the work itself progressed.

# The material culture of Mozambique

## Henrik Ellert

38 Rhodes Highway, Kwekwe, Zimbabwe

Zimbabwean, born 16 January 1946. General manager of a small factory.
Educated in Zimbabwe and Portugal; diploma (History, Language and Culture)
from University of Lisbon in 1974.

This project proposes to record and describe the rich and varied artifacts of
Mozambique's greater ethnography by: a thorough investigation of the artifacts
collected and transported to Portugal during the colonial era; research in a
number of ethnological institutions in Portugal, Mozambique, Zimbabwe and
Malawi, and on materials published in Portugal; and by field work in the
countryside. The final study will take the form of an illustrated catalogue with
texts describing the multifaceted aspects of Mozambique's culture, for publication
in English and possibly Portuguese.

There is an urgent need to implement this project soon, in view of the
continuing social upheaval in Mozambique which has driven thousands of
peasants from traditional living areas to take refuge in camps in neighbouring
Zimbabwe. A traditional system of rural peasant life is rapidly changing and
there is a danger that important aspects of Mozambique's cultural heritage will
be lost; consequently, the Government is emphasizing the preservation of the
national patrimony.

### Mozambique – A brief historical overview

The name Mozambique derives from an island of the same name which was
settled by the Arabs from around the tenth century. Mozambique Island and
Sofala, farther to the south, served as trading centres with the African people of
the interior. The arrival of the Arabs and later the Portuguese in Mozambique
was predated by Iron Age African society during which cultural affinities
evolved with what is now Zimbabwe. The Portuguese period of Mozambique's
history began in the late fifteenth century, and by 1606 the colonial period had
overcome all opposition. Portuguese preoccupation with the quest for gold
during the sixteenth and seventeenth centuries contributed much to our
knowledge of contemporary African society in the lands then known as the
Empire of Monomotapa – extending from north-eastern Zimbabwe to the sea
and bordered in the north by the Zambezi River and to the south by the Sabi.

Comparison between artifacts described in certain Portuguese documents of the sixteenth and seventeenth centuries and those in village use today reveal remarkable similarity. Indian settler-traders arrived on Mozambique Island in 1686 bringing cultural traditions, some of which have been absorbed into the national culture; the best expression of Indo-Portuguese traditions may be found in the style of carving wooden camphor chests.

For the purpose of this study, the country will be divided into three separate regions, northern, central and southern corresponding to the ethnic distribution and geographic features.

## Northern region

Three ethnic communities predominate: the Maconde, the Macua and the Yao of the interior (also found in Malawi). Arab culture is evident in the local ethnomusicology, examples being the *tufo* dance which is common along the entire East-African coastline, and the *nsope* dance. Traditional African musical instruments which accompany these performances are the range of membrano-phones known as the *taware* and also the chordophone or string *tchakare*. As Arab-Swahili traders moved into the interior, many Africans converted to Islam; these cultural traditions are evident in dress styles, artifacts and knives and swords used by the Yao. The exquisite wood carving of the Maconde, ethnically related to the people of southern Tanzania, has attracted worldwide attention.

The populations of Querimba and Mozambique Islands were also influenced, over the centuries, by the Arabs and Portuguese, who brought admixtures of Indian and Indo-Portuguese culture. It is hoped to include in the project a section on Mozambique Island, which lies off the coast of Nampula Province, as it occupies a unique place in the ethnohistory of the country. Until the nineteenth century, it was the capital of Portuguese colonial interest in East Africa, an important station for the India traffic and the centre of the Portuguese slave trade. The island is a veritable living museum of sixteenth, seventeenth and eighteenth century Portuguese buildings and still standing is a fortress built in 1545; there is evidence of European, Indian and Arabic influence. After the provincial capital was transferred inland to Nampula, however, the island's importance declined and, severely neglected, many valuable historical buildings have fallen into serious disrepair.

## Central and southern regions

The Sena and Ndau people are the major ethnic groups in the Manica and Sofala provinces; the Korekore, Nyanja, Chikunda, Vadoma and Barue people predominating in the northern Tete province. Portuguese expansion into the Empire of Monomotapa from the early sixteenth century is well documented, and a wealth of information about traditional African customs and artifacts is available. The material culture of this region is extremely varied and the many artifacts will provide important insights into the past history, trade patterns and social structure of the African people.

The main linguistic group of this southern region is the Shangaan, followed by the Ronga, the Chitsua, the Chope and the Bitonga of the Inhambane district. The history of the stone-built Zimbabwe-style settlement at Manyikeni and that

*The cutting instruments shown here are of the type described by the Portuguese chronicler and priest Father João do Santos in 1561 during his journeys in Mozambique between the Zambezi and Sabi rivers.*

*The form of xylophone, known in Mozambique as the Mbila, is an instrument of the ideophone type. It was probably introduced into Mozambique by seafarers from Indonesia some 1,000 years ago.*

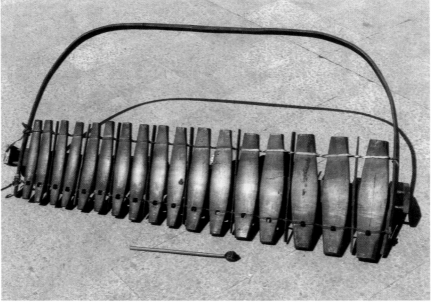

of the earlier Iron Age site at Matola will be reviewed with emphasis on the archaeological finds uncovered during excavations. The Inhambane district is famed for its xylophone, marimba or timbila instrument which, according to ethnomusicologists, was introduced by Indonesian seafarers over 1,000 years ago. The people of the Gaza province are largely Shangaan and their cultural traditions are akin to those of the Zulu and Swazi people to the south.

# Theodolite measurement and computation of megalithic astronomical alignments in Ancient China

## *Jean-Pierre Voiret*

9 Luziaweg, 8807 Freienbach, Switzerland

French, born 12 December 1936. Researcher, writer and translator. Educated in Switzerland, Taiwan and China. Doctorate (Metallurgy) from Federal Institute of Technology, Zurich in 1968.

Frequent reference to astronomy in relation to agriculture and social power structures in Ancient Chinese texts has led me to suppose that, in China – as elsewhere – life was regulated by a megalithic astronomy – nowadays "forgotten". In 1984, I discovered remains of this astronomy and my aim is now to organize an expedition to measure the megalithic astronomical alignments.

### Background and scope of activities

Archaeo-astronomy (also called astro-archaeology) has, over the past two decades, finally been accepted by the academic world as a science in its own right. Whereas earlier research in this field, such as the studies made by Sir Joseph Norman Lockyer in Greece, Egypt and England (Stonehenge) at the turn of the century, were never accepted as serious – even though later verification has demonstrated that most of Lockyer's hypotheses were correct – recent archaeo-astronomic research in Europe and Latin America has evidenced that archaeo-astronomy is an indispensable tool of modern archaeology, and actually helps achieve a better understanding of many gaps in our knowledge of ancient history.

On many occasions, my attention had been attracted to the likelihood that Ancient China – in the same way as other ancient civilizations – must have had a "forgotten" megalithic astronomy, and it was from this that my project evolved. The oldest surviving texts from those times (i.e. the oldest transcripts of archaic oral traditions, such as Shujing, Liqi, Chunqiu, Zhouli, etc.), often refer to astronomy in connection with agriculture and the formation of social power structures. This appeared to indicate that these two highly significant aspects of human existence must have been governed by megalithic astronomy. As a result, I carried out a reconnoitering trip to China in autumn 1984, during which I discovered a number of megalithic astronomical alignments. In particular, I was very interested by the strange monolith that stands near the tomb of Yu, mythical emperor of the first (Xia) Chinese Dynasty, and became convinced that

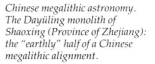

*Chinese megalithic astronomy. The Dayüling monolith of Shaoxing (Province of Zhejiang): the "earthly" half of a Chinese megalithic alignment.*

this monolith, with a tunnel-shaped hole bored through it, was used for astronomical sightings. However, when one looks through the slanted hole toward a clearly visible indentation in the jagged outline of the sacred mountain nearby, nothing special can be seen in the sky. This is only logical since the Earth's axis makes a conical revolution every 26,000 years and has changed position since the Xia Dynasty. Calculations show that constellations described in ancient Chinese texts were on the ecliptic about 2,400 BC. The Xia megalith's line of sight probably pointed towards these constellations. At that time, I did not have the possibility of making the necessary measurements; this is what I wish to rectify in my second planned trip.

Although megalithic astronomical "observatories" (mostly alignments) are quite numerous in many countries of the world, such "monuments" had not yet previously been discovered and identified as such on the territory of the People's Republic of China. Therefore, after studying historical, astronomical and etymological data I was able to formulate certain hypotheses, which I will describe, concerning Chinese megalithic astronomy. Its centres were the five holy mountains of Ancient China (Taishan, Songshan, Huashan, and the two Hengshans). Each alignment at a holy mountain was composed of two elements: one sighting monolith at the foot of the mountain, and one notch in the corresponding mountain ridge. One of the problems with Chinese astronomical alignments is that, very often, the position of the sighting monolith in the valley is today no longer known. However, analysis of some religious ceremonies held in ancient times at the holy mountains gives a rather exact description of the locations of certain monoliths of old, so that I have been able to reconstitute a number of alignments. These alignments must now be accurately surveyed in order to provide mathematical-astronomical proof of my hypotheses.

This project has the moral support of the History Department of the Swiss Federal Institute of Technology. The Chinese Academia Sinica will be officially informed and invited to join the project as soon as funding is obtained.

*Chinese megalithic astronomy. Notch in the Songshan mountain ridge near Denfeng (Province of Henan): the "heavenly" half of a Chinese megalithic astronomical alignment.*

### Proposed field work and methodology

Our team would need to spend one or two weeks at each Chinese holy mountain to determine, with a surveyor's transit theodolite, the risings and settings of stars, sun and moon, which may have corresponded to the discovered alignments, and to compare them with the stars whose calendric or religious functions are known from the ancient literature. To this end we plan a two- or three-month expedition to China in the autumn-winter of 1987.

A Kern astronomical theodolite will be used in our work, and to calculate the most interesting astronomical positions, i.e. those of the stars, sun and moon, we shall employ Aveni's azimuth-declination-predictor computer programme running on a Texas Instrument TI-59 calculator. Given the relevant declination, latitude and altitude, this programme can be used to find the azimuth; or given the latitude, altitude and azimuth one can find the declination. The programme corrects for atmospheric refraction up to 10° above the horizon. Sun and moon calculations are for the first and last gleam, lunar calculations also include parallax of the moon.

The measurement and computation of these ancient megalithic astronomical alignments will open up new horizons in our understanding of Ancient Chinese society, culture and religion.

265

# Recovering artifacts from the wreck of the Swedish East Indiaman *Drottningen af Swerige*

## *Jean-Claude Joffre*

Brettabister, North Nesting, Shetland ZE2 9PR, UK

Belgian, born 10 March 1945. Archaeologist. Educated in Belgium; Technical Diploma (Electronics and Electrical Engineering) in 1963.

Since 1974, when I came to live in Shetland, my aim has been to find a wreck which was well documented, had not been totally destroyed by the sea – as is usual in Shetland – and which contained a wealth of artifacts typical of the shipboard and trading life of the time, that once recovered, could be displayed as a complete collection in Shetland.

### The Drottningen af Swerige – **The ship to meet my ambitions**

Amongst the many unfortunate vessels which came to rest below the treacherous waters around the Shetland coast, the Swedish East Indiaman the *Drottningen af Swerige* (Queen of Sweden) met all the requirements needed to fulfil this ambition, and may well prove to be one of the major sites for marine archaeology in Europe. *The Queen of Sweden*, a vessel of approximately 950 t, was built in Stockholm for the Swedish East India Company for the trade with China. Carrying 30 guns and a crew of 130 men, she was the biggest ship the company had built or bought since its inception in 1731, and cost the company 152,480 silver dalers. In September 1741, she left the yard and on 10 January 1742 was ready to sail on her first voyage to China; however, on 12 January 1745, on her second voyage, outward bound to China, she was wrecked at the entrance to Lerwick Harbour in Shetland.

The Swedish East India Company was founded by Niclas Sahlgren, Henrik Konig, and two Scots, Colin Campbell and Charles Irvine. The two Scotsmen played a dominant role in the new company from the very beginning, Colin Campbell being its Director until his death. Campbell also received a special commission from King Frederick which made him the first ever Scoto-Swedish envoy to the Emperor of China. The Swedish company, unlike its other European counterparts, employed men from many nations, using their expertise and knowledge to create an efficient international trading company.

*On a copy of a page from the records of the Swedish East India Company lies a pair of brass dividers taken from the wreck of the Swedish East Indiaman* Drottningen af Swerige. *After 240 years in the waters of Lerwick Harbour, the iron points have rusted away.*

## Surveying and exploring the wreck

I located the wreck in September 1979, and then elaborated a new technique to survey and map the site – a method more appropriate to the complexities of the seabed around Shetland than those previously employed. Once this was completed, I began to remove the thick seaweed over small areas of the site and to carefully excavate the concretions below. As each artifact was removed, it was mapped and recorded. It became evident after the first season's work that I had found a very important source of material for the study of life aboard a mid-eighteenth century East India vessel. Because the site is in Lerwick Harbour, the extreme weather conditions and heavy seas had not taken their toll over a period of nearly 250 years, as has occurred in many other wreck sites in Shetland. Since, at the time of the wrecking, the representative of the Crown had his residence adjacent to the wreck site, interference by local residents was impossible.

The local museum offered to conserve the artifacts that were being recovered but it was clear by the end of the first season that they could not cope with the quantities of organic material such as leather seaboots, wooden ship's fittings and wine bottles, some with their contents, that I was finding. The quantity of wine bottles alone meant that I had to undertake some of the conservation myself and, in doing so, I found a simple and reliable method for stabilizing the glass.

The following year the conservation of wooden artifacts was well under way; among the findings made at this stage was that although softwood would conserve well using the polyethylene glycol method, another method needed to be found for hardwood. A new method was subsequently devised and used successfully with ebony and olive wood.

267

*One of the divers surfacing with a beautiful pewter plate taken from the wreck of the* Drottningen af Swerige.

## Finding a home for the treasures

By this time, the work on the site, and the research in archives and elsewhere, had stretched my budget to its limit. Moreover, a new addition to the family meant that my wife could no longer help as before, and it looked as though I would not be able to continue. The Shetland authorities were prepared to help financially; however, because the small local museum was already saturated, they could see no way of undertaking to display such a large and complete collection and therefore decided it was an exercise with no immediate future. Those were harsh times financially, but luckily the Manager of the local branch of the Royal Bank of Scotland was convinced of the importance of my work and agreed, against the security of our house, to lend us sufficient funds to continue. Various friends, who had either dived on the site or knew the importance of my work, also helped us out.

As a new, larger and more modern museum is the subject of a feasibility study at present, the Shetland Amenities Trust (an official body established by Shetlanders to use a part of the oil revenues to preserve local amenities of historical interest) has decided to purchase the entire collection. They have settled on a sum which will almost cover our bank loan and which is independent of the quantity and value of the totality of the artifacts recovered from the wreck. Consequently, I am currently searching for financial assistance to complete the final year's excavations and to start assembling all the data collected over the past six years with a view to publishing my findings and methods in the appropriate learned journals.

My aim is still unchanged. I am determined to see the entire collection placed in the Shetland Museum where it will be displayed and be available as a valuable source for further historical and scientific research.

# Nicaraguan folklore in music and song

## Salvador Cardenal

Radio Güegüense, Bo. Ciudad Jardin, Managua, Nicaragua

Nicaraguan, born 29 October 1914. Director of Radio Güegüense. Educated in Nicaragua; self-taught specialist on folklore and folkloric music.

My interest in the study of Nicaraguan folk music and song began some 50 years ago when I attended a Jesuit high school, where most of the priests were Mexican. I was a teenager when they introduced me to the folkloric music of Mexico, and that was the start of my musical career. I felt strongly that Nicaragua also should have its own folk music. I therefore set to work to do something about it, and by the time I was 18, had carried out my first piece of research. Since then I have never stopped, so that I am in effect a self-made folklore specialist and Nicaragua's only musicologist. I have also studied classical music and Radio Güegüense, of which I am the Director, broadcasts exclusively cultural programmes comprising symphonies, concertos, sonatas, etc., accompanied by spoken commentaries. I am also writing a history of music.

### Criteria for selecting the music and songs

The criteria I have adopted in my compilation of Nicaraguan folkmusic and song are that: it must be old music, yet not extinct, be anonymous or have been sung by the people for 80 years or more, and be currently in use among a large sector of the population. It must be transmitted orally from generation to generation and not be handed down as a written score. Not all "typical" and popular music, therefore, can qualify as "folk".

Since funds were not available to enable me to devote myself full time to the task of research and compilation, the first part of the project was completed in my leisure hours, while earning a living elsewhere. One of my sons has been collaborating with me for the past 25 years and another has become involved in this quest for the past five years.

### The research to be undertaken

I have already recorded ten one-hour cassettes and have written an explanatory booklet to accompany them. This music comes mainly from the Pacific coast of Nicaragua; there is also some from the north, but very little from the Atlantic coast. This project therefore aims to study and make a compilation of the folk music of the Atlantic coast of Nicaragua, an area somewhat isolated from the rest of the country and inhabited by four different ethnic groups: the Miskitos, Zumos, Ramas and the Blacks. They all have their own language and music and considerable research is therefore essential here.

The eastern region of Nicaragua is divided into three zones: north, central and south. The three zones present different cultural backgrounds, different ways of living and different customs. For this reason the research must be carried out independently for each of them. When the compilation has been completed, it will be studied and codified, in order to determine the areas which have a common background, and the differences among them and the various influences to which they have been subjected.

This region is the most extensive in Nicaragua, covering almost 40% of the country, as well as the most abandoned – which makes the investigation a difficult task. In this part of the country, the most common form of transport is by river, or by roads which are passable only in the dry season. A considerable amount of equipment will be needed to enable us to reach and record the music of these populations who are dispersed along the river banks, deep in the jungle, and along the Atlantic coast. For example, we will need a four-wheel drive vehicle and a motorboat in addition to a range of audio recording equipment. Work will be done in 30 towns in the area – towns in which music has evolved considerably since the revolution. A comparison between its present state and that of six years ago will be attempted.

### Revision and collation

My two sons, an assistant and an interpreter will do the field work which I myself will co-ordinate. Subsequently, in Managua, with the help of my sons, I will revise, collate and study the collection in order to carry out the next stage of our investigation.

*The cover illustration by L. Saénz for the booklet included in the box of records on Nicaraguan Music and Song produced by Salvador Cardenal.*

270

# Reconstructing the prehistoric environment of the Sahara and Sahel

## Henri J.F. Dumont

J.B. Callebautstraat 87, 1780 Affligem, Belgium

Belgian, born 8 February 1942. Head of Limnology Team, Zoological Institute, State University of Gent. Educated in Belgium; D.Sc. (Zoology) in 1968.

The fauna in relict waters of the Sahara and Sahel is directly related to the history of these environments. This project is making a biogeographic analysis of the area to obtain data about past pluvials and hyperarid phases, to provide new qualitative information about rapid climatic changes in Africa since the late Pleistocene, and to substantiate the hypothesis that, 3,000–5,000 years ago, the Sahara was much drier than today.

### Expeditions of adventure

In 1975, I started on a research programme to identify and sample the fauna of as many relict waters as possible in the Sahara and Sahel belts of Africa. My objective here was to plot out distribution patterns of species, compare these with the distribution of the same species outside the Sahara-Sahel belt and determine what past climates allowed such water fauna to establish themselves in areas which are now deserts or semi-deserts. It has long been known that over the past tens of thousands of years, Africa has been subject to drier periods alternating with wetter periods, more or less in parallel with glaciations and post-glacial climatic fluctuations in Europe and North America. However, my concept was that aquatic relicts might be more numerous than hitherto believed, and have a story of their own to tell (be able to furnish information not obtainable by other means). My plan was to cover the whole range of water fauna from crocodiles and fish down to zooplankton, adopting the approach that the chances of Daphnia surviving as a relict are much greater than those of a lion.

Between 1975 and 1981, I organized 11 expeditions lasting from three weeks to over three months and took part in all but one of them. By 1981, I had managed to cover most of the Sahara-Sahel, except the very east and some important mountain chains (Tibesti, Ennedi) in Chad, which were not accessible for political reasons. After 1981, I began filling in remaining gaps in selected areas, such as the Tassili-n-Ajjer in central Algeria and the Republic of the Sudan, which proved to be an exceptionally fertile area for the type of studies I was undertaking.

## A new theory of climatic change in the Sahel

In the course of the first years of my research, I had begun to realize that my original biogeographical objectives were too narrow. I was puzzled by the fact that central Saharian mountains, such as the Hoggar and Tassili-n-Ajjer, have abundant fish populations of species of central African origin although mountains farther south lack fish completely, and came to the conclusion that the extinction of fish in the southern mountains was attributable to a period much drier than today and which I tentatively placed between 5,500 and 3,000 BP. The political implications of this are considerable: 3,000 BP is a date so near to us, that one can only conclude that since historical times the Sahel has become moister, not more arid and, consequently, desertification is more likely of human than climatic origin.

The task of substantiating this theory was much larger than anything I had previously undertaken. However, I was convinced that Malha, a crater in the Meidob Hills of Northern Darfur, might contain the information to prove my case, knowing that the sediments of crater lakes are influenced by local climatic conditions only, and can therefore reveal how the local palaeoclimates have evolved with time. In 1985, I undertook an expedition to core the sediments of Lake Malha.

While the cores were being taken, we discovered the ruins of four prehistoric cities. None showed signs of destruction, indicating that a sudden drought may have chased their previously sedentary populations south. I calculated that these four cities represent a population density of five people per square kilometre, i.e. about ten times the present density, and I concluded that precipitation must have been at least 500–600 mm per year, instead of 100–150 mm as at present. With such a palaeo-precipitation, the Wadi el Milk, now a dry river bed, must have been a permanent stream, and connected the Meidob area to the Nile. UNESCO-sponsored salvage archaeology along the Nile in Nubia

*An aerial view of one of the prehistoric cities (Umm Gerur) located during the surveying work round Lake Malha. 1. Acropolis; 2. Second-level stone huts; and 3. Lowest-level stone huts. (opposite)*

*Helicopter lifting the cores drilled at the Malha crater lake to analyze the lake sediments. It was during these aerial operations that we observed numerous circular stuctures which proved to be the ruins of a prehistoric city.*

has recently disclosed stone buildings in similar style there, and I hypothesize that they are of similar age, and represent a pre-meroitic culture.

All pieces of the puzzle now seemed to start falling into place. From the biogeography of the plankton, and also from fish fauna, we had known for some time that the biota of the Nile and Chad basin are so closely related that a recent connection between all these basins must have existed. Meidob is strategically situated at the water divide between Chad and the Nile and may have been on the pathway along which contact occurred. More important, this contact also applies to human cultures and there is evidence of Iron Age activity in the lowlands to the east of Lake Chad. What is needed next is: a further detailed study of the information contained in the Lake Malha cores; a systematic study of archaeological remains along the Wadi el Milk between the Meidob Hills and the Nile, and in the Zaghawa area west of Meidob.

## A last verification needed

Finally, at the end of the 1985 expedition, I briefly visited Jebel Marra, some 250 km south of Malha. Here, two more crater lakes occur and, curiously, the slopes of this high mountain are almost completely terraced, a form of agriculture uncommon on the African continent. The walls of the terraces are built in the same way as those of the Meidob cities, but many of these terraces are now disused. It could therefore very well be that the Meidob people, having deserted their cities, became re-established on Jebel Marra and cultivated this area, until the climate changed again. In order to test this idea, one of the lakes in the Dariba crater of Jebel Marra should be cored, and this forms the third future object for the continuation of my project, which I hope to start as of 1987.

# The fishes of Easter Island

## John Ernest Randall

Division of Ichthyology, Bernice P. Bishop Museum, 1525 Bernice Street, POB
19000-A, Honolulu, Hawaii 96817–0916, USA

American, born 22 May 1924. Senior ichthyologist, Bernice P. Bishop Museum.
Educated in USA; Ph.D. (Marine Zoology) from University of Hawaii in 1955.

I first became interested in the fish fauna of Easter Island (also known by the
Polynesian name Rapa Nui and by its Spanish name Isla de Pascua) in 1963
when I found a specimen of an undescribed species of the genus *Cantherhines*
from Easter Island misidentified as *Monocanthus cirrhifer* (a Japanese species) in
the National Museum of Natural History, Washington D.C. This stimulated me
to survey the literature on Easter Island fishes and I was surprised to find only
five papers on the subject, which together brought to 40 the total number of
fishes known from the island. Ten of these occur only there, thus giving a
surprising 25% endemism for Easter Island fishes. None of these authors had
made his collection using modern ichthyological methods and, since I knew that
many more species of fishes must occur at the island, I resolved to make an
ichthyological expedition there.

### Tripling the fish fauna of Easter Island

In 1968, I was able to make a month's stay on the island, we collected 109 fishes,
confirmed the existence of a further 15 and obtained their Rapanui names from
local fishermen. Although we had nearly tripled the fish fauna of Easter Island,
we knew that more extensive collecting would probably yield at least a few more
species. Nevertheless, it was apparent that the fish fauna is extremely
impoverished. Easter Island has the lowest number of fishes of any tropical or
subtropical island in the world. This is not unexpected in view of the extreme
isolation of the island, its small size, the paucity of marine habitats and its
location at latitude 27 degrees south. During an ice age, tropical species must
have disappeared; during warm periods, the reverse undoubtedly occurred.

The small number of species within any fish group has resulted in an unusual
depth-related distribution of the fish species at the island. At other localities
with numerous fishes, one generally finds a distinct zonation with depth within
a group of fishes. It was startling to observe species of damselfish or goby, for

*The wrasse,* Anampses feminus *Randall, which occurs from Easter Island to Lord Howe Island, is unusual in that the female is more colourful than the male. This species was named by John Ernest Randall.*

example, living in a shallow tidepool and encounter them later at 60 m and all intermediate depths.

## High level of endemism among Easter Island fish

An analysis of the fish fauna of Easter Island proved to be very interesting. The different components include: Indo-Pacific (i.e. occurring only at the island); southern subtropical; antitropical (occurring in the southern and northern subtropical or temperate latitudes but not in tropical waters); eastern Pacific (west coast of the Americas and nearby islands); cosmopolitan; and pelagic. No other place in the sea has more different zoogeographic components to its fish fauna. The endemic fishes, of course, have been of the greatest interest, since those not previously collected represented new species. Within the vast Indo-Pacific region, only the Hawaian Islands have a slightly higher percentage of endemic fishes.

## Efforts to establish a definitive species inventory

Knowing that my collecting efforts at Easter Island in 1969 had not resulted in the definitive fish fauna, I returned for two weeks in February 1984, and this trip resulted in 17 new records and seven new species of fishes. Yet, I was still not confident that I had all the fishes from the island. I especially needed the deeper-water fishes which required the help of Rapanui fishermen. Also I wanted to take more underwater photographs of the fishes, especially of a dark barred butterfly fish that had been sighted in 60 m of water. Beginning 31 January 1985, I made my third visit to Easter Island and managed to photograph the butterfly fish previously observed, and six other new records and three new species were obtained, along with additional specimens of other rare fishes.

## Plans for a book and marine sanctuaries

My major objective with respect to Easter Island is to write a book on the entire fish fauna of the island (155 species). All species will be illustrated, nearly all in colour, the inshore fishes from my underwater photographs. Separate English and Spanish editions are planned. Stanford University Press has expressed an interest in this volume.

A number of us are concerned with the over-exploitation of some of the marine resources by the Rapanui people. We have seen populations of the spiny lobster (*Panulirus pascuensis*), the cowry (*Cypraea caputdraconis*) and certain fishes such as *Girella nebulosus* and *Bodianus vulpinus* greatly reduced in recent years. We have proposed the creation of two marine sanctuaries, one at Motu Nui and Moti Iti, small rocky islets at the south-west corner of the island, and the other at Anakena-Ovahe. These preserves will provide for reproductive stocks of the exploited species to be sustained. Also they are exceptionally beautiful for diving and should be maintained in pristine form for those who want only to observe and photograph the marine life. In addition, it is hoped to establish a small marine museum at Easter Island, a major objective of which will be to educate the island residents in the principles of marine conservation so they will utilize their marine resources more wisely. The museum will also serve to introduce visitors to the unique marine life of the island.

*A new species of serranid fish of the genus* Caprodon *which was caught by hook and line off Easter Island.*

# The cave art of India

## *Vishnu Shridhar Wakankar*

Institute of Rock Art, Bharati Kala Bhawan, Madhav Nagar, Ujjain-456001, India

Indian, born 4 May 1919. Director, Institute of Rock Art. Educated in India;
Ph.D. (Archaeology) from University of Poona in 1972.

Indian rock paintings have not been well documented. This project will explore
a major part of the central and south Indian plateau, and survey a period
between ca. 40,000 BC and 500 BP. The paintings will be copied, photographed
and documented; analytical studies will be made of subject matter, chronological
styles and human life study; and a comparative study will be made with present-
day tribal art.

### A wealth of unsurveyed material

The existence of Indian cave paintings was first discovered by A. Carllyle as
early as 1870, and since then several explorers have discovered scattered rock
shelters from Keral to Kashmir and Hoshangabad to Mirzapur. Excavations by
the Archaeological Survey of India, Vikram University, Deccan College, Basel
University and M.S. University, Baroda, have provided evidence for dating
some of these paintings to the prechalcolithic period.

### A lack of photographic records

I, personally, started exploring cave and shelter paintings in 1950 and, since
then, I have explored more than 3,000 shelters covering a wide area of India;
nevertheless, a large part of the sandstone area still remains unsurveyed. So far,
I have prepared eye copies of most of these sites, but photographic records are
meagre. Indian forests are being cut to house the growing population and any
sites near inhabited areas, and especially those near urban localities, are in
danger of damage: consequently, more extensive photographic surveying is
essential and urgent. Moreover, there are many new sites which require
exploration, excavation and preservation.

My doctoral thesis dealt with a vast region covering the whole of India but this
was a general study; moreover, since 1972, much more research has been
undertaken and many new sites have been explored. In my capacity as an artist,
I have tried to copy many of these, and have established a collection of items

277

from over 2,000 shelters, which is now located in the Institute of Rock Art at Ujjain.

My plan is to explore a major part of the central and southern Indian plateau and survey the rock art ranging over a period from 40,000 BC to 500 BP. The project will be divided into three stages, each lasting a season and devoted to a different area in which the rock paintings will be copied, photographed and documented; analytical studies will be made of the subject matter, together with chronological surveys and human-life study. Throughout the whole survey, classification and interpretation of rock art will be accompanied by a study of the relationship between rock paintings and tribal art and tradition.

## Documenting the rock paintings

It has been observed that each geographic unit has a special style of its own in each period and this can be visualized by photographing or by sketches done on the spot. The most extensive painted rock shelters have been selected for each site, and these will be photographed in detail and traced on to plastic tracing paper; these tracings will then be transferred to paper. By sketching the separate stylistic composition, a composite picture of the subject painted can be obtained and studied.

The rock shelters in each area will need to be numbered as has already been done at Bhimbetka, Kharwai, Bhopal, Raisen, Putlikarar and other sites. All the sites will be documented photographically and equidistant photographs will be taken for larger groups. Although wide-angle lens views will be taken, multicentred photographic records will be extremely important since this is the only way a total picture of the mural compositions can be obtained; this will be done in colour as well as black and white. In addition, colour studies will be made of all the important compositions, individual figures or groups of figures.

*An excavated shelter with Acheulian deposits.*

# Exploration of submerged caves in search of biological treasures

## Jill Yager

c/o Biological Sciences Department, Old Dominion University, Norfolk, Virginia 23508, USA

American, born 20 November 1945. Doctoral student. Educated in USA; currently studying for Ph.D. (Biological Sciences) at Old Dominion University, Norfolk.

The cryptic realm of the submerged cave has been an environment totally unknown and unstudied until recently. However, advanced cave-diving skills and equipment have allowed safe access to the dark passages and recent exploration of this habitat has led to the discovery of an entire new ecosystem, the value of which we are only now beginning to understand. The object of our project is to continue our studies by exploring submerged caves in the Cook and Galapagos Islands and various aspects of the life and ecosystem in them.

### The discovery of living fossils

The most exciting find has been the very primitive crustacean class *Remipedia*, a blind, swimming centipede-like animal. Since finding the first remipede in a submerged cave in the Bahamas several years ago, we have investigated many such caves throughout the West Indies region and have collected at least eight additional new species of remipedes, representing a new family and several new genera. The characteristics of remipedes indicate that the group is very ancient, probably the most primitive crustacean living today. These "living fossils" are significantly changing the way in which crustacean biologists are thinking about crustacean ancestors and evolution.

Along with the remipedes, entire communities of cave-adapted organisms (troglobites) previously unknown to science have been revealed. The troglobites we have collected from these caves represent not only the new class, but new families, new genera and over 20 new species.

### Submerged caves – Windows on the past

The type of submerged habitat we are studying is called an anchialine cave, i.e. one that has a surface opening inland and with subsurface connections to the sea. Its environment is characterized by several layers of water of different

*The most exciting find in anchialine caves has been the very primitive crustacean class,* Remipedia, *a blind swimming centipede-like animal. Since finding the first remipede, Jill Yager's team has collected at least eight additional species.*

*Anchialine caves have a surface opening inland, with subsurface connections to the sea. These caves are a true "window on the past" and have represented a refuge for animals and allowed survival during periods of glaciation. (opposite)*

salinity with the surface water usually being a fresh to brackish layer separated from the lower, more saline water by a distinct density interface; the water beneath the density interface has a very low dissolved oxygen content. Remipedes and the associated animal community live below the density interface. They inhabit the dark, horizontal passages sometimes hundreds of metres from the surface opening. Because such environments can be accessed only by persons with special training and cave-diving skills they have, until recently, been largely unknown to scientists and undocumented.

Our project will explore submerged caves on selected islands in the South Pacific Ocean, to survey the life found in the caves and measure other ecological factors of the cave environment such as nutrients, salinity, dissolved oxygen and hydrogen sulphide. The data will be compared with those collected from cave habitats in other areas of the world.

Since there are very few cave-diving biologists, anchialine caves of the world represent relatively undisturbed, stable environments in which the porous nature of the rock has provided a habitat available for colonization by troglobites for millions of years. Submerged caves are a "window on the past" providing a refuge in which animals have survived during periods of glaciation. The existence of closely related cave species in caves separated by great distances is causing biologists to rethink ideas about the distribution of such marine life.

However, these caves are under threat worldwide from pollution and development on the land above them, and measurement of the ecological parameters in several caves throughout the world will give baseline data which can be used to monitor any further changes. The exploration of the submerged cave ecosystem also has an important social value. By increasing individual awareness of the unique, hidden environment, a conservation ethic can be established which will help to preserve this natural resource.

## Expedition sites and methods

We have chosen two locations in the Pacific for this expedition: the Cook Islands and the Galapagos Islands. The Cook Islands have many submerged limestone caves, especially on the island of Mangaia. The Galapagos Islands have lava caves, several of which are known to end in the sea. Neither of these two locations has been explored by cave-divers, so the potential for discovery of new life is excellent.

Water chemistry analysis will be done on the first dive, to ensure that an accurate, undisturbed measurement is obtained. Samples will be taken at the cave surface and then in the aphotic zones (several hundred metres from the entrance) at varying depths and measurements made of temperature, salinity, dissolved oxygen, hydrogen sulphide and nutrients. We will collect specimens of animals in the water column and of epifauna from the cave floor, ceilings and walls. Cave-floor sediment will also be sampled and examined for macrofauna and micro-organisms. Eventually a food web for anchialine cave habitats can be constructed. After completing each dive, animals will be sorted, photographed, and sent to appropriate specialists for identification and/or description. Remipedes, if found, will be retained for description and comparative anatomical study and scientific manuscripts will be written in co-operation with scientists worldwide.

It is hoped that the expedition we propose will result not only in the advancement of science, but that the public will benefit and that the photographs taken and the articles written will reveal to all the beautiful hidden world of the submerged cave.

# Chinese T'ang Dynasty tomb murals and their reproduction

## *Hongxiu Zhang*

Shaanxi Provincial Museum, Sanxue Street, Xi'an, People's Republic of China

Chinese, born 22 August 1940. Calligrapher, tomb-mural reproduction artist and writer. Educated in China; graduated (Traditional Chinese Painting) from Xi'an Institute of Fine Arts in 1962.

During the T'ang Dynasty in China (AD 618–906), mural art reached a peak of excellence, and the murals in tombs of this period are a Chinese cultural treasure. Important murals from the period have been found in Qianxian County in three large tombs – the tomb of Crown Prince Zhang Huai, the tomb of Crown Prince Yi De and the tomb of Princess Yong Tai, all grandchildren of Empress Wu Zetian and put to death at their grandmother's command because they expressed resentment of her dictatorship.

### An insight into life during the T'ang Dynasty

The large murals and various funeral objects give a picture of the luxury in which aristocrats and the royal family bureaucrats lived at the time and provide an insight into the acute political struggle taking place. "Guards of honour of women court attendants", "Hunting party under way", "Playing polo", "Male and female attendants" form the main content of the murals which, by the reality of their artistic expression and technique, embody the character of traditional Chinese paintings in their composition, line, modelling and colouring.

A feature of traditional Chinese painting is the author's use of line for modelling and the T'ang murals have been extremely successful in this respect. Nearly all of them have been drawn with vigorous and forceful lines of identical width, demonstrating the skill of the ancient artists in manipulation of their brushes. The lines themselves are very simple, but the figures they formed were true to life. A few forceful strokes outline a well-rounded and sturdy horse and vividly express its shape, posture and vitality.

### Murals in urgent need of preservation

The importance of these T'ang funeral murals as precious relics as well as great works of art, and the rarity of such masterpieces, make their preservation and renovation a matter of urgency. I have been entrusted with the task of copying

282

these murals and studying the techniques employed. Having survived for 1,300 years, the T'ang murals have suffered to varying degrees, due to the effects of humidity in particular. Lines have been obliterated and colours have faded and, in some cases, are even invisible to the naked eye.

Transferring the murals from the wall to paper without loss of the original artistic impact demands command of colour, application, line and the clothing patterns. Moreover, the copier has to ascertain by inference the true nature of lost or indistinct lines and coloured areas, thus restoring to their full glory the singing court women, the strong and vigorous military horses, the tall, heavily guarded watch towers, the majestic guards of honour and the busy male and female court attendants.

To this end, I started work on mural-copying in an exploratory way in my spare time in 1981 and so far I have made over 300 mural reproductions, and have acquired a wide range of theoretical and practical knowledge.

## Techniques of mural reproduction

The techniques involved entail erasing corrosion marks to restore the total harmony, and ensuring that the ancient murals appear as traditional Chinese paintings. By preserving both the artistic effect of the original and the qualities of traditional Chinese painting, I have been able to ensure that the reproductions are not only relics but also works of art. In addition, I have explored the techniques of line-drawing and colouring used by the original artist and have attempted to apply the knowledge acquired to mending the damaged parts of the original.

The line-drawing technique that was employed made much call on skill with the pen and competence in Chinese calligraphy and, consequently, I have attempted to expand my abilities in this field and, in doing so, have published a number of articles on calligraphy.

*The illustrations given here, and overleaf, show a reproduction of a Yuan Dynasty mural and an original mural from one of the T'ang Dynasty tombs.*

As far as the colours are concerned, I have arrived at the conclusion that importance should be given first and foremost to primary colours with the dark, light and wash being applied in a way that reproduces the appearance of an old wall. Moreover, water also has a part to play if an effective attempt is to be made to reproduce the impact of certain lost lines.

My hope is that mastery of method and skill in accurately reproducing the original, graceful lines, figures and harmonious colours will result in reproductions that are true to their 1,300-year old originals.

# Recording and transcribing traditional tabla drumming

## Jürg Wüthrich

20 Kasthoferstrasse, 3006 Bern Switzerland
*Swiss, born 26 December 1949. Lecturer, Basel Musicological Institute, and co-worker at Südwestfunk Experimental Studio. Educated in Switzerland and India; accepted as "Adept of Indian Classical Music" by Pandit Jnan Prakash Ghosh, Calcutta in 1980.*
This project aims to: establish a record of traditional tabla drumming, including many authentic documents (such as unique audio/video recordings of the old tabla-wizards and their performances); develop a new system of musical notation/transcription for the tabla; and research instrument construction (table, tanpura, etc.) so as to manufacture instruments for integration in the West.

# A speleonautic step into a geothermal future

## Jochen Hasenmayer

38 Herrenalberstrasse, 7534 Birkenfeld bei Pforzheim, West Germany
*West German, born 28 October 1941. Hydrospeleologist. Educated in West Germany.*
This project's hydrospeleological exploration of Swabian Alb karstic caverns has found evidence of widespread palaeokarstic structures under the whole pre-alpine Jurassic plate, subduced to a depth of up to 7 km during formation of the Alps. The thermal cave phenomena, with enormous geothermal capacity resulting from terrestrial heat flow, will be researched with a view to exploiting this clean energy.

# Traverses of Zanskar

## Per Erik Asson Löwdin

24A Luthagsesplanaden, 75225 Uppsala, Sweden
*Swedish, born 19 November 1949. Director of Studies, Department of Cultural Anthropology, University of Uppsala. Educated in Sweden; Filosofre Kandidat at University of Uppsala.*
This project has four main objectives: to explore the upper basins of the rivers Khurna chhu, Niri chhu, Tok phu chhu, and Zara chhu in the Zanskar region of India; to produce route descriptions of advanced treks in the Zanskar Mountains; to collect data on culture and society in Zanskar and Ladakh; and to publish a book describing the findings.

# The Bon religion – A living tradition of Tibet

## Charles Albert Edward Ramble

c/o The British Council, POB 640, Kathmandu, Nepal
*British, born 6 February 1957. Post-doctoral research worker. Educated in UK and USA; Ph.D. (Social Anthropology) from University of Oxford in 1984.*
This two-year project will study the Tibetan Bon religion as it is practised in Greater Tibet and in areas of indigenous Tibetan culture in Northwest Nepal, by participating in and observing the daily life of selected sedentary, nomadic and monastic communities in each main region. Daily secular and religious life, songs, oral traditions and changing material culture will be tape-recorded and photographed.

# The Minoan calendar, chronometer and four-year abacus

## Panayote Gregoriades

10 Aldou Manoutiou Street, 11521 Athens, Greece
*Greek, born 22 February 1947. Director of Athens Branch of Minos, a company producing solar heating systems, etc. Educated in Greece and UK; diploma (Film Directing) from School of Cinema, Athens in 1968.*

Among the finds at the Minoan Palace of Knossos were artifacts commonly described as "Gaming boards". This project has analyzed these museum exhibits and concludes that they are not simple gaming boards but "portable chronometers/four-year calendars", used over 3,500 years ago by the Minoans who followed a solar calendar based on the rising of Sirius, and which still functions today with absolute precision.

# A search for the traditional site of the Incaic "Ushnu" at Machu Picchu

## Raymond Edwin White, Jr.

Steward Observatory, University of Arizona, Tucson, Arizona 85721, USA
*American, born 6 May 1933. Associate Professor, Department of Astronomy, University of Arizona. Educated in Switzerland and USA; Ph.D. (Astronomy) from University of Illinois in 1967.*

This project proposes to excavate a portion of the ruins at Machu Picchu in order to find the historical foundation for the "Ushnu", the central pillar of Inca ceremonials. The excavation will be guided by a prediction evolved from an interpretation of the utility of the "Intihuatana Stone" to the Incas. Other extant forms of the Intihuatana Stone will also be searched for and documented.

# Exploring, preserving and classifying Patagonian late-palaeolithic rupestrian paintings

## Hugo Rafael Mancuso

5538 Santo Tome, 1408 Buenos Aires, Argentina
*Argentine/Italian, born 4 July 1961. Assistant Professor at University of Buenos Aires. Educated in Argentina; Licentiate degree (Literature and History of Art) in 1984.*

The present project consists in preparing the first systematic and comprehensive classification of known palaeolithic parietal art of Argentine non-Andean Patagonia (*Patagonia extrandina argentina*), and the classification of hundreds of caverns that have yet to be excavated and/or scientifically recorded. The material will be photographed, analyzed and interpreted, and reproductions will be published.

# Artistic and monumental atlas of the colonial epoch in Guatemala

## Juan Haroldo Antonio Rodas Estrada

4a Calle 15–22 Zona 1, Nueva Guatemala de la Asunción, Guatemala
*Guatemalan, born 25 May 1956. Director, Fray Franciso Vásquez Museum. Educated in Guatemala; Licentiate (History) from Universidad de San Carlos de Guatemala in 1982.*

This project consists in the establishment of an inventory of architectural monuments (both religious and civil) erected during the Spanish "Colonial Epoch" (1524–1821) in the area now covered by Guatemala. Each monument would be catalogued with an indication of location, structural details, materials used, etc., and the position of the monuments would be shown on a map of Guatemala.

# Social behaviour of Allen's swamp monkey

## Marina Ann Cords

Zoology Department, University of California, Berkeley, 4079 Life Sciences Building, Berkeley, California 94720, USA
*American, born 22 July 1957. Visiting Lecturer, Zoology Department, University of California. Educated in USA; Ph.D. (Zoology) from University of California in 1984.*

The Allen's swamp monkey has not been studied in its natural habitat but investigation of captured species indicates that they may live in permanent multi-male groups. This project proposes to study this monkey in a Zaïrian rain forest to determine how the groups are organized and the critical aspect of male-female relationships, to enhance our understanding of social organization in long-lived highly social mammals.


# Ornithological investigation of Peruvian-Brazilian border hills and low mountains

## John Patton O'Neill

119 Foster Hall, Louisiana State University, Baton Rouge, Louisiana 70803, USA
*American, born 12 April 1942. Co-ordinator of Field Studies and Artist-in-Residence, Louisiana State University of Natural Sciences. Educated in USA; Ph.D. from Louisiana State University in 1974.*

The hills and low mountains on the Peru-Brazil border at the headwaters of the Rio Shesha are probably the site of a Pleistocene speciation "refugium". This project proposes to study the avifauna of the area, collect specimens of birds and other vertebrates, take samples of vertebrate systematics for biochemical study, and make notes and tape recordings to serve for a book on the birds of Peru.


# Catcher in the rye – A recorded collection of minority languages

## Lili Pan

English Section, Changsha Communications Institute, Changsha, Hunan, People's Republic of China
*Chinese, born 1 July 1959. English teacher at Changsha Communications Institute. Educated in China; B.A. (Teaching English as a Foreign Language) from Hunan Agricultural University in 1981.*

In view of the danger that China's minority languages may be assimilated by Chinese and vanish, this project proposes to visit the 71 minority autonomous counties and record the 53 languages and dialects in use there. Two competent interpreters will separately make scripts for accuracy and future use. Copies of the completed recordings will be sent to institutes of linguistics in China and other countries.


# The joint services expedition around the world in search of traditional medicine

## Jerzy Michniewicz

2E Michałowskiego, 71–343 Szczecin, Poland
*Polish, born 21 July 1958. Physician. Educated in Poland; M.D. from Pomeranian Medical Academy in 1985.*

This project proposes to make an expedition to a number of developing countries in order to record and classify traditional methods of healing in use there. Particular attention will be devoted to the techniques employed in the preparation and administration of these medicinal products and the ritual surrounding the collection and processing of ingredients.

## Project Joy – Navigating the Northwest Passage in a solo kayak

*Subagh Singh Winkelstern*
1560 Warncke Road, Lyons, New York 14489, USA
*American, born 9 May 1944. Dentist and yoga instructor. Educated in USA; D.M.D. from Tufts University School of Dental Medicine in 1970.*
This project plans to undertake the first known solo kayak navigation of the Northwest Passage, covering some 3,000–4,000 km in a single summer (1988). The subsequent "sharing" phase will include: publishing a photographic and narrative account of the trip; lecturing; teaching ocean kayak techniques; marketing designs and equipment developed for this project; preparing for future related projects.

## The search for the mountain quail

*James Owen Merion Roberts*
Mountain Travel Pvt. Ltd., POB 170, Kathmandu, Nepal
*British, born 21 September 1916. Founder and Consulting Director, Mountain Travel Pvt. Ltd. Educated in UK; graduated from Royal Military College, Sandhurst in 1936.*
The mountain quail, *Ophrysia superciliosa*, is a small slaty-brown, partridge-like bird that was seen during the winter in the foothills of the Western Himalayas between 1846 and 1876. After 1876, it simply disappeared – although it still features in bird books. Its sudden appearance and disappearance remain an ornithological mystery. This project will try to rediscover this small bird in West Nepal.

## Locating the site of the first European settlement in Athabasca Country

*Gloria Joyce Fedirchuk*
304, 1725 Tenth Avenue S.W., Calgary, Alberta T3C 0K1, Canada
*Canadian, born 16 December 1946. Executive Director of a firm specializing in assessing the impact of industrial development on historical resources. Educated in Canada and USA; Ph.D. (Anthropology) from University of New Mexico in 1975.*
The Englishman Peter Pond was a key figure in exploring and opening up Athabasca Country in Western Canada in the late eighteenth century. This project aims at locating the settlement known as the "Old Establishment" built by Pond in 1778 on the Athabasca River, promote its preservation and development as a heritage site, make an archaeological search of the area and report the findings.

## Comparative physiology of Himalayan and Andean high-altitude natives

*Robert B. Schoene*
Harborview Medical Center, Division of Respiratory Diseases, ZA-62, 325 Ninth Avenue, Seattle, Washington 98104, USA
*American, born 4 December 1946. Associate Professor of Medicine, University of Washington. Educated in USA; MD from Columbia College of Physicians and Surgeons, New York in 1972.*
The Himalayan-Andean Research Expedition of 1986–1987 will carry out physiological studies to test the hypothesis that Himalayan natives who have lived at high altitudes for over 500,000 years have better adapted to the rigours of low oxygen pressure than Andean natives who have lived at high altitudes for 10,000–20,000 years and in whom there is a high incidence of chronic mountain sickness.

## Human/Dolphin Community

*James M. Nollman*
273 Hidden Meadow, Friday Harbor, Washington 98250, USA
*American, born 31 January 1947. Author, musician, director. Educated in USA; B.A. (English Literature and Music for Theatre) from Tufts University in 1969.*
The concept of an area where humans and dolphins meet to interact by sharing music and play has its roots in many ancient cultures. Following a decade of study of human/dolphin interaction, this project will, in spring 1987 and 1988, establish a Human/Dolphin Community site along the Bolivian coastline to further explore the community concept and cultivate a relationship between humans and dolphins.

## Botanical exploration of the world's richest rain forest

*W. Scott Hoover*
718 Henderson Road, Williamstown, Massachusetts 01267, USA
*American, born 20 November 1951. Research Associate, Missouri Botanical Garden. Educated in USA; B.A. (Biology and Philosophy) from Colorado College in 1974.*
The Chocó region of extreme north-western South America is the most species-rich area in the world; however, much of it remains unexplored. This project proposes a botanical exploration to obtain additional data that will contribute to the conservation of this unique tropical rain forest, and also help in clarifying several opposing theories put forward to explain the unique diversity of the region.

## Lost cities of the Tayrone

*Maria Eugenia Romero*
Apartado Aéreo 039372, Bogotá D.E., Colombia
*Colombian, born 11 April 1948. Anthropologist. Educated in Colombia and USA; M.A. (Anthropology) from Southern Illinois University in 1977.*
This project will prepare a documentary film on the ancient history of the Sierra Nevada de Santa Marta, Colombia, and the archaeological remains left by the Tayrona Indians, and give a contemporary view of the Kogi Indians and other descendants of the Tayrona. It will show where the Tayrona lived, the archaeological testimonies they have left, and a historical perspective of Tayrona cultural developments.

## Yarumela – Gateway to the Olmec jade trade in Central America

*Boyd MacNeil Dixon*
Department of Anthropology, U-176, University of Connecticut, Storrs, Connecticut 06268, USA
*American, born 4 August 1952. Graduate student of Latin American Archaeology. Educated in USA; B.A. from University of Alabama in 1983.*
Yarumela, in the Comayagna Valley, Honduras, was a strategic location on trade routes connecting the Pacific and Caribbean coasts, and became the largest centre in non-Maya Central America due to its unique position in the Olmec jade sculpture trade. This project proposes to document this gateway community by intensive survey of the valley and extensive excavation of elite and ceremonial architecture.

# Marine cave fauna of the Indo-Pacific

## Thomas Mitchell Iliffe

Bermuda Biological Station, Ferry Reach 1–15, Bermuda
*American, born 14 August 1948. Research associate, Bermuda Biological Station. Educated in USA; Ph.D. (Biochemistry) from Marine Biomedical Institute, University of Texas Medical Branch in 1977.*

The marine cave habitat, accessible only through specialized diving techniques, is one of Earth's last faunistic frontier regions and serves as a refugium to ancient "living fossil" species and to animals closely related to the deep-sea organisms. This project proposes to conduct an expedition to islands in the Indo-South Pacific for an investigation of the marine fauna of limestone and volcanic caves.


# Searching for remnant populations of the endangered northern white rhinoceros

## George Walter Frame

c/o Tropical Forests Office, International Union for Conservation of Nature and Natural Resources, avenue du Mont Blanc, 1196 Gland, Switzerland
*American, born 2 August 1943. Post-doctoral Research Fellow, International Union for Conservation of Nature and Natural Resources. Educated in USA; Ph.D. (Wildlife Ecology) from Utah State University in 1985.*

The northern white rhinoceros, *Ceratotherium simum cottoni*, is nearly extinct, and conservationists are trying to protect the remaining 35 rhinos in the Garamba National Park of Zaïre. This project proposes to search for other remnant populations of the northern white rhinoceros and assist the responsible governments in establishing adequate conservation measures to increase these animals' survival chances.


# Evolutionary status of the chambered nautilus

## William Bruce Saunders

Department of Geology, Bryn Mawr College, Bryn Mawr, Pennsylvania 19010, USA
*American, born 12 November 1942. Professor of Geology, Bryn Mawr College. Educated in USA; Ph.D. (Geology) from University of Iowa in 1971.*

The chambered nautilus is regarded as a rare, reclusive relic, restricted to a few remote Pacific sites, and an evolutionary holdover. This project hypothesizes that renewed evolutionary differentiation, leading toward speciation, is in progress within this ancient lineage. It proposes to study the nature of this differentiation and measure and analyze it morphologically, genetically and geographically.


# Investigating 3.5 million year old human-ancestor footprints at Laetoli, Tanzania

## Donald Carl Johanson

Institute of Human Origins, 2453 Ridge Road, Berkeley, California 94709, USA
*American, born 28 June 1943. Director, Institute of Human Origins. Educated in USA; D.Sc. (Hon.) from John Carroll University in 1979 and from The College of Wooster in 1985.*

Fossil evidence has shown that the origin of bipedal locomotion was the hallmark of human evolution, antedating the expansion of the brain and the elaboration of material culture. This project proposes further excavation and study of the fossilized early human footprint trails discovered at the 3.5 million year old site of Laetoli, Tanzania, to better understand these footprints and their implications.

# Rehabilitation and social integration of primitives in Papua New Guinea

## Alessandro M. Strohmenger

7 Bastioni Porta Volta, 20121 Milan, Italy
*Italian, born 19 May 1914. Retired industrialist and voluntary missionary scholar. Educated in Italy; graduated (Plant Engineering) from University of Milan in 1938.*

This project has been carrying out humanitarian work amongst the population of the jungle region of the Torricelli Mountains in Papua New Guinea. It has explored unknown regions, founded churches, hospitals, dispensaries and laboratories, installed sanitary, communications and production facilities, set up a range of schools and run vocational-training and job-creation programmes.

# Rescue excavations at Carthage

## Simon Patrick Ellis

Robins Court, 54 Fields Road, Alsager, Stoke-on-Trent, UK
*British, born 6 April 1954. Archaeologist. Educated in UK; D.Phil. from Lincoln College, Oxford in 1984.*

In the face of increasing threats of modern development to the ancient city of Carthage, this project plans a series of rescue excavations to recover important information without permanently blocking construction of modern amenities. Hopefully, it will encourage co-operation between developers and archaeologists, and promote joint archaeological ventures to overcome shortages of funds.

# Diversity of tropical forest plant communities

## Alwyn Howard Gentry

Missouri Botanical Garden, POB 299, St. Louis, Missouri 63166, USA
*American, born 6 January 1945. Associate Curator of Missouri Botanical Garden and Adjunct Professor. Educated in USA; Ph.D. from Washington University of St. Louis in 1972.*

This project is studying the composition and diversity of tropical rain forests using a large series of 0.1 ha samples, and has now compiled data sets for 71 sites from 23 countries on six continents. Most of the data sets are from the lowland Neotropics. It is planned to extend these data sets to include a series of altitudinal transects of Andean cloud forests and several additional palaeotropical sites.

# Cycling through the USA to study community norms, values and mores

## Steve Robert Gill

5 Park Drive, Thornton, Liverpool L23 4TL, UK
*British, born 18 September 1948. Teacher, free-lance writer and photographer. Educated in UK; B.A. (Sociology) from Grey College, Durham in 1970 and Postgraduate Certificate in Education from the University of Wales in 1971.*

The aim of this project is to make a cycling and camping voyage through every State in the USA and chronicle the observations and discoveries made during this endeavour. The results will be formulated in a manner useful for those studying primarily sociology, social psychology and economic history. In addition, an account will be written of the travels and adventures experienced.

## Amazing maze – The Gundestrup cauldron and the maze of Notre-Dame de Chartres

*Bernadette Guyot-Jullien*
1 rue du Canal, 91160 Longjumeau, France
*French, born 20 January 1940. Sales representative with Air-Inter. Educated in Algeria.*
Having analyzed the meaning of the Gundestrup cauldron and related it to the maze of Notre-Dame de Chartres, this project plans to examine a number of churches, and study the evolution of medieval astronomical knowledge, looking in particular at its influence on Romanesque architecture. An attempt will be made to reconstruct the astronomical instruments which were used at that time.


## Disabled youth to swim seven seas and the English Channel both ways

*Taranath Shenoy*
197 Ganpatrao Kadam Marg, Lower Parel, Bombay-400013, India
*Indian, born 10 June 1959. Clerical employee, Central Railways, Bombay. Educated in India; diplomas in screen printing and textile design in 1980 and 1981.*
This deaf, dumb and partially blind youth has already swum the following waters dividing two countries or continents, or joining two seas: the Palk Straits; and the English Channel (three times). He now plans to swim the Straits of Gibraltar; the Straits of the Dardanelles; the Straits of Bosphorus; and finally the Panama Canal from the Atlantic to the Pacific Ocean.


## Late Stone Age and Early Iron Age residential patterns in Mozambique

*Leonardo Adamowicz*
Centro de Investigação Arqueologica, 16A rua dos Combatentes, 520 Nampula, Mozambique
*Polish, born 10 July 1945. Director, Archaeological Research Center, Nampula. Educated in Poland and Sweden; preparing Ph.D. thesis (Anthropolgy) at Uppsala University.*
This project is studying Late Stone Age and Early Iron Age residential patterns in the region between the Lurio and Ligonha Rivers in the Nampula Province of Mozambique. Ethno-archaeological methods are being used to reconstruct the ecology of the sites, in relation to the present environmental habitat, with special references to hunting activities, land-use patterns, etc.


## Windows into the past – Videotaping interviews on the Mosquito Shore of Honduras

*Frank Griffith Dawson*
Hughes Hall, Cambridge University, 3 Eltisley Avenue, Cambridge CB3 9JG, UK
*American, born 29 September 1934. Fellow of Hughes Hall, Cambridge and Lecturer on Latin American Law and History. Educated in USA and Guatemala; LL.B. (International Legal Studies) from Yale Law School in 1960.*
The Mosquito Shore of the north Caribbean coast of the Republic of Honduras is a wilderness of jungles, swamps, lagoons and winding rivers in which three major non-Hispanic ethnic groups have survived. This project will videotape interviews with the older generations before they die and take with them priceless, unwritten memories of historical events, botanical knowledge and cultural traditions.

# The Environment

The projects described in this section were submitted under the category "The Environment" which was defined in the Official Application Form for The Rolex Awards for Enterprise 1987 as follows:

*Projects in this category will be concerned primarily with our environment and should seek to protect and preserve, or to improve, the world around us.*

# A search for the Sumatran rabbit

*John Etheridge Cormack Flux*

Ecology Division, DSIR, Private Bag, Lower Hutt, New Zealand

British, born 20 December 1934. Scientist with the New Zealand Department of Scientific and Industrial Research. Educated in UK and Kenya; Ph.D. (Zoology) from University of Aberdeen in 1962.

The Sumatran rabbit, *Nesolagus netscheri*, was first described by Prof. H. Schlegel in 1880, "To my utter astonishment, it proved to belong to a totally unknown species (with) a system of coloration as beautiful as it is uncommon among the hare tribe, the upper parts being largely striped and crossed with black and the greyish general tint of the fur passing, on the hind part of the animal, into a fine rusty tint". This most unusual rabbit has apparently always been extremely rare. It is confined to mountain forests at an altitude of 600 – 1,400 m in Sumatra, and no fossils have been found to indicate that it ever had a wider distribution. Although evidence from forest clearance suggests people have been living in Sumatra for at least 7,000 years, there is no native name for the rabbit. In 1914, a major zoological expedition to the Kerinci area (where the rabbit has been recorded) found none, despite three months of intensive search. The total of all known specimens is 15, so it is clearly one of the world's rarest animals.

Zoologists recognize the Sumatran rabbit as a specially interesting link between the primitive fossil forms of the Myocene and the highly evolved species of today. These examples of steps in evolution are more valuable to scholars than even such dramatic "end points" as the Californian condor or blue whale, which receive so much public support. There is the practical consideration that a tropical rabbit could be of great benefit as a protein supply in climates where malnutrition occurs; and the Sumatran rabbit is known to be easy to keep in captivity on a wide range of food.

### Previous surveys and sightings

There have been only two reported sightings by zoologists since 1916. The first was by Dr. M. Borner, who studied the Sumatran rhino from 1972 to 1975. He saw one rabbit in 450 days of field work in north Sumatra, in an area well studied by scientists, so the rabbits if still present must be very scarce. The second sighting was in 1978 by Dr. J. Seidensticker from a bus at night near Mt. Kerinci,

295

but he did not formally publish this observation because details were too scanty. Locals assured him domestic rabbits were not kept in the area, but I saw multicoloured domestic rabbits in hutches at Kerinci in 1982, so the record remains inconclusive.

A thorough survey for many rare mammals was carried out in 1983 and 1984 by Blouch, who reports "We did not encounter any direct evidence of Sumatran hares but found three places where local people described the animal well enough for us to conclude that it occurs there. In the settlement of Way Laga, south of Liwa, on the border of Bukit Barisan Selatan National Park, it was reported that a group of four, including small ones, was once seen near the edge of the forest in recently cleared land that was about to be planted with coffee. People living on both the north and south sides of the Gumai Pasemah Wildlife Reserve in Sumatra Selatan say that hares are fairly common in the reserve at an altitude of around 1,600 m, and one was once caught and killed by a dog. People in the town of Kurotidur in Bengkulu about 40 km north of the provincial capital also report that there are hares in the mountainous protection forest east of the village.

"It seems likely that hares are sparsely distributed throughout the length of the Barisan Mountain chain in southern Sumatra. Their survival depends on the continued existence of their mountain forest habitat. Whether they could live in disturbed forests is a moot point since, in mountainous areas, there is little selective timber cutting: either the forest remains in a more or less undisturbed condition or it is cut down completely and converted to agriculture. Apparently they are rarely hunted, probably because there are so few of them and in such remote areas that it is not worth the effort."

The International Union for Conservation of Nature and Natural Resources (IUCN) has a Species Survival Commission (SSC) to advise on conservation priorities. Their Lagomorph Specialist Group selected the Sumatran rabbit as its top priority, and a project proposal was drawn up in 1979, but fell through partly for lack of funds. In 1982, en route to an IUCN meeting in Helsinki, my wife and I paid a private visit to Sumatra to examine conditions first hand. We went from Padang to Sungai Penuh by bus (150 km in 14 hours) and spent a day on foot in mountain forest on Mt. Kerinci at about 2,000 m. Much of the forest below this level has been cleared and clearance was continuing. The pace of change will become more rapid with the programme to resettle 500,000 people a year from Java to Sumatra. Our short survey showed that an expedition to locate a population of Sumatran rabbits was both urgent, and feasible.

### An expedition to find the Sumatran rabbit

Hence the present project proposal, the aim of which is to visit all locations in the six regions where rabbits have ever been reported and to search carefully for them using modern techniques. Our main method will be to explore an area thoroughly by daylight on foot, looking for browsing on *Cyrtandra* (the favourite food plant) and droppings. The latter are characteristic and there are no other wild rabbits in Sumatra to cause confusion. Then at night the same area can be searched with a low-powered red spotlight and night vision equipment. A camera can be attached to record any animals seen. My wife and I have worked together in the field for many years and could undertake this project alone.

However, at the IUCN meeting in Edmonton in August 1985, Dr. C. Santiapillai, who works for the World Wildlife Fund at Bogor, Java, offered to accompany us, and his local experience would be very useful.

**Future plans**

If any Sumatran rabbits are found, the next step would be to map and assess the size of the populations. It is reasonably likely that some will occur in existing National Parks, but suitable protection for the animals should be ensured. Then IUCN could supervise a more detailed study later. If there are enough rabbits, some could be kept in zoos, such as those at Antwerp, Jersey and Mexico, which have had success in breeding rare rabbits.

*The Sumatran rabbit,* Nesolagus netscheri, *first described in 1880. It has always been extremely rare and is confined to montane forests in Sumatra at altitudes of 600-1,400 m; no fossils have been found to indicate it has wider distribution.*

# The Buddhist perception of nature – A new perspective for conservation education

 *Nancy Lee Nash*

5H Bowen Road, 1st Floor, Hong Kong

American, born 7 May 1943. International co-ordinator, Buddhist Perception of Nature Project. Educated in USA; considerable field experience in pioneering conservation projects.

This ongoing project constitutes in itself, and as a blueprint for other cultural groups, a new perspective for conservation education, employing traditional teachings to raise awareness of the need for conservation to improve attitudes towards protection of the earth's natural environment.

Responding to the world crisis of disappearing nature and natural resources, conservation efforts have largely focused on biological problems and techno-logical solutions. Efforts have overlooked, for the most part, cultural, social and individual attitudes which have played a role in creating the problems but which, if employed effectively, could help bring about long-term solutions. This project takes as its scientific foundation the consequences for the earth of destruction of our natural resources continuing at the present rate. It uses ethical, religious and cultural traditions as a basis for the work which will involve Buddhists from all parts of the world and all walks of life.

## The role of education and religion in conservation

Education from grassroots to leadership level is recognized as the single most important factor for improved environmental protection. Religion as one of the earliest forms of education and, as one of the main sources of instruction today, has a major role to play. The importance of recognizing mankind's interdepen-dence with all forms of life varies from religion to religion, just as interpretations of the codes vary from person to person. However, there always exists some obligation to protect the earth and all things living. More than half of the world's population adheres, to some degree, to a religious faith, and religious teachings hold powerful messages for proper conservation.

*Nancy Lee Nash, Rolex Laureate – The Rolex Awards for Enterprise 1987, at work in her study preparing future efforts in her project on the Buddhist perception of nature.*

## The Buddhist perception of nature

Buddhism was selected for a pilot project because it is influential in Asia, a part of the world which is home to an estimated 75% of the earth's animal and plant species – many of which are threatened with extinction. At the grassroots level, Buddhist social structures are often the main or sole source of education. Buddhist teachings embody themes of awareness and compassion. In Thailand, a number of species threatened with extinction have been saved through Buddhist intervention.

This new approach to conservation education evolved in response to the teachings of His Holiness the 14th Dalai Lama on Universal Responsibility and to my own experience of wildlife conservation work. Following intermittent research over a number of years, I produced the outline for the project at the end of 1984. Two research teams were formed in 1985, and work began in the middle of that year. The project was formally announced in the winter of 1985.

The project covers three stages: research and compilation of traditional Buddhist teachings regarding mankind's interdependence with, and responsibilities to, the natural environment; production of efficient teaching materials and application of the materials in established educational systems; and use of the project as a blueprint for similar projects involving other faiths.

## Research methods and materials to be produced

Project personnel have the task of locating and compiling the literature to produce comprehensive and efficient teaching tools widely acceptable to faithful Buddhists. A Thai team has been set up by Wildlife Fund Thailand in Bangkok to gather the Theravada traditions, whilst the Mahayana research is directed by the Council for Religious and Cultural Affairs of His Holiness the Dalai Lama, in Dharamsala, India. Leading scholars not directly involved with the project are contacted, as required, for clarification of texts, and recognized experts review all resulting materials before production.

The project also addresses the merit of symbolic acts such as releasing birds into the air and turtles into water compared with attitudes and actions which actually save life. Codes of conduct will be examined for their current significance for development activities such as forestry sciences, agriculture and human settlements.

The main teaching tools in the early stages are books and audio-visual aids; these are being produced in non-technical language, in Thai and Pali for Theravada traditions, and in Tibetan and English for Mahayana. They will be used initially in Thailand, where plans have already been made to introduce the "Buddhist Perception of Nature" into the nation's 36 teacher training colleges, and in the traditional system of wats (temples), which is still the main source of education in rural areas. Mahayana material will be used in the Tibetan refugee school system and targeted areas of the Himalayas. The traditional system of education involving monasteries will be employed. Materials will also be made available to His Holiness the Dalai Lama and the Thai Royal Family to use as they choose in published material and speeches to encourage the protection of nature.

## Long-term objectives

The importance of expanding the project work into Japan, and other areas of the world where Buddhist teachings may influence people to become better conservationists, has been recognized and is part of the project outline. Finally, the project also provides a blueprint for similar work involving other faiths such as Christianity, Hinduism and Islam.

*Tibetan researchers study both the modern scientific basis for better conservation of nature and the ancient Buddhist teachings highlighting humankind's interdependence with the natural environment.*

*Nancy Nash's project addresses Buddhists of all ages and all walks of life from grassroots to leadership levels, employing ethical and cultural imperatives already in place rather than imported formulas.*

# The four seasons of lynx

## *Michel Strobino*
**Honourable Mention**
**The Rolex Awards for Enterprise – 1987**

1961 Hérémence/Riod, Switzerland

Swiss, born 3 September 1931. Independent wildlife film director/cameraman, specializing in Alpine fauna. Educated in Switzerland; attended Ecole des Arts et Métiers, Geneva from 1947 to 1951.

---

This project plans to produce a documentary which will be the second part of a study devoted to the lynx. The first documentary has just been completed under the title : *Vous avez dit: Lynx?* (Did you say "lynx"?). It will be presented to the general public during 1986 and will show mainly the work of two Swiss biologists who have been studying wild lynx in Switzerland since 1982, by capturing and equipping them with radio transmitters.

In this new documentary, I plan to ask a number of key questions about the place and desirability of the lynx in our environment. To achieve this, I will follow, over a period of two years, a number of lynx which have been equipped with these transmitters and thus show to the public various aspects of lynx behaviour such as rutting, hunting, education of young, etc.

### Putting the lynx on film

I realize that, in order to make this documentary attractive to the general public, I will need to shoot some sequences of captive subjects; however, I want to limit these to a minimum. For instance one such scene will be that showing the first days of young lynx. For the first six weeks after a female lynx has given birth it is impossible to get a sight of her and her litter (even in parks). Consequently, in order to try to film her behaviour, my intention is to equip, beforehand, a den both with film and TV cameras. Using the TV camera I will be able to monitor the action inside the den and then, whenever interesting behavioural activity occurs, I will fire my film camera which will then receive its image through optical fibres running into the den.

The film will show the relationship between the lynx and its prey and describe changes in the behaviour of prey in territories taken over by the predator, such as, for instance, the falling concentration of female chamois with young in established "spring nurseries".

The film will also offer examples of the geographical spread of this predator and its need for a large and independent hunting territory typified by the case of the female lynx which is established near Spiez and her offspring which have settled near the Pillon Pass over 50 km from Spiez. The relationship between the lynx and domestic animals will be highlighted by filming interviews with farmers – especially sheep owners – whose animals have been killed by lynx.

## Relating the lynx to society

Another interesting point that I want to develop in this documentary is the regulating rule played by lynx on our wild game, and especially on deer and chamois. Lynx "break up" large concentrations of these mammals and, in doing so, they offer our forests a better chance of harmonious development suffering as they very often do from excessive grazing by wild game.

We have now provided for the management of our major game species which are present in larger numbers than for decades; however, it is now necessary to take a closer look at the problems of ecological balance, and make some critical decisions about the possible rehabilitation of their natural predators. In doing so, we also need to analyze and, if necessary, change human attitudes – and especially those of hunters – towards animals such as the lynx. And this is what my film will aim to do.

## A daunting but feasible task

I am fully aware that I am launching myself into one of the most difficult productions I have undertaken to date but I am also convinced that, with the necessary resources, it will be possible to devote to this documentary more time than was feasible for previous productions and that by using the latest sophisticated (and expensive) filming techniques I will successfully complete this project.

*(Illustrations overleaf)*

*Michel Strobino with his cameras in the mountains preparing to film an elusive lynx.*

*A lynx photographed while living in semi-freedom in the Langenberg Park in Switzerland.*

# A demonstration farm in the dry zone of Falcón State, Venezuela

## Silvia Diana Matteucci

Edificio Torre Orión, Apartamento 10-D, Callejón San Bosco, Coro 4101, Venezuela

Argentine, born 11 August 1941. Full-time Associate Professor, Department of Plant Productivity, Francisco de Miranda National Experimental University. Educated in Argentina and USA; Ph.D. (Plant Physiology) from Duke University in 1970.

In 1976, we started a research project to identify and describe the problems and capacities of the land in Falcón State, in order to recommend a plan of action for the different ecosystems, based on the local characteristics of the terrain and its inhabitants. Although the State's arid zone was in a critical situation, it represented only 4.5% of Venezuela's territory; thus, we recognized that its agricultural development could not be considered a matter of national priority. Even so, we recommended that action be taken to prevent desert encroachment towards the south.

### A cause for concern

Five years later, when we had completed an ecological study, it became clear that the dry area had almost doubled. There was, however, little official concern. Enough public information exists to show what is needed to prevent and even reverse desertification, so we realize we must make every effort to awaken public awareness, so as to promote government action. Therefore we are planning a project to serve as a practical illustration of what can be done to remedy the situation.

The climatically arid and semi-arid zone comprises about 9,200 km², almost 40% of Falcón's surface. However, the tract of dry land is doubled when assessed on the basis of desertification trends. A considerable proportion of land has suffered some degree of desertification which will continue as long as policy-makers maintain the present development strategy, unsuitable for a tropical environment with such ecological characteristics, because it promotes the use of traditional technology. Despite the decrease in land productivity, a considerable proportion of the rural population dwells in the dry zone, where the main activity is goat-herding, at the expense of the deciduous seasonal forest, thorn woodland and scrub, without any pasture management. Subsistence rain-fed

305

agriculture is practised and also handicrafts.

Although governmental action is centred on dam construction and the establishment of irrigation schemes for commercial mono-cropping, in fact livelihoods depend as much on the supply of wood as that of water. Wood as a resource has been ignored in development plans, yet it is the main and often only energy source and the most important raw material for building, fencing and the fabrication of equipment. Thus shifting occurs more in the quest for wood rather than because of a shortage of water, and it is wood depletion that is causing the advance of desertification.

## A project to improve the situation

To prove successful, a project in this area must be small scale, ecologically sound, labour-intensive, promote participation, and ensure mechanisms for transfer to other areas. Initially, it will be located near the university campus, and research will be undertaken by teachers and students within the farm or in relation to it. A diversified system of land management will be introduced based on soft technology adapted to the local conditions, in order to improve land productivity and reverse desertification. The 50-ha field station will serve as a demonstration and testing unit.

A site was chosen on the boundary between desert and woodland, to represent the various situations encountered within the coastal plains and has an annual rainfall of 364–500 mm. It comprises three different landscapes: a denuded alluvial plain, an impoverished patchy thorn woodland, and a secondary deciduous seasonal forest. To supplement the local activities of goat-herding and subsistence agriculture, it is intended to introduce silviculture. Afforestation with the double purpose of land reclamation and windbreak and shelter-belt establishment, and an agrosilvicultural system for forage and wood production will be the main pursuits. Species already present on the site will be used for these activities, and – initially – only one new one, *Vigna aconitifolia*, will be introduced. Since some mechanization will be needed, animal traction, using available donkey-power, will be used with simple, inexpensive, locally manufactured equipment.

Activities will be oriented towards rainwater storage and soil conservation and reclamation. Tree species will be replaced from the edges of the forest presently occupied by the thorn woodland, towards the centre, and afforestation with multipurpose woody species will serve to enlarge the silvopastoral area and reclaim desertified lands. The products obtained from the forest will be used in the other activities, e.g. construction of small weirs for soil erosion control.

The patchy thorn woodland will ultimately be transformed into a silvopastoral system and the silvopastoral area subdivided to achieve grazing rotation. Local slopes on the denuded lands will be used to lay down the cropping systems and a run-off storage tank will be located in the centre of each catchment to collect the excess water during the rainy season. In the dry season, irrigation could be applied by pumping water from the storage tank. One of the purposes of the ridge and furrow system to be adopted is to improve soil infiltration and storage capacity, which are impaired by soil compaction. Crops will be seeded on the flat ridges, and between furrows, depending on the crop, intercropping will also be tried. The northern edge of the denuded lands will be afforested for shelter-belt establishment, using multi-purpose trees to provide wood for fuel or construction. Water storage reservoirs for the animals will be modified to introduce the compartmental system, a technique which reduces surface area and water temperature, decreasing evaporation, and enables the maintenance of the reservoir. Certain erosion control measures will be taken in the gullied spots.

The system should be self-perpetuating, each improvement leading to the next; and monitoring of the whole system is essential in order to adjust each innovation to its evolution.

*Wooden logs are also used for building water-diversion and water-distribution systems, fencing and crop-drying and crop-threshing structures.*

*In residential areas of the Falcón State arid region – where wood is gathered for a variety of purposes – the perennial vegetation has been impoverished. Wood and water gathering, performed by women and children, occupies a major part of the day.*

# Antarctic contamination – A barometer for world pollution?

## Marco Morosini

Antarctica '85, 27 boulevard Albert Premier, 98000 Monaco, Monaco

Italian, born 12 August 1952. Journalist. Educated in Italy; degree (Chemistry and Pharmaceutical Technologies) from State University of Milan in 1977.

This project is co-ordinating wide-ranging studies of Antarctic contamination with xenobiotics (such as DDT and other halogenated hydrocarbons), which could provide reference values for planetary minimum levels of contamination, and help evaluate patterns and trends in the global diffusion of pollutants.

### The discovery of Antarctic pollution

Following the discovery of the pesticide DDT in Antarctic penguins in 1964, DDT had been banned in many countries ten years later. Nevertheless, the "Antarctica '85" expedition aboard the sloop *Basile* discovered DDT and other halogenated hydrocarbons in samples of Antarctic Peninsula flora. This finding raised a number of questions about world diffusion of chemical contaminants that no single research project could answer in isolation.

What is the time scale for the global diffusion of a chemical and how long will the substance persist in the environment? To what extent are the legislation and recommendations on pollutants really being enforced? What are the degradation rates and patterns for different chemicals? What is the relative distribution between air, water, soil and biomass, and the geographic distribution between oceans and continents? Are certain chemicals concentrated by biological activity (e.g. feeding chains) or geophysical phenomena? Could some of the xenobiotic compounds discovered in the Antarctic be endogenous (i.e. from the permanent stations located there) and consequently not a significant parameter from the planetary point of view? Can we use simple, standard techniques for systematic, routine measurements in order to identify possible trends? Can we investigate the historical dispersion of chemicals by, for example, analyzing biological and geographical deposits?

To help answer some of these questions, we established a co-ordinated study that would stimulate awareness and, perhaps, promote action to slow down the environmental dispersion of persistent chemicals. The project comprises three arms: the compilation of existing environmental contamination data; the measurement of contamination during a winter expedition along the Antarctic Peninsula; and dissemination of information about Antarctic pollution.

## Compiling existing data and collecting new data

The project's scientific committee will carry out a number of activities to co-ordinate existing data by the establishment of a data bank, by information exchange amongst specialists in the fields of ecology, pollution and pollution control, etc., by promoting reviews, publications and meetings and by encouraging the study of simple methods of environmental monitoring.

To collect new data, a scientifically equipped and specially built 23-m sailing sloop with a crew of ten will undertake an 18-month 1,300 km survey of the Antarctic Peninsula shores from the periantarctic islands to Marguerite Bay or even farther south. The expedition will carry out an extensive scientific research programme covering animal and vegetable biology and historical environmental analyses to compare our reports with those of other ship-based expeditions and to cut ice carrots to allow analysis of contamination trends over recent decades. Current environmental degradation will be assessed by the collection of samples of air, snow, water, ice, fauna and flora and by their analysis for the detection of xenobiotic contamination.

Finally, a specialist in geophysics and cartography will exploit the unique opportunity that this expedition offers to achieve an understanding of the nature of any environmental degradation that may be encountered in this area.

*The scientific research vessel* Basile *surrounded by ice flows off the Antarctic peninsula.*

### Disseminating information about Antarctic pollution

The main thrust of the dissemination activities will be through the drafting of a scientific report for the competent authorities and the scientific community, and the production of a book and a film for the public at large. My own personal experience as a journalist and lecturer on problems of Antarctic ecology has taught me that a message is easier to put across if it is backed up by the impact of a personal testimonial and spectacular images. The film entitled *Verso il Sud* (Southbound), a co-production of the Swiss State Television and our 1985 expedition, proved fascinating for millions of television viewers and drew their attention to the problems of the Antarctic environment. We will consequently adhere to this same formula of "informing whilst fascinating" for the film that will be produced during the current Antarctic Peninsula expedition, and the impact achieved will be further heightened by the adventurous nature of the objectives, methods and difficulties involved.

By reaching the Poles, man has, this century, reached the ultimate goals of his geographic exploration of the earth. Simultaneously, he has for the first time created a global risk for the environment – both acute, in the form of nuclear weapons, and chronic, in the form of environmental pollution. Researching, stimulating public awareness and promoting governmental action on the subjects of these global hazards is for me the new frontier of adventure.

*A member of the project team hard at work with the* Basile *in the background*

# Rescuing the dorado in the Paraná, Paraguay, Uruguay and Plate River basin

## *Manuel Pereira de Godoy*

**Honourable Mention**
**The Rolex Awards for Enterprise – 1987**

3039 ave. Prudente de Moraes, 13630 Pirassununga-SP, Brazil

Brazilian, born 24 March 1922. Professor of Natural History and Biology. Educated in Brazil, France, West Germany, Sweden and UK; graduated as Professor of Natural History from University of São Paulo in 1950.

As early as the sixteenth century, Cabeza de Vaca, a Spanish explorer, drew attention to the virtues of the dorado fish from the Paraná River, commenting on its excellence as food and recommending in particular the head, which provided an oil claimed to cure leprosy. In the literature, the dorado, *Salminus maxillosus*, is always commented on for its size (at up to 116 cm in length and 31.6 kg in weight, it is the largest scale fish in the Plate River basin), its succulent flesh, its beautiful golden-yellow colouring, its economic importance, and its qualities as a game fish. In Argentina alone there is an annual catch of 675 t of dorado, whereas the figure for Brazil is some 400 t.

## My study of the dorado

Since 1943, I have carried out studies centred on the physicochemical environment, the ecology and biology of numerous fish species exposed to environmental changes.

Over the period 1954–1963, I tagged 27,000 fishes (including a high percentage of dorado) in the Upper Paraná River basin to obtain a picture of migration, reproduction and feeding localities, interdependence of rivers in the fish ecology patterns, etc. The tagging studies carried out have shown that the dorado migrates between 1,200 and 1,400 km/year (about 600 to 700 km/year upstream to reproduce; and about 600 to 700 km/year downstream to feed). The data collected indicate that the dorado and related fishes have a "reproduction home" and a "feeding home", in the Mogi Pardo Grande ecosystem of the Upper Paraná River basin. Other research in the calmer waters of the Paraná and Plate rivers in Argentina, shows that a dorado can migrate about 3,000 km/year (some 1,500 km/year upstream and 1,500 km/year downstream).

## Environmental changes affecting the dorado

Throughout the Plate River basin, major changes have taken place in the

*Professor de Godoy with a female dorado taken at the Itaipu Reservoir on the Paraná River.*

environmental conditions due to deforestation and bad agricultural practice which have resulted in soil erosion and silting of rivers, lakes and reservoir beds. There has also been destruction of marginal lagoons where the dorado's eggs incubate, and overfishing during the spawning period. Finally, the construction of hydroelectrical plant dams ranging in height from 30 to 185 m has changed the waters from lotic to lentic, and this has affected the migratory and rheophilic fishes which, over millions of years, have migrated, reproduced and fed under lotic conditions.

However, it is perhaps the major dam projects that are the greatest threat to migratory fish like the dorado since they prove to be insurmountable barriers to fish movement. Fortunately fish facilities are planned for the dams, and this may be a new force in final decisions being made in Argentina on the conservation of the dorado and other migratory fish.

In Brazil, however, the stipulations are that fish facilities have be provided only in certain dams under 15–16 m in height; on the bigger dams of the Upper Paraná River basin, fish facilities have been and still are lacking. Consequently, I am now submitting to Centrais Elétricas do Sul do Brasil SA a proposal for a fish ladder for the future Ilha Grande 18–m high dam on the Paraná River.

## Future efforts

The future objective of this project is to complete the collection of the following data about the dorado: spawn habits, egg fecundation, embryological development, ovum, larva and post larval phases until adulthood, food chain, parasites, catch, and sport and commercial values. It is planned to draw up a map showing the current status of the dorado in river basins covering an area of 3.84 million km$^2$ and involving five countries (Argentina, Bolivia, Brazil, Paraguay and Uruguay). Moreover, a comprehensive survey will be made of physicochemical conditions in the Itaipu Reservoir and its upstream waters and a complete list of

*A male dorado weighing 1.65 kg and measuring 51 cm in length, caught in the Paraná River near the site of the future Ilha Grande reservoir.*

the fishes in the area will be established to cast light on the role of the lentic and lotic water ecosystems for the dorado. All this will be put together in a book placing special emphasis on dorado conservation in areas where there are major dam and man-made lake projects; it will call for the provision of fish ladders, and will demand other protection measures such as pesticide control and the conservation of natural-lagoons containing the eggs and larvae of the dorado and related fishes. Proposals will also be made for controlled and improved artificial dorado breeding.

Efforts will continue to obtain approval for the construction of an 18–m high fish ladder at the Ilha Grande dam located between the Itaipu and the future Port Primavera reservoirs for the conservation of the migratory fish in the area. It is also intended to continue studies, started in 1943, on the physicochemistry of the waters in the Mogi Pardo Grande ecosystem and on the ecology and biology of some 100 different species of Characoidei, Siluroidei, etc., that have already been located there, and where I have already observed 34 different fishes spawning in the Mogi Guassu River, where the dorado is the most famous game fish.

# Reversive hormonal contraception – An alternative to culling free-ranging lions

*Humphrey John Leask Orford*

POB 895, 9 Anderson Street, 9000 Windhoek, Namibia

Namibian, born 4 April 1938. Head, Department of Obstetrics and Gynaecology, Windhoek State Hospital. Educated in South Africa and UK; M.B.B.S. from St. Mary's Hospital, London in 1965.

The creation of game reserves has led to unexpected increases in animal numbers, which often leads to culling – a paradox, for animals are now being killed in large numbers in the very areas rnan set aside for their protection.

### Launching a contraception programme for lionesses

In 1980, the lion population of the Etosha National Park in northern Namibia was estimated at 500 lions and game counts suggest that whereas the number of other predators has decreased over the past 50 years the number of lions has increased. The Park authorities therefore decided that there were too many lions in Etosha and that their numbers must be controlled. Consequently, we undertook to evaluate long-acting contraceptives as an alternative, hoping the method would prevent the killing of lions in Etosha and eventually lead to the abandonment of the practice.

Etosha has an area of 22,270 km², and its major feature is a vast, flat, saline depression known as the Etosha Pan, covering an area of 4,590 km². This investigation was confined to the south-west edge of the Pan, an area of 470 km² which contained five lion prides.

The evaluation of the contraceptive necessarily involved not only measuring the effectiveness and the complications of the drug but also a far wider study of the lions' special social structure, behaviour and feeding habits to assess whether it could be applied to free-ranging individuals. We thus permanently marked 25% of Etosha's lions and since 1981, aided by radiotelemetry, the travels, lives and deaths of these animals have been closely followed.

### Contraception methodology

The area contained 59 lions; three had natural markings and were regarded as uncaptured controls. The remaining 56 lions were immobilized, and individually hot branded. The 32 lionesses were immobilized; 22 serving as untreated controls and ten being treated with a melengestrol acetate silastic implant inserted in the neck muscle. Melengestrol acetate is a progesterone and when mixed with silastic powder forms a long-acting contraceptive implant which, depending on dosage, causes sterility in zoo lionesses for a period of up to five years. The treated animals and controls were, on the whole, similar in age, weight, condition and steroid hormone levels (progesterone, oestrogen, testosterone, thyroid-hormone and cortisol). The treated lionesses were re-captured and no changes had occurred in weight and condition but there was an initial fall in serum cortisol, and the serum progesterone fell progressively on treatment. Neither finding appeared biologically significant and no pathological changes or deaths could be causally linked with the contraceptives.

The ten treated lionesses did not have cubs in the first three years of the study whereas in the same period the controls produced 19 litters comprising 39 cubs, demonstrating that the drug worked effectively as a contraceptive. To test its reversibility, three lionesses were recaptured and their implants removed, after which they ovulated on days 18, 21 and 36 respectively; all three copulated, became pregnant and produced a litter of normal healthy cubs. The melengestrol acetate implants were therefore shown to prevent pregnancy and at the same time to have reversible effects. Fearing that the influence of the melengestrol acetate implants might lead to behavioural changes in the members of the pride, and possible pride break-up we divided lion activities into 13 mutually exclusive categories measuring how much time the treated and untreated lionesses devoted to each category. No statistically significant difference was shown in participation in pride activities by treated and untreated animals in over 1,000 hours of observation.

Natural mortality among lions is high and a slight decline in fertility would cause a sustained decline in the population; thus a contraceptive could be judiciously used to manipulate population trends but would be reversible if the situation altered. The branding having allowed us to identify with certainty the

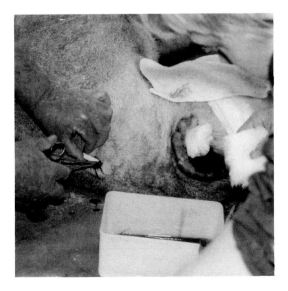

*Helped by his son John Dr. Orford places the contraceptive pellet (melengestrol acetate in silastic rubber) into the incision made in the neck muscle of a sleeping lioness.*

315

*Dart gun in hand, Mark watches while his father, Dr. Hu Berry of the Etosha Ecological Institute, listens to the heart beats of a large male lion that has just been immobilized.*

59 lions on more than 3,000 occasions, the re-sighting of marked lions enabled us to demonstrate an unexpected fall in lion numbers. This requires explanation, underlines the inherent danger of irreversible culling and emphasizes the value of contraception as an alternative. We found that the number of lions in the study area has declined by 30% over four years, and the total lion population of Etosha Park by 50%; the reason for this is not yet apparent but the treated lionesses are unlikely to have contributed significantly. However, had culling proceeded in 1981 it would have had disastrous consequences.

## Conclusions

Melengestrol acetate implants cause temporary sterility in lionesses for up to five years depending on dosage. No changes in metabolism or behaviour could be demonstrated and we believe our study has shown that culling of lions is no longer an acceptable means of controlling lion populations. Among numerous advantages of contraception over culling are that it is reversible, natural selection is less disturbed, and the practice is much more ethical.

In short, contraception in lions is practical, can be used to control their numbers, will reduce in-breeding and resultant genetic drift and contribute to the survival of wild lions.

# Rehabilitating marine mammals and sea turtles

## Robert Schoelkopf

3625 Brigantine Boulevard, Brigantine, New Jersey 08203, USA

American, born 4 October 1946. Director, Marine Mammal Stranding Center. Educated in USA; graduated from US Navy Underwater School in 1966.

Each year over 2,000 dolphins, whales, seals and sea turtles strand on the East Coast of the United States. Many of these creatures are endangered species and all are protected in the United States by the Marine Mammal Protection Act of 1972. In 1976, the Marine Mammal Stranding Center began its unofficial existence. That year, a total of five animals were reported to State conservation officials and, in turn, it became the responsibility of my wife and myself to recover those animals. The Center became incorporated in 1978 with an average annual stranding rate of 35 animals.

### Stranding – A growing problem

The word "stranding" pertains to any marine mammal or sea turtle which is no longer able to maintain a normal existence with its own species. Several major causes contribute to this problem. Obviously there are the natural causes such as old age, pneumonia, parasites and predators. However, in the past five years, a growing number of strandings have been directly attributed to human inter-vention factors such as propeller cuts, collisions with large ships, commercial fishing net entanglements, and ingestion of plastic products (the latter being a world-wide problem involving not only coastal species but also pelagic species such as sperm whales which are stranding in increasing numbers after having ingested various types of plastic product).

In view of the wide variety of ailments with which they present, each injured or sick animal received at the Center is treated in a different manner, and ever expanding international co-operation among the different rehabilitation facilities ensures that the latest developments in medication can be used to increase the animal's chances of survival. When the animals have recovered, every effort is made to release them back into their natural habitat; here, the use of electronic tracking devices ensures that the scientific community can glean more information about the migratory patterns of the marine mammals in question.

317

## A research involvement

Although strandings are reported more rapidly and in increasing numbers each year, most of the stranded animals are dead before our team reaches them. All dead animals are removed from the beach for two reasons: first, this lessens the potential health hazard to the thousands of tourists who frequent our coastline in the summer months; second, it enables us to study the cause of death, the animal's food consumption and other biological information pertaining to that species. In this way, not only are we able to gather vital statistics about the stranded specimens, but also, by the removal and in-depth study of various organs, we are able to accomplish promising advances in human medicine. The eyes are studied in relationship to human glaucoma, and the fact that this disease does not occur in whales. Bone samples of various age groups of marine mammals are sent to researchers to help them in their studies on bone disease in human infants. Recently we received a request for the larynx, trachea and lungs of whales from a well-known hospital carrying out studies of "sudden infant death syndrome" in humans.

## A rapidly expanding Center

Each year, the Center receives a growing number of requests from researchers, and, each year, more and more live animals are washed ashore. As a result, the Stranding Center has now grown from a handful of volunteers to over 500 members throughout the United States. Nevertheless, for our whole 10 years of existence we have relied on the resources and generosity of our members and the general public; the entire operation is perpetuated by their donations.

At the present time, we have: a small indoor pool and holding tanks for seals; a museum in which visitors can look at and actually touch bones and teeth from various animals, and see actual photos of both strandings and animals in their

*Robert Shoelkopf in the Center's rehabilitation pool walking a dolphin rescued from a New Jersey beach and treated at the Center for two weeks. Someone was in the water with the dolphin at all times. (Photo by Ray Fisk)*

natural habitat; and an office building that also houses volunteers when they are needed for shifts in the pool with animals that need assistance in swimming. In the future, we hope to add a large indoor pool to allow us to rehabilitate larger whales and to initiate a research project for the rehabilitation of autistic children in which the children will be able to interact with dolphins and other small cetaceans. In-house laboratory facilities are also being planned to expedite the treatment of injured animals.

Many secrets remained locked in the ocean depths. The study of marine mammals and sea turtles during their recuperative stay at the Marine Mammal Stranding Center may give us a key to unlock some of those secrets. This work also gives our many volunteers the satisfaction of helping a species that, without our intervention, may be headed for extinction.

*Robert Schoelkopf with an infant grey seal that was brought to the Center from Virginia where it had been abandoned on the beach by its mother. The animal died after one week of treatment. (Photo by Ray Fisk)*

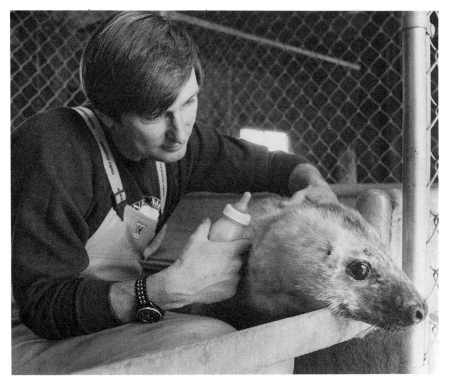

319

# "Bild-Dokumentation WALD" – Photographic documentation of forest disintegration in Switzerland

## Christian Mehr

24 Worbstrasse, 3075 Rüfenacht, Switzerland

Swiss, born 7 August 1953. Photographer and free-lance journalist. Educated in Switzerland, Poland and USA; studied (Photography and Journalism) at Newport School of Documentary Photography and Journalism from 1976 to 1979.

The forests of Switzerland are sick and everyone knows it, but most of us do not have a clear understanding of what this means. Our idea of this phenomenon is shaped by the disturbing pictures of destroyed forests in Germany and Czechoslovakia. In comparison, Swiss forests look healthy. But appearances are deceptive. Slow decay is insidious.

### Dying forests – An elusive issue

At the beginning, changes are slow and far from spectacular. We have become so used to seeing dead trees that we hardly notice the slow disintegration of our forests. Because we lack tangible comparisons, we fail to observe the profound changes in the landscape, even where decay is far advanced. Forestry experts fear that we may already have reached the point where disintegration will accelerate dramatically. The large-scale collapse of forests has become a very real prospect and would inevitably have far-reaching consequences for the Swiss economy.

Restoration of the ecological balance is essential but action depends, ultimately, on widespread public awareness and willingness to demand intervention. New, creative and convincing information campaigns are needed to overcome current widespread indifference towards the issue of dying forests; habit and acquiescence lead us to avoid confrontation with reality. Ways must be found to make reality more real. The photographic documentation on the dying forests that we have compiled is an attempt to develop illustrative material to render the issue more tangible.

*Switzerland's forests are dying. The dead trees are easily spotted by their reddish-white colour. By the time this stage has been reached, the bark beetles, that can kill off a tree in a matter of days, have long left the dead shell.*

## Documentary photography as a tool

The decay of a forest is a slow and barely perceptible process. Documentary photography offers a wide-ranging approach to demonstrating the various forms of decay, their development, relationships and long-range consequences. It can provide precise visual evidence of the different disease symptoms. Time-lapse photography makes it easy to recognize the different stages of disintegration; and a series of pictures provides a basis for comparison (healthy-sick/before-after). Such comparisons can serve to correct errors of sensory perception (e.g. highlight changes in a landscape that would otherwise be scarcely perceptible). Key pictures can be used to confront the viewer's lack of awareness, prejudice or illusions with hard facts. Methodically planned, our series of photographs will explain the relationships between different and seemingly unconnected facts (e.g. dying forest – erosion – flooding). Individual photographs can document the need for and effectiveness of reconstructive measures; sequences of photographs are able to create an understanding of the economic importance of the forest.

This type of structured and professional collection of photographs is practically non-existent today or is hidden away in the private collections of a handful of forest rangers and amateur photographers. Our photographic documentation of the dying forests attempts to close this gap by producing and classifying a new systematic series of photographs in a professional manner, and collecting, updating and cataloguing existing photographs. The photographs must fulfil the requirements of science while at the same time meeting the quality standards of the leading print media with regard to information and design. In order to provide early initial records for a later comparative series, work on this photographic inventory must be initiated immediately. Comparable photographs of affected sites provide convincing evidence of the extent and the speed of forest disintegration. Any delay in the production of such records means losing important links in the total chain of evidence.

321

## "Bild-Dokumentation WALD" – For effective publicity campaigns

"Bild-Dokumentation WALD" (BDW) aims to provide effective photographs on the current state of Swiss forests and a differentiated, factual presentation of the different aspects of dying forests in the various regions of Switzerland. The process of forest decay will be demonstrated by detailed, long-term documentation of selected situations. The studies, covering limited but representative cases, will serve to clarify statements made about larger regional developments. It will also attempt to improve the technical aspects of photographic forest documentation and facilitate professional exchanges between photographers and, wherever possible, will try to co-ordinate various ongoing documentation projects, increasing the number of uses and, therefore, the value of the photographs. BDW files will also offer high-quality up-to-date illustrations to support information campaigns by scientists, politicians, ecology-oriented corporations and media workers.

Access to the BDW and its photograph collection is basically unrestricted. It supplies illustrations for authors and producers of articles, TV films, books, brochures, schoolbooks, exhibitions and slide shows and will even provide assistance to those who carry out their own research. Furthermore, in addition to its service functions, the BDW team is also trying to initiate its own productions in the various media.

*Since avalanches have always been a hazard in Alpine valleys, housing was built away from the danger zone. However, forest disintegration along avalanche pathways poses a growing threat to existing residences.*

# Re-establishing mangrove forests on the coasts of the Arabian peninsula

## Motohiko Kogo

**Honourable Mention**
**The Rolex Awards for Enterprise – 1987**

3-29-15-1003, Honcho, Nakano-ku, Tokyo 164, Japan

Japanese, born 3 January 1940. President, Al-Gurm Research Centre. Educated in Japan and UK; B.Sc. from Department of Agricultural Chemistry, Tokyo University of Agriculture in 1964.

The mangrove has an unusual physiology which enables it to live and grow in salty water; and mangrove forests proliferate on the shores of tropical and subtropical seas.

### Arabian mangrove forests in antiquity

However, Sumerian inscriptions indicate that rich mangrove forests flourished in Arabia in ancient times, and Eratosthenes of Cyrene (276–194 BC), the Alexandrine geographer, and Nearchus, an admiral of Alexander the Great, both give descriptions indicating that they had seen mangroves growing in the Arabian Gulf area. The mangrove forest has presented a suitable environment for living since ancient times. Our research has shown major cities on the coast located near mangrove areas, and we have also found numerous ancient ruins, some dating from 5,000 years ago, in mangrove areas or in areas where mangroves are considered to have disappeared.

Today, most of the coast line of the Arabian peninsula is barren although we did find a scattering of poorly developed mangrove forests. Nevertheless, the mangrove forests continue to be of importance to the inhabitants, providing firewood, building material and fodder for camels.

The Arabian peninsula is one of the most arid areas in the world and has, to a large extent, resisted efforts made so far to afforest it. We have, therefore, taken up the challenge of developing mangrove forests along the coastal areas as a limited approach to this problem. Our object is to recover the mangrove forest of ancient times, and even though it may prove impossible to re-establish forests of the dimensions that were present in Arabia under the humid conditions existing before the third millennium BC, we believe that densities that were found under the subsequent arid conditions are still feasible.

*The red-coloured leaves of one-year-old* Rhizophora stylosa *seedlings rising on their stems from the waters of Ras al Khafji in a project carried out by the Al Gurm Research Center under commission from the Arab Oil Company.*

### Putting an idea into action

The Al-Gurm Research Center (*Al-Gurm* meaning "mangrove" in Arabic) was set up in early 1978 to study mangrove afforestation in Arabia. So far, we have surveyed public and governmental attitudes to attempts at mangrove afforestation in the region, researched the distribution, ecology and local uses of mangrove forests in Arabia in the present and past, identified suitable species for plantation and established the techniques for mangrove cultivation.

In 1981, we began the experimental cultivation at Ras al Khafji on the northeastern coast of Saudi Arabia for species trials and the establishment of plantation techniques, and in 1983 we commenced in the same way on Mubarras Island in Abu Dhabi; both of these areas were completely barren. Trials were made with the seeds collected from some ten mangrove species in India, Pakistan, South-East Asia, Djibouti, etc. However, the temperature extremes were too great: some seeds did not germinate and those that did died within a few months. However, we were able to confirm that some species could stand up to these severe climatic conditions, and determined the three main factors that inhibit growth in the Arabian environment: sea water salinity which is over 4.2% in the Arabian Gulf and the Red Sea in comparison with some 3.6% in the Indian Ocean; temperature which may range from 3 to 45°C; and the quality of the soil which comprises only sand and gravel with no organic matter. Finally, we have now identified three mangrove species that can grow under such severe conditions: *Avicennia marina, Rhizophora stylosa* and *Ceriops tagal*.

### Future activities and prospects

About 12,000 mangrove seedlings are currently growing in Khafji, with the tallest two-year old seedlings having reached 100 cm in height. On Mubarras Island, no winter damage has been apparent and, as at February 1986, about

*One of the prime achievements in 1984 was determining the best method of protecting young mangrove seedlings from the elements. Motohiko Kogo believes that this method will bring the project close to its objective of mangrove afforestation in Ras al Khafji.*

10,000 seedlings were growing along the coast. Furthermore, we have established additional small-scale experimental cultivations in Salalah (Oman) and Corangi creek (Pakistan) in 1983.

Our experiments have confirmed that some mangrove species can grow in the severe environmental conditions of Arabia and that mangrove afforestation is a valid option. We have two more projects for the near future; finding more suitable species to grow in Arabia, and making a forest of at least 100,000 mangrove trees in co-operation with the local government. We have received financial support for our activities on mangroves from some foundations in Japan and some oil companies, but this is a private enterprise, and one that I consider to be an adventure.

# *Trafficking* – A family board game

## *Peter Thomas Spinks*

2 Crown Road, Twickenham TE1 3EE, UK

British, born 28 March 1926. Free-lance designer. Educated in UK; attended Pitman's Business College, London.

Research on the drug problem, sponsored by the Central Office of Information in the United Kingdom, has indicated that there are strong arguments for a carefully thought-out, long-term drug control media campaign with both advertising and educational elements which would have the aim of de-glamourizing drug abuse and arming young people with appropriate information and knowledge about heroin and spelling out the mental, psychological, physical, social and financial consequences of heroin misuse. In response to these research findings, this project has developed a board game specifically designed to produce an anti-drug reaction and aimed at 12–15 year olds who are not presently involved in drugs.

Research was done prior to designing this game which confirmed the enormous complexity of the drugs problem, the difficulty that authorities have in devising ways to combat it, and the slowness of their response. It has been acknowledged that early government media campaigns based on shocking or frightening potential drug users have failed. I therefore decided not to make an obvious and blatant anti-drug approach. The problem cannot be solved by a mere game, but if a small positive contribution can be made over a long period of time, its cumulative effect will be worth while.

### *Trafficking* and how it is played

Just one aspect of the drug problem is tackled, without making any attempt to portray drugs as unpleasant, or causing visible and deleterious effects. The very heart of the drug business is MONEY. The drug trade does not exist in order to give users pleasant feelings or experiences. It exists to make its operatives rich, without regard to the effects on consumers. The fact of the customer's likely addiction only makes it more attractive to the trafficker, and I have chosen to expose this factor.

The game comprises: a board of customary size; six tokens of people (Mr. Big) which are identical except for each being a different colour; six tokens of cars, identical except for each being a matching colour to a Mr. Big; two dice; paper money; 26 cards each with a face illustration with the legend "Addict" (and also with the words "Every user is at risk"); a further card with the legend "Undercover Agent, Police Drug Squad" plus the words "Go directly to jail"; one further card with the legend "Hit Man" and a suitable illustration, plus certain instructions; six tokens marked "Heroin £50" and six tokens marked "Cocaine £100".

The board displays an oval track, divided into a number of squares, and play proceeds according to the throw of the dice from square to square. Players take the part of Mr. Big, drug trafficker, choosing a token person (Mr. Big) of a particular colour, and a matching "Courier" (car token). Movement around the board represents the journey of a drug courier, in the course of which drugs are bought at a low cost (tokens), but most squares require the player to pay the heavy expenses typical of a trafficker's life – hotels, travel, gambling losses, bribes, preparation of cars for carrying drugs, robbers, blackmail, default on money owed, etc. Money is paid to a "syndicate" Banker.

In addition, a few squares enable the player/drug trafficker to collect "Addict" cards, and on one square with the legend "User entices friend" two "Addict" cards may be claimed. "Addict" cards may also be claimed on certain of the above expense squares, especially where the Courier is securing services such as changes to car, or gambling (the inference being that any form of association with drug operatives puts one at risk of addiction). On reaching a square at the end of the journey designated "VICE DEN", the drugs bought earlier may be sold at a higher price which is multiplied by the number of "Addict" cards collected by the player. Drugs (tokens) are handed in, with "Addict" cards, in exchange for money from the "syndicate" Banker.

The tokens representing Mr. Big normally reside on the board adjacent to the "VICE DEN" square, and are only used on the death of a Courier. This may occur by landing on one square designated "Courier dies of overdose" or by another player using against you the card with the legend "Hit Man" which is again secured by virtue of landing on a square labelled "Make a contact with Hit Man" and payment of a charge to the Banker.

On having a Courier die or liquidated, a player must recover his car from the square where this occurred by playing with "Mr. Big" token in its place. For Mr. Big all the expenses of the board are doubled, but on returning to the "VICE DEN" square with the car, Mr. Big is returned to the safety of the adjacent square (the inference here is that Mr. Bigs never expose themselves to risk if it can be avoided). A player using the "Hit Man" card to liquidate an opponent's Courier may claim any "Addicts" which are held (the inference being that a Mr. Big without drugs to sell cannot retain his addicts). There are one or two similar instances where "Addicts" can be lost to another player.

The game is structured with expenses being extremely high. For most of the players the capital they receive at the beginning of the game will be exhausted within one hour or so, depending on the sum issued. The winner is the surviving player.

## Public reactions and future plans

The reaction of the authorities, organizations and individuals to the proposal to market this game has ranged from a recommendation that the project should be

*A board game for all the family, called* Trafficking, *designed by Peter T. Spinks to counteract the appeal of drug taking.*

abandoned to the view – from persons of equal prominence – that it is only a game and is more likely to help than hinder. It must be said, however, that all those persons or organizations who expressed unfavourable views were, at the same time, not prepared to play the game or take more than a superficial view or cursory inspection.

I do not accept that the game will encourage thoughts of using drugs to get rich. This fact is already well known. The game shows clearly that the risks are high, and those involved are quite ruthless in their pursuit of money. Many messages are contained in the game, some quite subtly, including: the addict is a loser who is being used to make others rich; addicts can die through adulterated drugs, be rehabilitated, enticed by friends, enticed by free trials; couriers may be subjected to robbery, murder, death by overdose, hepatitis and prison. Mr. Big succeeds, but only at the cost of murder and mayhem on the other Mr. Bigs. Market research shows that children, brought up on television, are quite unperturbed by these events. In all these respects, the game follows quite closely to the real situation. Very few Mr. Bigs are ever apprehended! The Central Office of Information research repeatedly emphasizes the need to be realistic in any media campaign.

However, until the game has earned public acceptance it is classed as not commercially acceptable. Not only will games manufacturers not be interested in making it, but large chain retailers will not be prepared to offer it for sale. I would therefore like to publish the game for sale in limited quantities in specialized outlets and for free distribution in schools in combination with a research study so that the effectiveness of this unusual approach to a social problem can be evaluated.

328

# Disease-free buffalo herds for food and power in African developing countries

## John Beatty Condy

15 Collins Avenue, PO Chisipite, Harare, Zimbabwe

Zimbabwean, born 6 April 1927. Consulting veterinarian. Educated in UK and Switzerland; M.R.C.V.S. from Edinburgh University in 1950.

We believe that the African buffalo, by its geographical location, its resistance to disease and its food and power potential, could be trained to become an appropriate technological asset in most of developing rural Africa.

### A reservoir of foot-and-mouth disease

During our research into foot-and-mouth disease in wild life, we found that the African buffalo, *Syncerus caffer*, appears to be nature's natural host for the Southern African territories' three types of foot-and-mouth disease virus. Buffalo carry the virus for at least five years and, although it has no effect on them, it does turn them into a reservoir of infection for domestic livestock. Our research also showed that young buffalo calves are protected from live carrier virus by high levels of maternal antibody for the first three months of their life.

Once they acquire the carrier virus there is no known way of ridding them of it. However, if calves caught in the wild at a young age are reared in isolation, and subsequently kept in isolation in an area where foot-and-mouth disease does not exist, they will remain free of the carrier virus and acceptable to veterinary authorities and cattlemen who are traditionally suspicious of many species of wildlife as reservoirs of disease for their domestic livestock.

### A tame and trainable animal

During the course of establishing this first herd of foot-and-mouth disease free buffalo, we noticed that many animals became exceptionally tame. The African buffalo is a very different animal from the water buffalo, *Bubalus bubalis*, which is commonly found in the East from India to China. The latter has been domesticated for thousands of years but, until we carried out this work, it had generally been believed that the African buffalo was untrainable. It has even been referred to as the most dangerous of big game.

We first trained the young buffalo calves to be led and not to fight against a rope being put around their horns. At about 14 months of age, they were taught

329

to accept a yoke on their necks and to drag a branch of a tree. As their confidence built up, they were gradually given heavier work to do. The older they became the more reliable they were, and when fully adult at four years of age, they would stand patiently when required to do so and would pull carts and a plough on command. African buffalo are very intelligent and more powerful than domestic cattle. They are also more resistant to endemic disease. Our association with them has been very close and continuous and we believe that any human who is genuinely interested in animals should have no difficulty in training them.

### An invaluable natural resource

Independent African countries are rapidly progressing towards a peasant economy. Agencies aiding agricultural development have not yet considered using this natural resource, which is found in most of Africa's remote areas, as a method of improving the quality of lifestyle. Agricultural aid often includes tractors (usually with few spares) which go to unsophisticated people who live in remote areas where fuel is expensive and servicing facilities minimal. We believe it would be of greater benefit to rural African peasant agriculture to develop the domestic potential of the African buffalo. The animal is not only a more practical source of power, but would also provide a significant food source.

### A potential substitute for conventional cattle

In many areas of Africa the prevalence of tsetse fly and its associated disease of trypanosomiasis prevents peasants from keeping the cattle they need as a source of food and as power for ploughing. The African buffalo (unlike the water buffalo) is resistant to, and not affected by, trypanosomiasis.

*Training time for members of Dr. Condy's disease-free buffalo herd. A pair of buffalo getting accustomed to a working-yoke.*

330

Use of domesticated buffalo would also be a good method of instilling a realization of the value of wildlife – a realization which is essential if we are to combat traditional attitudes that wildlife is an inexhaustible, heaven-sent, free gift to be cropped indiscriminately by anyone.

From our research on a limited scale in Zimbabwe, it is clear that the African buffalo could play a far more important – in some cases indispensable – role in the development of rural African agriculture and lifestyle. It remains for governments and organizations interested in furthering African development to be apprised of the potential of this widespread natural resource, in order for it to be exploited on a wider scale.

*His Royal Highness, Prince Charles, The Prince of Wales, talking to Dr. Condy and inspecting buffalo on the occasion of his visit to confer independence to Zimbabwe in March 1980.*

# Conserving the desert-dwelling elephant and rhino by involving the local tribal communities

## Garth Leslie Owen-Smith

POB 3596, 9000 Vineta, Namibia

South African, born 22 February 1944. Free-lance nature conservationist.
Educated in South Africa.

The elephant and black rhino of the Kaokoveld in north-western Namibia are exceptional because they spend much, if not all, of their lives in the Namib desert, where the rainfall averages less than 150 mm per annum. In order to survive in this extremely arid environment, they have made behavioural and perhaps physiological adaptations and have acquired intimate knowledge of the food and water resources within their home range which is passed on from generation to generation. Thus it is extremely unlikely that, if the present desert-dwelling elephants and rhinos were exterminated, they could be replaced by the translocation of animals from other areas.

The whole of the Kaokoveld was proclaimed a game reserve in 1907 and remained as such until 1970, when the South African Administration deproclaimed all but a thin strip along the coast in order to create tribal homelands for the Herero and Damara people.

Having lived in and been administratively responsible for the agriculture of the Kaokoveld, I am convinced that the arid western parts of the region are ecologically unique and this, coupled with the spectacular desert scenery and the fact that it is very marginal for human settlement, give it the potential to be one of Africa's finest and most important national parks. After the Kaokoveld's deproclamation, I therefore recommended that the western parts of the region retain their conservation status and be incorporated into the adjoining Skeleton Coast Park to provide a sanctuary for the desert-dwelling elephant and rhino and other large mammals. These subsequent pleas by myself and leading conservationists were ignored by the South African authorities.

While I was resident in the Kaokoveld, I developed a close association with its tribal peoples and was particularly impressed by their generally harmonious relationship with potentially dangerous species such as elephant and rhino. Other game species were only hunted when the people were in need or, in the case of predators, when they threatened livestock.

In the Kaokoveld, as in other parts of Africa, large-scale illegal hunting for ivory and rhino horn took place during the 1970s and, by the end of the decade, there was a flourishing black market trade out of Southern Africa. This was a great temptation to the local inhabitants whose pastoral economy had been undermined by the worst drought on record, and as a result, by 1981, the desert-dwelling elephant and rhino of the Kaokoveld were well on the road to extinction. Realizing this, the African Elephant and Rhino Specialist Group of the International Union for Conservation of Nature and Natural Resources gave the Kaokoveld populations of both species their top priority for conservation.

However, in 1982, when I returned to the Kaokoveld as the field officer for the Kaokoland/Damaraland Desert Project of the Namibia Wildlife Trust (a non-government conservation organization set up to assist the State authorities in their fight against illegal hunting), the Namibian authorities still had stationed only a single officer, Chris Eyre, with one assistant in the region. The situation I found was catastrophic. Fewer than 300 elephants and 60 rhino had survived in the entire region, and almost all other big game populations had also been decimated by drought and uncontrolled hunting. Unless something was done about the situation fast, the Kaokoveld's magnificent wildlife was doomed.

Realizing that we did not have sufficient manpower to adequately patrol the whole area we set out to gain the support of the local inhabitants by a campaign of conservation education which resulted in both the Herero and Damara Representative Authorities totally banning hunting in the region. This was a major breakthrough as poachers would now also be breaking the laws of their tribal leaders, and contraventions would have social implications that would be more serious to the hunters than going to prison or paying fines.

In mid-1983, in conjunction with Herero headmen, I started the "auxiliary game guard system" by which headmen appointed local tribesmen as game guards who then received basic training and regular supervision. The Namibia Wildlife Trust and later the Endangered Wildlife Trust supplied the guards with staple rations and a small monthly cash allowance.

Their main function was to notify us of any hunting that might have taken place in their areas; however, they were not undercover informers and all their

*Traditional Himba pastoralists – the nomadic human inhabitants of the northern Namib. The man in the centre is a member of the auxiliary game guard force which was created to assist the authorities in their fight against poaching.*

333

*A bull elephant gunned down from a helicopter on the banks of the Kunene River. The poachers used a chain saw to remove the tusks and feet from the carcass.*

activities were conducted in the open. When evidence of illegal hunting was found, the cases were discussed with the area headman who gave us invaluable support in our investigations and, with few exceptions, we were able to get successful convictions.

The auxiliary game guards have played a major role in detering would-be poachers and keeping us informed about general game and human movements. However, I believe that the most important contribution of the system has been to directly involve the local community in the conservation of their own natural resources. Ultimately, these people will rightfully be responsible for what wildlife survives in the Kaokoveld, and this augurs well for the future.

Currently, although there are more government nature conservation personnel in the region, the local support for conservation is still the key factor in controlling poaching; in fact, poaching for elephant tusks or rhino horn has virtually ceased in the Kaokoveld and the numbers of both species have increased for the first time in over 15 years.

Unfortunately, State funds are still not available to support this unorthodox system and, consequently, further financial assistance is still urgently needed to carry out further work of this nature, both in the Kaokoveld and other tribal areas where important wildlife populations are threatened.

# An expedition to the crocodile caves of Ankarana, Madagascar

## Jane Margaret Wilson

4 Oatlands, 69 Thame Road, Warborough OX9 8EA, UK

British, born 21 June 1954. House physician at Princess Margaret Hospital, Swindon. Educated in UK; M.Sc. from Oxford University in 1979, B.M. from University of Southampton in 1985.

Ankarana is a Jurassic limestone massif in the tropical north-east of Madagascar, remarkable for its huge river caves in which the local people hunt crocodiles and fruit bats, and bury their kings. Within the massif, and inaccessible except through the caves, there are ecological "islands" of lush virgin forest, walled in by sheer limestone cliffs rising to a height of 200 m. During the dry season, the luxuriant forests within the massif are maintained by the subterranean rivers while the surrounding basalt scrubland becomes parched.

### Main expedition thrusts

In 1981, we made a 10-day reconnaissance of Ankarana and discovered many new species of inverterbrates. However, no complete lists of species have been compiled and it is our project to return to Ankarana and, in collaboration with Malagasy scientists, compile the most comprehensive species list for any Malagasy reserve and make censual and behavioural studies on the most significant vertebrates. We also plan to assess interactions between the Antankarana people and their environment, considering the influence of helminths, arthropod vectors, gastropods and mammalian-disease reservoirs on public health, and the influence of man on vertebrate populations.

We will compile a comprehensive zoological inventory of the Ankarana area focusing particularly on the following groups: herpetofauna, lemurs, bats, invertebrates and mesites. The caves of Ankarana form one of the few remaining refuges for *Crocodylus niloticus*, and we will assess this crocodile's population and conservation status and study crocodile movement and behaviour in the caves. We will also catalogue and photograph the herpetofauna in the caves and the isolated pockets of forest, locate amphibia and record their calls.

A search will be made for further evidence of the broad-nosed gentle lemur, *Hapalemur simus*, a species on the brink of extinction, which was thought to be extinct locally until, in 1981, its bones were found within the Ankarana massif. Species lists of bats will be compiled, and various bats will be captured,

335

photographed, sampled for ectoparasites and then released. Mass collections will be made of invertebrates, and speciation in the massif's isolated forests will be studied. We will also collect a few live butterflies, *Papilio dardanus meriones*, for genetic research. In our studies on cave ecology, we will collect data on the distribution of aquatic cavernicoles, many of which should be new to science; cave shrimps in this region display a striking species diversity and require further study. Botanical research will involve collecting material for the conservation of genetic resources at the Kew Seed Bank, and we will also provide duplicates for archiving in Madagascar.

In the field of public health, assessments will be made of bacteriological water quality and of water use patterns by the Antankarana of Andrafiabe, and the results will be related to the prevalance of water-related disease, e.g. diarrhoea, ascariasis, skin infections, etc. Schistosomiasis epidemiology will be studied and the urine and stool egg content of infected people will be measured and correlated with extent of exposure to infective cercaria, the population dynamics of snail intermediate host(s), and the production of cercaria by infected snails. Antihelminthics for the treatment of ascariasis and schistosomiasis will be administered to any Andrafiabe villager who wishes it, and stools may be analyzed at the start and end of the expedition to check that eradication of infestation has been achieved.

**Significance of the research**

Ecological studies in Madagascar have been largely confined to the principal species in a few well-known areas; there is no comprehensive inventory for any Malagasy reserve and little information on the ecology of northern Madagascar. We believe that our intensive study of one reserve – Ankarana – will contribute towards the understanding of the unique ecology of Madagascar. We anticipate that the parasitological work will further improve our knowledge of the

*A male crowned lemur,* Lemur coronatus, *emerging from a cave water hole in the Ankarana massif. This species had not previously been photographed and studied in the wild.*

336

*This blind white goby is a new species discovered by members of the Crocodile Caves of Ankarana Expedition in 1986. It has yet to be named by taxonomists of the British Museum.*

aetiology and control of these diseases. The expedition will benefit nature conservation since we will assess the impact of the local people on lemurs, crocodiles and fruit bat populations which use the caves for shelter, and will suggest management policies which would enable continued cropping without threatening the survival of these species. These studies will be valuable for stimulating local interest in conservation, and will enable us to produce relevant educational materials. The expedition will also offer immediate benefits to education in Madagascar since I will be available to offer lectures whenever they are required after the expedition. Duplicate slides taken during the expedition, and copies of publications resulting from the expedition, will be offered to Malagasy institutions.

Plans are afoot to produce slide-sound sequences on animals, plants and their conservation. These will be soundly based on the comprehensive study of the Ankarana reserve, and on the interactions that the Antankarana people have with it. It is intended that the material will be made freely available to conservation bodies and the World Wildlife Fund. Duplicates of all animals and herbarium specimens collected will be deposited at the relevant Malagasy institutions.

# Semi-Arid Lands Training and Livestock Improvement Centre Kenya (SALTLICK)

## Robert Percival Slade

POB 77, Rumuruti, Kenya

British, born 17 February 1936. Senior Complex Manager, Agricultural Development Corporation, Mutara Ranch. Educated in UK and Canada; Certificate of Agriculture from Lackam College of Agriculture in 1953.

Arid and semi-arid lands account for 75% of the total surface area of Kenya, approximately 50% of all the country's livestock, and roughly 25% of its population, thus representing a major challenge to all concerned. The Government is currently emphasizing these areas through the Arid and Semi-Arid Lands programme (ASAL), and considerable preliminary planning has been done. At present, these lands contribute little to the national economy, and improvements – within the ecological restrictions – will come only with careful planning.

Most of the people occupying these arid and semi-arid lands are ranching pastoralists whose life style, traditions, food and beliefs are centred on their livestock (cattle, sheep, goats, camels and donkeys) on which they depend for their livelihoods. For them, development of a crop programme is a far less secure investment than livestock, on account of the harsh climate and fine ecological balance in these areas; it is obvious, however, that the ASAL region will become increasingly sedentarized and that the pastoralists will eventually settle. It will thus be essential to equip them with the knowledge they need for successful ranching. There are also large numbers of new settlers with agricultural backgrounds in the ASAL region, who must be taught dry-land farming, the cultivation of suitable crops and how to avoid crop failures (which often happen with newcomers, and then necessitate famine relief measures).

### SALTLICK and its objectives

The general objective of the Semi-Arid Lands Training and Livestock Improvement Centre Kenya (SALTLICK), a non-profit organization, is to assist in the overall development of the areas concerned, in particular: livestock marketing and upgrading; preservation of indigenous genetic material; water development; use of agro-forestry; land and range management; animal health; dry-land crop production; soil and water conservation; and other related skills suitable for the development of the local economy. Training programmes on all these aspects are also provided.

*Camels being watered in the semi-arid lands of northern Kenya.*

The concentration of the different livestock varies with the fineness of the ecological balance. Cattle are of key significance for the pastoralists and play a traditional role in many rituals and ceremonies. Goats are less harmful to pastures than sheep, and goat improvement should be fostered. Camels have many advantages and, in particular, they need water less frequently and continue to produce milk throughout the year. Ranchers of the ASAL should be helped to improve the quality of their animals, and the main emphasis should be on better management of and selection within the existing stock. However, without a regular supply of breeding animals, particularly males, it will be difficult to make rapid and lasting improvements.

The ASAL region's future depends on the large-scale preservation and production of trees for forage, firewood, commercial products, etc. Trees are essential for the ecological survival of the area and, as sedentary ranching increases, will be crucial to livestock for forage during drought periods. In addition, to allow the pastoralists to supplement their livestock products, the teaching of dry-land farming should have priority. Much can be achieved by terracing, micro-catchments, etc. Water is crucial and, although many ASAL areas receive low rainfall, they have a relatively high water table, and many retain rainfall run-off; there is water at accessible levels below the river beds. Water conservation methods should therefore be introduced and/or promoted.

The success of any livestock improvement programme in the ASAL regions depends on the provision of training programmes to equip the people with the knowledge and ability to cope with the harsh environment and recurring droughts. Vocational training should also be provided in such skills as carpentry, masonry, metalwork, tailoring, home economics, etc. A training centre will be set up for this purpose.

### SALTLICK project proposals

Projects envisaged by SALTLICK include: specialized camel research; training in the use of horses, mules, oxen and donkeys and in the breeding of these animals; the provision of a small tannery for teaching purposes, etc.; and the organization of vocational training courses of one or two years' duration. SALTLICK proposes that the projects be carried out in three phases. The first will cover the leasing of land to be operated on a commercial basis to demonstrate ranching and to generate funds for the following phases. The second phase will encompass the preservation of breeding stock; in Kenya the genetic material is outstanding but is in danger of being lost. The third phase will be devoted to setting up the training centre mentioned above.

If these SALTLICK proposals can be implemented, they will make an outstanding long-term contribution to lifestyles and living standards in arid and semi-arid land areas.

*The pastoralists in the semi-arid lands of northern Kenya – "people matter more than things".*

# For a free Pyrenean migration of European birds

## Joël Tanguy Le Gac
**Honourable Mention**
**The Rolex Awards for Enterprise – 1987**

Lasclaveries, 64450 Thèze, France

French, born 2 April 1945. Biology and geology teacher. Educated in France;
Agrégation de sciences naturelles in 1970.

---

The valley of Larrau, Basque country of south-west France, is a topographic funnel for the European migratory birds that cross the Pyrenees by millions every autumn on their journey to the Mediterranean and Africa. For some years, our consumer society has exploited this international heritage by auctioning out passes and crests to hunters and, for example, the 17 passes of the valley of Larrau are let by the intercommunal authorities of Soule to 193 hunters every third year.

In 1979, a group of ornithologists got together to rent a pass at a price of 20,000 FF a year, to ensure that, at one point at least, the migrators could escape the murderous fire. It was in this way that "Operation Orgambideska Free Pass" was born, and allowed hundreds of observers from all over Europe to study the transpyrenean migration and the extent of hunting pressure for three years (1979–1981). The studies have shown that the Larrau Valley concentrates up to 15% of the migrators, especially birds of prey. Every autumn, from the Orgambideska Pass we can observe more than 20,000 birds of prey of 20 different species, thousands of cranes, several hundred thousands of wood pigeons and millions of songbirds, etc., of more than 100 species. It is one of the two or three most important migratory passes in Western Europe. The hunters in the passes have dumped over a tonne of lead each year in the nearby mountain pastures, firing about 50,000 shots, killing 3% of the wood pigeons, not to speak of the other species, no matter whether they are protected or not.

The next six years proved a contest of wills between the ornithologists and the hunters who tried by all means to regain their Orgambideska hunting grounds; whilst the ornithologists attracted more and more adepts, collected detailed statistics of bird movements over the crest and, finally, formed themselves into an association, the Orgambideska Col Libre – Pertuis Pyrénéens.

## Our scientific achievement

Here we have made something of a discovery, since the Orgambideska crest has allowed us to study in depth a major and representative segment of European autumnal bird migration. The data we have collected have been computerized and analyzed and the results of our observations have been published and widely disseminated – all on the basis of voluntary efforts by our co-workers. In the past three years, we have been able to extend this activity – by means of the Transpyr programme launched and organized by François Sagot – to cover all the Pyrenean passes used by migrating raptors and pigeons. Obviously our chain of Pyrenean birdwatchers can be further extended to cover a larger area for a longer portion of the year but it is already of sufficient density for satisfactory deductions to be made. As far as the Orgambideska crest itself is concerned, our migratory data are complete and only the installation of a radar system could improve the information collection; this in itself is a feasible project. What is needed, however, is a long-term presence so that migration population dynamics can be studied year after year. The scientific freedom we have acquired has had to be paid for and won; but many of the hunters in France would like to deprive us of this freedom.

**Our conservation achievement**

The space our association has protected is minute when one considers the large number of crests in the Pyrenees and constitutes but a small breach in the field of fire laid down by hunters in the Western Pyrenees. However, in clearing the route over the Orgambideska crest we have opened up a field of action that goes far beyond the boundaries of the Pyrenees.

Two ministers have already promised to close 10% of the migrating passes to hunting. Alas, neither of them kept that promise. The next minister may promise less but certainly cannot deliver less. In the meantime, whilst waiting for these promises to be put into effect, our association has ploughed ahead and has given birth to similar ventures using Orgambideska as a model: six further

*Orgambideska Pass, a key section of the route taken by migrating birds each year on the way to the South had become an ambush firing range where tonnes of lead were pumped out to kill thousands of birds.*

*The efforts of the Orgambideska Col Libre Association, which outbid the hunters to rent the pass, have now ensured that hunters' guns have been replaced by bird watchers' binoculars.*

sites have been set up in France to study migrating birds and protect them from the onslaught of the hunters and others will be established in the autumn in Spain and Italy. Our venture has proved infectious and has been communicated to others.

### Our educational achievement

Certainly, our very presence on Orgambideska has been a far more powerful educational tool than the publication of any amount of scientific results or newspaper articles. Several hundred ornithologists of all levels have followed training courses on the Crest.

Several thousand visitors have spent between a few minutes and a few hours with us on the pass, receiving answers to their questions and several hundred school children have visited the pass with their teachers, for practical instruction on bird migration and nature protection. However, for this activity to flourish, we once again need the guarantee of continuity.

343

# Development of an International Crocodile Bank

## Zahida Whitaker

Madras Crocodile Bank, Mahabalipuram Road, Vadanemmeli-603104, India

Indian, born 21 April 1954. Honorary Secretary, Madras Crocodile Bank.
Educated in India; B.A. (English Literature) from Madras University in 1983.

In 1975, starting out with muggers, *Crocodylus palustris*, mostly from aquaria and exhibits, and 50 juveniles hatched from wild-collected eggs, my husband and I set up a trust, the Madras Crocodile Bank, with the object of conserving crocodilians through captive breeding, research, field surveys and public education. Visitors to the Crocodile Bank, 50% of whom are children, are treated to what is probably their first look at crocodilians as interesting reptiles and not merely objects of fear. An effort is made to provide each group with an informed guide. All the work at the Bank is done by villagers recruited locally and trained on the job for this unusual vocation. Located 40 km south of Madras in South India, the Crocodile Bank covers an area of some 3.5 ha with stone and brick walls surrounding the six large breeding enclosures, seven rearing pens and 20 nursery pens.

### The Crocodile Bank's facilities

Adult muggers are housed in a large enclosure, surrounded by a 180 m circumference wall; half the area is a landscaped pond 3 m deep, while the other half is well-planted dry land. Juveniles are housed in 3 m x 3 m nursery pens for the first six to eight months, and yearling crocodiles are kept in large enclosures of 50 m circumference with a water channel 1–2 m wide and 80 cm deep. Turtles (mostly *Melanochelys trijuga*) which are kept with the juvenile crocodiles, consume left-over food on the bottom of the ponds in the breeding enclosures.

Muggers mate in December and lay their eggs from February to April; the first hatchlings appear in April and the last in June. We routinely leave the eggs in the nests for 50 days; thereafter, they are transferred to styrofoam boxes, an optimum technique for controlled-temperature incubation. The crocodiles have a diet which is varied as much as possible; hatchlings and young animals are given tadpoles, frogs, small fish and crabs; they also feed on insects attracted by the lights near each pond at night. The larger animals are fed the seasonally most economical food which is tilapia and other species of fish one half of the year and buffalo meat the other. Breeding animals are fed large quantities of rats

344

caught by local tribals.

Adult mortality has been due solely to fighting and tunnel collapses; sickness occurs most commonly up to the age of two years and has included respiratory infection, liver damage and paralysis (the latter we think due to a toxic legume sometimes ingested by small crocodiles). Overall mortality among small crocodiles has been 5–10% in hatchlings and under 5% for yearlings and above.

## The International Crocodile Bank

The Crocodile Specialist Group of the International Union for Conservation of Nature and National Resources has approved the concept of internationalizing the scope of the Bank, and we have been encouraged to start breeding exotic species such as spectacled caymans. We are now building up breeding groups of crocodilians which are under extreme pressure in their own countries so that, when countries decide to protect their crocodiles, offspring can be obtained from the Crocodile Bank. Action has thus been started to establish the Crocodile Bank's credibility as a recognized international breeding centre and to start accumulating breeding stock of all the other species. Various zoos on a number of continents have agreed to send us seed stock of crocodilians from their respective countries and institutions. The Bank also offers its services in trapping crocodiles that are threatened by development projects or, occasionally, have become a public nuisance – and in such cases, we retain some or all for breeding.

The housing and care of the exotic breeds will follow the same lines as those for indigenous species, but there will be various modifications in habitat and feeding to meet the species' preferences.

*Mugger crocodiles hatching at the Madras Crocodile Bank.*

345

*Adult female gharial basking on the beach at the Madras Crocodile Bank.*

### Research, documentation and education

The availability of several species of crocodilians at one site has proved attractive to crocodile researchers, and a number of scientists have already taken advantage of our facilities. We expect to expand the research programme, and efforts will be concentrated on improving the technology of captive crocodilian husbandry, breeding biology, behaviour, growth, phenomena affecting hatching success, hatching survival and sex determination by temperature. Crocodile behaviour and the studies being done on various aspects of crocodile biology at the Bank are being documented on 16-mm colour film. It is intended to use this accumulation of relevant footage on little known aspects of crocodile life history to produce a documentary for Indian and international audiences.

Over 500,000 visitors have visited the Crocodile Bank to see the crocodiles and learn something about their positive role in the world. With proper landscaping and attention to detail, a display of the world's crocodilians, all at one place, will be an exciting educational attraction giving everyone the unique opportunity to see the range of forms and sizes these ancient reptiles have evolved into.

### Future plans and expansion

Because of the tourist value of the Crocodile Bank, the Government of Tamil Nadu has decided to acquire adjacent open land for the Crocodile Bank and increase the available area from 3.5 to about 6 ha, and it is hoped that income from tourism will keep pace with rising operating costs, thus guaranteeing self-sufficiency for the future.

346

# Using the snail kite to control schistosomiasis in Egypt

## Marc Bennett Garnick

Dana-Farber Cancer Institute, 44 Binney Street, Boston, Massachusetts 02115, USA

American, born 1 August 1947. Associate Professor of Medicine, Harvard Medical School. Educated in USA; M.D. from University of Pennsylvania Medical School in 1972.

Schistosomiasis, a human disease caused by infestation with schistosome worm, *Schistosoma haematobium*, affects nearly 200 million people. The major forms of schistosomiasis cause extensive morbidity and mortality in numerous developing countries: Africa, South America, the Middle East and the Caribbean and in China, Japan, South East Asia, North America and Europe.

A key factor in the epidemiology of the disease is the life cycle of the schistosome worm which is vectored by a freshwater snail that flourishes in still and slow-running water. There is a very realistic possibility that in future years schistosomiasis infection will increase as Third World nations and less-developed countries experience continued land and agricultural development, with the construction of complex water irrigation systems and new dams. Such alterations provide a favourable breeding place for freshwater snails, a critical link in the propagation of the schistosomes.

This project therefore proposes to introduce into Egypt, from the Florida Everglades, a number of snail kites to act as natural predators for the snails and thus control both the schistosome and the disease.

### Schistosomiasis and current control approaches

The spectrum of pathological conditions caused by schistosomes is varied but one of the most severe expressions of the disease is to be found in the development of urinary bladder cancer. The endemic infestation of rural Egyptians living along the lower Egyptian Nile Delta, who have contracted schistosomiasis, poses an extraordinary public health burden. The medical, emotional and financial implications of the loss of human life from bladder cancer pose a major challenge to medical and governmental facilities alike.

Although the association of schistosome infection with the eventual development of bladder cancer dates back to ancient Egyptian recordings and has now been studied more scientifically, control of the non-human reservoir of

347

schistosomes has moved at a "snail's pace". Efforts to control the snail population have included environmental control by altering water flow at irrigation sites, chemical control with molluscicides and, rarely, biological control by introducing natural predators of the snails themselves or the schistosomes. Unfortunately, the task of adequately controlling the snail populations which harbour the infective schistosomes (the vector snails) has been frustratingly difficult. Instead, the main emphasis of control efforts has now been transferred to the early detection of individuals with schistosomal infestation and the identification of patients with early carcinoma of the bladder. Clearly, the identification and control of complications of schistosomal infection do not address the more basic question of control and eradication of the parasitic worm itself.

## The snail kite as a natural predator

The purpose of this proposal is to provide a schema for a novel approach to controlling the snail population – a critical link in the overall life cycle of the schistosome – by the introduction and establishment of a breeding colony of one of the snail's natural predators – the snail kite, *Rostrhamus sociabilis* (also known as the Everglades kite) – with the objective of decreasing and eventually eliminating the freshwater snail population which allows *Schistosoma haematobium* to reproduce in the lower Nile Delta in Egypt. The project would entail the following steps: transporting a colony of six to eight snail kites from the Everglades (Florida) to the small Egyptian rural village of El-Shahawi; assessing the snail population density before and after the successful introduction of the snail kite; assessing the impact on the prevalence and incidence of human schistosomiasis in El-Shahawi before and after the introduction of the snail kite; and assessing the long-term changes in bladder cancer incidence and prevalence associated with a, hopefully, decreased rate of schistosomiasis.

*The Everglades or snail kite,*
Rostrhamus sociabilis.

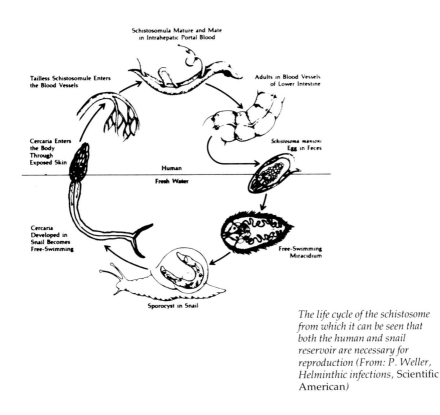

The life cycle of the schistosome
from which it can be seen that
both the human and snail
reservoir are necessary for
reproduction (From: P. Weller,
Helminthic infections, Scientific
American)

In the absence of a snail host to allow continued replication of the schistosomes, the risk of transmission of the infective schistosome cercaria to human hosts does not exist. Although individuals can be infected, they pose little risk for transmission to others, and the overall incidence of schistosomiasis should decline.

### The beneficial outcome of the project

The benefits expected by the successful realization of these objectives are three-fold: a decrease in parasitic schistosome infestation in man; a reduction in the incidence of cancer of the bladder – the most common form of cancer in Egypt today; and further expansion of our knowledge about biological ecosystems resulting from the successful establishment of natural predators.

If the proposed project were to be carried out and prove successful, there would be a substantial reduction in human disease and suffering. Once proved effective, the programme could be applied to endemic populations of schistosomal snails in other parts of the world, offering the possibility of improved health and quality of life for major sectors of the world's population.

# A process for regenerating water by aeration

## Thomas Engel

Haldenhof, 6287 Aesch, Switzerland

West German, born 10 May 1927. Process engineer, Head of
Engel-Verfahrenstechnik. Educated in West Germany.

The process of enriching fluid with dissolved gases by introducing very small bubbles has been known for many years. Gas is dissolved into the fluid by means of a diffuser – a device which produces small bubbles. As the bubbles rise a gaseous exchange takes place between the bubbles and the fluid. Gas can be dissolved in the fluid only up to a saturation point which varies with the type of gas, the fluid, the pressure and the temperature. The bubbles reach the surface of the liquid at a rate which increases with their size and this, in turn, reduces the time of their contact with the fluid. Therefore the optimum effect is achieved with the smallest possible bubbles. As the diffuser is limited in size, it has proved technically difficult to achieve a sufficiently high infusion of gas to make the purification process economically sound. The extent of the activity of such an installation lies only between 10 and 20%.

This project has developed a new unit which promises to be more effective.

### Using oxygen for water purification

In the case of drinking water, the most modern purifying methods require considerable quantities of oxygen to render water drinkable. Even pure natural water requires a regular supply of oxygen before it can support animal and plant life. This is brought about by natural processes. An aquarium can be ventilated by forcing air through a porous stone so that minute air bubbles are emitted which then rise to the surface. This is the system which is used industrially. This technology can be used in projects for improving the quality of lake and river water and for purification of water from nuclear power and sewerage plants.

Aeration and how it works can be seen in sewage reprocessing. To clean and recycle household sewage, micro-organisms are mixed with the sewage in concrete tanks where they metabolize the sewage and convert it to suspended matter which is then deposited, leaving the clear water to be channelled off. Because of its high chemical content, sewage can be regarded as more or less "dead", and needs to be activated to create conditions in which the bacteria can live and work. This is done by feeding in, from below, a continuous supply of

*A myriad of minute bubbles of oxygen streaming upwards out of the horizontal diffuser panel and through the liquid being treated. The small size of the individual bubbles ensures maximum installation efficiency.*

fine bubbles of oxygen. However, if these bubbles are too large, they immediately rise to the surface without dissolving and are lost. Small bubbles are far more effective; however, they are very difficult to produce.

### Reducing aeration bubble size

The best solution, therefore, would be if the whole floor of the tank could be one entire diffuser. This would produce a huge "carpet" of bubbles and result in very effective aeration without increasing the speed at which the bubbles rise to the surface. My new technique has achieved this objective.

In this system, the diffusers consist of hollow panels of modified polyethylene which are finely perforated on one side; they are closed at the ends but have a connection through which the air can be introduced. Optimum hole size is between 80 and 100 micron. It is, technically, almost impossible to drill holes of this size and, consequently, a new technique employing special high-temperature needles was used to perforate the diffuser and produce extremely fine bubbles. These needles are like a corkscrew and after perforating the panel wall they remove a small amount of polyethylene to ensure that the hole remains open. The holes in the diffuser are arranged in a chequered pattern and are sufficiently spaced to prevent collision between the bubbles.

Bubbles with a diameter of less than 0.5 mm fed into the liquid from a depth of 3 m will be 95% effective. Even though it is not yet technically possible to produce bubbles of such a small diameter, this new diffuser is to a large degree capable of producing this ideal situation. Furthermore, it has been found that bubble formation can be enhanced by feeding the air into the panel intermittently, thus achieving a pulsating inflow which frees the bubbles more rapidly from the diffuser surface and reduces bubble size.

351

## A diffuser with wide-ranging advantages

The new diffuser technique offers marked advantages. It costs far less than a conventional system and will therefore appeal to medium-sized industries.

This new "bubble carpet" is acid resistant and low in weight. It can be built into existing installations and is, moreover, simple to clean. It can be employed in the chemical industry, in medicine and in agriculture, and of course in sewage treatment and lake and river purification. It has an important role to play in environmental protection and in the efforts being made to keep our water pure.

*The oxygen vaporizers forming part of a water treatment installation set up to regenerate a lake. The installation has a daily throughput capacity of 4.5 t of oxygen.*

# Ethno-ornithology – Studying the names of and cultural beliefs about birds in Kenya

*Aneesa Kassam*

**Honourable Mention**
**The Rolex Awards for Enterprise – 1987**

POB 40319, Nairobi, Kenya

Kenyan, born 26 May 1949. Staff member, Department of Literature, University of Nairobi. Educated in Kenya, Madagascar and France; Ph.D. (Ethno-linguistics) from University of Paris III (Sorbonne Nouvelle) in 1984.

Kenya is a bird-watcher's paradise, and almost every scientific aspect of the avifauna has been extensively studied. However, remarkably little attention has been paid to cultural attitudes and beliefs about birds amongst the peoples of Kenya and, with one brief exception, no systematic study has been undertaken of the vernacular names and traditional beliefs about birds. Yet, in Kenya, as elsewhere, birds play an important role in the cosmology, religion, social, economic and political life and in the oral literature of the different ethnic groups. How are birds perceived, named and classified in traditional systems of thought? What do they mean? What links do they provide between the different realms of culture? How can we use this cultural information to protect the bird population and environment? These are some of the many questions which this project hopes to answer.

## Project objectives and multidisciplinary approach

My project will be divided into a number of phases and have the following objectives: to collect data for a handbook of local bird names, with their English and scientific equivalents; to study bird taxonomy and topography; to record the cultural beliefs about birds in the major ethnic groups of Kenya; to publish a book of Kenyan folk tales on the theme of the bird; and to produce an educational slide show.

Data will be collected amongst both adults and children. In particular, a questionnaire especially designed for use by school children will collect data through the magazine of the Wildlife Clubs of Kenya (*Komba*) and through the children's columns of the Kenyan press; this will be used to refine the questionnaire for use in schools.

A card index of the 1,090 reported species of birds in Kenya will be opened at the Ethnography Department and all the ethnographic literature and language dictionaries will be scanned for references to birds. All this cultural information will be added to the cards according to ethnic group. To extend my own

*The white feather of the male ostrich is, among other things, a symbol of power for many Africans. It is worn here by a Gabra Oromo in the ceremony of the "Killer" when a man has proved his virility by felling an important trophy animal.*

*Verreaux's eagle owl,* Bubo lacteus. *For many Kenyans the owl is often a bird of ill-omen and an augur of death and misfortune. (Photo by John Karmali) (opposite)*

knowledge of bird life, I will also attend the weekly bird walks led by an ornithologist at the National Museum of Kenya and will participate in other excursions and trips organized by the Kenya Museum Society and the Natural History Society where an ornithologist is present.

Before publication, all language data will be checked by a professional linguist or linguists. Cultural information collected will be published in the form of a bird "dictionary", with introductory chapters on taxonomy and bird topography for each of the groups studied. Folk tale data will also be annotated for publication. It is possible that further fieldwork will have to be carried out to collect and check data for this phase of the study. Bilingual versions of the tales will be presented and they could either be illustrated by drawings done by children or professionally illustrated. In the final phase of the study, the scientific, cultural and ecological data collected in the previous phases will be used to provide commentary for a bird slide show. The background sound could consist of bird song, classical music based on the work of J.L. Florentz, a French composer who has transposed Kenyan bird song into his music, or traditional music recorded in the field.

### Publication and utilization of findings

It is hoped that the study will not only have academic value but also provoke more general interest, and be of more practical use and relevance to the nation as a whole. In Kenya, with rapid urbanization, social change and the breakdown of traditional forms of education, much of the cultural heritage of its peoples, of which birds are only one aspect, is rapidly being lost. By focusing on birds and by systematically recording all the traditional knowledge connected with them, an important step will have been made towards documenting these traditional systems of belief, and salvaging them from oblivion. The data would also help the Department of Ornithology at the Museum to answer questions from

354

government authorities and academic and commercial organizations in Kenya and abroad. In the Museum of the future, the slideshow could provide another dimension to the bird display, and could "travel" to other regional museums and abroad, popularizing birds and creating awareness about them and thus protecting them through cultural mechanisms.

By encouraging young student researchers to document the subject in their own cultures, the project will contribute to their training in the field and provide them with a research methodology for the future if they continue in this line of study. A book of folk tales centred on the theme of the bird, supported by cultural data, will be invaluable to teachers and students of oral literature and provide interesting comparative data for the study of folklore and religion in the world, where the image of the bird is universally present.

# Toxic waste – An ocean dilemma

## *John Christopher Fine*

150 Puritan Drive, Scarsdale, New York 10583, USA

American, born 12 October 1943. Attorney-at-law, writer, underwater photographer and film maker. Educated in USA; LL.B-J.D. from Notre Dame Law School in 1967.

My interest in the ocean dates from my earliest recollections, and I started diving at the age of six years. This fascination for the oceans, combined with my writing skills, led me to enter and win local and national literary prizes and awards, and regularly write about things and creatures I discovered in the environment around me.

### Realization of environmental deterioration

With increasing concern I discovered the rapid deterioration of the ocean environment, and this led me, with a colleague, to be the first to report the massive fish kill in the Atlantic in 1976 following the increased volume of ocean dumping in the New York Bight. Yet, efforts by concerned public officials, conservation groups and even amateur divers and sport fishermen were not enough to stem the tide of ecological destruction of water resources that I saw at close quarters as a diver. Moreover, as a Senior Diplomatic Official attached to the US State Department, I obtained a first-hand view of the world's hunger problems and observed the famine resulting from the failure of our environment to produce food, and the inadequacies of a feeble food chain.

On my return to New York to assume the duties of Assistant Attorney General in Charge, Organized Crime Task Force, I did not foresee that my profession would mesh with my avocation of concern for the sea and authoring books and papers about the marine environment; however, in one of those coincidences that puts a person in a special position at the right time, this convergence did take place. Well water was contamined, Love Canal had received dangerous toxic wastes, and an important wide-ranging investigation I initiated into organized, criminal take-over of the carting, landfilling and toxic waste industry in the United States led to the discovery of an environmental holocaust, the dimensions of which have not yet been fully estimated.

*John C. Fine at the site of illegal dumping of toxic wastes into a protected marshland which led eventually into the Atlantic. As Chief Prosecutor in Charge of the Organized Crime Task Force, John C. Fine pioneered investigations into organized criminal dumping of toxic wastes.*

## Investigations into illegal waste dumping

My investigations showed official corruption in government and, as Counsel to a special grand jury, I returned a report which for the first time detailed the extent of the environmental menace caused by toxic waste discharges into the environment, the ramifications to human and animal health, and the contamination of land and water resources. Corrupt political figures were linked to ownership of companies whose illegal business it was to dump the poisoned wastes directly into the ocean, streams, rivers, village sewer treatment systems, landfills built in marshlands or on harbours; in all cases, these persons were linked with criminals associated with organized crime.

Detectives working for me were threatened with guns, driven off the road in their police cars; my life too was threatened and my professional career menaced. I refused to give in to the building political pressure to stop the investigations which were daily revealing the involvement of elected and appointed political figures with organized crime, bribery and corruption. Persons who figured prominently in the ABSCAM corruption investigation owned waste companies which I had under investigation and which we filmed dumping dangerous chemicals into a river leading to the ocean.

Nowadays, the extent and danger of toxic waste contamination of the environment is evident but my investigations began in 1977, when government refused to admit that war wastes, biological, nuclear and chemical residues were dumped, knowingly, by officials into landfills which now contaminate the water resources. My investigations were blocked at every turn – yet, with a few loyal and honest detectives, I succeeded in obtaining arrests and executing search warrants on major toxic waste sites. I subsequently became Counsel to the Senate Committee on Toxic Wastes and Hazardous Substances and continued my documentation and investigation of the criminal, improper and unlawful disposal of dangerous wastes into the environment.

357

Throughout my experience in this field, I was called upon to testify as an expert witness before legislative committees and senate bodies investigating the area. Major newspaper series were written about my work, television aired the results of these investigations and three books reported on my findings and work. However, the work is not finished and I continue to film and photograph the results of this contamination and publish articles in various journals, magazines and newspapers.

### Culmination of my efforts

A book and a professional 16-mm film entitled *Toxic waste – An ocean dilemma* will be the culmination of this work and will present the danger of and a solution to the problem that has made it feasible and profitable to dump dangerous materials directly into the environment. It will show the hidden face of ocean pollution from toxic contaminants by diving into the polluted sea, observing the outcome of deliberate abuse and convenient neglect and issuing a brief for co-operative action to remedy the harm.

The oceans are a vast reservoir of food and there is no doubt that the world will soon look to the oceans as a source to feed the hungry; but the assault on their ability to support life, and the contamination of fish and seafood by heavy metals and other toxic contaminants is putting these resources in peril.

*The explosion and fire at the Chemical Control Company in Elizabeth, New Jersey located alongside the Elizabeth River. Millions of litres of toxic wastes poured into the river and were carried into the Atlantic. The case was investigated by John C. Fine.*

# Reducing mortality and increasing fertility in Burmese timber elephants

## Michael Henry Woodford

84 Maycross Avenue, Morden SM4 4DB, UK

British, born 27 September 1924. International wildlife veterinary consultant. Educated in UK; Postgraduate Doctorate of Veterinary Medicine from University of Zurich in 1976.

Burma has a total land area of 676,500 km$^2$, of which 387,200 km$^2$ (57%) is forested, mixed deciduous forest constituting 39% of total forest area, and teak some 10–12% of the growing stock. It is estimated that Burma has 75% of the world's teak reserves; in 1983, 848,000 m$^3$ of teak was felled and the Burmese timber industry earned 26% of the nation's foreign exchange.

### Use of elephants in the timber industry

Over one million tonnes of timber are extracted each year, 900,000 t by a combination of elephants and buffaloes, or elephants and machinery. About 5,400 captive elephants work in the timber industry, all of which – with the exception of a few bred in captivity – are caught in the wild. Burmese forests are, in the main, managed cyclically under the selective logging system, with a logging cycle of 30 years. This system is dependent upon the natural regeneration of teak and other hardwoods, which will not occur if the forest environment is damaged. The superiority of elephants over machines in minimizing environmental damage during timber extraction is obvious. Indeed, one of the most important logging operations known as "Ve Lite" can be undertaken only by elephants.

### Help in the healthier management of elephants

The Burmese have more expertise than any other nation in the management of captured elephants for work in the timber industry, so this is not an area where foreign expertise can be of assistance. However, these animals currently have an unacceptably high mortality rate, particularly in the post-capture period, and poor reproductive performance in captivity. Therefore the project will employ a broad range of modern veterinary diagnostic and therapeutic techniques to reduce the high losses (25%) occurring amongst newly captured young elephants, which are thought to be due to the stresses of capture and post-

*Domesticated Asiatic elephant at work in a teak plantation.*

capture handling and to injuries received during restraint. In addition, concurrent subclinical infections, such as trypanosomiasis may become pathogenic under stress conditions. The 6% mortality rate among adult working elephants needs to be investigated and the causes identified so that it can be lowered. Training of Burmese counterpart veterinarians in modern diagnostic techniques for use under field conditions must also be given priority.

The poor reproductive efficiency of the female working elephant is due partly to the separation of the sexes during the six-month mating season when the females are turned loose in the forest where, in the past, they often met a wild male in the forest and became pregnant. Now that the number of wild males is much reduced, the chances of a female being thus served are small. Oestrus in the female elephant occurs at approximately 16-week intervals and is not accompanied by any overt signs. What is needed is a simple field test, using the female elephant's urine or saliva, to indicate the onset of hormonal changes which presage oestrus, upon detection of which she could be served by the nearest captive male.

Current research in America suggests that certain reproductive pheromones are excreted by female elephants at the time of oestrus and that detection of these by analytical means may provide the necessary information. As elephants excrete very little progesterone in their urine or milk, studies are under way to see whether it can be monitored in the animal's saliva. The project has contacted pheromone and progesterone assay researchers in the USA and the UK and will co-operate with them in test development.

Male elephants are able to detect by olfactory means changes in the female's reproductive status and, before a chemical assay becomes available, it may be necessary to present a sample of the female's urine at regular intervals to a test-male until he exhibits the required response. Another approach would be to attempt artificially to provoke oestrus by the injection of prostaglandins. If this were successful it would be possible to synchronize breeding and thus regulate the production of batches of recruits of similar age class.

*Elephants at work in a teak plantation.*

## Need for a wild elephant population census

Whatever the success of the veterinary component in reducing mortality and improving fertility, there will be a continuing need to recruit replacement animals from the wild. Rough estimates suggest that the wild elephant population is about 6,000, and declining. To sustain a population at this level, annual offtake should not exceed 150 animals (2.5%), but it is still over 250 with a bias towards females due to their greater tractability. To continue at this level will rapidly deplete the existing wild stock making it impossible to provide the recruits needed.

In order to set a realistic annual offtake at a sustainable level, an accurate census of elephant numbers and distribution is urgently required, and the project will undertake a country-wide census of the Asian elephant population in Burma. Provided the excessive offtake can be reduced, there is no reason why this endangered species should not survive in the wild in Burma so that, if the project is successful, it will assist in the conservation of an endangered species.

# Systematic research on the ground beetles of Nepal

 *Pierre Morvan*

71 route du Pavé Blanc, Résidence "La Chaumière", Bat. Q, 92140 Clamart, France

French, born 8 June 1935. Taxi driver. Educated in France; self-taught entomologist.

When not at the wheel of his taxi, Pierre Morvan devotes his time to the study of insects. In fact, for some 20 years, he has spent his holidays travelling the mountains of Asia collecting beetles (Coleoptera) and, in particular, ground beetles (Carabidae) from which, he feels, much can be learned about speciation, i.e. the formation of biological species and the processes involved therein.

In recent decades, considerable progress has been made in the study of biological speciation mechanisms; in particular, research on geographic variations in animal populations has shown that isolation is the sole determinant of speciation, and that a species may, in fact, be defined as an isolated gene pool. Although this isolation may depend on various factors (behaviour, habitat or reproduction), it is now widely accepted that all forms of isolation were originally preceded by isolation of a geographic nature. Biological differentiation in a population group results from a division of the species' gene pool; once geographically isolated, a population group will inevitably develop its own specific characteristics. The isolation barriers at the origin of these mechanisms are, therefore, of considerable interest. Species variation is thus related to the ecology and topography of the area in which the species is distributed; hence, the interest of studying species in highly divergent regions. The study material must, however, meet certain requirements and, in particular, it is preferable to work with a species that is morphologically variable and which belongs to groups which have been subject to systematic study.

### Significance of the Carabidae in speciation studies

The Carabidae (or ground beetles) meet these criteria particularly well; I have specialized in the species which live underground and which are so environment-dependent that they are somethimes referred to as "environment indicators".

*Pierre Morvan, Rolex Laureate – The Rolex Awards for Enterprise 1987, with part of his collection of beetles.*

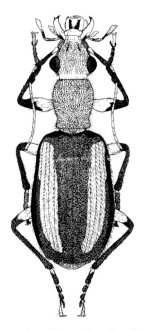

*A drawing by Pierre Morvan of a specimen of* Desera lineola *encountered in Nepal.*

These species are not only affected by the slightest environmental changes but are also sensitive to genetic factors; this results in multiplicity of species and geographic races in the same region, and offers an outstanding field for research on links between geographic variations and variations in extrinsic factors.

The Trechinae, an "environment indicator" subfamily of the Carabidae, undergo intense speciation; research has linked their current distribution to continental movements, and attempts have also been made to explain certain local distributions on the basis of palaeogeographic data. I myself believe that the Platyninae, from the main group of Colpodes, offer the same advantages as the Trechinae from the palaeogeographic and biogeographic point of view. My project is therefore to carry out biogeographic studies on this group in the Himalayan region – which is especially attractive since it is at the interface between the Palaearctic and Indo-Malayan zones, is of irregular topography, and has a fauna and flora which are largely unstudied.

## Biogeographic attraction of the Himalayan region

The southern Himalyas display an astonishing acceleration of the transition between two biogeographic zones and, therefore, are a meeting point of ecologically different formations of transition. For example, in the Kali Gandaki Valley, in the southern part of the Dhaulagiri massif, within a space of less than 10 km as the crow flies, there is a transition from a tropical formation to an Alpine zone offering interesting prospects for the comparative distribution of Coleoptera Trechinae and Carabinae species – which are exclusively palaearctic. This region is also of interest in view of the palaeogeographic origin of the Indian Peninsula which, having collided with Asia following its detatchment from the ancient continent of Gondwanaland, has a fauna completely different from the Eurasian fauna.

364

*Pierre Morvan photographed on the Jhala-Jele pass against a background of Mt. Churen in the Dhaulagiri Massif during one of his expeditions to Nepal.*

Mountainous massifs are of particular interest when they form the boundary of an area occupied by an animal group, since they contain a high density of the geographic isolation factors at the origin of speciation mechanisms and concentrate a rich potential for research into a small surface area. It may even be possible to partially reconstitute and explain the geographic distribution and variation of a given species or a species group. The Alps have been the subject of several biogeographic studies in this respect and it will be interesting to determine similarities between the southern Alps and the southern Himalayas. The study of palaearctic relics high on isolated massifs in a subtropical zone will certainly bring to light Trechinae or Carabinae to demonstrate that they were distributed farther south in the Pleistocene ice age.

Finally, our knowledge of the Himalayan fauna is very limited, and even though recent expeditions have given us a tantalizing glimpse of the entomological resources of the Nepalese massifs, the Carabidae of large areas remain unknown. Nevertheless, the increasing number of organized expeditions has encouraged me to compile a book entitled *The Carabidae of Nepal*. Nepal seems to contain its own special fauna and it will be necessary to determine the limits of these typically Nepalese elements. Our knowledge of the Trechinae and Platyninae is still too fragmentary to hazard any conclusion but we know that members of the Carabidae family from Kashmir are found as far away as the Jumla region whilst an exclusively Nepalese member is to be found in Annapurna. Nepal is not lacking in regions which are unexplored by entomologists and offers great promise of interesting discoveries.

365

# Wild plant derivatives as an alternative to conventional insecticides

## Angel Lagunes-Tejeda
**Honourable Mention**
**The Rolex Awards for Enterprise – 1987**

Juan Escutia No. 7, Tezcoco, Mexico

Mexican, born 20 March 1943. Professor of Economic Entomology. Educated in Mexico and USA; Ph.D. from University of California, Riverside in 1980.

Although much has been published about the use made of plants as medicines in prehispanic Mexico there is very little information about plants with insecticidal activity. Clearly empirical research at that time was focused more on medicinal than insecticidal properties. Natural plant products are a source of various bioactive substances that were used as models for such modern insecticides as the carbamates and pyrethroids. One of the best known natural insecticides is derived from the flowers of pyrethrum which was used against the human louse in the time of King Xerxes of Persia. Other plant-derived substances that have been used as insecticides are nicotine, rotenone and sabadilla.

## Plants and pests in Mexico

Some of the native plants which were used for their insecticidal properties in Mexico include: *Haplophyton cimicidum* for fruit flies in the orange, mango and guava; *Microsechium helleri* for white grubs in gardens; *Artemisia luduviciana* for corn weevil; and *Trichilia havanensis* for seedcorn maggot.

The introduction of synthetic organic insecticides interrupted development of natural-based products; however, with the spread of insecticide pollution in Mexico and other developing countries, the use of natural-based products would have numerous advantages: these materials are derived from renewable resources; the environmental contamination risks are minimal because the plant preparations are not persistent; plant materials and, in particular, wild plants, are cheap and easy to obtain and prepare; insect resistance to these substances develops only slowly in view of the low level of residues; and this "technology" can easily be adopted by the small-scale farmer because it fits in well with his way of life.

This ongoing project has as its main objective to draw up recommendations for small-scale farmers on how to use powders and water extracts of wild plants growing around them to combat the insect pests of major crops (corn and beans), that have the most destructive effect on Mexico's economy. It comprises seven major segments: collection and drying of plants, preparation of plant material, laboratory testing, greenhouse testing, field testing and dissemination of results.

The main insect pests that have been selected as targets are: the army-worm, *Spodoptera frugiperda*, and the fall army-worm, *Pseudaletia unipuncta*, which attack corn in the field; the corn weevil, *Sitophilus zeamais*, the angoumois grain moth, *Sitotroga cerealella*, and the larger grain borer, *Prostephanus truncatus*, which attack grain during storage; the Mexican bean beetle, *Epilachna varivestis*, which attacks beans in the field; and the common bean beetle, *Acanthoscelides obtectus*, and the Mexican bean weevil, *Zabrotes subfasciatus*, which attack beans in storage. Between them, these pests are responsible for at least 80% of the losses caused by insects to corn and bean in Mexico.

## Plant collection and screening

Plants have been collected at flowering time and a sample weighing approximately 1.4 kg is hung in a storehouse to dry. Each plant is then processed to produce three different types of product: some 500 g is ground to a fine powder for testing on storage pests; a 5% solution is prepared by boiling 50 g of plant in 1,000 g of water; and 50 g of plant is mixed in a blender in 1,000 g of water. The water extracts are allowed to settle in a flask overnight and, after the solids have been strained off, the solutions are used for testing.

## Laboratory and field tests

For army-worm and fall army-worm, the test solutions are mixed with artificial diet and placed together with larvae in vials. If larval mortality in the test vials is high in comparison with that in control vials, the treatment is retested; if the effect is confirmed, the substance goes forward for greenhouse testing. Larval weight reduction caused by the plant solutions is also taken into account; if the average weight of treated larvae is less than half that of controls, the treatment is considered promising. In the case of the Mexican bean beetle, larvae are placed on bean leaves that have been soaked in a treatment solution; plant solutions that result in over 50% mortality go for further tests.

To test the effectiveness of treatments on pests that attack stored corn and beans, 100 g of corn is mixed with 1 g of treatment powder and placed in a glass container with 10 male and 10 female insects; parent mortality is then evaluated after 15–20 days and first generation mortality is assessed after 40–50 days. Promising powders once again go on for further testing.

Subsequently army-worm and fall army-worm treatments are applied to the foliage of greenhouse corn to which larvae are then added. Damage produced by the larvae over a period of one week is used as the evaluation criterion. Treatments for Mexican bean beetle are applied to potted bean plants 25 days after emergence; the damage caused 15 days after larvae placement is used for evaluating effectiveness. The powder solutions that proved most promising in laboratory and greenhouse tests will now go on to field testing in 10 different geographic areas of Mexico using conventional evaluation procedures and the results will be published in bulletins and/or pamphlets.

## Overall achievements and future prospects

So far, over 400 plants have been tested in the laboratory and more than 40 have been found to have promising properties. Field tests are still at an early stage but, already, four plants have shown promise against the fall army-worm and two against the Mexican beetle. However, an additional important achievement is that already 10 scientists have graduated doing research on this project, and a further 26 persons have been trained on the project work – all of which bodes well for future progress.

*Corn plants infested with armyworm,* Spodoptera frugiperda. *(above)*

*The mashed roots of* Hippocratea *sp., a wild, medicinal plant used to control insect pests in stored corn and beans.*

# Versatile ricehull-based building material to combat ricehull pollution

## Roman Gammad S. Barba, Sr.

Barba Research Laboratory, Cattaggaman Nuevo, Tuguegarao, Cagayan 1101, Philippines

Filipino, born 23 February 1941. Inventor, researcher and research director. Educated in Philippines; B.Sc. (Physics) from FEATI University, Manila in 1964.

Each year, millions of tonnes of rice are produced in the Philippines; however, the ricehulls – which are a major waste product of rice milling – have become a significant environmental problem since they are widely disposed of by dumping in rivers or landfills or by burning in the field. Ricehulls are, nevertheless, processed for use as fuels, abrasives, etc.; but such applications are infrequent.

### Turning a waste product into a building material

At the same time, the construction boom in the Philippines is making a heavy drain on indigenous raw materials, depleting the forests, encouraging massive sand and gravel quarrying activities, and rapidly increasing the cost of building materials. This gave me the idea of utilizing the ricehulls (which are mostly silica) for the manufacture of a high-quality construction material. Research began in 1977 and resulted in the development of a product called BARCRETE – a concrete material for general construction purposes made from a combination of ricehulls, sand, Portland cement, chemical additives and/or admixtures.

Ricehull is a valuable raw material for the construction industry since it has a high silica content, is rot and decay resistant, termite-proof and light in weight. When the material is mixed with Portland cement, etc., it has a high adhesion, for example, to steel reinforcement bars and wire mesh. When ricehulls are used in BARCRETE, their minute hairlike projections give the finished material high tensile and compressive strength, and these characteristics are further enhanced by the addition of small quantities of glass-fibre reinforcement. BARCRETE also has thermal and acoustic insulation properties, is quite flexible, when compared with ordinary concrete and, in view of its relatively low weight, it has less inertia than ordinary concrete; it is therefore well suited to the construction of high-rise buildings and low-cost earthquake-resistant structures.

369

## A material with outstanding characteristics

BARCRETE combines the properties of wood and concrete and can be sawn, drilled, sandpapered and planed; however, it is non-flammable, highly fire-retardant and unaffected by wide temperature changes. It can be reinforced with steel bars of minimal diameter and can be used with wire-mesh reinforcement, especially in the construction of domes. Its mass density can be varied at will, making it a very versatile material to distribute the weight (deadloads) of high-rise buildings, i.e. with the density being very high at the base of the building and decreasing towards the top; it is highly workable and readily mouldable for the manufacture of hollow bricks, prefabricated panels, floors, roofs and tiles and for the fashioning of outdoor furniture and statues; and it can be made available in premixed forms and can be terrazo-ground, tool-finished, textured, coated with resins and varnishes and/or painted.

The materials used in the manufacture of BARCRETE include: ricehulls that are free from straw and leaves, clean river sand, Portland cement, salt- and oil-free water, chemical additives or admixtures such as set retarders and set accelerators, pigments and, if desired, glass-fibre reinforcement. The mixing process is similar to that for concrete, and pigments or fine coloured glass or marble-chip aggregates can be added to enhance the appearance of the finished product.

BARCRETE can be applied in the same way as ordinary concrete, i.e. placed in moulds for hollow blocks or prefabricated panels, poured *in situ* into concrete shuttering, pumped through a concrete pump and sprayed for the construction of domes, etc. Once cured, BARCRETE can be terrazo-ground and/or sanded to produce a glasslike finish. Imaginative architects and structural and civil engineers have already used BARCRETE for a number of residential and monumental structures.

*The rice plant is a major food source in numerous countries of the world. However, it can also be a source of durable shelter when the ricehull is converted into BARCRETE.*

*These giant statues have been moulded from BARCRETE as have also parts of the wall behind them. They are located in an area exposed to winds of up to 200 km/h.*

### Increasing the market for BARCRETE

To fully demonstrate the validity of BARCRETE, it will be necessary to erect a pilot processing plant with an output capacity of 2,000 hollow-blocks (100 mm x 200 mm x 400 mm) or a minimum of 16 t of mixed BARCRETE per eight-hour day. This will also to serve to research the improvement of BARCRETE technology and provide a clearing house for all BARCRETE problems.

Finally, to achieve the pollution control objectives of BARCRETE production, Government policies should be introduced to require ricemillers to install BARCRETE processing facilities to utilize their ricehull waste, or to make the delivery of a ricemilling licence dependent upon transferring the ricehulls to Government operated BARCRETE plants. In addition, tax incentives should be given to encourage contractors and future homeowners to use BARCRETE, and BARCRETE manufacturing businesses should be tax exempt.

# Rescuing endangered lemurs in Madagascar

## Roland Albignac

Laboratoire de Biologie et d'Ecologie Animale, Faculté des Sciences, route de Gray, La Bouloie, 25030 Besançon, France

French, born 26 October 1940. Professor of Animal Biology and Ecology, University of Besançon. Educated in France.

A number of lemur species in Madagascar are endangered by actual or pending irreversible destruction of their natural habitat owing to deforestation for agricultural exploitation in particular. Attempts could be made to provide protection by enlarging existing reserves; however, it is not realistic to systematically forbid the population from felling forests in order to acquire new agricultural land.

**Proposed rescue strategy**

One of the solutions to this problem would be to capture individual lemurs whose habitat is endangered and then free them in protected areas where their vital and essential needs are met. Consequently, our project proposes to relocate two categories of lemur populations in Madagascar: lemur colonies which are too small and/or colonies that are over-concentrated in small and threatened areas. Scientific data have already been collected for defining natural reserves to which the colonies could appropriately be relocated; in particular, such reserves would have a biotope which is perfectly suited to these species, and the type of natural barriers that impeded lemur migration in the past. We are, of course, aware of the danger of genetic contamination and will, therefore, take appropriate measures.

The species and/or subspecies of lemurs that may disappear over the next ten years include:
- *Propithecus verreauxi coronatus*: found solely in forests along rivers in the midwest region near Lake Kinkony and only a hundred or so specimens have survived;
- *Propithecus verreauxi majori*: there remain only a few dozen of these in two forests each of a few hundred hectares, both in the south;
- *Propithecus diadema perrieri*: this species, which was "rediscovered" by our team ten years ago, is found in only a few areas of dry forests in the north, and less than a hundred specimens are left;

*Propithecus verreauxi majori is to be found in at most two forests extending over a few hundred hectares in the south of Madagascar. Probably only a few dozen remain. This specimen has been fitted with a radio-collar for tracking.*

- *Indri indri*: this is the largest living lemur and its future is seriously jeopardized by human pressure;
- *Lemur macaco flavifrons*: this lemur was also "rediscovered" by our team five years ago in the north of Madagascar, and only a few hundred specimens are to be found in a shrinking forest encroached upon by crops;
- *Hapalemur simus*: this lemur is found in bamboo forests in the south-east and its numbers are limited to a few hundred; and
- *Daubentonia madagascariensis* or the aye aye: this nocturnal lemur is the most intriguing and endangered species, and is now found only in a few forests along the coast.

### Identifying suitable reserves

In collaboration with the World Wildlife Fund, the Malagasy authorities have already established reserves which are, in principle, able to provide a home for these lemurs and those that I consider suitable are Nosy Mangabe, Nosy Be Lokobe and Ambohitantely.

Ten aye ayes were successfully released on the 520-ha densely forested and humid island of Nosy Mangabe between 1972 and 1975 and it would now be possible to release specimens of *Propithecus d. perrieri* and *Indri indri*. The 750-ha Nosy Be Lokobe natural reserve is a humid forest area with a well-defined dry season, isolated from Madagascar by a channel, and its biotope would accommodate such lemurs as *Daubentonia madagascariensis*, *Propithecus perrieri* and *Hapalemur simus*. The vegetation of the mid-west Ambohitantely reserve is exceptionally well preserved but the lemurs have practically disappeared; administration of this new reserve by the World Wildlife Fund would allow rehabilitation of *Propithecus v. coronatus*, *Lemur macaco flavifrons*, *Lemur fulvus*, *Avahi laniger* and *Lepilemur*.

373

*This lemur,* Propithecus diadema perrieri, *was "rediscovered" by Professor Albignac's team some ten years ago. It is found in the dry forest in the north of Madagascar; however, the size of the population is now well below 100 specimens.*

### Capture and transfer techniques

We propose to start the programme as early as 1987. The animals will be captured by immobilizing them with an injection of ketamine, delivered in a light hypodermic syringe shot from a compressed-air blowtube which has an accurate range between 3–30 m and is sufficiently accurate to hit the fleshiest part of the animal's body. Ten years of experience have shown this to be the safest technique; it has already been used to capture or recapture over 300 lemurs ranging from the 600–700 g avahi, to the 8–9 kg indri. The ketamine anaesthetic used is sometimes mixed with Valium to sedate the animal, and the dosage is varied depending on the animal's bodyweight. The captured animals will be examined and marked by a notch whilst anaesthetized; determination of their age, weight and sex will allow us to define population structure at the time of the capture and provide a good way of estimating any subsequent structure destabilization. The captured groups of animals will maintain their original social structure and will be released as soon as possible in their new environment.

The notched animals will be fitted with a collar incorporating a radiotransmitter; by using the official breeding centre at Ivoloina, near Tamatave, as a relay station, it will be possible to track the movements of certain of the animals over the first few months. Finally, control animals will be used to monitor the population and estimate their chances of survival, especially by observation of diet and their territorial and social organization.

# Field research and photography for a book to help protect the world's bats

## *Merlin Tuttle*
**Honourable Mention**
**The Rolex Awards for Enterprise – 1987**

Brackenridge Field Laboratory, Austin, Texas 78712, USA

American, born 26 August 1941. President of Bat Conservation International. Educated in USA; Ph.D. from University of Texas in 1974.

Nearly a thousand kinds of bats constitute almost a quarter of the world's mammal species. However, most people, including conservation planners and public health officials, know little or nothing about the values and plight of bats nor how to solve apparent conflicts between bats and people. In fact many people fear bats so intensely that they attempt to kill them on sight, often using poisons that do not solve perceived problems, but instead create serious environmental and public health hazards. General ignorance and the extent of inappropriate responses needlessly threaten both people and bats. As a result, public health is often seriously compromised, and – environmentally – vital bat populations are threatened. The consequences are potentially disastrous and make immediate research and education imperative.

### Victims of ignorance and superstition

Despite widespread ignorance and superstitious fear, most bats are harmless and highly beneficial, or even essential for a healthy environment. They play an important role in seed dispersal and pollination, they are the major predators of night-flying insects, bat guano is one of the world's best natural fertilizers, and bats are increasingly important as subjects of medical research. However, despite their value, bats are misunderstood and killed nearly everywhere, and their populations are declining at alarming rates.

Bat Conservation International (BCI) was founded by Dr. Tuttle to help resolve bat/human conflict and to preserve important bat species and their critical habitats. It has emphasized thorough documentation of the ecological and economic values of bats and has educated and assisted the public as well as larger private and government organizations. A variety of publications have been produced to increase public awareness about the need to protect bats as a valuable and irreplaceable resource, and several of the world's most important bat populations, ranging from the United States to Australia, American Samoa, Thailand and Trinidad have been saved.

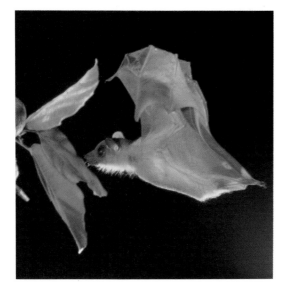
*A dwarf epauleted bat,*
Micropteropus pusillus, *flying towards a fig tree branch.*

### Preparing a major book on bats

One of the primary goals of BCI is to produce a major work entitled *Bats of the World* that will be the first book on bats in which the author personally will have visited and photographed bats on every continent, including all of the most important species.

A combination of new techniques and knowledge has allowed Dr. Tuttle to obtain photographs and stories never before documented. The use of a night vision scope and an illumination system designed by Dr. Tuttle has allowed him to make new discoveries of bat behaviour. By studying the activities and interactions of bats in their natural state and by developing methods of hand-taming and training wild caught bats, Dr. Tuttle has succeeded in photographing previously unseen behaviour in this travelling studio. This portable photographic studio, invented by Dr. Tuttle, can be rapidly erected, complete with authentic-looking sets, in which trained bats can be photographed pursuing their natural activities. This ability to hand-tame and train wild bats within hours of their capture has resulted in unique, highly acclaimed photographs. Dr. Tuttle's collection of bat photographs already is by far the world's largest and contains the only documentation of many species and their intriguing behaviour.

Much of the work for this publication has already been completed, including research on numerous bat populations and 50,000 slides taken during expeditions to Asia, Africa, Australia, Central America and the Pacific Islands.

These expeditions, funded by such bodies as the National Geographic Society and the Chapman Foundation, have produced photographs and detailed studies of unique and rare species of bats and have led to increased public awareness of the bat's ecological importance and even to legislation on the conservation of certain species.

To complete coverage for the book, expeditions have still to be undertaken to Central and South America, Borneo, Java, New Guinea and New Zealand.

*A Gambian epauleted bat* Epomopharus gambianus *flying towards Dr. Merlin Tuttle and his camera.*

Funding from the New York Botanical Gardens is anticipated for a South American trip to further document the importance of bats as vital seed dispersers and pollinators of Latin American rain forests. The final phase of research for the book could be completed with funding for the expeditions to Borneo, Java, New Guinea, New Zealand and Central America. In Java, the world's largest bats, fruit-eating species having 1.9 m wingspans, still need to be studied and photographed. In Borneo, some of the world's largest bat caves contain a variety of important species including the hairless bat, the world's largest insectivorous bat, as well as unique bat-dependent life forms and ecosystems. The world's only burrowing bat lives in New Zealand and in Central America the beautiful Honduran white bat, the carnivorous false vampire bat and other species of New World bats need to be documented.

The expeditions themselves will have a direct impact on conservation and research via increased scientific and media attention, while the information and photographs obtained will become invaluable long-term educational tools. The book *Bats of the World* will be the ultimate educational publication about bats and thus a key to bat preservation throughout the world.

# Managing the maleo

## Renatus Wilhelmus Rembertus Jozef Dekker

Maleo Research Project, Dumoga Bone National Park, POB 006, Kotamobagu,
Sulawesi Utara, Indonesia

Netherlander, born 27 September 1957. Project investigator, Maleo Research
Project. Educated in Netherlands; graduated (Biology) from Free University of
Amsterdam in 1984.

Megapodes, or thermometer birds, all of which are confined to the Indo-
Australian region, are different from all other birds. They do not physically
incubate their eggs themselves but instead use fermentation, volcanic or solar
heat by burying their eggs in mounds of fermentating leaves or in ground where
the sun or hot springs act as natural incubators.

*Macrocephalon maleo*, the endemic megapode of Sulawesi, is one of the most
beautiful members of the group, being mainly black with bright salmon
underparts. On the back of the head it has a big black knob, the cephalon (hence
the scientific name *macrocephalon*), and the naked skin around the eye is yellow
and red. It has the simplest breeding strategy of all megapodes and just digs its
eggs into the ground in the tropical rain forest at communal egg-laying grounds
close to hot springs or at sun-exposed beaches. Both the male and the female
engage in digging the nesting hole and, once the chicken-sized female has laid
her enormous egg, which is about five times the size of a chicken egg, the pair
cover the nesting hole again with sand and from that moment on take no further
care of the eggs or the chicks. The chicks hatch after a period of two to two-and-
a-half months, and struggle towards the surface, often having to dig themselves
out from a depth of a metre. Immediately after hatching, they are able to fly.

### A bird to study and protect

Although the breeding strategy of the maleo is well known, its general ecology is
poorly documented and in spite of being protected by law since 1970, it is
nevertheless severely threatened by human egg hunters and destruction of the
tropical rain forest. It is listed in the IUCN Red Data Book as an endangered
species. This project has therefore closely combined research and management
in an attempt to stop this rapid decline and protect the maleo by establishing
hatcheries; carrying out research; training Indonesians to work in the project,
and informing and educating the public.

## Management and research

Two egg-laying grounds inside the Dumoga Bone National Park have been chosen for protection and management, and two hatcheries have been built on the egg-laying grounds of Tambun and Tumokang. During the egg-laying season, eggs are collected daily, by the four Indonesian co-workers from the Dumoga Bone National Park, and are reburied in the hatchery, where they are safe from egg collectors and egg predators. After hatching, the chicks are released in the forest thus guaranteeing a new generation of maleos each year. So far, 150 chicks have been released while another 250 eggs will hatch within two months. In the future, chicks raised in the Dumoga Bone National Park will be reintroduced at other poorly populated or abandoned egg-laying grounds.

The first research phase involves: studying the population dynamics and general ecology of two maleo populations to make recommendations on future management; collecting data on egg-laying rhythm and quantities to define reproductive potential; and marking birds by wingtags. Daily observations at the egg-laying grounds during the second phase, when the young birds start egg laying for the first time, will provide information on the age at which the birds start laying, the number of eggs a female can lay in a season, whether males and females stay together more than one season, the number of birds using a particular egg-laying ground, and the level of juvenile and adult mortality. Food choice is being studied by analyzing faeces and the stomach contents of dead birds and by observations in the jungle. Long-term records are made of ground temperature fluctuations to investigate the influence of heavy rains and day and night rhythm upon hatching time and hatching success. The hatcheries provide data on hatching time, hatching success and the relation between egg weight and chick weight. Factors determining the suitability of ground for egg-laying are being analyzed and a regular search is made for new egg-laying grounds and one beautiful undisturbed site has been discovered.

*The maleo lays its eggs, that are five times bigger than those of a chicken, in a hole in the ground close to hot springs or on sun-exposed beaches – and leaves them to incubate on their own.*

Activities started during the first phase will be continued into the second and will be supplemented by radio tracking of adult hens if funds become available. An innovation will be the use of infrared satellite photographs of the area, if obtainable, to locate hot springs in the jungle, which will be visited to find new egg-laying grounds.

## Training, information and education

The Dumoga Bone National Park has seconded four staff members to be trained in management and research activities. They patrol the area, collect eggs, supervise the hatchery, raise chicks, etc., and provide valuable information by counting the egg-laying maleos to make population forecasts, by recording egg and chick weight and by searching for wing-tagged birds. Without the involvement of the Dumoga Bone National Park, it would not be possible to guarantee project follow-up. Public information and education are vital to the success of a nature conservation project. Last year, the BBC visited North Sulawesi to film local wildlife, and the maleo and this project figured prominently in the film; in addition, the English newspaper *The Guardian* has published an article on the project. Indonesian television, too, has shown interest in the project. It is planned to distribute posters to schools, police stations and airports all over Sulawesi, and information about the maleo and its habitat will be made available for primary and secondary schools. The Tambun egg-laying ground could well become a tourist attraction for the Dumoga Bone National Park.

*The maleo,* Macrocephalon maleo, *or thermometer bird, is the endemic megapode of Sulawesi and is one of the most beautiful members of the group, being mainly black with bright salmon underparts.*

# Large mammals and biological conservation – Collecting data and applying them to other species

## Joel Berger

POB 14096, Reno, Nevada 89507, USA

American, born 22 December 1951. Associate Professor of Wildlife Ecology, University of Nevada. Educated in USA; Ph.D. (Biology) from University of Colorado, Boulder in 1978.

Baseline data are needed on the genetic structure and reproductive biology of fragmented populations of large mammals threatened with extinction, so as to develop wise conservation strategies. This project is using the North American bison as a "model" species for data collection and for determining the extent to which individuals vary in their genetic contribution to the next generation.

### Reproduction patterns in fragmented populations

Although some 97% of the earth's mammals have breeding systems in which a small proportion of males monopolize the majority of matings, the effects of such reproductive patterns on the genetic structure of populations are still poorly understood. Moreover, we are fast approaching an era of unprecedented biological extinction, and because many large and well-known mammals (e.g. pandas, giraffes, lions and bison) now live in island-like populations many hundreds of kilometres apart, the spread of genes from one group to another is prohibited; the possible genetic and environmental effects of this could further diminish such populations.

The American bison (*Bison bison*) is a good example since it survives in scattered and remnant herds in reserves, national parks and zoos and only two non-hunted, non-implanted herds are in existence.

Clearly, bison are not unique. Virtually all the world's large mammals (for example, Kalahari wildebeest, mountain gorillas, and Indian blackbuck to name but a few) are undergoing dramatic reductions, some similar to the one suffered by bison a century ago. The net result of this is that population sizes are reduced, and recent evidence points to serious inbreeding in natural populations; about 40% of the male caribou on Slate Island in Lake Superior (Canada) no longer have antlers while Florida mountain lions have kinked tails, spotted shoulders and "ridgebacks".

*Bisons in an island-like national park.*

*Bison bulls in the Badlands National Park, USA. (opposite)*

### Study of bisons as a model for other species

Populations are so totally fragmented that it is unclear today what a wise management strategy is. Incredibly, there has never been detailed study of population structure in various sizes of reserves, the genetic consequences of the breeding system, and the factors which influence reproduction. This project is therefore studying bison in the Badlands National Park (South Dakota, USA) to determine how individuals vary in their genetic continuation to the next generation, and whether non-random processes ensure that extreme inbreeding does not occur; the objective here will be to quantify, for the benefit of zoologists, environmental planners, geneticists, wildlife conservationists, etc., the genetic consequences of breeding systems, and clarify the roles various factors play in inbreeding.

Bison, however, can do more than just offer information about the results of abuse; they can also provide an outstanding "model" for other species currently being reduced to fragmented populations. They are ideal for data collection purposes because the saga of bison is well known and new information about bison genetics is likely to be reported; bison are also eminently suitable because, since they already exist in isolated populations of varying sizes and genetic relationships, they are an untapped, yet experimental, reservoir of material for comparative investigation and because truly unique situations are available for continuing the collection of genetic data about bison at Badlands National Park.

The necessary data will be derived from a novel (yet natural) experiment which can be conducted only in Badlands National Park, where a very large population of bison are roaming free over a large area of their native North American prairie.

382

## Significant expansion of knowledge in this field

This study will enable me to pursue answers in a relatively new area of environmental sciences, biological conservation. In doing so, I will (and am) acquiring new knowledge to deal with topics that are becoming increasingly important for the preservation of the natural world. Because I am dealing with issues in genetics and conservation, I am interacting with a segment of the scientific community to which I had not been exposed in the past. My prior research has been concerned with identifying pressures promoting adaptive strategies in animals, whereas the present focus offers chances to broaden my experiences by dealing with a new set of issues. Second, I am interested in finding novel approaches to solving problems in wildlife conservation. The tactics to be adopted here are direct field measures. As such, scientists from other nations may be willing to view the data with a greater degree of confidence than those obtained in past studies. If, by using bison as a model species, I can reach scientists in other countries and they adopt sound measures to protect their species, then the effort will have been worth the trouble.

# The black robin – Back from the brink of extinction

## Donald Vincent Merton

21 Benge Crescent, Upper Hutt, New Zealand

New Zealander, born 22 February 1939. Principal Wildlife Officer (Endangered Species), New Zealand Wildlife Service. Educated in New Zealand; New Zealand Wildlife Service Technical Training Diploma.

The black robin, *Petroica (Miro) traversi*, is endemic of and was formerly widespread in the Chatham Islands, 850 km east of the New Zealand mainland. However, following European colonization early last century, subsequent clearance of forest and scrubland and, in particular, the introduction of rats and cats, the robins, together with many other indigenous bird species, have disappeared from the larger islands. Miraculously, however, a remnant black robin population of about 25 birds persisted for the subsequent 90 years in less than 5 ha of scrub forest on top of a 200 m sheer-sided rock-stack, Little Mangere Islet.

In the 1970s, the woody vegetation atop Little Mangere degenerated rapidly with the result that the robin population plummeted from 18 birds in 1973 to seven (two pairs and three males) in 1976 when the survivors were relocated to nearby Mangere Island (130 ha), where a revegetation programme had been carried out to provide additional habitat for the robins and other indigenous wildlife.

### Placing robin eggs with foster parents

During the final three years on Little Mangere chick survival to breeding age was minimal and, although it improved following the transfer (five chicks in four years), the skewed age-structure of the population meant that recruitment of young was off-set by natural mortality of old birds. Unaided, no rapid recovery was possible; further urgent management was called for since, in view of its low reproductive rate, the species lacks the ability to recover quickly when its population is reduced. However, the fact that black robins can be renested increases their potential productivity; consequently, in 1979 I proposed cross-fostering as a means of capitalizing upon this potential so as to boost productivity and quickly restore the population to a viable level.

Five birds, including only one effective breeding pair, existed in September 1980. However, an intense management programme developed since then has

384

*Rick and Elsa, two five-week old black robin fledglings being raised by Chatham Island tits.*

resulted in a spectacular recovery to over 30 birds. This recovery can be attributed largely, if not entirely, to innovative management which has involved developing and refining techniques for safely and effectively manipulating robin nesting cycles, and fostering eggs and young to other species such as warblers and tomtits. In this way, egg production has been increased by over 100%, while nest protection and security at both robin and foster nests has virtually eliminated accidental losses during incubation and nestling periods.

Subsequently, tomtits were found to be more suitable foster parents than warblers and they became the backbone of our programme. However, since tits do not occur on Mangere Island, eggs for fostering had to be conveyed 15 km by sea to South East Island.

### Results

In 1983, I sought and was granted permission to attempt to establish a robin population on South East Island (210 ha) where extensive areas of woodland exist. Two pairs of robins were transferred to South East Island in 1983, and this event proved to be a turning-point in the species recovery, for the major population is now found there. Furthermore, the need to transport eggs and birds between islands has diminished. About 30 pairs of tomtits breeding on South East Island are managed each spring so as to ensure a continuity of secure foster nests is available throughout the robin breeding season.

To my knowledge this is the first time that cross-fostering has been used in the management of an endangered song-bird living in the wild. However, techniques developed during the black robin programme have been adapted for use in the management of other species in New Zealand. Interest has also been shown in our techniques by endangered species managers and researchers in other countries.

The black robin conservation programme has involved a party of from two to

*Donald Merton and Old Yellow, the elderly male black robin from which all but one of the surviving robins are descended.*

four people in the field for approximately four months each spring and summer since its inception in 1980, and has proved a relatively inexpensive yet highly successful undertaking. The annual budget, in the order of NZ$ 20,000, has been met almost exclusively by the New Zealand Wildlife Service. The programme has created unprecedented interest from both within New Zealand and overseas. Its success can be attributed to the patience, perseverance, attention to detail and very high level of commitment by the small dedicated team – together with the obvious co-operation of the robins and tits, and of course more than a fair measure of good luck! However, perhaps the most remarkable feature of the black robin story is the incredible endurance and outstanding vitality the birds have displayed in spite of intense inbreeding over a very long period. Survival of the tiny population isolated for almost a century on the windswept summit of a rock-stack in mid-ocean is no mean feat of endurance for any animal.

## The future

Following the 1986–1987 breeding season, the robin population should be sufficiently strong to continue its historic recovery unaided. Re-establishment of the species on a major island in the Chathams group will then become the priority. Pitt Island (6,270 ha), the second largest island in the group, is rat-free and therefore suitable for this, and plans are already in hand to eradicate its feral cat population. If funds can be found, the New Zealand Wildlife Service intends to start this ambitious and relatively costly project in 1987, for such is the only means by which the medium and long-term survival of the black robin – and other endangered Chatham Island species – could be ensured.

# The Signatus Project – A strategy for wolf conservation in Portugal

*Francisco José Petrucci Gutteres da Fonseca*

**Honourable Mention**
**The Rolex Awards for Enterprise – 1987**

R. Adelino Amaro da Costa 3, 1°B, Paço d'Arcos, 2780 Oeiras, Portugal

Portuguese, born 28 January 1953. Assistant, Department of Zoology and Anthropology, Lisbon University. Educated in Portugal; graduated (Biology) from Lisbon University in 1979.

The wolves found in Portugal and Spain form one population, divided into one major and three minor sections; they belong to a sub-species of the grey wolf, *Canis lupus*, and bear the name *Canis lupus signatus*. Wolves were numerous in Portugal during the nineteenth century but, by 1910, their numbers were already on the decline, the main reason being human expansion and habitat destruction. No census has ever been taken and reliable data are not available but the current rate of reported killings is some 40 per annum; when illegal killings are included the figure must be at least 50 wolves per year. On this basis, comparison with figures from other countries leads us to tentatively estimate the wolf population on Portuguese territory at some 150 animals.

There are a number of positive and negative factors affecting wolf survival. The positive factors include continuing genetic variability, intelligent interest in wolf conservation amongst a small but growing segment of the population, and various conservation measures that have already been undertaken such as according the wolf game status, and the formation of a wolf group, the *"Grupo Lobo"*. The negative factors include the attacks made on livestock and domestic dogs by wolves, due mostly to lack of natural prey, traditional hostility amongst the public, and a dangerously low population level.

## A new impulse to wolf conservation

Nothing was really done about wolf conservation in the Iberian peninsula until 1981, when top priority was given to a project to carry out a survey and establish a conservation strategy. Due to technical and financial limitations, the project was confined to the area around Bragança (north-west Portugal).

However, when the project ended, research came to a standstill and the information gathered so far is insufficient for evaluating the real situation and for promoting adequate conservation measures. It is, therefore, essential to pursue the research, obtain more specific population data, and launch a public information campaign primarily in areas where wolves still survive.

Research is now being extended beyond the area around Bragança and is gathering useful information on wolf ranges and life-style, and the delimitation of feeding sites has reduced the occurrence of attacks on livestock. On the other hand, suspicion and apprehension persist in rural areas, poaching has occurred and we have been held back by a lack of manpower.

To preserve the wolf would require a population of at least 50, and preferably 100, animals; however, even though this number currently exists, continuing survival really depends on changing public attitudes to the wolf, a task that has already been started by the *Grupo Lobo*, and others, using such means as car-stickers, posters, a competition in schools (supported by the Ministry of Education) and a planned television series. If and when funds become available it is intended to hold meetings and show films in all the areas affected by wolves.

To conserve the wolf would require a population of at least 500 animals – a figure which is certainly met by the combined populations in Portugal and Spain. Conservation would thus require close collaboration between the two countries and effective dual management control. Preliminary contacts have already been made by the *Grupo Lobo*. A natural reserve large enough to ensure a viable population is not possible in Portugal, or in Spain, or in the two countries together. Therefore, the plan must resolve the problem of wolf/man relationships; man must learn to live alongside wolves as wolves have learned to live alongside man. This implies a radical change in governmental and popular attitudes.

## A two-phase plan

This project has therefore been established to ensure the survival of the wolf in Portugal by operating in two phases. In phase one, it will carry out field surveys

*The Iberian wolf,* Canis lupus signatus, *which Francisco José Petrucci Gutteres da Fonseca is studying in his "Signatus Project". (opposite)*

*Radiotracking of wolves is an important element in the "Signatus Project" survey programme.*

to establish more accurate information on status and habitat requirements, and determine the relationship between wolves and human populations, especially with reference to the extent of damage caused to domestic animals, and interactions with stray and feral dogs. In phase two, it will attempt to pursue a comprehensive education campaign, mainly in those areas inhabited by the wolf. Next, it is intended to create a wolf museum, in order to show the role of the wolf in traditional Portuguese culture, and to improve the understanding and appreciation of wolves as important and useful elements of natural ecosystems.

An assessment will be made of the possibility of establishing wolf "havens" or "sanctuaries" as areas with full legal protection, within which the wolf population would be regulated according to ecological principles to minimize conflicts with other forms of land use. This envisages the creation of "wolf-free" and "wolf-inhabited" zones, together with intermediate zones, belonging to different categories according to the local situation. An attempt will also be made to promote wolf-related tourist activities, such as: photography, howling and "howl-ins", and identification of wolf-signs both as a way of raising funds for the wolf-related activities and to stimulate public interest in wolf conservation.

Finally, recommendations will be made with a view to ensuring the survival of the wolf and the proper management of the existing wolf population.

389

# Studying and conserving bats in France

## *Jean-François Noblet*

Château de Rochasson, 52 ch. de Rochasson, 38240 Meylan, France

French, born 17 June 1951. Press attaché, Rhone-Alps Federation for Nature Protection. Educated in France; self-taught specialist in ornithology, mammalogy and herpetology.

The 30 species of bats that exist in France account for about one-third of all the country's wild mammals. Yet little or nothing is known about their distribution, biology and ecology, and there are no professional French scientists working specifically in this field. What is more, public attitudes to the bat are far from positive. However, these animals are useful predators of insects and constitute good biological indicators of the quality of our natural environment.

### The status of the bat in France

The status of the bat is degenerating seriously and of the 30 species in France, 25 are in regression and 20 of these are on the verge of extinction. Some 15 years ago, I started work on the study and protection of bats in France and soon became acutely aware of the lack of fundamental information about these animals. The French national atlas of mammals which appeared recently bears witness to the enormous gaps in our knowledge: do the Nathusius pipistrelle and Brandt's murina breed in France? Is Cestoni's molossus migratory? These were just a few of the multitude of questions with which I was confronted and which will have to be answered before we can really launch any measures to protect the bats in France.

### Getting things started

An important step in our efforts to study and conserve bats in France was to build up a widespread network of young scientists and enthusiastic amateurs with a particular interest in what is, after all, a mammal that suffers from considerable public prejudice and even aversion. This network has, however, gone from strength to strength and has eventually become a full-fledged association with one of its prime objectives being the establishment of an inventory of the populations of bats thoughout the country, the setting-up of artificial hatcheries and the protection of hibernation sites.

## Establishing a bat-protection programme

The programme we have developed is aimed at determining the distribution of bats in France – especially in the national and regional parks – establishing the status of the species, estimating the evolution of this status, and, where the species is threatened, making an attempt to save it.

The project involves extensive field work in which we question the public, church vicars, foresters, roofers, speleologists and we visit potential roosting sites in caves, mines, churches and ruins, underneath bridges and in hollow trees. Some of these visits have turned out to be adventures in themselves and we have had to make use of some rather unusual means to obtain access to the habitats that we wish to observe; firemen's turntable ladders and aerial baskets are no longer a mystery to us.

In addition, with the aid of ultrasound detectors, we are planning to make systematic studies of the droppings (guano) made by animals in flight at night. To minimize disturbance to reproduction sites, we chose to capture the bats at night on their hunting grounds using nets; annual counts made in sample areas have provided information on important factors such as pesticides, predators, etc.

One of the steps that I have taken to help facilitate our work is to organize study groups for voluntary naturalists and national park personnel and these are attended by approximately a hundred people each year.

*Television has been a major component of the campaign to educate the French public about bats. Here a cameraman is at work filming bats for French television under Jean-François Noblet's supervision. (Photo by Tixier)*

Often, many years of work are needed to analyze and assess the population in a given region and to know whether it is hibernating or whether it is possibly, probably or definitely reproducing there. Once the situation has been evaluated, an attempt is made to understand why the bat's existence is threatened; hypotheses are sought and, where necessary, experiments carried out by analyzing corpses, studying diets, etc., with the aid of specialized laboratories.

In the Department of Isère we are attempting to establish artificial hibernating sites under bridges or in trees, for example, and efforts have been made to protect the bats' cave habitats by placing gratings across the openings.

### Gaining public support for bat conservation

We soon discovered that our work could not be fully constructive without the support of the public. In 1984, we launched a major public information campaign to achieve the rehabilitation of European bats. Over 300 newspaper articles, several television programmes, interviews, a book, posters, slide shows and various documents have been produced and widely disseminated. It has now been decided, moreover, that 1986 will be the year of the bat in France.

*The search for bats is an adventure in itself and may entail having recourse to unexpected technology. Here Jean-François Noblet has called out the local fire brigade to gain access to bats lodged in tall trees. (Photo by Leroux)*

# Ngare Sergoi Rhino Sanctuary

## Anna Hepburn Merz

c/o Lewa Downs Ltd., Private Bag, Isiolo, Kenya

British and Swiss, born 17 November 1931. Collaborator in the running of the Ngare Sergoi Rhino Sanctuary. Educated in UK; B.A. (Philosophy, Law and Economic History) from Nottingham University.

Demand for rhino horn as a decorative material and as an ingredient of "medicinal" potions is high in a number of countries – and the supply is often met from the horns of illegally hunted animals. When my husband and I moved to Nairobi from Ghana in 1976, rhinoceros poaching in Kenya was at its height. Its horrors left an indelible mark on my mind and made me determined to do something about this traffic as soon as circumstances permitted. Later when my financial situation improved, I undertook to help protect these animals by constructing a sanctuary; however, my funds were not sufficient to buy land, and even if they were, non-Kenyans are not allowed to own more than about four hectares.

Nevertheless, in September 1982, I was fortunate enough to meet the Craig family, owners of Lewa Downs, a 20,000 ha cattle ranch in the arid north of Kenya, where game, other than rhino, is both abundant and well protected – an ideal rhino habitat. Moreover, with great generosity and trust, the Craigs agreed that I use some 2,800 ha of their land to try to create a rhino sanctuary, provided I agreed to act on the advice of Peter Jenkins, Senior Management Officer of the Game and Wildlife Department. For my part, I fully admitted that I knew nothing about rhinos except their urgent need for help, and willingly accepted this condition.

### Starting a sanctuary from scratch

The first requirement was an electrified fence to delimit the sanctuary. This was designed by Peter Jenkins and, in January 1983, work started on construction of the fence and all the other infrastructure required, such as roads, water, staff quarters, etc. We moved in January 1984 and, in March 1984, our first rhino was brought to the holding enclosure, to be released in April 1984 when the fence was completed. We now have 12 rhinos, including two calves born here; one of these was deserted by her mother at birth and I am consequently raising her by hand.

The object of the sanctuary is to breed black rhinos and allow them to lead natural lives protected only from poachers and restricted only by the fence but, as a spin-off, the project also provides paid employment for the local Ndrobo tribesmen who act as our security force and take a great pride in their work and a great interest in the rhinos. With the aid of my Ndrobo tribesmen, I usually manage to see all the rhinos daily and make notes of where they are, what they are doing, and whether they are alone or with other rhinos. In this way, I am building up a picture of their ranges, feeding habits and companions, and am increasing my general knowledge and understanding of their behaviour.

## Learning about rhino behaviour

I have found that, like all the other great mammals, they are highly intelligent and neither antisocial nor aggressive unless they are wounded or frightened – in fact, the two that have never been hunted are incredibly gentle animals. It is interesting to note that one male, probably between six and seven years of age, is still with his mother, which must indicate that learning how to behave in rhino society is a prolonged affair.

The abandoned female calf, Samia, that I am hand-raising is now one year old; however, my intention is that she should lead a normal life with the other rhinos and consequently she is free by day although confined to a stable by night. Each afternoon, I take her out to allow her to get to know the area around the house, to introduce her to as many food plants as possible and, above all, to get her acquainted with the scent and scrapes of the other rhinos; when encouraged, she will deposit her droppings on these scrapes so that the other rhinos become accustomed to her scent, and I have noted how other rhinos listen when she calls. There have been reports on the number of vocalizations made by the Indian rhino; our rhinos, however, are normally silent with the exception of Samia, who has an ever increasing vocabulary of sounds. I have been trying to

*Samia, a female calf that Anna Hepburn Merz is raising by hand, is free by day but still confined to a stable by night. She is providing an interesting insight into rhino behaviour. (opposite)*

*Morani, an adult male black rhino quenches his thirst at a watering spot. One of Anna Hepburn Merz's objectives is to bring more water into the Ngare Sergoi Rhino Sanctuary to provide more pools and wallows for the inmates.*

394

understand their significance and hope that when Samia reaches adulthood and is leading a normal life with the other rhinos, I may be able to follow her on moonlit nights and learn more about the behaviour of these animals during the period when they are most active.

## Plans for the future

My plans for the future fall into three parts. First, I wish to obtain financial support to enhance the sanctuary's facilities and capacity by improving the water supply to provide water holes and wallows so that the whole area can be used more efficiently. At the same time, the water would allow me to replant a variety of local acacias, either by seedlings in the traditional manner and/or by placing goat and elephant manure (which contains acacia seeds) into furrows and growing the plants from seed.

Secondly, I wish to undertake some sound behavioural studies on the black rhino but I would need some help from a scientist in analyzing my notes and pulling my findings together. Finally, I feel it necessary to increase public interest in and sympathy for rhinos in general and the black rhino in particular. If it were realized that the rhino is intrinsically as beautiful and intelligent as other great mammals and if the general public had the same attitude to the rhino as it does to whales, tigers and pandas, public opinion might prove strong enough to force the horn-consuming countries to control this traffic. That a magnificent animal should be rendered extinct because of loss of habitat is bad enough but that it should be obliterated to satisfy the lust for a status symbol dagger handle or a medicine whose efficacy is dubious is, in my opinion, utterly shameful.

# Achieving maximal genetic variation in the cheetah and establishing an endangered-species embryo bank

## Bruce Clement Davidson

Department of Medical Biochemistry, University of the Witwatersrand, York Road, 2193 Park Town, Rep. of South Africa

British, born 4 March 1950. Lecturer, Department of Medical Biochemistry, University of the Witwatersrand Medical School. Educated in UK and South Africa; Ph.D. from University of the Witwatersrand in 1986.

In view of its shrinking world population, and the encroachment of man into its environment, the status of the cheetah as an endangered species is not a matter of question. Only in east and southern Africa does the cheetah now seem to exist in significant numbers. In East Africa, the situation is deteriorating due to territory encroachment, poisoning, trapping and poaching; however, even though things look a little better in southern Africa, in Zimbabwe the population is thought to be diminishing, and in Botswana the numbers are definitely decreasing. In certain areas of South Africa, the cheetah is still classified as vermin and thus threatened with indiscriminate shooting. Only in Namibia is the population apparently increasing, although this may be a statistical artifact.

### Genetic peculiarities in the cheetah

The cheetah exhibits a very narrow range of genetic variation and, apparently, the species suffered a population crisis some 10,000 years ago, and insufficient time has elapsed for the diversity of the species' gene pool to be re-established. Even though cheetah numbers have not yet reached the critical non-survival level, the gene pool may be close to this point. Our project plans to generate as wide a cheetah gene pool as possible by importing stock of East African parentage, thus ensuring preservation of a representative sample of what little genetic variation remains. We will also study the diet of captive carnivores – so as to make recommendations concerning supplementation where necessary. Finally, we will establish the procedures for embryo transplantation and storage as a means of ensuring species survival.

*Cheetah mother and cubs aged one month.*

## Special dietary requirements

Due to a genetic lesion, the Felinae lack the enzymes (desaturates) required for further desaturating the plant polyunsaturates, linoleic and alpha-linoleic acid, to the long-chain polyunsaturates they need for normal function and health; consequently, the polyunsaturated fatty acids in lipids of animal origin are an essential part of their diet. Evidence to date shows conclusively that both the domestic cat, *Felis catus*, and the lion, *Panthera leo*, lack these enzymes; however, evidence for the cheetah is less conclusive.

None of the other members of the Felinae, or indeed the rest of the order Carnivora, have as yet been examined for this genetic lesion. Yet, whether it is a characteristic just of the Felinae, the Felidae, or all the Carnivora is a question of importance for the dietary maintenance of captive carnivores, and we are currently investigating this point. In the wild, the animal lipid requirement is usually satisfied by eating other animals, especially the internal organs and tissues. Unless captive carnivores are fed carefully tailored and supplemented diets, they may develop essential fatty acid (EFA) deficiency symptoms. When dealt with at an early stage, these symptoms can be reversed easily and quickly by the administration of EFA-rich oils such as evening primrose oil, blackcurrant oil and certain fish oils; however, if the symptoms are not controlled, the result may be self-mutilation, distorted birth sex ratio, and ultimately death. We have shown in domestic cats fed diets of differing degrees of EFA deficiency that only in those animals fed the most complete diet did growth prove normal; similarly the females on the best diet were the only ones to come into oestrus.

## Implanting fertilized cheetah ova in domestic cats

Felines ovulate only on copulation; thus artificial insemination is difficult and the timing critical in most cases. The technique of induced ovulation is reported

397

to have been successfully practised on captive cheetahs, thus it is possible to obtain ova from this species; spermatozoa are usually readily available by electro-ejaculation. We intend to perfect the techniques of induced ovulation, external ova fertilization and implantation on domestic cats (subjecting half the batch of ova to embryo freezing, thawing and re-implantation) so as not to further endanger any wild species. Thereafter, we will apply the procedure to cheetahs, with whatever slight modifications are necessary. We will, however, not re-implant into female cheetahs but into female domestic cats. One embryo only will be implanted per female, to allow ample space for full development. The cub will be delivered at term by Caesarean section because the birth canal would be too small for a cheetah cub, and will be fed by the host mother but with supplementation by modified bottled milk formula.

The procedure could then be applied to other endangered felines (e.g. the snow leopard) thus maintaining population numbers. It would also be possible to re-establish the species in old areas from which it has disappeared, and even introduce it into carefully selected new environments. Ultimately it may be possible to generate a bank of frozen ova, sperm and embryos of endangered felines (and other species), thus acting as an insurance against future extinction, or massive population drop.

*A pair of cheetahs during the mating phase of the oestral cycle.*

# A contribution to the protection of the chimpanzee species

## Margaret Elspeth Lea Templer

"Can Miloca", Breda, Gerona, Spain

British, born 2 November 1920. Head of a Zoological Centre for Chimpanzee Rehabilitation. Educated in Egypt and Britain; attended University College of Bangor from 1938 to 1940.

My husband and I started this project in 1979 – three years after our retirement to Gerona Province, Spain – when we learned of the widespread use of chimpanzees by Spanish beach photographers to attract clients, and the resultant illegal import of these animals. Our objectives are: to alert the Spanish authorities to the survival crisis facing the chimpanzee as a consequence of abuse both by beach photographers in Spain and by biomedical research; persuade the authorities to halt the trade by effective legislation and to confiscate the illegally imported chimpanzees; restore the latter to health at our rehabilitation centre in a forest near Gerona; and return the integrated group to their natural environment in Africa.

For every young chimpanzee caught in Africa which reaches Spain alive, at least nine die during capture and transportation. Of the survivors, 40% die during the first six months in Spain, those remaining being killed at the age of four, when they become too large and strong for safety. We brought the matter to the attention of the World Wildlife Fund International, which authorized me to make an assessment for them of the numbers and location of the animals in use in Spain by photographers. In 1982, I visited Alicante and Malaga Provinces, Tenerife, Grand Canary, Ibiza, Majorca and the Costa Brava, and came up with a figure of approximately 155 to 190 animals affected, a number which has since increased.

### Spreading the word

From the start, we publicized the matter as widely as possible, both in Spain and internationally. Many leading Spanish and 124 European newspapers co-operated fully; the European national offices of the World Wildlife Fund (WWF) gave us willing and highly effective collaboration; and there was extensive coverage on television and radio. We attended certain international meetings and, in 1984, wrote to all known Spanish conservation, protection and ecological societies, as a result of which a collective appeal bearing 127 signatures representing thousands of individuals, was sent to the Ministry of the Interior.

## Galvanizing government authorities

Early in our campaign, we visited the mayor of Lloret de Mar, who gave us a copy of a very comprehensive edict he had issued barring captive animals from beaches and other public places, denying licences for their use to photographers and providing for confiscation and a fine if the order was disregarded. Armed with a copy of the edict, we were able to persuade all other mayors in the tourist areas of Catalonia to issue similar decrees. Subsequently we visited all the relevant authorities in the country and were given assurance that appropriate action would be taken to halt the trade. Unfortunately, despite the various official decrees, orders and instructions issued over the years, the concrete results did not, on the whole, match the promises. In our view, the continuation of the beach chimpanzee trade may be ascribed largely to the indifference of the higher authorities and the efforts of the photographers to corrupt the lower echelons. It is hoped that, once Spain has completed the necessary formalities for accession to and ratification of the Convention on International Trade in Endangered Species of Wild Fauna and Flora (CITES), expected in 1986, it will put an end to the beach chimpanzee trade.

## Chimpanzee rehabilitation centre

Rehabilitation activities began in 1981 when a confiscated baby chimpanzee was placed in our care. Early in 1982, we took steps to legalize our status and in November of that year became an official "zoological centre", committed to accepting all confiscated beach chimpanzees. The aim of the rehabilitation process is to produce a compatible group through provision of time and conditions for the formation of an integrated community as independent and self-reliant as is feasible in semi-captivity. By 1984, the Centre had received 22 chimpanzees, of which eight had been returned to Africa; ten others are

The "Beach-chimp photography business". In addition to chimpanzees, lion, tiger and bear cubs are used as bait by photographers to attract tourists. The cubs are killed at around four months of age, but chimpanzees are not put out of their misery until the age of four years. (opposite)

Margaret Templer during the process of introducing six beach-chimps from Spain into the resident group in the Gambia.

scheduled to join a three-year scientifically controlled rehabilitation programme in the Ivory Coast, their costs to be paid by us. From 1983 to 1985 the Spanish national office of the WWF contributed £3,275 towards the maintenance of the chimpanzees at our centre.

## Biomedical research

The second menace to the survival of the chimpanzee is the demand for them by biomedical research on account of their close relationship to man. The chimpanzee is considered essential for research programmes on such diseases as hepatitis-B and AIDS. As this research is banned in the United States, certain US scientific units have set up laboratories in Central Africa in order to circumvent the ban. One New York biomedical institution suggested that we lend the confiscated chimpanzees for a year to its research unit in Liberia, for a fee, to demonstrate the safety of the hepatitis-B vaccine; and the WWF proposed the donation of the confiscated chimpanzees to biomedical research for breeding purposes only. Neither proposal was acted on.

While it is obvious that the confiscation and return of a group of chimpanzees to a natural environment will do little to mitigate the threat to the species, it serves to focus attention on the need to prohibit effectively the use of the wild chimpanzee for any purpose whatsoever.

# Adaptive agriculture

## *François Jean-Marie Couplan*

5 rue Albert de Lapparent, 75007 Paris, France

French, born 5 January 1950. Teacher and writer on ethnobotany. Educated in France and USA; diploma from l'Ecole Pratique des Hautes Etudes, Paris in 1983.

Nowadays it is common practice to adapt the soil to suit the needs of a limited number of standard fruits and vegetables; however, many wild plants – now considered weeds – were eaten with pleasure and profit by our ancestors. The concept of "adaptive agriculture" has been developed for the cultivation or semi-cultivation of a wide range of spontaneous and subspontaneous plant species – especially on land now considered unfit for agricultural purposes. It is also a means of improving the soil yields.

### Adaptive agriculture for soil improvement and food

Adaptive agriculture could also be termed "adaptive gardening", since it is often applied to relatively small surfaces and since it entails a large number of plants being grown together. In good soils, the cultivation of spontaneous and subspontaneous plants will conserve the biological character of the soil, already in natural balance. Growing many plants together duplicates what occurs naturally in any given environment, with obvious advantages. Depleted soils require treatment to bring them "back to health" and local plants or introduced plants from similar environments will provide ground cover and improve the soil by creating a humus layer.

A certain number of the plants that grow naturally in any given environment are potentially edible. Moreover, since they are the hardiest vegetables and fruits that can be grown in the environment in question, they can be used as crops in areas formerly considered to be unproductive. Many of these adapted plants have low water and/or nitrogen needs and therefore require little or no irrigation or fertilizers, and no soil preparation. Moreover, they are relatively disease and parasite resistant.

Adapted or wild species growing in their natural environment are extremely rich in vitamins, minerals and other nutrients. They tend to satisfy the appetite more rapidly and with less volume than cultivated plants and do not contain harmful chemical residues found in conventionally grown crops. Some of these

402

**Sambucus nigra.** *Elder grows extremely fast and produces flowers in May-June; it fruits in late summer and autumn giving a very high fruit yield.*

**Tussilago farfara.** *As early as February, coltsfoot displays its golden yellow flowers which are an aromatic vegetable. A few months later, they are replaced by an amazing number of leaves that can be prepared for the table in a variety of ways. (below)*

403

plants are amazing protein producers: 1 ha of comfrey, *Symphytum uplandicum*, yields 1,800–8,500 kg (4,500 kg on average) of crude protein per year in comparison with 500–700 kg of wheat protein and 150–200 kg of meat protein. Adapted plants generally have plenty of flavour. Since several dozens, if not hundreds, of different species can be "grown" in a given environment, the extraordinarily wide range of tastes coming from using this method is quite significant. In conclusion, adaptive agriculture proposes a low-entropy system of producing high-quality food.

## Putting adaptive agriculture into practice

The process starts with an ethnobotanical study of the local vegetation to select the plant species which are the most promising from the point of view of nutrition, taste, culinary quality, potential yield and soil improvement; however, it is also possible to introduce known adapted species from similar environments. Nature's tendency of forming a three-layered type of vegetation (trees, shrubs and herbaceous plants) is an example to be followed as often as possible. A good combination consists of fruit and nut trees, berry-bearing shrubs, with shade-loving vegetables at ground level.

Adaptive agriculture can be used in all environments in all parts of the world. However, the most interesting and spectacular results are likely to occur in regions with unfavourable growing conditions, limited by soil, water, climate or other factors. Unlike modern agriculture, it requires little or no financial investment and is accessible to all. The people most likely to be concerned are those living in poor agricultural areas, obliged to live on what they manage to squeeze out of the land.

## What we have achieved to date

I have been studying, lecturing and writing on adaptive agriculture for some 15 years and have, for five years, been "growing" various wild and cultivated species on a small plot near Paris; in 1984, we bought 70 ha at Haut Ourgeas in the southern Alps, where we began cultivating and semi-cultivating local and introduced plants. Since then, we have been carrying out a number of activities for the development of adaptive agriculture including: workshops, seminars and training courses; lecturing and public education through the media; research and the establishment of experimental farms elsewhere.

Adaptive agriculture is especially suited for countries with low technology and can be helpful in reducing malnutrition. Disseminating information in these countries about our methods will therefore be one of our priority objectives. First of all, ethnological studies must be conducted locally, adapted plants identified and their "cultivation" introduced in collaboration with the local population.

Now that we have been using and experimenting with wild plants for a number of years, we clearly see the need to find a balance between spontaneous and cultivated plants. The results of our efforts – adaptive agriculture – can, we believe, produce high-quality food with minimum inputs even in unfavourable areas and help create a world where man and nature can live in harmony.

# The Newark Collaboration Group – A public-private partnership

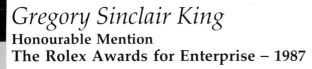

## Gregory Sinclair King

**Honourable Mention**
**The Rolex Awards for Enterprise – 1987**

The Newark Collaboration Group, Inc., 303–309 Washington Street, Newark, New Jersey 07102, USA

American, born 6 September 1948. Manager, The Newark Collaboration Group Inc. Educated in USA; M.P.A. (Public/Private Management) from Harvard University in 1980.

A universal problem for all cities is how better to manage and co-ordinate the critical and long-term decisions about the future at both macro- and micro-levels. The multifarious problems that confront the nation's largest cities have shown that there exists a real need for collaboration in the management of urban socio-economic change, and there is now a growing recognition that it is possible for communities to achieve consensus on certain issues and to benefit from collaboration.

### The Newark Collaboration Group is born

In the 1660s, a group of migrants from New England, in an effort to create a model community, settled the region of what is now Essex County in New Jersey. Inspired by the biblical story of Noah, they called their settlement "Newark", because they believed that it could provide both a refuge from some of nature's hardships, and an opportunity for growth and progress. Now we are in the decade of the 1980s and the inhabitants have changed, and so have the problems. For years, Newark has been looked upon as the symbol of the worst in America's urban malaise – its problems seemingly insuperable: unacceptably high unemployment; a faltering housing sector; a declining middle class; and a population riddled with crime and dependent on welfare.

Therefore, in order to address some of the above problems, the Newark Collaboration Group (NCG) was formed in May 1984. An exceptional and ambitious enterprise, founded on the principle of co-operative decision-making, the NCG is an active forum of leaders who represent a variety of public and private organizations, institutions and interests in the City of Newark, County of Essex and State of New Jersey. Leaders from every sector are meeting to discuss and hammer out a common vision of Newark's future. It is the first effort of its kind in the city's history to draw all sectors into the process of improvement on a comprehensive scale. Utilizing the decision-by-consensus

405

*A mural by local Newark high school students expressing the City's rebirth.*

method to develop common agendas for the revitalization of Newark, the NCG is confident that its strategies and recommendations will be acted upon and produce substantial results. The NCG is composed of representatives from over 200 organizations located in or serving Newark; all sectors – public, private and non-profit, are well represented. Over 260 volunteers are participating in its work.

Key leaders including the Mayor, other senior officials and the President of the Chamber of Commerce serve as *ex-officio* members of the Executive Committee. Other community leaders involved include university presidents, foundation and corporate executives, government officials, etc., and this level of participation ensures that the time invested will bring results; indeed, the NCG has successfully secured the support of and substantial contributions from a number of important public and private institutions by means of which activities are being fostered in such crucial areas as jobs, housing and neighbourhood development. NCG members believe that Newark is capable of considerable progress, and that the time is right to move forward in a collaborative effort. The city has been slowly planting the seeds of its own rebirth and already has impressive socio-economic assets including, for example: a thriving airport, shipping port and important bus and rail services; five higher education institutions, major corporations, etc. More than US$1 billion worth of development is planned for the city, most of which is in progress.

### How the NCG functions

The NCG is organized as a non-profit corporation, and has a 15-member Executive Committee selected by the NCG membership to advise on and suggest organizational policy. Four major programme committees and an administrative committee are headed by vice-chairpersons of the Executive Committee.

Much experience has been garnered from the implementation of a collaborative consensus-building process in Newark. Key points to bear in mind in order to duplicate the NCG experience in other urban communities include: the collaborative decision-making process, and the commitment of resources by major decision-making organizations; collaboration must be educational, must produce immediate successes in order to demonstrate its legitimacy and effectiveness and must be open and visible. Our purpose is to create the social and economic conditions for the rebirth and human revitalization of the City of Newark, and to do this, we must be able to inspire commitment and confidence, and provide leadership. Perhaps one of the best ways to envision the distinction between NCG methods and those that have been used in the past, is to describe collaboration as an "accordion" process of planning and working together as opposed to a "linear" process, signifying that all the parties who would be affected by a decision are engaged at the very start and collaborate closely throughout each phase. This has enabled the NCG to demonstrate to both State and Federal Governments that the City is receiving the support of all those engaged in developing solutions to community needs. Such co-operation is essential to our success.

*Gregory King, Managing Director of the Newark Collaboration Group Inc., against a background of the skyline of downtown Newark.*

407

# Help for do-it-yourself building in Argentina

## Jaime Nisnovich
**Honourable Mention**
**The Rolex Awards for Enterprise – 1987**

Guatemala 4148, 1425 Buenos Aires, Argentina

Argentine, born 25 May 1933. Director, Programme of Assistance to
Independent Do-It-Yourself Building. Educated in Argentina; diploma
(Architecture) from University of Buenos Aires in 1960.

The United Nations General Assembly has proclaimed 1987 as the "International
Year of Shelter for the Homeless" to focus attention on the critical housing
shortage throughout the world, and to seek a solution. It is clear that low-
income populations in need of housing will have to do their own building. With
this in mind, in 1984 we started a Greater Buenos Aires Programme of
Assistance to Independent Do-It-Yourself Building.

**The do-it-yourself housing movement in Argentina**

In Latin America, as in most other developing countries, the urban poor live
largely on the fringes of the cities, often lacking infrastructure and services, and
low-income families build their own houses on plots of land usually held
illegally. Argentina has a deficit of 2.5 million houses; moreover, a large
proportion of the existing houses are in a state of disrepair and require
renovation. This shows clearly that independent housing construction is here to
stay. We, therefore, propose to assist do-it-yourself builders, since their
activities affect both the quality of our urban surroundings and the well-being of
our people. This self-help building is individual, spontaneous and independent
of any organized system or plan, and movement has occurred because vast
sectors of the population can neither afford to purchase a house nor wait for one
built by the State. Although not an ideal solution, the phenomenon is
widespread and it would be absurd not to support and assist it. Moreover, as it
has been largely ignored so far by policy planners, independent builders
construct their houses without financial help and without appropriate design,
with the result that many houses remain unfinished, and overcrowding, poor
hygiene and faulty technical design are perennial problems. We consider these
deficit houses and neighbourhoods to be a social waste.

Although there are certain measures which can only be taken by the State,
technical design and assistance can be provided by small groups of technicians
and professionals. Such help is essential for those who, in general, learn to build

their houses as they go along, with the attendant costly mistakes and poor results. Our Programme was therefore designed and implemented to centre around technical assistance and seeks to foster the changes needed in the field of financial and legal support. We hope the Programme will instruct official organizations on possible low-income housing policies and that the proposed do-it-yourself building organizations will carry enough weight to promote these changes. Building one's own house with few resources is a formidable enterprise, requiring enormous physical effort and economic sacrifice. The families involved have little or no savings capacity, and funds have to be found from basic needs resources. It does, however, offer certain advantages to such families: a measure of security, the personal satisfaction of creation, a good, safe investment which can be undertaken gradually and at low cost, and possible new economic potential through the development of complementary activities (e.g. a shop).

## A Do-It-Yourself Handbook

Do-it-yourself building is an activity carried out at weekends by people scattered over wide areas and thus not easily reached, which makes it impossible to offer large-scale advice through professional technicians, We therefore created a Do-It-Yourself Handbook developed from a survey of the type of house most commonly used, as well as current construction methods. It is presented in comic-book style, instructions are complete, simple and clear, and cover not only building techniques but also related problems arising in do-it-yourself building. In order to avoid the potential communications difficulties between the professional adviser and the small builder, given their very different back-grounds, we recruit our technician-adviser from the same neighbourhood as the do-it-yourself builder. Highly experienced in the field – for example he may be a

*The outskirts of many South American cities are lacking in infrastructure and services but, nevertheless, form the residential areas for much of the urban poor population.*

409

*Building one's own home through one's own labours and with few resources is an immense task demanding courage and endurance to attain the final objective.*

retired bricklayer – he receives special training on the Handbook. Thus, with the Handbook as our means of communication we are able to cover wide areas and remote localities. From a central nucleus of the highest technical level (architects, builders, construction experts) knowledge is passed on to the zonal groups through the neighbourhood adviser to the do-it-yourself builder.

## A Do-It-Yourself Club

The above-mentioned operations obviously call for organization, and we suggest that do-it-yourself builders' organizations be modelled on that of a club, an autonomous, open institution fostering participation, integration, and better solutions to common problems, thus promoting the general welfare of the community. The name we chose for such a club was "El Hornero" – the oven-bird – a symbol in Argentina and neighbouring countries of what can be achieved with perseverance and few resources.

During its second year, our Programme has been carrying out pilot experiments to test, evaluate and make adjustments to the Handbook, the advice system and the idea of the club. Other community development and training projects to enrich the work done through the "El Hornero" club are scheduled or have already started.

# How I became a "mother gorilla"

## Yvette Leroy

Maya-Maya, Aeroport, BP 2892, Brazzaville, People's Republic of the Congo

French, born 4 August 1941. Employed with a hotel and catering management company. Educated in France.

During my six years of work in the Congo, in charge of the victualling of work camps in the bush, I have started to acquire some knowledge and understanding of the tropical forests along the Congo-Cameroon border – and their inmates. It was at one such camp, located at Sembe, that I made contact with a variety of animals that had been brought in for care and attention. These animals were lonely and in need of affection which the men at the camp did not always have time to give them. The outcome was that an arrangement was made to send the gorilla babies, brought to the camp, to me in Brazzaville, where I was to become their "mother".

### It all started with Albin

Albin, my first gorilla baby, was six months old when he came to me, and he proved a difficult initiation to gorilla motherhood. He was suffering from diarrhoea and spent most of his day clinging to me; to be able to work, I had to put him in a large box with a pillow so that he could play and, when I went out, I had to leave him in the dark where he felt more secure. I hoped that with time he would become less dependent and more like the other monkeys; but my hopes were in vain and, two years later, even though his weight had increased from 4 to 20 kg he was still as dependent on me – if not more so. My expectation was that he would one day return to his natural environment in the forest but he had taken me as his mother; he bestowed all his affection on me, knew how to console me when I was sad and, when he had been fed, would sit with me and gently scratch my head.

Communication had been established between us but I knew that a solution would have to be found for Albin's future. It was then that I saw on television an animal programme starring Lord Aspinal and his "gorilla paradise" in England. Contact was made with Lord Aspinal and negotiations initiated between the British and the Congolese authorities; these proved very time-consuming in view of the quarantine laws in the United Kingdom and the fact that the legislation on endangered species in the Congo prohibits the export of gorillas.

411

Nevertheless, Albin's case was presented and accepted as a life-or-death operation and authorized.

Albin and I travelled together to England and after I had seen him installed in his palatial quarantine quarters in a two-room apartment at Lord Aspinal's castle, and had entrusted him to Lord Aspinal's assistant, Julie, for the six-month quarantine period, I left to return to the Congo. It was a heart-rending experience – like taking a child to boarding school, but seven months later when I had the opportunity to visit him, he immediately recognized me and showed me the same affection as before.

## My gorilla family grows

It was then that Lord Aspinal asked me to continue my work of saving baby gorillas, and promised personally to provide for their future. Back in the Congo, the authorities proved most co-operative and gave me a free hand to adopt orphan gorillas and give them the care they needed – in fact, there was no one else to do it, and even the zoo did not have the necessary resources. From that point on, I encouraged my friends in the bush to keep their eyes open for stray or captured gorilla babies; they also reported on the circumstances so that the authorities could carry out an inquiry and arrest people who had been hunting gorillas.

My family now comprises five gorilla babies, all named after the villages in which they were found: Sounda, three weeks old; Pokola, 12 months; Kouilou, two months; Kandeko, six months; and Ndindi, six months. It takes some 30 to 40 bottles a day to feed them and I have to vary the ingredients to suit their ages and tastes. The smallest, Sounda, has had to be nursed like a premature child and fed on an intravenous drip; fortunately, when Lord Aspinal heard of this, he sent me his vet, a specialist in gorillas, and Sounda probably owes her life to this gesture.

*Yvette Leroy surrounded by her family of gorillas. (opposite)*

*Ndindi seeks comfort from his adopted mother, Yvette Leroy.*

My gorillas will not be able to stay in the Congo: they need a family atmosphere such as that found in Lord Aspinal's "gorilla paradise" but the male:female gorilla ratio there is already too high. Moreover, my gorillas have already formed their own family unit and could not be broken up until they are older. A ray of hope has, however, come through the American Embassy and World Wide Primates, which have shown interest in the protection of my babies. Nevertheless, the manager of the Chicago Zoo who visited me and offered my family a home in the USA, agreed that they should not travel to Chicago until they are two years of age.

### Improving the situation in the Congo

The publicity that has been given to my family has helped improve the situation in the Congo, where mother gorillas were frequently killed when protecting their territories against the encroachment of roads, etc. Laws have now been enacted banning hunting for half the year and protecting endangered species such as gorillas. However, my idea of a gorilla sanctuary is still a long way off. In the meantime, to ensure that I can reconcile my work with the care of my gorilla family, a young Congolese, Jean, has joined me to help and share the experience, and he has to some extent taken on the father role in the family.

Certainly, my life with my gorilla family has been so revealing and so full that I really need to write a book to tell the whole story. But I am so busy looking after everyone! Being a mother is certainly hard work – but how exciting and rewarding!

# Portawalk safety apparatus

## John Corica

POB 730, 435 West Elkhorn, Estes Park, Colorado 80517, USA

American, born 7 August 1930. Disabled. Educated in USA.

The Portawalk is a patented, fully mobile, rotary bridge for use in emergency and non-emergency situations where evacuation and/or access are essential.

The device comprises a series of linked structural segments, initially stored on a rotatable reel but extendable at a variable elevation angle, and rigidized in the extended position by a tensioned cable. The storage structure is mounted on a rotating platform which permits extension in various azimuthal directions, as the need dictates. Installation of the entire assembly on to a flat-bed truck or other conveyance provides the mobility needed for transportation to sites of emergency or permanent installation.

### Structural segments forming a bridge

The Portawalk utilizes a series of segments to form an arched structure over an obstacle. The arched configuration is formed by a tapering of the vertical sides of a segment, resulting in a shape which is trapezoidal when viewed from the side. Segments are linked together by a pinned joint at each end of the upper side of the segment.

The length of each segment is arbitrary but a range of approximately 1.8 m to 2.4 m is currently under consideration. If we assume that the span to be cleared by the Portawalk is some 21 m, that the centre height is some 4.2 m and that the supports at each end are approximately 1.8 m, then we arrive at the following dimensions for the installation: a length of arc of some 22 m, nine segments each of some 2.44 m in length and an angle between the sements of 5.72°.

### Use as an aerial ladder

When the Portawalk is extended from its stored position, or when it is used as an aerial ladder, there is no support available at the extended end and it will therefore behave as a cantilever beam. Consequently, the segment structure will be designed with sufficient strength to resist the structure's own weight plus a light live load in the cantilever configuration. However, for moderate-to-large live loadings, an additional support will be required at the extended end. When

414

*An example of the use of the Portawalk in an emergency situation to rescue patients from a hospital in which a fire has broken out.*

*An example of the use of the Portawalk for a rescue operation to permit the descent of two skiers trapped on a blocked ski-lift.*

a vertical support (reaction) is provided at the extended end, a positive bending moment will develop in the segment structure.

### Resisting positive moment

Without strengthening or rigidizing the structure in some way, the segments do not have the inherent capability of resisting the positive moment. Arched structures typically derive their strength or rigidity from the fact that there are abutments at each end. These provide horizontal reaction forces which, in conjunction with the vertical reactions, negate the bending moments in the arch except at the location of applied loads. For permanent installations, the Portawalk may employ an abutment (e.g. a concrete anchor) at both ends. However, for temporary service the structure must have the integral stiffening/strengthening provided by the tensioned cable if it is to withstand the bending moment.

### Prestressing by a tensioned cable

This stiffening is derived from the prestressing provided by the tensioned cable. The cable introduces a built-in negative moment (pre-load) into the Portawalk structure. Service loads, which are subsequently applied, will tend to introduce positive moments which must overcome the pre-load before failure can occur.

This effect requires that sufficient external service load (positive moment) must be applied to overcome the internal compressive preload in the lower chord before separation of the abutting faces occurs.

The drawings (on p. 415) illustrate various features and applications of the Portawalk when used for emergency situations.

# A new future for the Belgians – Making Belgium a truly polyglot country

## *Jean-Pierre Gailliez*
**Honourable Mention**
**The Rolex Awards for Enterprise – 1987**

2 chemin de l'Apitoire, 7078 Le Roeulx, Belgium

Belgian, born 5 May 1944. English teacher.

---

Belgium has two main groups of people: one speaking French and the other Dutch; in addition, there is a small German-speaking community in the northeast. The country is divided by its so-called "linguistic border", to the north of which Dutch is spoken and to the south, French. An important part of Belgium's recent political life has developed in a context of permanent struggle around that border. The country's three official languages are Dutch, French and German but although most representatives of the Dutch- and German-speaking communities have acquired French, few representatives of the French-speaking population have ever properly mastered Dutch.

In the hope of changing mentalities and of developing closer communication between the different communities, I initiated – as a service to the community – a non-profit language centre which for 11 years has received substantial State support. Through this centre, we have been able to launch a wide range of activities employing, in many cases, a variety of modern communications.

### Individual and group youth exchanges

An early finding was that French- and Dutch-speaking Belgians had few chances to meet, and knew little about each other. Our first effort, therefore, was to organize a radio programme on either side of the "linguistic border" to broadcast messages by means of which young people from both communities were put in touch with each other through the provision of names, addresses and telephone numbers. In nine years this venture has resulted in some 4,300 individual exchanges involving 8,600 youngsters.

In 1978, our centre developed a programme to encourage exchanges between schools belonging to the two communities, and this initiative has now involved some 86,000 youngsters. We organize annually a large "find-a-partner-school-for-an-exchange" meeting, attended by teachers from both communities, with the objective of helping them to find a partner and start an exchange project.

Having had positive experiences with meetings on boats, where a special atmosphere can be created, we set up, with the help of two British cultural institutions and the Townsend Thoresen Ferry Company, a "find-a-partner-

*On the early-morning train, businessmen travelling to work exercise their linguistic abilities by joining in guided discussions about the morning's press.*

school-for-an-exchange" meeting aboard a large Dover-Zeebrugge car ferry, in which 150 British and 200 Belgian teachers participated. There were 26 such school exchanges in 1982, 11 of which are continuing. Subsequently, with the help of the Netherlands' Minister of Education, we organized a similar meeting aboard a Netherlands passenger boat during a symbolic trip from Maastricht in the Netherlands to Liège, Belgium, and back, in order to develop contacts and exchanges between Dutch teachers of French and Belgian teachers of Dutch. A new meeting of the same kind with British schools has already been scheduled. However, the fact that the overwhelming majority of British schools are twinned with French schools in France leaves little chance of their developing fresh links with Belgium. As Welsh schools, however, have fewer links with France, we are developing contacts with Wales, and a first experimental study week, in that country, for 22 Belgian students, is scheduled.

### Language teaching on commuter trains

Persuading Belgian youth to acquire a foreign language is far from easy unless parental interest is also stimulated. It therefore became urgent to launch a major project for adults. As Belgian administration is highly centralized in Brussels, the capital, thousands of workers commute daily from the provinces. Our Centre's information service discovered that many adults wished to improve their command of a second language, but lacked the time.

Hearing of language-teaching experiments on main-line trains in Britain, I was particularly interested in the so-called "brain train" on the Brighton-London run, feeling certain that hundreds of Belgian commuters would be interested in a similar service. A statistical study on the main Belgian commuter lines showed that 10% of the commuters would, in fact, be ready to participate, and the first programme was launched in 1984 on the Mons-Brussels line, in which some 15% of the commuters participated.

418

*Walloon French-speaking children practising their Dutch during one of the numerous "linguistic discovery" expeditions organized by the Centre set up by Jean-Pierre Gailliez.*

The activity has been extended and a subsequent even more successful programme was started on the Liège-Brussels run, followed by a programme in Dutch-speaking Belgium, on the Hasselt-Brussels line, where the enthusiasm was just as great. Teachers are either volunteers who are regular commuters, or contracted under an official "jobs creation" programme and paid by the Belgian Ministries of Budget and Employment.

### Other activities and future perspectives

We have developed a number of other activities: daily language practice at lunchtime, offering four languages, a number we hope will grow to include as many languages as possible making our centre a true "tower of Babel"; a bimonthly international press review in three languages; translation of popular songs; and international exhibitions on the teaching and learning of foreign languages.

Many of the programmes we have devised enjoy support from major institutions, the political parties, and we have even attracted the interest of the King himself. One component, however, is lacking: the funds needed to extend our project and make the Belgians truly polyglot.

# Atoll wildlife conservation in the Republic of the Maldives

## Paul Adrian Webb

c/o Elke Seeger, 12 Mühlenstrasse, 4330 Mülheim, West Germany

British, born 28 November 1951. Free-lance wildlife writer and photographer. Educated in Singapore.

Although the Government of the Maldives is concerned about its country's environment, it is unable to divert its limited funds from its human-needs programme to wildlife and conservation work. In particular, having seen a copy of my book on wildlife in Bahrain, the President of the Maldives expressed the opinion that a similar volume on the Maldives would do much to generate interest both locally and internationally in the country's endemic wildlife.

Consequently, at my own expense I travelled to the remote southern atolls to investigate the wildlife, and soon realized that there was a wealth of material to be studied and photographed but that conservation work was urgently needed to protect it. Before leaving the Maldives, I drew up a set of proposals, for the Ministry of Atolls, on the flora and fauna of the islands concerned, and dealing in particular with: the protection and investigation of turtle breeding islands; the study and conservation of seabird colonies; the experimental translocation of white terns to benefit the human inhabitants of remoter islands; cataloguing of the flora and fauna of the remote atolls; the establishment of a Department of Wildlife and Conservation; and production of a book on the wildlife of the Maldives. These proposals form the essence of my project.

### Turtle breeding islands and seabird colonies

Over-exploitation of sea turtles is a critical problem, and the one-time large populations have now disappeared from certain islands. Although villagers once managed sea turtles as effectively as domestic animals, and harvested only the numbers of eggs and live animals required to meet their needs, eggs are now taken by commercial dealers and the turtles themselves are killed for their shells. The intention is to reintroduce a balance to the system by setting aside certain uninhabited islands as turtle breeding sanctuaries and educating near-by villagers to realize the value of the turtles as a resource.

The remoter islands harbour massive colonies of seabirds such as frigate birds (*Fregata minor* and *Fregata ariel*), blue-faced, red-footed and brown boobies (*Sula dactylatra, Sula sula* and *Sula leucogaster*) and the lesser noddy (*Anous tenuirostris*),

420

*The courtship of two black-naped terns, one of the many examples of the tern family encountered in the Maldives.*

at least eight species of tern, three species of tropic bird and probably many other unrecorded species. These colonies have never been visited by naturalists and would offer remarkable unspoilt subjects for investigation. They have so far come under slight pressure but, since it is known that bird colonies may sometimes desert their nests on remote islands "en-masse" after disturbances, recommendations should be made to ensure the necessary protection, whilst taking into account the needs of the villagers in these remote areas, for whom the eggs are a valuable source of protein.

### Terns to scare the crows

The Indian house crow (*Corvus splendens*), which has recently arrived on the remote islands, has proved a considerable troublemaker by stealing fish the islanders put out to dry in the sun and any fresh vegetables or fruit the villagers may have cultivated. However, the observation that the highly aggressive white terns (*Gygis alba*) on Adu Island refuse to allow any dark-coloured birds invade their territory has led me to propose that a small number of young white terns be translocated from Adu atoll to Lamu atoll where the house-crow problem is acute, in the hope that they will effectively clear the island of the erring crows. All these efforts require to be followed up by the establishment of a Department of Wildlife and Conservation.

### A book on the wildlife of the Maldives

This is my ultimate ambition and the reason I first visited the Maldives. The Government is certainly interested and such a volume would be a major contribution to our knowledge of these islands and, hopefully, would make the Maldivians and tourists alike look at their environment with renewed interest and sympathy. Few parts of the world are in such a pristine and natural

421

*The natural splendour of a Maldive sunset provides a glowing background to this island wildlife paradise.*

condition as the Maldives and the book would hammer home the theme that they should stay that way.

The area comprises over 2,500 islands grouped in 23 atolls spread over more than 1,000 km of Indian Ocean and, consequently, the project would not be short-term. Twelve months would be spent systematically exploring the islands, and then individual islands of greater interest would be visited for longer periods with regular conservation recommendations and suggestions being made to the Government throughout. The greatest logistic problem is the lack of suitable craft for island hopping and exploration and the purchase of a medium-sized seaworthy craft, such as a 5-m rigid-hull inflatable with adequate storage space, is essential for the project. There would be little difficulty linking up with the solar-powered radio communications network used on the islands and, by eating the same simple fare as the islanders, problems of food supply would be overcome; drinking water is available on all inhabited islands but a good medical kit is essential as outside of the capital there is no medical aid whatsoever.

In the long-term, the Government plans to develop the remote southern atolls as a tourist area and establish resort islands in the vicinity of many of the turtle and seabird islands. This obviously will have a dramatic effect on both the wildlife and human population of the region. Consequently, the opportunity of implementing adequate conservation measures, before it is too late, to ensure the continuation of such an undisturbed and beautiful part of our world along with its remarkable fauna and flora makes this, I believe, a worthwhile project of enterprise.

422

# Cartographic survey of karstic areas in Wallonia

## Claude De Broyer

Commission Nationale de Protection des Sites Spéléologiques ASBL, 124 avenue de la Floride, 1180 Brussels, Belgium

Belgian, born 23 March 1942. Biologist specializing in oncology. Educated in Belgium; D.Sc. (Zoology) from University of Louvain-la-Neuve.

From an examination of draft land use plans, it appears that speleological (or karstified) sites, both subterranean (caves, underground rivers) and surface (dolines, swallow-holes) have been almost entirely ignored in Belgium. Karstic areas of considerable importance, as yet unprotected by law, are being used increasingly, by official decree, as rubbish dumps, sewage outlets, etc., demonstrating complete ignorance of the environmental consequence. This project, therefore, proposes to make an accurate cartographic survey of karstic sites, underground rivers and artificial corridors in Wallonia, and to put forward concrete proposals for the modification of land use plans in order to protect the environment. The basis for the survey already exists in a systematic but partial inventory made in 1978, which identified over 400 karstic sites and former chalk quarries. This inventory having remained incomplete for lack of funds, a considerable area still remains to be surveyed, especially caves and swallow-holes. It is hoped that the publication of such a survey will contribute to the improvement of land use planning in Wallonia, and become an effective instrument for the conservation of the most interesting karstic sites and artificial corridors, and for alerting the public authorities to the need for prevention of future misuse.

### Scope of the survey

The survey will cover 15 land use plans, giving an explanatory text for each, and 80 map-boards. The latter will show the external limits of calcareous and dolomitic areas in the case of karstic sites, the entrances and extensions of underground corridors and, where required, give information about the perimeters of the protection zones. Over 1,747 sites have already been counted. Both desk and field work will be carried out, and the authors will visit most of the sites personally.

### Evaluation criteria and practical use of survey

The general criteria to be used in the evaluation of the scientific interest of the sites and their designation for protection are: their absolute or relative rarity, the diversity and abundance of their natural and anthropological phenomena, and the size and didactic value of the site; hydrological aspects will be mentioned since any survey of underground waters should take them into consideration. The speleological significance of a site will take into consideration its scientific interest and its interest as an underground landscape and as a place for subterranean exploration. The term "scenic interest" will be reserved for surface sites. The current state of the site will be mentioned where necessary.

Land use planning policy in karstic areas must take into account the conservation of nature and of typical landscapes, protection of underground water, the quality of subsoil (for housing and other construction), and quarry exploitation. The survey will supply information useful for decision-makers concerned with land management in karstic areas.

### Status of sites in land use plans

Surface sites (swallow-holes, cave entrances) and surface over-hanging cave corridors and subways will be categorized as "natural areas of scientific interest" in the land use plans. This status will be claimed for all karstic sites either conserved or deserving of conservation, present and future natural reserves, large hydrogeological networks, tourist caves and, more generally, karstic sites and artificial subways offering an obvious scientific interest. Within these areas, any activity or works likely to alter the site's integrity either on or below the surface, should be prohibited. Major hydrogeological works can also be delimited by a perimeter "protection area for underground natural resources" (or "natural underground area"), stamped on the land use plans. These

*The Cave of Rosée, near Liège, Belgium: a protected site endangered by industrial pollution. (opposite)*

*The fascinating but fragile world of cave minerals.*

424

perimeters will correspond either to the limits of the hydrogeological basin or, when these are too broad, to those of the calcareous stretch (area of direct absorption) containing the sites in question. So far, the survey has defined the perimeters of about 20 "natural underground areas" in seven land use plans and recommends that, within these areas, such restrictions, as may be necessary, be imposed for their protection.

With respect to landscape conservation, wooded karstified hollows isolated in the middle of open fields and meadows offer a real interest as landscapes, shelter many animal species and present special micro-climates favourable to original plant groups. In order to conserve the elements typical of limestone landscapes, the survey will recommend that the filling of large holes, dry valleys and cave entrances be prohibited. Landscapes visible from the big historic cave sites will be categorized as "areas of scenic interest" in order to maintain them in an adequate setting.

Today, limestone masses supply about 75% of the groundwater piped in Wallonia, but the characteristic water circulation in those masses makes the underground water vulnerable to pollution. Land planning organization must therefore take every precaution to ensure water preservation. The survey will indicate all swallow-holes and dolines located in inhabited areas and call attention to the risk of soil instability. Karstic sites situated in quarry exploitation zones will also be indicated.

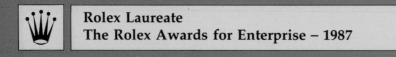

# The Seabird Colony Creation Project

## Stephen W. Kress

159 Sapsucker Woods Road, Ithaca, New York 14850, USA

American, born 5 December 1945. Research biologist, National Audubon Society. Educated in USA; Ph.D. from Cornell University in 1975.

The Seabird Colony Creation Project began in 1973 in an attempt to restore Atlantic puffins, *Fratercula arctica*, to Eastern Egg Rock, a former nesting island in Muscongus Bay, Maine. Nesting colonies of Atlantic puffins were once common in the Gulf of Maine but, as a result of intensive hunting, most of them had disappeared by the late 1880s. Puffins lay only one egg each year, and the single chick usually fledges from its burrow when it is about six weeks old and then spends the next two to three years at sea. A key factor for the restoration plan was the fact that puffins often return to their natal island when they are about two or three years old (natal-site tenacity), but do not breed until they are at least four years old.

In 1973, six two-week-old puffin nestlings were taken from the large puffin colony on Great Island, Newfoundland and, having reached fledging age, were transplanted to Eastern Egg Rock where until about 1885 there had been "considerable" numbers of Atlantic puffins; in 1974 and 1975, a further 145 nestlings were transplanted.

### Luring puffins with decoys

Since two-year-old puffins usually return to existing colonies before they breed, 50 wooden puffin decoys were placed atop conspicuous rock outcrops, and a four-sided mirror box was displayed to hold the attention of returning birds until a critical mass of puffins assembled at the island. Puffin chicks from the 1975 transplant began to return to Eastern Egg Rock in 1977, and this was the first evidence that transplanting nestlings would work. Puffin transplants at Eastern Egg Rock from Great Island, Newfoundland, have continued through 1985, by which time 1,000 chicks had been transplanted from Newfoundland to Maine. To date, 88 of the transplanted puffins have visited Eastern Egg Rock: in 1981, five pairs bred at the island and the colony has since increased to 20

*Stephen W. Kress, Rolex Laureate – The Rolex Awards for Enterprise 1987, takes a moment of relaxation afloat whilst preparing the next stage of his Seabird Colony Creation Project.*

427

breeding pairs. The re-established colony has been very successful at producing young, with an average fledgling success of about 90% each year. This experiment has shown that natal-site tenacity is learned sometime during late chick development or shortly after fledging and, if true for other species, could prove of value in managing seabirds endangered by introduced predators. Subsequently, in 1984, we began to re-establish puffins on Seal Island in Penobscot Bay so as to test the site-transfer technique by replicating a restored colony.

## Extending the project to terns

In 1978, the Seabird Colony Creation Project began working with Arctic terns, *Sterna paradisaea*, at Eastern Egg Rock which had been an important nesting island for terns until 50 years ago. To encourage terns to recolonize the island, 100 tern decoys were set out early in the nesting season, and tape recordings of tern courtship calls were played near the decoys to help bring the terns into breeding condition. It took three years of playing tape recordings among the decoys for the terns to recolonize the island, but the tern colony has now grown to over 1,000 pairs – the largest tern colony in Maine. In addition to Arctic terns, the colony also contains common terns, *Sterna hirundo* and roseate terns, *Sterna dougalli*, an endangered species. The Project has also worked with Leach's storm-petrel, *Oceanodroma leucorrhoa*, using automatic tape recordings of petrel courtship calls and artificial petrel burrows. This technique has since been replicated with Leach's storm-petrels on three other former petrel nesting islands.

These experiments with unrelated species of seabirds demonstrate that colony formation is usually initiated by a few unusual individuals who take the risk to start colonies in places where there is no recent history of breeding success. Most members of colonial species prefer to nest in well-established colonies and this is why many highly colonial species are slow to start colonies, even if the causes for the extinction of former colonies have been eliminated.

## Using the techniques for endangered species

The research to date with non-endangered species points to the usefulness of these techniques for assisting endangered species. Currently, two endangered species are under consideration for assistance, using some of the techniques mentioned above. The Hawaiian dark-rumped petrel, *Pterodroma phaeopygia sandwichensis*, is one of 12 endangered seabirds in the genus Pterodroma and it is threatened by mammal predators that have been introduced to its remote nesting islands. With adequate funding, the Seabird Colony Creation Project will initiate a recovery programme for the dark-rumped petrel by attracting these rare birds to a safer nesting island.

With this ample experience behind us, we are ready to extend our horizons to other species and other geographic regions, and a collaborative project is already envisaged for the short-tailed albatross, *Diomedea albatrus*, which has its only nesting colony on the slopes of an active volcano on Torishima Island, south of Japan. The establishment of a new colony on a non-volcanic former nesting island would be an ideal opportunity for sharing our techniques with others.

*An inquisitive puffin takes a good look at itself in one of the four-sided mirrors set up by Stephen Kress to attract the birds to their new nesting grounds.*

*Stephen Kress places fledglings into the portable transport container ready for transfer to their new site.*

# A decade of integrated crane conservation efforts in the Indian subcontinent

## *Steven Erling Landfried*
**Honourable Mention**
**The Rolex Awards for Enterprise – 1987**

Route One, Highway 59 East, Evansville, Wisconsin 53536, USA

American, born 1 November 1944. Adult education officer. Educated in USA; Ph.D. (Curriculum and Instruction) from University of Wisconsin, Madison in 1978.

The number of Siberian cranes, *Grus leucogeranus*, migrating along the Indo-Asian flyway to Bharatpur, India, has dwindled to approximately 37 birds as a result of habitat destruction, hunting, etc. Unless all habitats crucial to the crane's survival can be identified and protected, this breeding group of the Siberian crane is almost certainly doomed to extinction.

The task is complicated by such factors as: the Siberian cranes' low population base and slow breeding characteristics, the vagaries of international politics, population pressures, lack of environmental awareness, a long-standing history of crane hunting by Pathan tribesmen in Pakistan and Afghanistan, the absence of any tradition for protecting migratory cranes along the flyway, and the virtual absence of meaningful scientific information about the migration routes over the 5,700 km journey to Bharatpur, India, from breeding areas in western Siberia.

In view of these difficulties, the International Crane Foundation (ICF) decided to focus attention on other areas with better prospects of success; however, I decided to try to arouse government and public understanding and develop an international project of education, research and conservation strategies, which, since 1980, has passed through three successive phases: exploration and propaganda; activism and implementation; and consolidation.

## Exploratory and propaganda phase: 1980–1982

The first step was to publicize the fact that the number of Siberian cranes observed at the Keoladeo Ghana Bird Sanctuary in Bharatpur, India, had dropped to 33, and to investigate the potential consequences of the growing number of domesticated cattle and their human attendants in the sanctuary. My participation in an international environmental conference in Bangalore, India, provided the opportunity of corresponding with Indian conservation leaders, meeting with and making audiovisual presentations to journalists, government officials, conservationists and the general public, and helping in drawing up a series of recommendations to study the threat posed by cattle in the Keoladeo

Ghana Bird Sanctuary, have a Siberian crane stamp issued by the Indian Department of Posts and Telegraphs, and develop educational materials for use in schools and conservation groups. A major step forward occurred when the Prime Minister, the late Mrs. Indira Gandhi, and a key journalist, Mr. Khushwant Singh, took personal interest in the situation leading to nationalization of the sanctuary and removal of the domestic cattle.

About the same time, I began to question the hypothesis that Siberian cranes flew non-stop over 1,000 km from Bharatpur to Lake Abi-Estada south-west of Kabul, Afghanistan; it seemed certain that they had to alight in Pakistan. My sleuthings revealed that Pathan tribesmen in the Northwest Frontier province caught cranes live and that top government officials kept captive cranes as pets and "watch dogs". Travelling to Pakistan to investigate the situation, I expressed my concern to the governing board of the World Wildlife Fund Pakistan, but found that government officials and conservationists lacked information about cranes in general, and the Siberian crane in particular. A second visit to Pakistan in 1982 highlighted the social significance of crane hunting in the Bannu area, and indicated that the proliferation of this sport starting in the late 1960s and its export to Baluchistan might be related with the fall in the number of Siberian cranes wintering in Bharatpur.

### Activist and implementation phase: 1983–1985

The next phase called for: an evaluation of crane hunting and hunter motivation; an assessment of the adequacy of existing game and hunting laws for the protection of the Siberian cranes; education of hunters, high- and mid-level government officials, wildlife conservation staff, and the public about the dangers this hunting posed to Siberian cranes; inducement of hunters to tag or band live caught cranes for migration studies; the production of a documentary about crane hunting in the Kurram Valley and Baluchistan; and development of educational materials for diverse audiences.

At this point, I took leave of absence from my teaching duties and spent the next five months in India and Pakistan working full time on the project. In India, presentations were made about crane hunting in Pakistan to the International Crane Conference at Bharatpur, India, and resolutions were submitted for the protection of all migrant crane populations in South Asia and for the release of Siberian crane stamps by all flyway countries. In Pakistan, a survey of crane hunters was carried out and educational presentations about cranes were made to hunters – stressing the importance of their releasing and reporting the capture of any white cranes to wildlife authorities. Legislation banning the hunting of Siberian cranes was introduced, hunting licences and bag limits were established for demoiselle and common cranes, and shooting of all crane species was prohibited. The Government of Baluchistan also agreed to enforce a total ban on crane hunting in that province. Work on a slide, audio-tape and text programme for public education was started and further attempts were made to interest hunters in captive breeding.

At this time, two stimulating events occurred: the number of Siberian cranes increased to 41 birds, and an American film crew arrived in Pakistan and promised to spread the crane and wetland conservation messages throughout the region on completion of their film in 1986.

431

## Consolidation phase: 1986–1990

In spite of six years' progress, the Siberian crane is still on the brink of extinction with the number of birds falling to 37. Moreover, it seems that the demoiselle, Sarus and common cranes all face problems similar to those of the Siberian crane. Efforts must be redoubled to understand the habitats upon which these birds depend and create an awareness of man's self interest in the fate of birds and wildlife generally. These things don't just happen. Only hard work will produce them; anything less will probably condemn these wonderful creatures – the cranes of the subcontinent – to a dismal fate.

*A line of crane hunters demonstrate their technique for launching their soiia – a 10-m long lead-weighted nylon cord, twirled around the head before being thrown skywards. As many as 30 hunters will throw these lead-weighted cords simultaneously at the landing cranes.*

*The critically endangered Siberian crane is the only white crane found in the Indian Subcontinent. At one time, as many as a thousand of them may have migrated here. However, their numbers have now dwindled to a mere 37 birds.*

# Reclamation of quarry wasteland – An integrated approach

## René Daniel Haller

Baobab Farm Limited, POB 90202, Mombasa, Kenya

Swiss, born 18 December 1933. Managing Director, Baobab Farm Limited.
Educated in Switzerland; diploma (Tropical Agronomy) from Basel University in
1955.

Open cast strip mining or quarrying annually lays to waste vast tracts of land the
world over. Most of the successful reclamation projects that have been initiated
are located in areas of favourable climate and soil conditions, where population
densities have necessitated rehabilitation of the land for safety reasons or for
purposes of alternative developments. This often involves filling or restoring top
soil to create suitable conditions and this precludes reclamation in areas where
the value of the minerals mined does not justify the expense; consequently,
many abandoned open cast mines remain wasteland.

Over the period 1954 to 1985, the Bamburi Portland Cement Company had
excavated 350 ha of coral limestone to a depth of 6 m at its mining activity 10 km
north of Mombasa, Kenya, and this was creating an ugly scar in the otherwise
touristic setting of this East African coastline. In 1971, the company voluntarily
established a quarry reclamation project and Baobab Farm Ltd. was entrusted
with carrying out a demonstration reafforestation project.

### Reafforestation

It was decided that success would depend on using plants which had already
naturally established themselves on the quarry floor; 27 species of trees were test
planted and a seedling nursery was established. The most successful combination proved to be the *Casuarina equisetifolia* and the *Conocarpus lancifolius* from
Somalia, both of which produce valuable timber. The Casuarina proved to be a
very aggressive pioneer colonizer. Tolerant of the saline condition and difficult
rooting conditions, trees grew 2–3 m per year and reached a croppable pole size
in 4-5 years. Another successful tree species was of the Algaroba variety. This
was used as a natural screen for the quarry walls and as a source of pollen for
bees which produce 12–15 kg of honey per hive per year.

Shrubs, grasses and ferns established themselves everywhere except under
the Casuarina trees; however, research identified plants that would grow in this
location and, once a nucleus of these had been established, it acted as an
epicentre for dispersal.

*Part of the peaceful pond area where many of the animals come to drink and graze.*

*An aerial view of the landscape on which the quarry reclamation project has been carried out and where Baobab Farm Limited has undertaken a demonstration reafforestation programme. (opposite)*

### Restoring wildlife

As various food niches developed so compatible animals were introduced. Others such as small antelope, monkeys, bush buck, rodents and reptiles all found sanctuary in the forest. Over 130 species of birds have now been recorded. As the ecosystem grew, attempts were made to stabilize conditions. Frog populations flourished in the rainwater pools and snakes and monitor lizards were introduced to control frog numbers. A mongoose was then released to keep the snakes in check. When longicorn beetles were found to be attacking the trees eagle owls were introduced as natural predators. Similar biological control measures were instituted for other aspects of the developing forest.

Larger animals such as eland were introduced to feed on the lower branches of the trees and oryx and buffalo grazed on the developing grasslands which were also kept closely cropped by Sally, a 12-year-old orphaned hippo, who adorns the forest's main pond and is now the project's mascot. Grass around the water edges and in areas where the water table is high were untouched by other animals, so water buck were brought in.

### Fish farming

Pools that had formed were stocked with fish (primarily tilapia) for mosquito control; and experiments with fish farming led to a pilot fish farm. The tank culture technique used is now internationally recognized and this "Baobab System" is finding application elsewhere in the tropical world.

### Integrated farming

Integration and simplicity have been key concepts. For example the fish farm has been combined with an irrigation project so that water flows by gravity

434

through the fish farm, aerated by cascade turbulence and can be re-used three times before wasting. Flowing water keeps the crocodile pens clean and cool and the crocodiles are fed on trash fish and dead farm livestock.

Most of the fish farm waste water flows into sediment tanks to settle heavy organic particulates which although not sufficient for economic biogas production are suitable for manure in the landscaping nursery.

## Future projects

The site now attracts many visitors including school and college students on educational outings. The animal orphanage is being expanded and a museum and demonstration poster hall will show techniques employed in reafforestation. A recreation site and licensed fishing lake are under construction and a canteen and restaurant facility to cater for visitors.

To do justice to the 15 years of research on this project, a guide should be published to help others implement some of Baobab Farm methods. Funds for such a venture are limited but it is hoped that a would-be publisher can be found. It is not often that one can turn wasteland into a "Garden of Eden" and we look forward to sharing our experience.

# Community-based sanctuary for the black howler monkey

## Robert H. Horwich
**Honourable Mention**
**The Rolex Awards for Enterprise – 1987**

Rd 1, Box 96, Gay Mills, Wisconsin 54631, USA

American, born 31 December 1940. Resident ethnologist, International Crane Foundation. Educated in USA; Ph.D. from University of Maryland in 1967.

Starting from the premise that only a limited amount of tropical rain forest can be preserved in its pristine state and that large tracks of rain-forest land are already, or soon will be, under cyclic cultivation, this project has established a scheme to complement attempts to preserve uninhabited forest areas. What may be considered a unique experimental approach to the conservation of a wild life species has been adopted, since it involves volunteers working with local agricultural landowners on a management plan for their private lands and thus aiding in conservation of the black howler monkey, *Alouatta pigra*.

The project began as a pure research study on various aspects of howler monkey behaviour; however, it soon became evident that the black howler was in need of conservation. The situation in Belize, however, was found to be more favourable in view of the tolerance displayed towards the monkeys by the sparse human population there. In particular, the villagers in the area called the "Bermudian Landing" were well disposed to the howlers which the local Creoles call "baboons".

### Launching the sanctuary concept

After a preliminary enquiry in 1984, a petition was drawn up requesting support for the concept of a community sanctuary for the howler monkeys. This was circulated in the village of Bermudian Landing and was signed by 16 owners of land on which howlers resided and by the seven members of the village Council. The support of the area representative of the Government of Belize and of the Ministry of Natural Resources was also obtained together with permission to begin the project.

In 1985, the sanctuary was formally launched with financial support from the World Wildlife Fund (USA), and the concept of a community sanctuary was presented to a Bermudian Landing village meeting attended by the area representative, with stress being laid on the voluntary nature of the programme. The support of the Council was obtained, and the villagers gave permission to begin what came to be known as the "Community Baboon Sanctuary". Formal

*A male black howler monkey,*
Alouatta pigra, *in the*
*Community Baboon Sanctuary at*
*Bermudian Landing, Belize.*

work commenced with the mapping of an area of some 780 ha north and south of the village on the west side of the Belize River. Vegetation maps were constructed, the howler population was censused and a study was started of the riverine forests including the successional stages following cultivation.

At the end of the three-month study, maps of the individual lands were drawn up, together with appropriate management programmes. After any points unacceptable to them had been removed, a number of landowners signed voluntary pledges to abide by a programme designed to provide optimum benefit for the howler monkeys and for the area as a whole – especially from the point of view of river bank maintenance. The overall plan will attempt to maintain a continuous forest along the river banks, connected to the strips alongside the cultivated fields, thus providing a strong reseeding base for the regeneration of the riverine forests and the nutrients they offer, and for maintaining a continuous gene flow in the monkeys.

## A multifaceted project

The project has three main aspects: conservation, education and research, which continually intermix. At an early date, an education programme about the black howlers was launched on three levels: in local schools, at the village level and at the professional and public level through the Belize Teachers' College and the Belize Audubon Society. Lectures were given to local schools, colleges and the

437

general public, a radio programme about the sanctuary was broadcast on Radio Belize, and 500 copies of a booklet on the black howler and its conservation were produced and distributed to villagers and landowners; the booklet was subsequently rewritten for high school students.

The project's most recent educational booklet is an illustrated guidebook containing: information about the importance of tropical rain forests and the establishment of the sanctuary; the history of the area; a description of the forest types and vegetation; census maps; facts on the black howler monkey; a key to trees in the sanctuary and a partial listing of the sanctuary's mammals, birds and reptiles. The retail mark-up on this will be used to finance updates.

Research has started on various aspects of howler behaviour and will be continued with greater emphasis on howler ecology and the interaction of farming practices, forest succession and howler usage of the forest. For example, a preliminary categorization of successional stages in the riverine forest will be continued, and data collection on seasonal usage of plants by the howlers has been started together with a study of local commercial use of the endangered river turtle, *Dermatemys mawi*. At the villagers' request, limited tourist objectives have also been pursued with the sanctuary being publicized through the media and through tourist agencies specializing in wildlife tours. In addition, volunteers have constructed a tourist shelter along with an introductory sign about the sanctuary.

## Planning to expand the project

In 1986, it is planned to extend both the area and philosophy of the sanctuary, and the guidebook – although designed for sale to tourists – will also be distributed to villagers and local naturalists to demonstrate what can be done on a low budget, and help spread the community sanctuary concept. Geographically, the objective for 1986 is to expand the sanctuary to some 4,660 ha up and down river from Bermudian Landing, and increase the number of landowners and villagers involved. Participating landowners will be formally presented with certificates during a general village meeting, and will receive T-shirts decorated with howler monkeys as a token of appreciation.

We also hope to develop a limited tree-propagation programme in which, with the permission of the participating landowners, students will help replant eroded areas along the river banks with fig or other trees. Further lectures will be given at local schools, and another attempt will be made to initiate a conservation-orientated film programme through the Bureau of Information. The publicity campaign will continue through news releases and radio and TV coverage to encourage tourism and to give positive feedback to the villagers; talks will again be given for tourists groups, and local people acting as sanctuary guides will be given formal training. Finally, work on an educational film about the village and the project will be pursued, and preliminary scenes will be shown to the villagers in 1986.

# Protection of Jentink's duiker in Liberia

## Vivian John Wilson
**Honourable Mention**
**The Rolex Awards for Enterprise – 1987**

Chipangali Wildlife Trust, POB 1057, Bulawayo, Zimbabwe

Zimbabwean, born 31 October 1932. Director, Chipangali Wildlife Trust and Chipangali Wildlife Orphanage. Educated in South Africa and UK; M.I. Biol. from Institute of Biologists, London in 1971.

The Jentink's duiker, *Cephalophus jentinki*, is restricted in distribution to a small part of the lowland forest zone of eastern Liberia and to another small section of the western Ivory Coast. Probably only a few hundred still exist in the wild, however, no estimate is reliable since only very few specimens have ever been observed and nothing whatsoever is known of this animal's natural history and biology. Jentink's duiker is perhaps the rarest and least known of all the antelopes of the West African rain forests and its elusive habits and the closed habitats in which it lives make it almost impossible to study.

Although the Jentink's duiker did not figure among the top 12 most endangered animals in the world (not only mammals) listed in the *Species Survival Commission Newsletter* of May 1985, it was nevertheless cited as a runner-up. The greatest threat to the survival of this endangered species is a loss of its forest habitat and the fact that it is poached extensively for its meat and skin. Consequently, the species is in danger of extinction, and it could well disappear before we even know anything of its behaviour and ecology. A survey of the distribution and status of the endangered Jentink's duiker has, therefore, been planned for the second half of 1986.

### A programme to survey Jentink's duiker

Base camps will be established in several areas in eastern Liberia, and two to three weeks will be spent in each area. Surveys on foot will be made along creeks and rivers in the forests and along as many existing footpaths, roads and tracks as possible. However, no attempts will be made at this stage to cut our own transects. All signs of tracks made by Jentink's duiker, scats (droppings) and sightings will be recorded, and very detailed information kept on periods of activity, food and feeding habits, etc. Skulls from prey remains, scats and any other material will be collected for later examination. The use of local guides, trackers and hunters will be essential at this stage if sound results are to be obtained.

439

*The zebra duiker (Cephalophus zebra) is another species of forest duiker that will be studied by Vivian Wilson in the west African rain forests.*

*The rare Jentink's duiker (Cephalophus jentinki) that will be the prime subject of Vivian Wilson's study in the forests of Liberia. (Photo by Karl Kranz) (opposite)*

"Bush meat" markets will be visited as often as possible in the towns and villages, and duiker carcasses found for sale along the roads will also be examined and identified. Official records will also be examined for evidence about poaching of Jentink's duiker and local hunters, park guards, etc., will be interviewed. Leopard scats will be collected throughout the survey and analyzed to determine the prey the animal has eaten and to ascertain what percentage of Jentink's duiker remains they contain. Night-time searches will also be made to try to locate the presence of Jentink's duiker after dark. Stomach contents, reproductive tracts and as much other biological material as possible will be collected from any dead duiker encountered, and all carcasses will be measured and weighed, and skins, skulls and both internal and external parasites will be collected.

The whole procedure will certainly be a very difficult and tiring exercise; but, by the end of five months, it should be possible to give some idea of the distribution and status of the Jentink's duiker in Liberia. It may also be necessary to employ different survey techniques from one area to the next, and other local methods of detecting the presence of the duikers may be discovered. Moreover, it should be emphasized that seven duiker species exist in Liberia and detailed information will also be collected about any species encountered or collected, and the field study will not be restricted to the Jentink's duiker.

### Governmental collaboration with non-governmental agencies

The Government of Liberia has clearly demonstrated its desire and determination to protect the country's wildlife; the establishment of the Sapo National Park and the decision to draw up a National Conservation Strategy are concrete examples of this concern. This governmental interest combined with the rarity of the Jentink's and various other duikers in Liberia, offer an excellent opportunity to demonstrate that external agencies could also help by providing the manpower for surveys of the country's important wildlife species.

There are many factors to justify a survey of the duikers of Liberia. No detailed surveys have ever been undertaken of the rare duikers of Liberia, and the ecology, biology, distribution and status of many of these species are unknown. More duiker species occur in Liberia than in any other African country with the possible exception of the Ivory Coast. When more is known about the duikers of Liberia, effective conservation measures can be proposed for implementation by wildlife authorities. The Liberian Development Authority has already pointed out that duikers are a very important source of meat for the majority of rural people in Liberia, and that overhunting combined with habitat destruction is threatening these species. Finally, it may be possible, and certainly desirable, to establish a Duiker Research and Breeding Centre in Liberia where many of the rarer species could be bred and studied in captivity.

## Building on the initial study

It is anticipated that the present proposed survey will be a preliminary one from which a research protocol and plan could be developed for future studies to be carried out on free-living duikers. It is therefore encouraging that the Wildlife Authorities in Liberia have indicated their willingness to assist in every way possible, and that the proposed visit to Liberia will be part of the overall plan of the ten-year survey of the duikers of Africa with several additional surveys planned for West Africa.

# European scientists to study the Amazonian rain forest at Maracá

## John Henry Hemming
**Honourable Mention**
**The Rolex Awards for Enterprise – 1987**

Royal Geographical Society, 1 Kensington Gore, London SW7 2AR, UK

Canadian, born 5 January 1935. Director and Secretary, Royal Geographical Society, London. Educated in UK and Canada; D.Litt. from University of Oxford in 1981.

This project will take one of the strongest teams of European scientists ever to work in Amazonia to the uninhabited and largely unexplored 92,000 ha riverine island of Maracá in the Uraricoera River, northern Brazil, to undertake a detailed ecological survey of the island and four research programmes on forest regeneration, soils and hydrology, medical entomology, land development and ecological surveying and management.

### Forest regeneration

Every year, hundreds of thousands of hectares of rain forest are felled. Much is soon abandoned, and it is vital to try to bring back rain forest to cleared land and thus achieve the likely benefits for climate, species diversity and exploitable forest products. Surprisingly, the rain forest is so rich in species and so complex that it does not easily regenerate after being destroyed. Consequently, the Maracá Rain Forest Project will try to learn more about the processes of regeneration, in order to help forests grow again. Once the initial surveys are made, we plan to set up and regularly monitor experiments to yield basic information on how rain forests function, which will be essential for any conservation or land management plan for the region.

### Soils and hydrology

Rain forests flourish only in a combination of tropical heat and heavy rainfall; to understand such jungles, it is essential to learn more about their hydrology and understand how forest soils absorb and release nutrients. Because rain forests are evergreen, they constantly produce a litter of leaves, twigs and dead trees but competition among the millions of seeds and thousands of trees is so intense that almost all the nutrient from this litter is recaptured by the growing biomass. Termites and fungi rapidly break up fallen litter. The nutrient is then recaptured by a near solid mat of tree roots, so that very little nutrient passes into soils

442

beneath the forest. A vigorous rain forest thus has a closed nutrient cycle. We can measure any "leakage" of nutrients from this cycle by examining water coming off hill slopes and percolating deep into the ground. Maracá Ecological Station is at the edge of a natural boundary between forest and savannah. It is therefore a perfect place to study the mysteries of why rain forest stops and gives way to grasslands.

## Medical entomology

Human life in Amazonia has always been blighted by tropical diseases, and the problem is growing worse. However, although we know that malaria, for example, is transmitted by the *Anopheles* mosquito, other diseases are less understood. The project therefore includes strong teams of scientists to study the disease-transmission role of such insects as: black fly which is known to transmit onchocerciasis and mansonelliasis; reduviid bugs which are vectors of trypanosomiasis or Chagas' disease which is virtually incurable; sandflies which are carriers of leishmaniasis; diptera (biting flies) that transmit disease and debilitate both humans and livestock; and *Anopheles* mosquitoes in relation to malaria.

## Ecological surveying and management

The Brazilian Environment Secretariat (SEMA) which administers the Maracá reserve and has built a permanent research station on it, needs to have an inventory of the animals, insects and plants on this large island. Once Maracá's ecosystem is better known, SEMA can divide the island into natural zones and plan integrated research in them. The ecological survey that we plan to carry out will include: the recording, classification and collection of the hundreds of species of trees, vines, ferns, mosses, orchids, fungi, etc., that inhabit this rich

*One of the expedition's tasks will be to establish an inventory of the animals, such as this jaguar, insects and plants on Maracá Island to help draw up a management plan for the conservation, future study and possible recreational use of this nature reserve (Photograph WWF/Y.J. Rey-Millet).*

443

*The rain forest is so rich in species that it does not easily regenerate after being destroyed. It is essential to learn more about the process of regeneration, in order to help the forests grow again (Photograph WWF/Paul Foster).*

jungle; recording of various animal species; and experiments in animal behaviour and relationship with other life forms. Where British and Brazilian experts are not available, specialists will be called upon to help. This inventory will be used to draw up a management plan for the conservation, future study and possible recreational use of this beautiful nature reserve.

### Land development

Millions of settlers are moving to the frontiers of Amazonian forests in a desperate search for land and at a rhythm which is too fast for any planning to be done on a scientific basis. Many pioneer colonists fail since the forests they try to clear prove unsuitable for farming, ranching or even forestry and plantations. General information is available to help Brazilian planners make better assessment of land potential but more detailed data are needed on spontaneous or directed settlement to make colonization more beneficial to the settlers and less damaging to the environment. The area around Maracá Island is a good location for such a detailed study and will look at the nature of land occupation, current land-use practices, proposals for alternative development strategies and the effect of current land-use practices on the environment.

All this work should be of real practical value, both to the people of Amazonia for the eradication of tropical diseases, the improvement of human frontier settlement, and the better understanding and management of the tropical rain forest.

444

## The great sharks – Over-exploited and headed toward extinction?

### Samuel Harvey Gruber

Rosenstiel School of Marine and Atmospheric Science, 4600 Rickenbacker Causeway, Miami, Florida 33149, USA
*American, born 13 May 1938. Professor of Marine Sciences, Rosenstiel School of Marine and Atmospheric Science, University of Miami. Educated in USA; Ph.D. (Marine Science) from University of Miami in 1969.*

This project aims to document the life history of the large, predatory sharks with a view to showing that, like the great whales, these unique life forms are at great potential risk through the irrational exploitation of their stocks by man. It will then create public awareness of these facts by dissemination of scientific information within the marine fisheries community and the general population.


## Establishing an offshore-island marine biological station without State funding

### Matt Murphy

Sherkin Island, County Cork, Ireland
*Irish, born 21 May 1935. Owner/Director, Sherkin Island Outdoor Pursuits Centre and Sherkin Island Marine Station. Educated in Ireland.*

This project has set up Sherkin Island Marine Station on a privately owned island with the objectives of: establishing baseline data on local marine life and recording natural changes in flora and fauna; introducing young people to sea-shore studies, bird-watching, etc.; interesting schools and universities in doing marine fieldwork; and encouraging individual scientists to carry out projects in the area.


## Rescuing children addicted to cocaine in the Amazonian jungle

### Federico Raúl Jerí

1491 Av. Javier Prado Oeste, Apartado 5281, San Isidro, Lima 27, Peru
*Peruvian, born 24 November 1918. Professor of Neurology, San Marcos National University. Educated in Peru and UK; degree in Medicine from San Marcos National University.*

Thousands of children are nowadays abusing cocaine, in the form of coca paste, in the jungle areas of Bolivia, Colombia and Peru. This project is trying to rescue these children by modifying the environmental factors that contribute to the development of this lethal form of drug abuse. It proposes the creation of a pilot centre for the diagnosis, prevention, treatment and rehabilitation of children who abuse cocaine.


## *Butterflies of the World* – A multi-volume masterwork

### Bernard Laurance D'Abrera

2/157 Bluff Road, Black Rock, Victoria 3193, Australia
*Australian, born 28 August 1940. Author/naturalist. Educated in Australia; B.A. from University of New South Wales in 1965. Fellow of the Royal Entomological Society of London.*

This project is an attempt to offer workers in genetics, animal behaviour, etc., an illustrated systematic guide to all the known species of Rhopalocera (true butterflies) of the world in synoptic volumes (three of which have already been published). This work, when completed, is expected to be the largest published work in any field of natural history ever undertaken by a single author/illustrator.

## Traditional pest control and food production in central and southern Uganda

### Steven Allen Nyanzi

c/o Mr. Samuel Kaddu Makumbi, Uganda Tea Authority, POB 4161 Kampala, Uganda
*Ugandan, born 16 July 1956. Intern at the International Organization of Consumers' Unions. Educated in Uganda and Kenya; preparing M.Sc. degree (Environmental Chemistry) at the University of Kenya.*

The Baganda, an agricultural community in central and southern Uganda, have traditionally practised non-chemical methods of protecting their crops against pests; however, these methods have never received support or publicity. This project plans to examine and publicize the unexplored indigenous knowledge on pest control currently in the hands of old peasant farmers before this knowledge is lost.

## The Raptor Education Foundation's living raptor collection

### Peter Reshetniak

925 East 17th Avenue, Denver, Colorado 80218, USA
*Australian, born 21 June 1950. President, Raptor Education Foundation. Educated in USA; Bachelor of Fine Arts from University of Colorado in 1974.*

This project plans to expand the activities of the Raptor Education Foundation in its efforts to educate the public about birds of prey (raptors) by establishing a national collection of injured raptors that have been rehabilitated but that cannot be released because of their injuries. These permanently damaged animals would be a powerful educational tool and also constitute a captive gene pool.

## Biofer – Biotechnology for agriculture

### Luis Vazquez Noriega

215 R. Vega Sánchez, Pachuca, Hidalgo 42060, Mexico
*Mexican, born 7 October 1927. Agronomic engineer, and Director of Agricultura Regional S.A. Educated in Mexico and USA; graduated (Agronomic Engineer) from Escuela Particular de Agricultura in 1952.*

Over 60% of the world's soils have a high pH and/or salt content. This project has developed the "Biofer" technology to recover soils of this type that have lost their productivity. The substance used comprises powdered sulphur, impregnated with specific micro-organisms which, when added to soil, results in acidification and the availability of sulphur to significantly increase crop yield and quality.

## Sun effects and building orientation in Dar es Salaam, Tanzania

### Fahrudin Teskeredzic

34 Bosanska, 41000 Zagreb, Yugoslavia
*Yugoslav, born 10 May 1933. Architect. Educated in Yugoslavia and Tanzania; M.A. from University of Dar es Salaam in 1972.*

This project is studying the relationship between building orientation and the effects of the sun. It is attempting to help adapt buildings to their thermal environment by calculating the quantities of solar radiation energy affecting vertical surfaces of a building located at various orientations in Dar es Salaam, Tanzania, by measuring solar radiation incidence and by rating sun effects for every possible building orientation.

## Re-establishing rain forest on degraded lands in the Amazon Basin

*Carl Frederick Jordan*
Institute of Ecology, University of Georgia, Athens, Georgia 30602, USA
*American, born 12 December 1935. Research scientist in ecology. Educated in USA; Ph.D. (Botany) from Rutgers University in 1966.*
Large areas of east-central Amazon Basin rain forest are being deforested, grazed with cattle for a few years, and then abandoned. This project proposes to examine methods of restoring native forest; it will also study the survival and growth of seeds of native rain forest species, the costs of various reforestation techniques and the importance of revegetation pattern in re-establishing native wildlife.


## Captive breeding to preserve the genetic diversity of the Sumatran rhinoceros

*Francesco Nardelli*
No. 03–16 Mount Faber Lodge, 27 Mount Faber Road, Singapore 0409, Rep. of Singapore
*Italian, born 5 September 1953. Zoo Curator and Managing Director of the Sumatran Rhino Project. Educated in Italy; course (Natural Science) at Rome University.*
The two-horned Sumatran rhinoceros is one of the world's most endangered animals. This project proposes to conserve these animals as viable populations in sufficiently large areas of protected native habitat. An educational campaign will be run to enhance public awareness and support, and a captive propagation programme will be established to preserve the genetic diversity of the Sumatran rhinoceros.


## Family food production and nutrition project in the Pacific

*Paul Sommers*
c/o UNDP, P.M.B., Suva, Fiji
*American, born 10 December 1952. UNICEF Regional Project Manager. Educated in Philippines and USA; M.Sc. (Nutrition) from University of the Philippines in 1978.*
Population growth, urbanization, unemployment and increased reliance on a cash rather than a subsistence economy have reduced standards of living and health for many Pacific Islanders. The Family Food and Nutrition Project was created to improve the nutrition and health status of Pacific Islanders through promotion of ecologically balanced and sustainable agriculture based on principles of multi-storey mixed gardening.


## South American sighting and stranding network for the right whale

*Alfredo Alejandro Lichter*
Fundación Vida Silvestre Argentina, 968 Leandro N. Alem, 1001 Bueno Aires, Argentina
*Argentine, born 13 February 1955. Wildlife researcher. Educated in Argentina; Bachelor degree at De la Salle College, Buenos Aires.*
This project aims to provide scientists with more information about the migrations of southern right whales (*Eubalaena australis*). Investigators from Brazil, Uruguay, Argentina and Chile send information on the presence of this cetacean in their respective areas to the project co-ordinator who computer-processes the data and publishes a compilation in half-yearly reports.

# Floating reception facilities for liquid oily residues from ships

## Hugh Daniel Williams

POB 120, 4 Torstadbakken, 1364 Hvalstad, Norway
*American, born 14 February 1938. Technical Director, Norpol Environmental Services A/S. Educated in USA; M.Sc. (Chemical Engineering) from University of Maryland in 1968.*

The International Convention for the Prevention of Pollution from Ships, 1973 (known as MARPOL 73/78), requires contracting parties to provide adequate ballast and slop reception facilities for tankers and other vessels. This project is developing floating reception facilities utilizing surplus large tanker hulls which will receive liquid oily residues from ships and, in particular, dirty ballast water from tankers.

# Aiding the elderly struck by natural holocausts

## Jan Reban

Leninova 117, 37341 Hluboká n/Vlt., Czechoslovakia
*Czechoslovak, born 18 January 1940. Physician and geriatrician. Educated in Czechoslovakia, Italy, USSR and Romania; M.D. from Charles University, Prague in 1967.*

Recent natural catastrophes, such as those of Mexico and Colombia, have devastated living conditions and interpersonal ties, especially of the elderly, as a result of broken family structures, the loss of children and parents, etc. This project plans to analyze the health, social and psychological needs of the elderly in such areas and draw up recommendations for governments on how to meet them.

# Technology to fight the inferno – Road-tanker safety

## Christian S. Welzel

20 Friedrich-Lau-Strasse, 4000 Düsseldorf 30, West Germany
*West German, born 24 December 1936. Mechanical engineer. Educated in West Germany; graduated (Mechanical Engineering) at Darmstadt in 1975.*

Highway accidents involving road-tankers carrying flammable or other hazardous fluids can result in major catastrophes. This project proposes various mechanical safety devices – such as steel guards for the external tank area and spring fenders at front and rear, together with electronic safety systems such as optical warning signals, rear-view closed-circuit television in the driver's cab, etc.

# Arousing public awareness to save the lagoons and marshes of the Llobregat Delta

## Ramon Planas i Torres

13–15 Castella, El Prat de Llobregat, Barcelona, Spain
*Spanish, born 14 March 1955. Management and manpower analyst, and part-time author and publisher. Educated in Spain; studied (Economics) in 1974 and (Law) in 1979 at University of Barcelona.*

This project plans to overcome the menace to the natural aquatic ecosystems of the Llobregat Delta near Barcelona, Spain, by a public information and education campaign to raise the collective awareness of the Delta's inhabitants. The campaign will use a book containing colour photographs of the ecosystem, its fauna and flora, combined with a simple explanatory text to stimulate concern about this ecological heritage.

## Ecology and status of pilot whales exploited off the Faroe Islands

*Geneviève Marie Desportes*
19 rue du Père Flavigny, 76620 Le Havre, France
*French, born 30 June 1958. Research worker at the Centre d'Etudes Biologiques des Animaux Sauvages et Antarctiques Français. Doctorat de Troisième Cycle (Animal Biology and Physiology) from University of Poitiers in 1985.*
This project forms an integral part of a larger-scale programme on the ecology of pilot whales, aimed at the development of rational management for these animals. The project will study population dynamics, obtain information on the movement of the animals, and examine the transfer of certain pollutants from prey species to the pilot whales themselves, and their final consumers – the islanders.


## Ecology and management of the Patagonia puma in southern Chile

*William Lloyd Franklin*
124 Science II, Department of Animal Ecology, Iowa State University, Ames, Iowa 50011, USA
*American, born 31 July 1941. Itinerant wildlife mammalian ecologist, author and explorer. Educated in USA; Ph.D. (Wildlife Science) from Utah State University in 1978.*
This project aims to study the Patagonia puma, *Felis concolor patagonica*, at the 160,000 ha National Park of Torres de Paine in southern Chile. Radiotelemetry, ground tracking, visual observation, etc., will be used to determine the animal's social organization, geographical distribution, movement patterns, population dynamics, predatory behaviour and food habits, and develop management recommendations for the Patagonian region.


## Spectacled bear research and habitat protection

*Juan Antonio Bravo-Perea*
Calle 14 No. 8–79, Of. 509, Bogatá, D.E., Colombia
*Colombian, born 7 September 1953. Official governmental translator. Educated in Colombia and USA; studied at Universidad Javeriana, Bogotá.*
Owing to indiscriminate shooting, the spectacled bear is near to extinction. This project plans a campaign to protect the bear by studying its social behaviour in the ecosystem, organizing an educational programme to stimulate public awareness, and protecting the bear's habitat. The project also plans a small reserve for interaction between leukaemic children and the offspring of endangered species.


## Distribution, abundance, behavioural ecology and sounds of Hector's dolphin

*Stephen Michael Dawson*
Cetos Research, Wainui, R.D. Duvauchelles, Banks Peninsula, New Zealand
*New Zealander, born 29 September 1957. Research biologist. Educated in New Zealand; M.Sc. (Zoology) from Auckland University in 1982.*
Having conducted a population survey of Hector's dolphins around the South Island of New Zealand, and launched an examination of ecological and behavioural factors, this project will study the dolphin's acoustic behaviour and sound production, with particular reference to the physical structure of the sounds, the relationship between sounds and behaviour, and the anatomy of the sound-producing organs.

449

## Using fungal disease to eradicate a termite colony and reduce pesticide use

*Heinz Helmut Hänel*

80 Tannenwaldallee, 6380 Bad Homburg v.d.H., West Germany
*West German, born 3 November 1955. Chemotherapy research biologist. Educated in West Germany, Australia and Malaysia; Ph.D. (Bee Parasitology) from J.W. Goethe University in 1985.*
Those using chemical pesticides to control termites are confronted with environmental protection problems and pesticide resistance in termites. This project has developed a technique by which a fungus, *Metarhizium anisopliae*, that grows on dead termites, is used to fatally infect a termite colony. It is planned to document the method, promote its use and supply free samples of the fungal spores.

## Wildon energy research project

*August Raggam*

60 St. Margarethen, 8403 St. Margarethen b. Lebring, Austria
*Austrian, born 8 October 1937. Head, Institute for Alternative Energy Research. Educated in Austria; Ph.D. (Pulp and Paper Engineering) in 1973.*
This project is developing a system by which agricultural biomass can be converted to a fuel source for small and medium-sized heating systems. Crop material will be pelleted and sold to users in Graz or used in the area of Wildon, Austria. The ash will be recovered, supplemented with nutrients, pelleted in the same facility and redistributed to farmers as fertilizer.

## New solutions for saving tortoises and turtles

*Claude-Henri Pavard*

50 rue Croix Bosset, 92310 Sèvres, France
*French, born 19 December 1942. Film producer and director. Educated in France; graduated (Sociology) from University of Grenoble and (Economy and Finance) from Grenoble Institute of Political Studies in 1969.*
This project wishes to adopt an innovative approach to the conservation of endangered species by presenting a new look at the relationship between animals and man – who is frequently a "natural predator". A sizeable expedition will be organized to Europa Island to film the life cycle of the green turtles there, with particular emphasis being placed on predatory functions.

## Conserving the demoiselle crane in Morocco

*Javier Antonio Alonso*

Cátedra de Vertebrados, Facultad de Biología, Universidad Complutense, Ciudad Universitaria, 28040 Madrid, Spain
*Spanish, born 5 July 1953. Professor of Vertebrate Zoology and Avian Ecology, Complutense University of Madrid. Educated in Spain; Ph.D. (Zoology) in 1980.*
Sightings indicate there is a relict population of breeding demoiselle cranes, *Anthropoides virgo* – one of the world's most endangered birds – in Morocco. This project proposes to discover the lost sanctuaries of these birds in the Atlas Mountains and preserve the last couples. The data collected will be presented to the Moroccan Government with an official recommendation for conservation measures.

# Fuel pellets from water hyacinth

## Lorenzo B. Ballecer

Suite 1113 – 11th Floor, National Life Building, 6762 Ayala Avenue, Makati, Metro Manila, Philippines
*Filipino, born 8 October 1944. President, Sunrise Industries Development Incorporated. Educated in Philippines, West Germany and USA; M.B.A. from Asian Institute of Management, Makati, Metro Manila in 1973.*

The ecological balance of the Laguna de Bay Lake near Manila has been disturbed by the uncontrolled proliferation of water hyacinth, *Eichhornia crassipes*, which is causing environmental decay. This project proposes to produce fuel pellets using these hyacinth plants as raw material, so as to tackle the environmental degradation problem whilst producing valuable fuel. A pilot plant is being developed.


# Fodder troughs to increase animal production and decrease environmental degradation

## George Hayward Craven

Noorspoort, POB 29, 6250 Steytlerville, Rep. of South Africa
*South African, born 23 June 1941. Farmer. Educated in South Africa and USA; Ph.D. (Plant Physiology) from Cornell University in 1972.*

Faced with the problem of feeding livestock in semi-arid areas, this project has developed a system in which fodder plants are grown in fixed or movable fodder troughs covered with wire mesh forming part of a closed hydroponics system that ensures that plants experience no water or mineral deficiencies and have maximum growth. The wire mesh covering allows growing plants to protrude and be eaten by animals but prevents trampling.


# The Elephants in Distress itinerant exhibition

## Francis Lauginie

Cocody Les Deux Plateaux, Ilot 7, Villa 347, 01 B.P. 932, Abidjan 01, Ivory Coast
*French, born 20 November 1947. Veterinary surgeon and ecological engineer. Educated in France and Ivory Coast; veterinary degree from University of Toulouse in 1977.*

This project has developed an exhibition entitled Elephants in Distress to alert the public to the rapid decline in the African elephant population. Following display of the exhibition in Abidjan, it is planned to produce multiple copies for use in other African countries and Europe. An Elephant project will be launched to develop proposals on territory management for elephants.


# Classroom under the sea

## Ian Gregory Koblick

51 Shoreland Drive, POB 787, Key Largo, Florida 33037, USA
*American, born 12 July 1939. President, Marine Resources Development Foundation. Educated in USA; B.A. (Science) California State University at Chico in 1964.*

This ongoing project aims to offer people of all ages the opportunity of experiencing an underwater habitat by living in comfort as a family some 10 m below the surface of the ocean for a short period, and thus becoming part of and learning about the marine environment. Should funding be obtained, additional habitats for education, recreation and science will be made available for use by the diving public.

## "Zig Zag" project

*Maurizio Costantino*
251/2 Via dell'Eremo, 34100 Trieste, Italy
*Italian, born 21 April 1948. Social worker. Educated in Italy and France; graduated from the Ecole des Hautes Etudes en Sciences Sociales in 1985.*

In an effort to provide reintegration for individuals who are excluded or isolated from society, this project raised funds, purchased, refitted and operated a sailing boat, the *Califfo*, for mental-hospital patients and drug-addicts. It offers these people the experience of achieving an objective and of building new, unexplored relationships between the healthy and the ill, and between the "normal" and the "deviant".


## Timba forest sanctuary – From wasteland to wonderland

*Indubhai Patel*
Madhuban, Opp. Electric Sub-Station, Gotri Road, Vadodara-390007, India
*Indian, born 14 November 1921. Industrialist. Educated in India; Matriculate from Bombay University.*

This project has, over a period of seven years, transformed a derelict and abandoned quarry – Timba – into a sanctuary and a water reservoir. It is now envisioned, in the near future, to attract tourists to this haven and bring man closer to nature, to help him know what it is to live amid the peace and quiet of natural surroundings.


## Royal scientific light expedition to the tropical African rain forest

*Ramón Antor Castellarnau*
Viviendas Enher, Ainsa (Huesca), Spain
*Spanish, born 5 January 1963. University student. Educated in Spain; fifth-year student (Biological Sciences) at Universidad Autónoma de Barcelona.*

This project plans a two-man expedition in West Africa (Cameroon, Guinea, Gabon, the Congo Republic and Zaïre). The expedition will study the ecology of the tropical rain forest and explore its remotest and most uninhabited forests by canoe and on foot. The montane ecosystems and the mangrove swamps will also be investigated, and biospeleological exploration of the unknown caves of this region will be undertaken.


## Saving the western North American population of the migratory Monarch butterfly

*Christopher Dike Nagano*
The Monarch Project, 10 Southwest Ash Street, Portland, Oregon 97204, USA
*American, born 28 December 1956. Biologist for the Monarch Project. Educated in USA; Master of Environmental Studies, School of Forestry and Environmental Studies from Yale University in 1985.*

The western North American population of the Monarch butterfly, *Danaus plexippus*, is threatened with destruction due to human intervention in its wintering and roosting sites. The object of the Monarch Project is to safeguard this butterfly in a three-phase operation: location of overwintering sites; measurement of environmental conditions at roosts; and protection of endangered sites.

# Name Index

455

# Country index

459

USA
  Allen, Jr., B. L. 140
  Bach-y-Rita, P. 39
  Berger, J. 381
  Bonaventura, J. 134
  Borman, K. L. 133
  Bournias-Vardiabasis, N. 134
  Bradner, H. 127
  Chabbert, R. J.-A. 251
  Claxton, R. J. 136
  Cords, M. A. 287
  Corica, J. 414
  Cox, J. M. 118
  Diamond, J. M. 166
  Dixon, B. M. 289
  Fine, J. C. 356
  Franklin, W. L. 449
  Garnick, M. C. 347
  Gentry, A. H. 291
  Goodman, S. M. 181
  Gruber, S. H. 445
  Hawkes, G. 109
  Hay, A. G. H. 106
  Heller, R. M. 103
  Hoover, W. S. 289
  Horwich, R. H. 436
  Johanson, D. C. 290
  Jordan, C. G. 447
  King, G. S. 405
  Kirk, R. L. 130
  Kiselewski, D. L. 64
  Koblick, I. G. 451
  Kress, S. W. 427
  Landfried, S. E. 430
  Langford, III, J. S. 36
  Lomax, P. 139
  McDonald, M. B. 46
  Miller, T. E. 218
  Mims, III, F. M. 79
  Nagano, C. D. 452
  Nollman, J. M. 289

O'Neill, J. P. 287
  Randall, J. E. 274
  Reshetniak, P. 446
  Rimland, B. 94
  Román, G. C. 112
  Rosheim, M. E. 9
  Sammon, R. 172
  Saunders, W. B. 290
  Schmieder, R. W. 248
  Schoelkopf, R. 317
  Schoene, R. B. 288
  Schulz, A. M. 221
  Silva, R. M. 142
  Stephenson, L. W. 58
  Taylor, Jr., O. R. 138
  Tuttle, M. 375
  Wells, R. A. 196
  White, Jr., R. E. 286
  Willard, M. J. 27
  Winkelstern, S. S. 288
  Yager, J. 279

Venezuela
  Arocha-Piñango, C. L. 175
  Matteucci, S. D. 305

West Germany
  Hänel, H. H. 450
  Hasenmayer, J. 285
  Krahn, K.-H. 142
  Kunz, J. F. 206
  Webb, P. A. 420
  Welzel, C. S. 448

Yugoslavia
  Teskeredzic, F. 446

Zimbabwe
  Condy, J. B. 329
  Ellert, H. 260
  Wilson, V. J. 439